INUYASHA

VOL. 44

Shonen Sunday Editio

STORY AND ART BY
RUMIKO TAKAHASH

CONTENTS

Long ago, in the "Warring States" era of Japan's Muromachi period, dog-like half demon Inuyasha attempted to steal the Shikon Jewel—or "Jewel of Four Souls"—from a village. The village priestess, Kikyo, put a stop to his thievery with an enchanted arrow. Pinned to a tree, Inuyasha fell into a deep sleep, while mortally wounded Kikyo took the jewel with her into her funeral pyre. Years passed...

In the present day, Kagome, a Japanese high school girl, is pulled down into a well and transported into the past. There she discovers trapped Inuyasha—and frees him.

When the Shikon Jewel mysteriously reappears, demons attack. In the ensuing battle, the jewel shatters!

Now Inuyasha is bound to Kagome with a powerful spell, and the grudging companions must battle to reclaim the shattered shards of the Shikon Jewel to keep them out of evil hands...

LAST VOLUME The battle rages on against the demon Naraku, who covets the shards of the Shikon Jewel. Naraku bestows rival powers to his heart (hidden inside Moryomaru) and to Inuyasha, in hopes they will exhaust each other—but his plan fails. Then Inuyasha sets out to learn how to truly master his blade Tetsusaiga. Unfortunately, the trainer he seeks—the Great Holy Demon Spirit—has problems of his own. Inuyasha agrees to retrieve the sage's stolen liver in exchange for fencing lessons, but now Tetsusaiga is sealed with

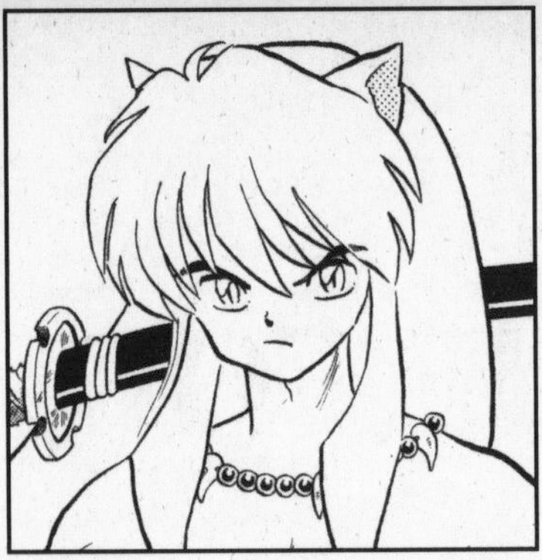

INUYASHA
Half-demon hybrid, son of a human mother and demon father. His necklace is enchanted, allowing Kagome to control him with a word.

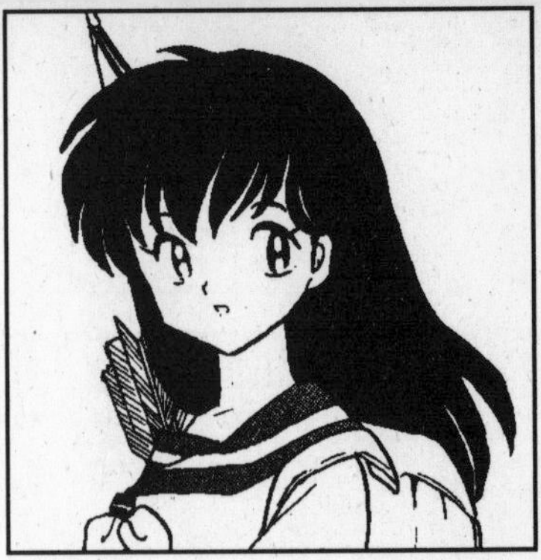

KAGOME
Modern-day Japanese schoolgirl who can travel back and forth between the past and present through an enchanted well.

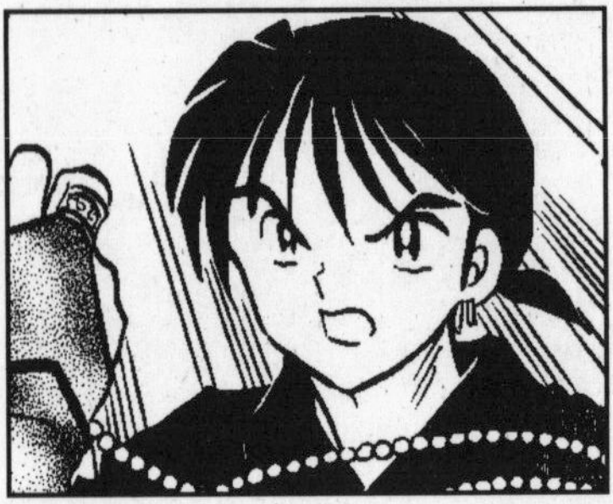

MIROKU
Lecherous Buddhist priest cursed with a mystical "hellhole" in his hand that is slowly killing him.

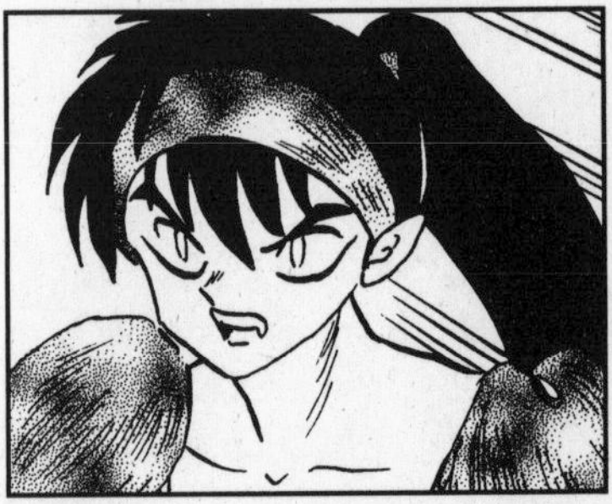

KOGA
Leader of the Wolf Clan, Koga is himself a wolf demon and, because of Shikon shards in each of his legs, possesses super speed. Enamored of Kagome, he quarrels with Inuyasha frequently.

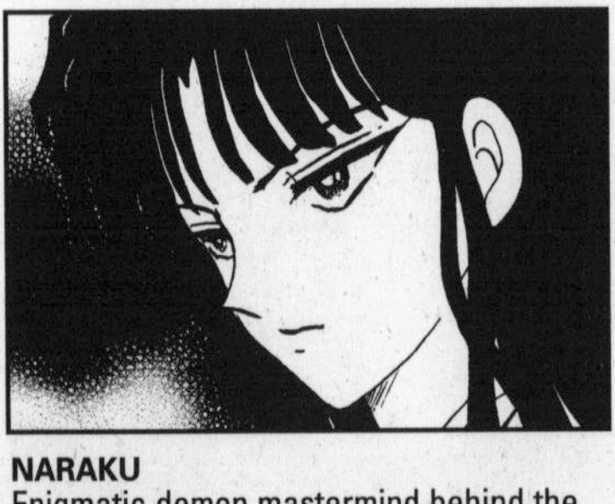

NARAKU
Enigmatic demon mastermind behind the miseries of nearly everyone in the story. He has the power to create multiple incarnations of himself from his body.

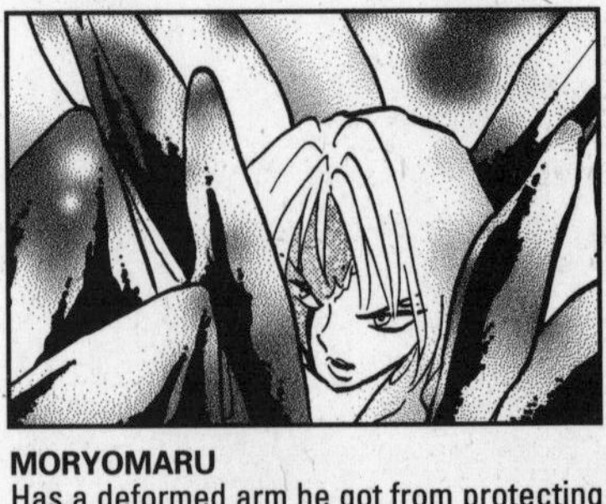

MORYOMARU
Has a deformed arm he got from protecting a shrine. In cahoots with Naraku. Immune to energy-based attacks.

SCROLL 1
THE TRUE FOE

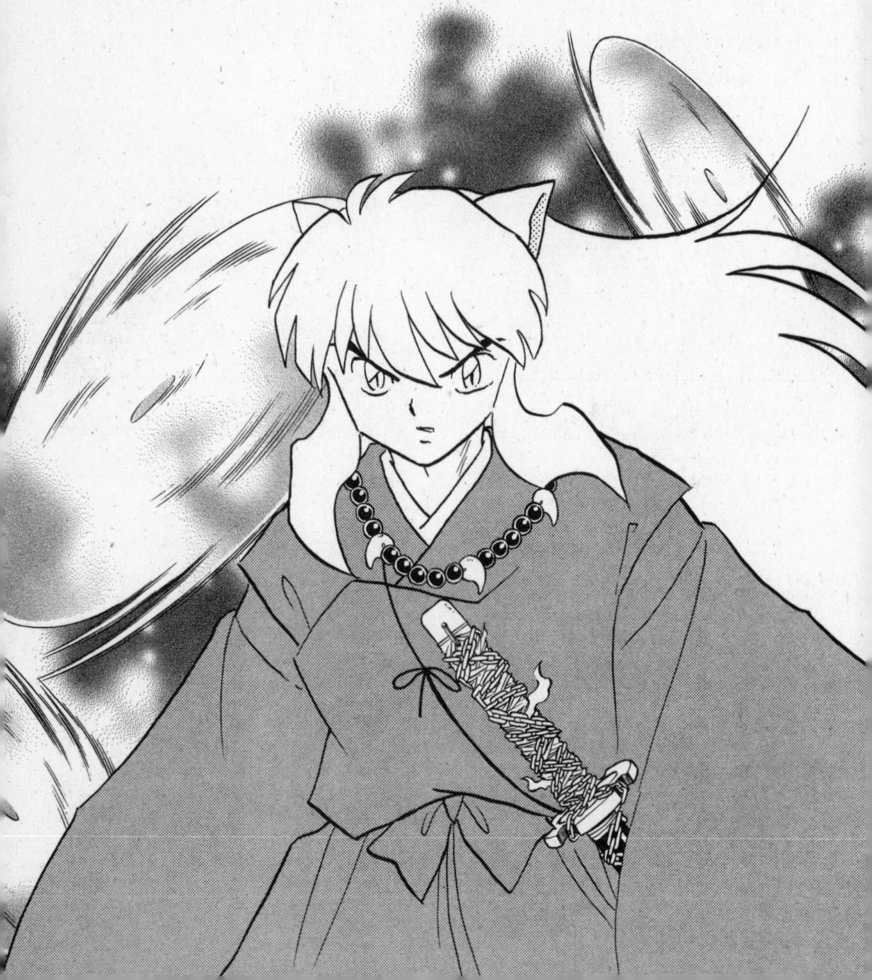

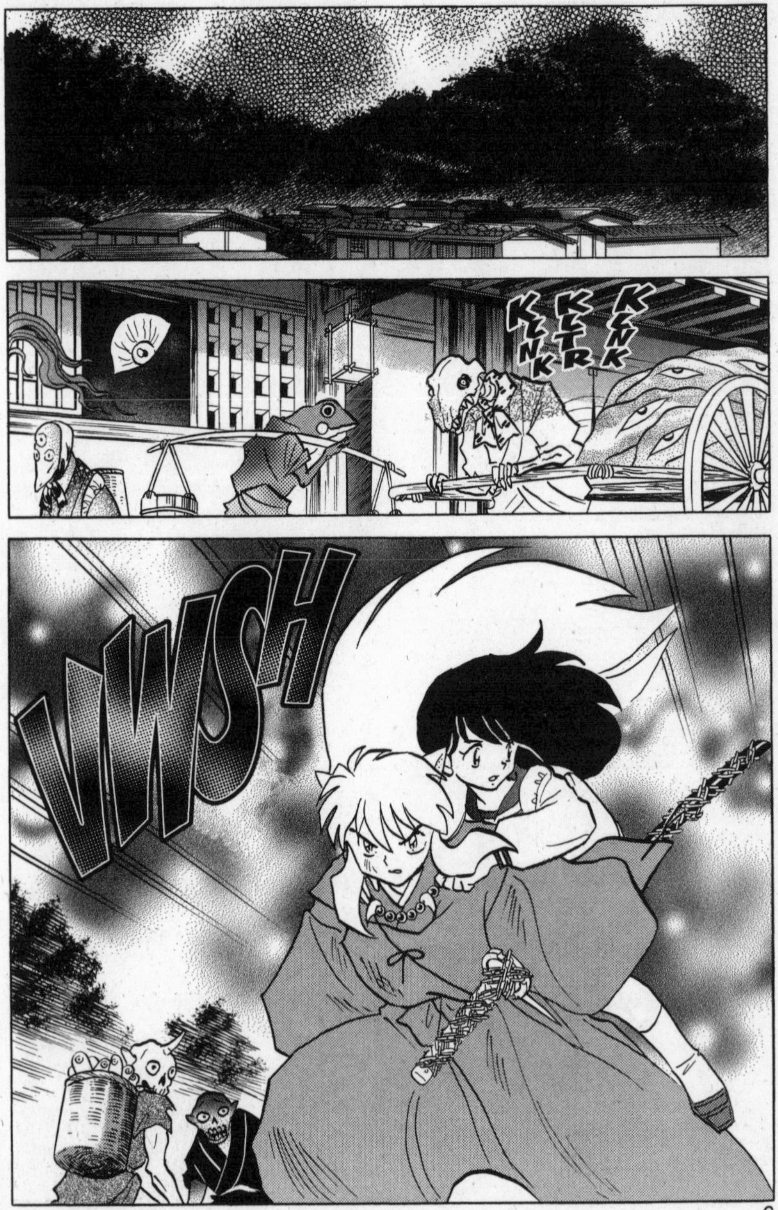
KLNK
KLTR
KLNK
VWSH

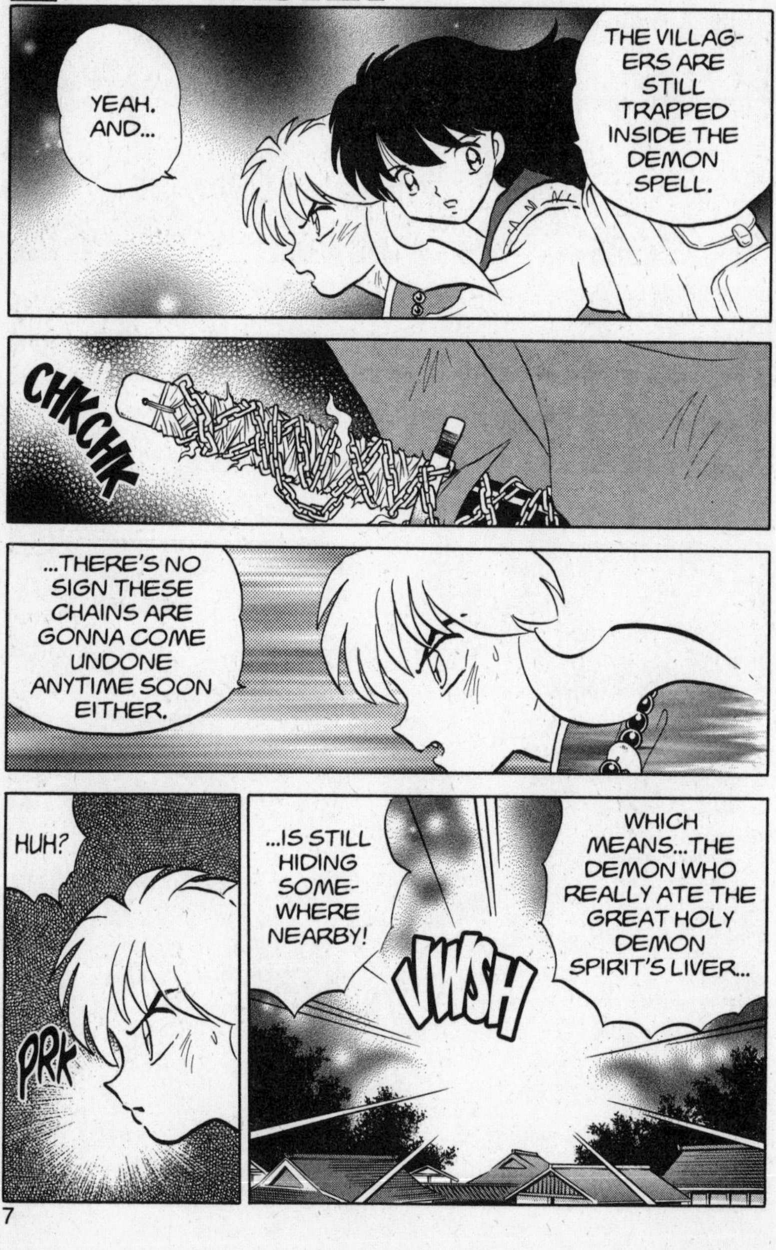
THE VILLAG-ERS ARE STILL TRAPPED INSIDE THE DEMON SPELL.
YEAH. AND...
CHKCHK
...THERE'S NO SIGN THESE CHAINS ARE GONNA COME UNDONE ANYTIME SOON EITHER.
WHICH MEANS...THE DEMON WHO REALLY ATE THE GREAT HOLY DEMON SPIRIT'S LIVER...
...IS STILL HIDING SOME-WHERE NEARBY!
JWSH
HUH?
PRK

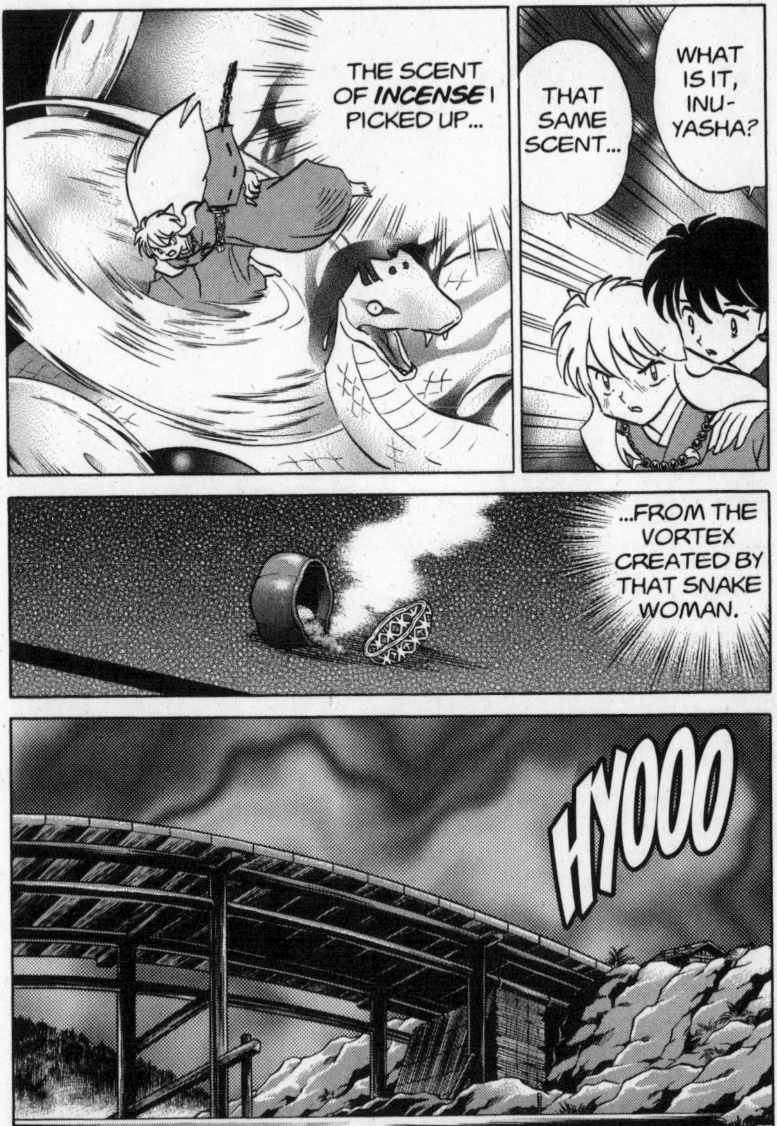
WHAT IS IT, INU-YASHA?
THAT SAME SCENT...
THE SCENT OF *INCENSE* I PICKED UP...
...FROM THE VORTEX CREATED BY THAT SNAKE WOMAN.
HYOOO

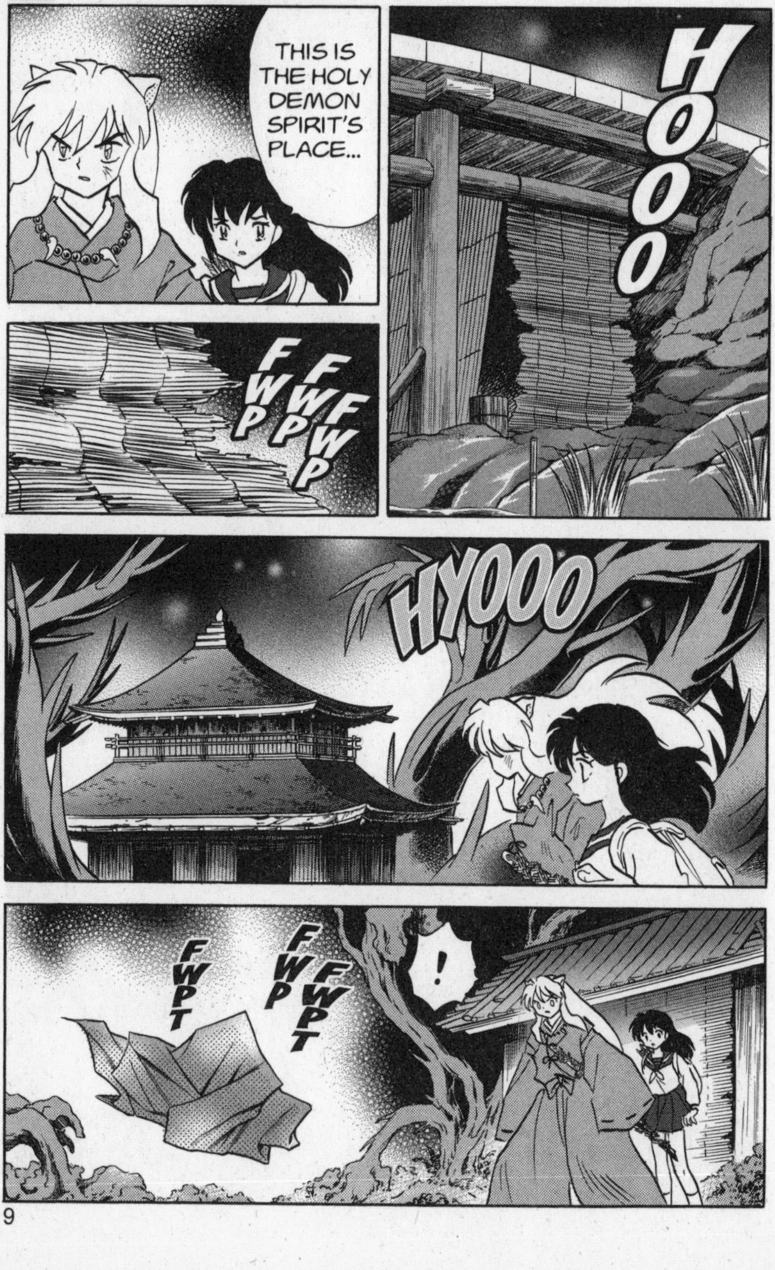
HOOOO
THIS IS THE HOLY DEMON SPIRIT'S PLACE...
FWP FWP FWP
HYOOO
!
FWP
FWPT
FWPT

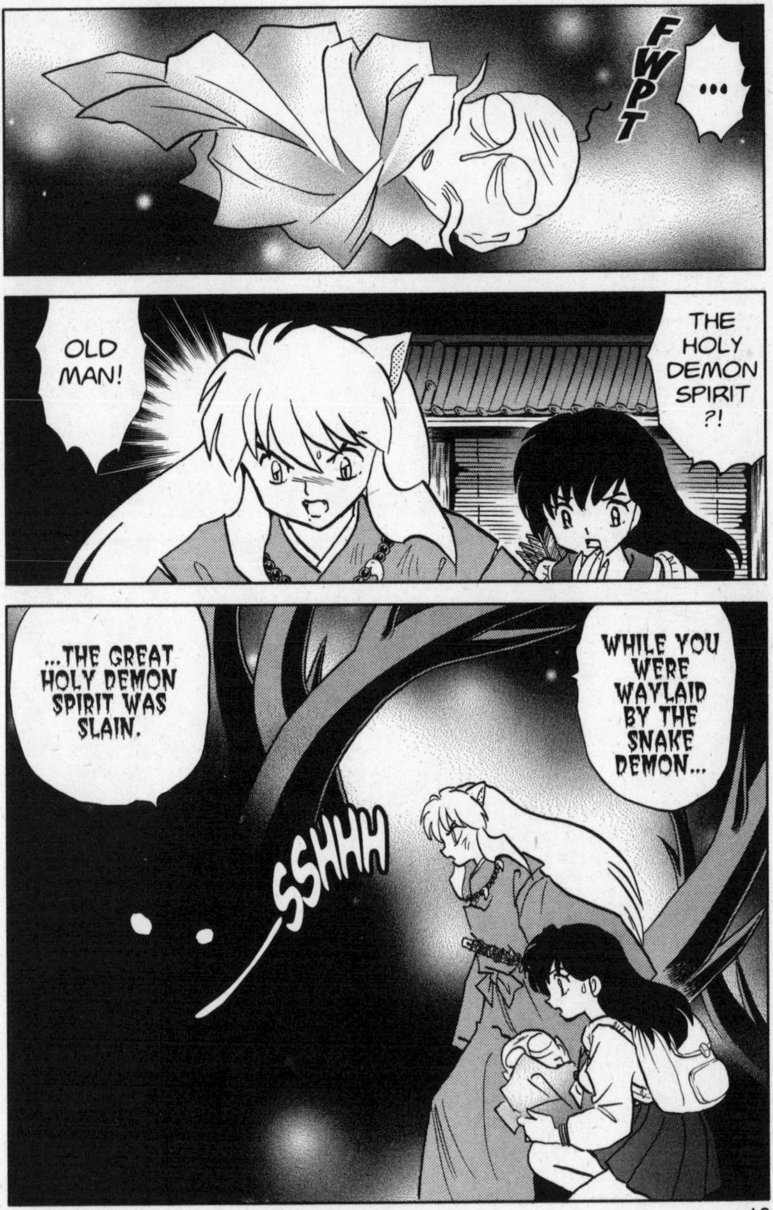
...
FWPT
THE HOLY DEMON SPIRIT ?!
OLD MAN!
WHILE YOU WERE WAYLAID BY THE SNAKE DEMON...
...THE GREAT HOLY DEMON SPIRIT WAS SLAIN.
SSHHH

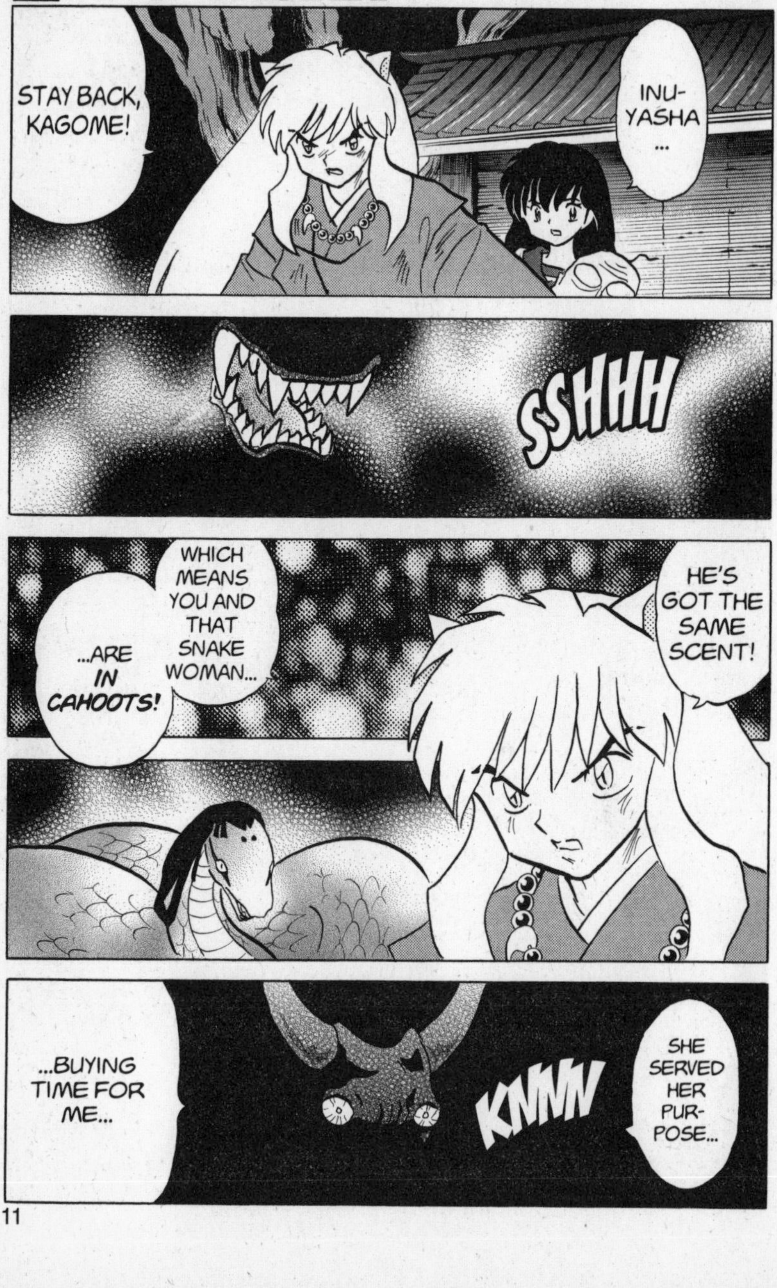
INU-YASHA ...
STAY BACK, KAGOME!
SSHHH
HE'S GOT THE SAME SCENT!
WHICH MEANS YOU AND THAT SNAKE WOMAN...
...ARE *IN CAHOOTS!*
SHE SERVED HER PUR-POSE...
KMMN
...BUYING TIME FOR ME...

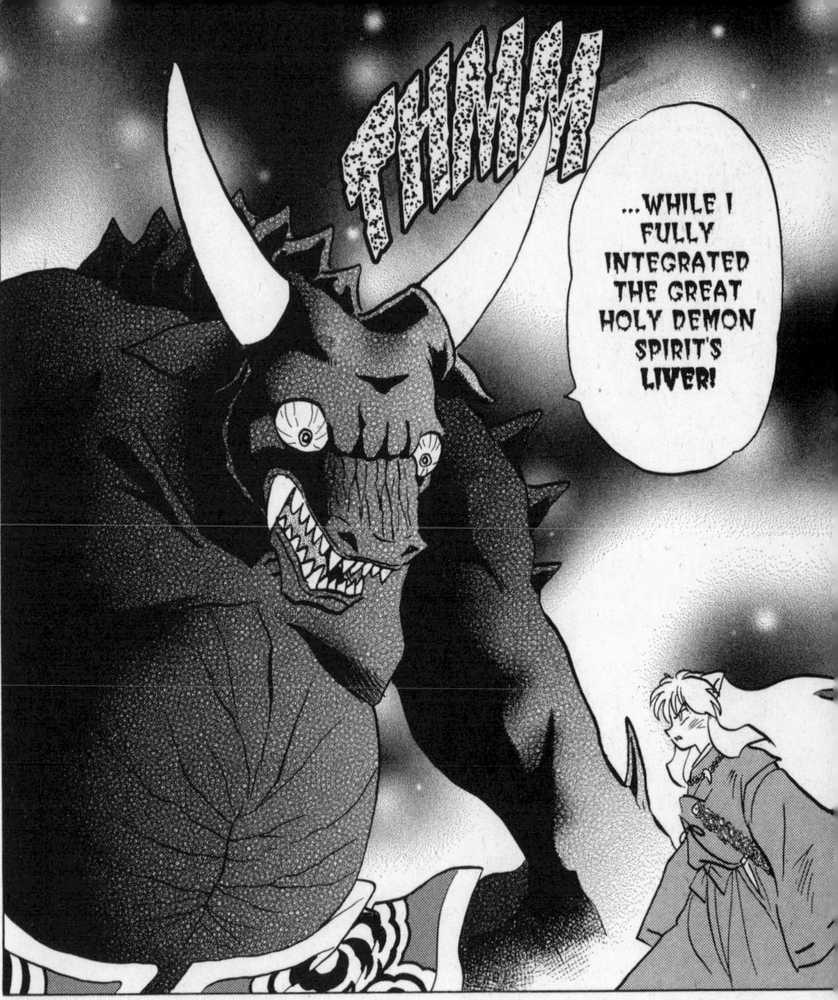
THMM
...WHILE I FULLY INTEGRATED THE GREAT HOLY DEMON SPIRIT'S LIVER!

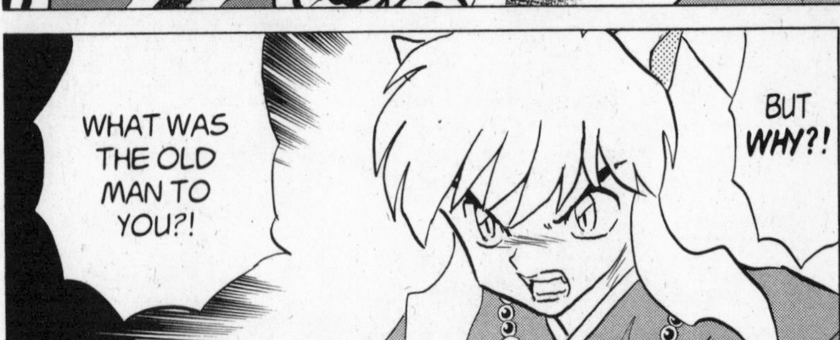
BUT WHY?!
WHAT WAS THE OLD MAN TO YOU?!

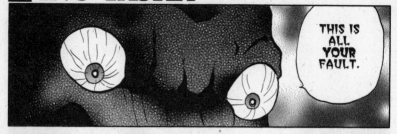

THIS IS ALL YOUR FAULT.
?!
HE'D BE ALIVE YET IF YOU HADN'T COME HERE TO TRAIN WITH HIM.
IT'S THAT BLADE OF YOURS.
!
IT ABSORBS OTHER DEMONS' DEMONIC ENERGY, YES?
CAN'T LEAVE A DANGEROUS BLADE LIKE THAT ON THE LOOSE...
...MUCH LESS LET IT KEEP GROWING STRONGER.

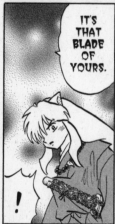

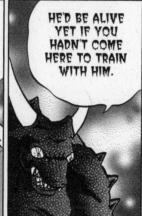

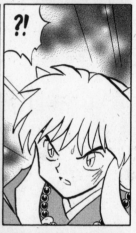

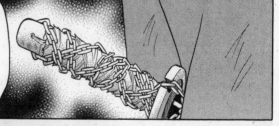

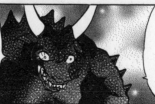

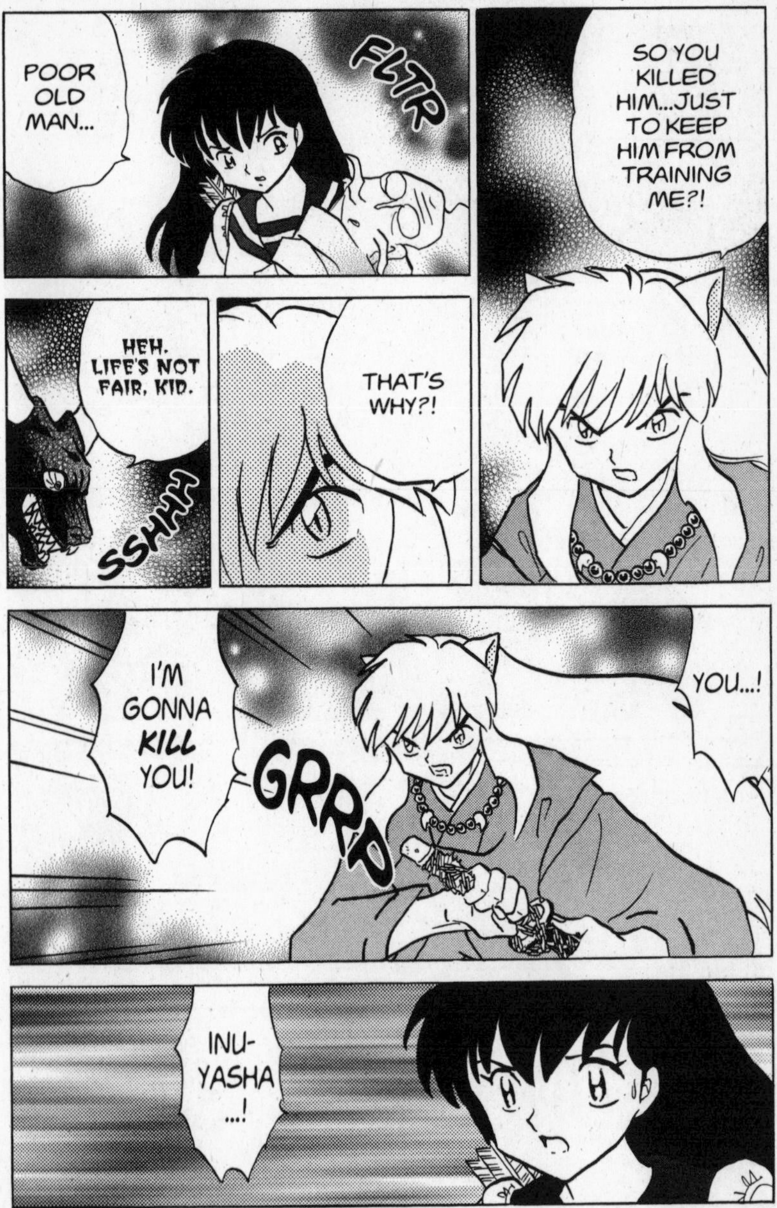
SO YOU KILLED HIM...JUST TO KEEP HIM FROM TRAINING ME?!
POOR OLD MAN...
FLTR
THAT'S WHY?!
HEH. LIFE'S NOT FAIR, KID.
SSHHH
YOU...!
I'M GONNA **KILL** YOU!
GRRP
INU-YASHA ...!

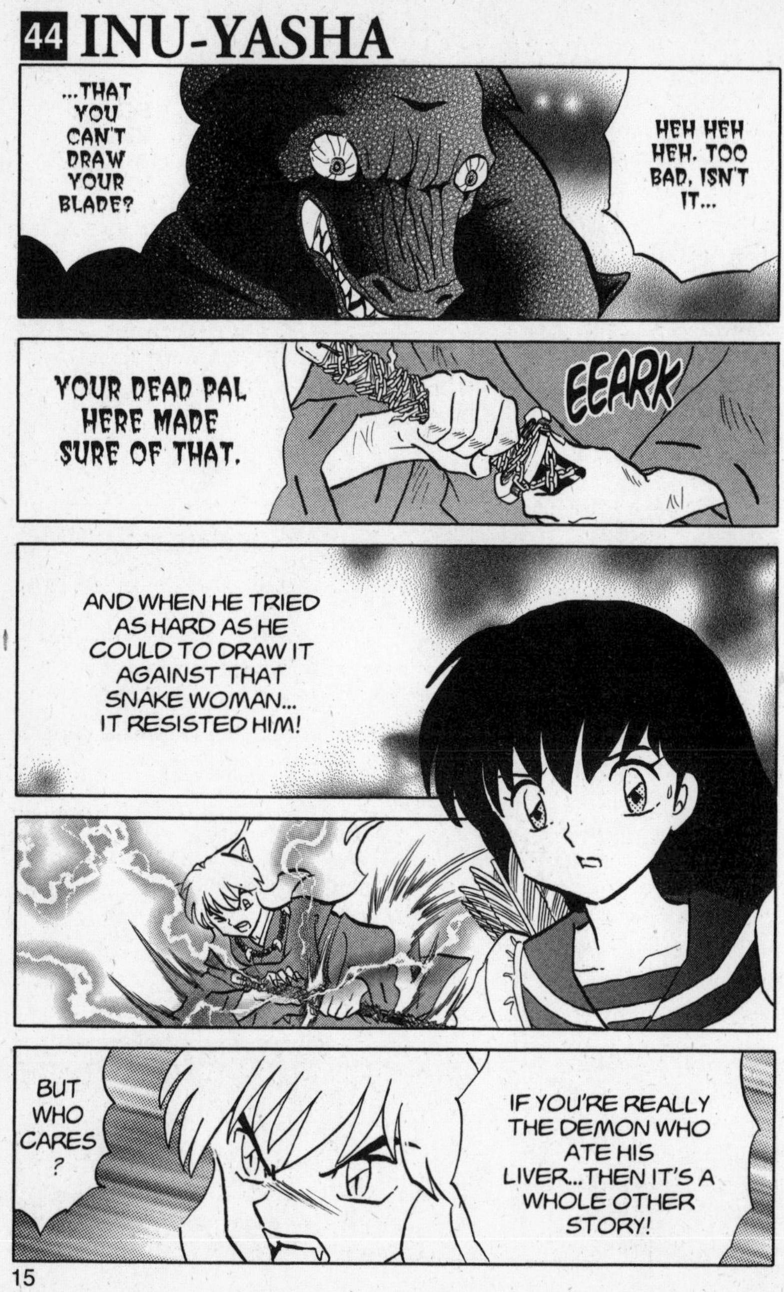
HEH HEH HEH. TOO BAD, ISN'T IT...
...THAT YOU CAN'T DRAW YOUR BLADE?
EEARK
YOUR DEAD PAL HERE MADE SURE OF THAT.
AND WHEN HE TRIED AS HARD AS HE COULD TO DRAW IT AGAINST THAT SNAKE WOMAN... IT RESISTED HIM!
BUT WHO CARES?
IF YOU'RE REALLY THE DEMON WHO ATE HIS LIVER...THEN IT'S A WHOLE OTHER STORY!

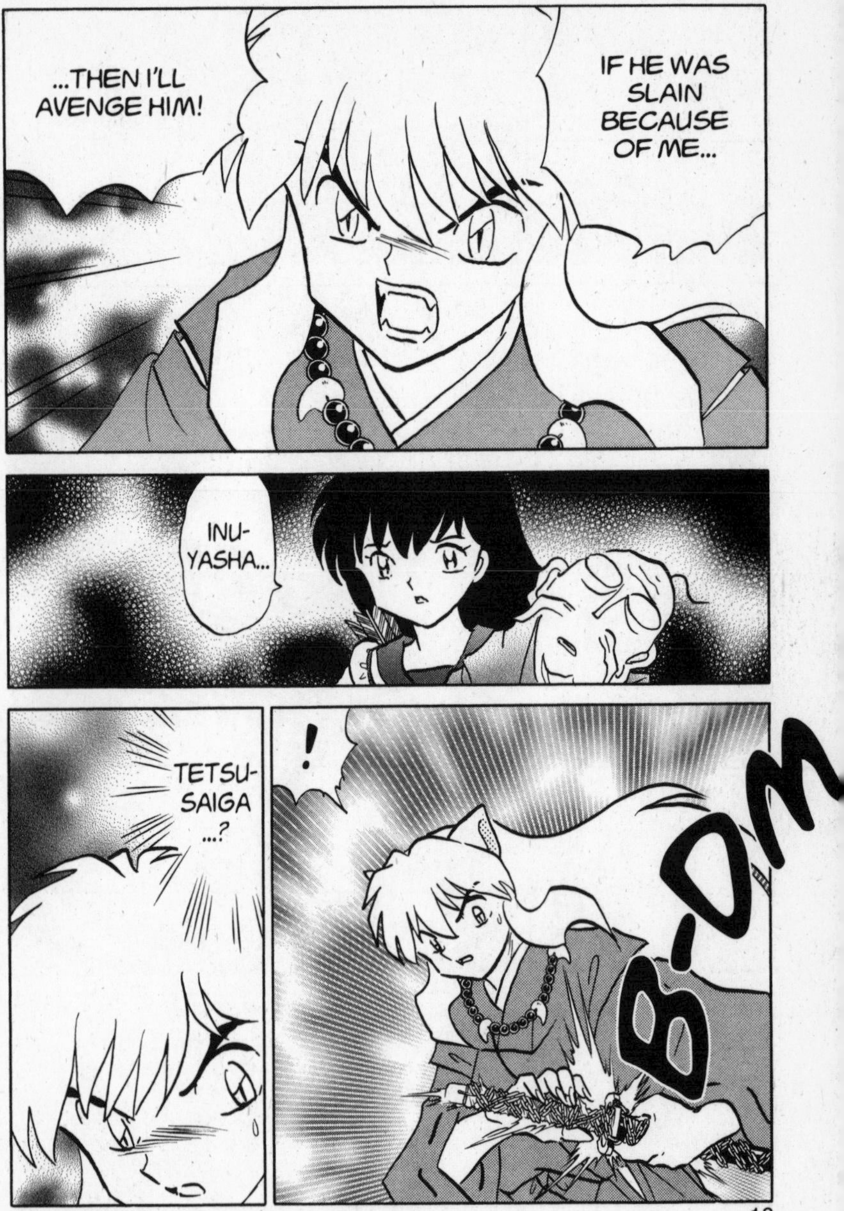
IF HE WAS SLAIN BECAUSE OF ME...
...THEN I'LL AVENGE HIM!
INU-YASHA...
!
B-DM
TETSU-SAIGA ...?

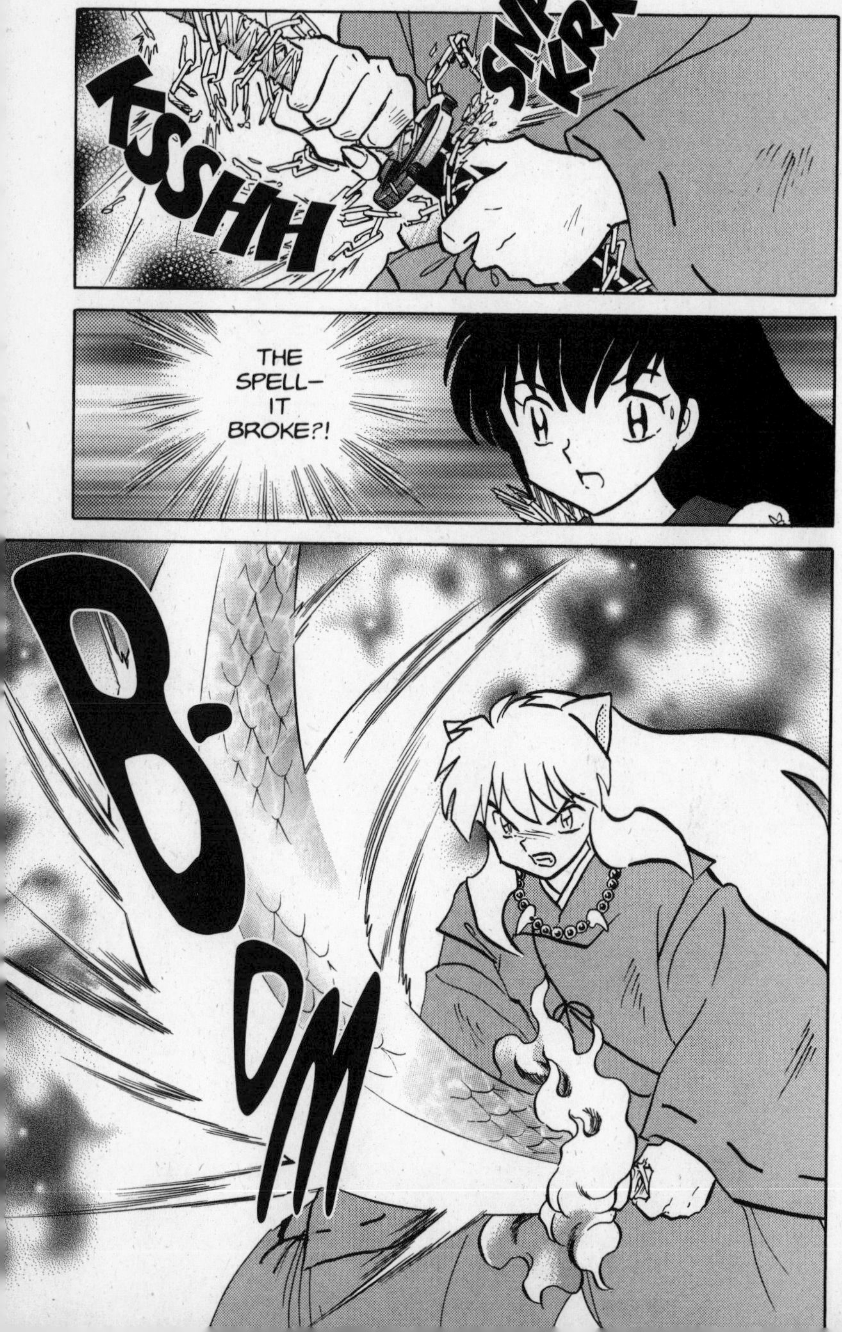
SNIP KRK
KSSHH
THE SPELL— IT BROKE?!
B-DOM

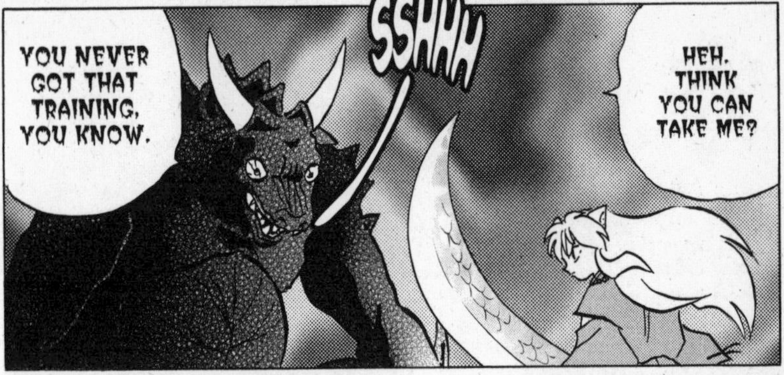
HEH. THINK YOU CAN TAKE ME?
SSHHH
YOU NEVER GOT THAT TRAINING, YOU KNOW.

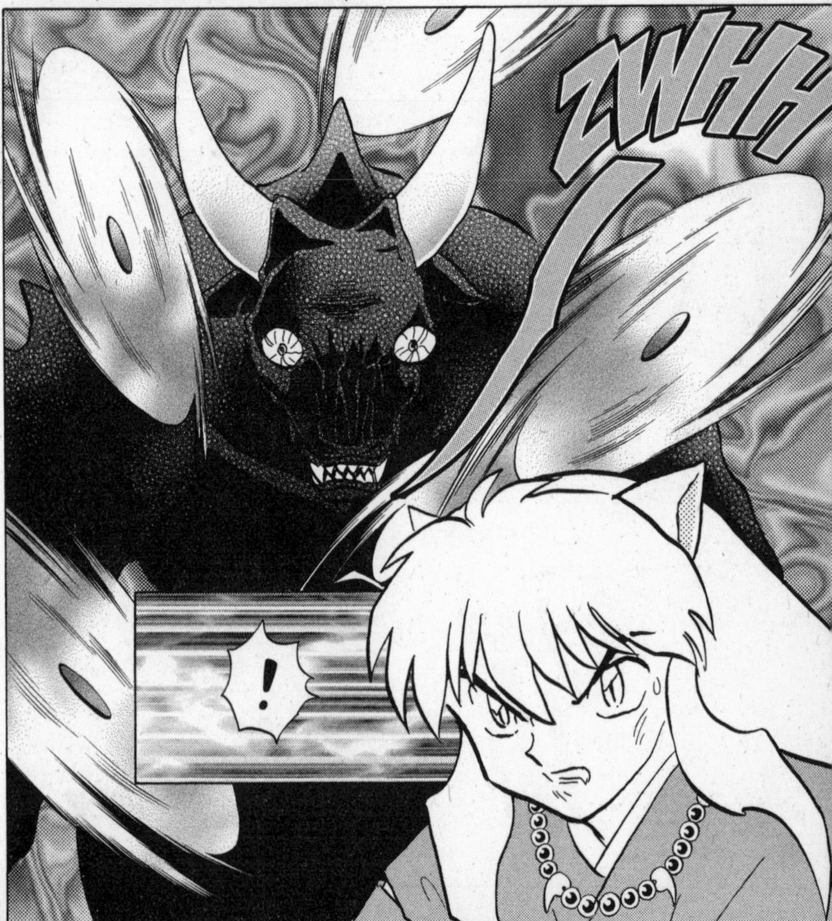
ZWHH
!

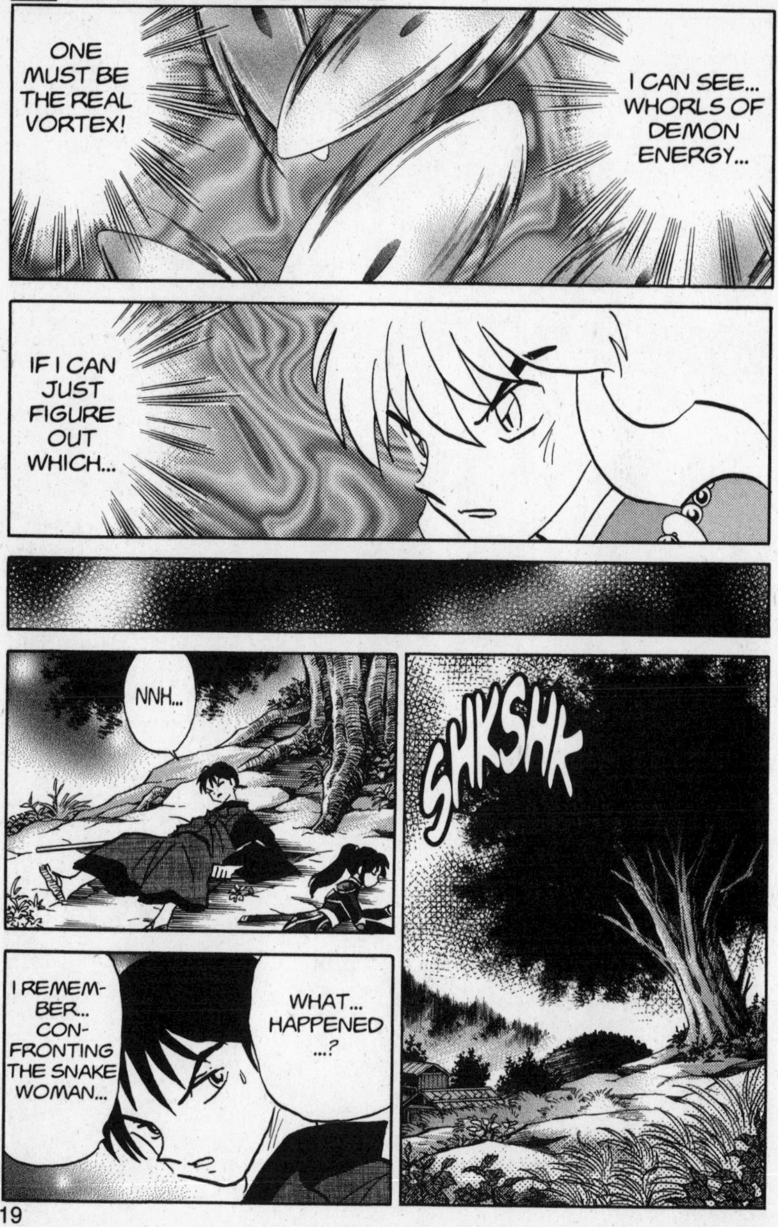
I CAN SEE... WHORLS OF DEMON ENERGY...
ONE MUST BE THE REAL VORTEX!
IF I CAN JUST FIGURE OUT WHICH...
SHKSHK
NNH...
WHAT... HAPPENED ...?
I REMEMBER... CONFRONTING THE SNAKE WOMAN...

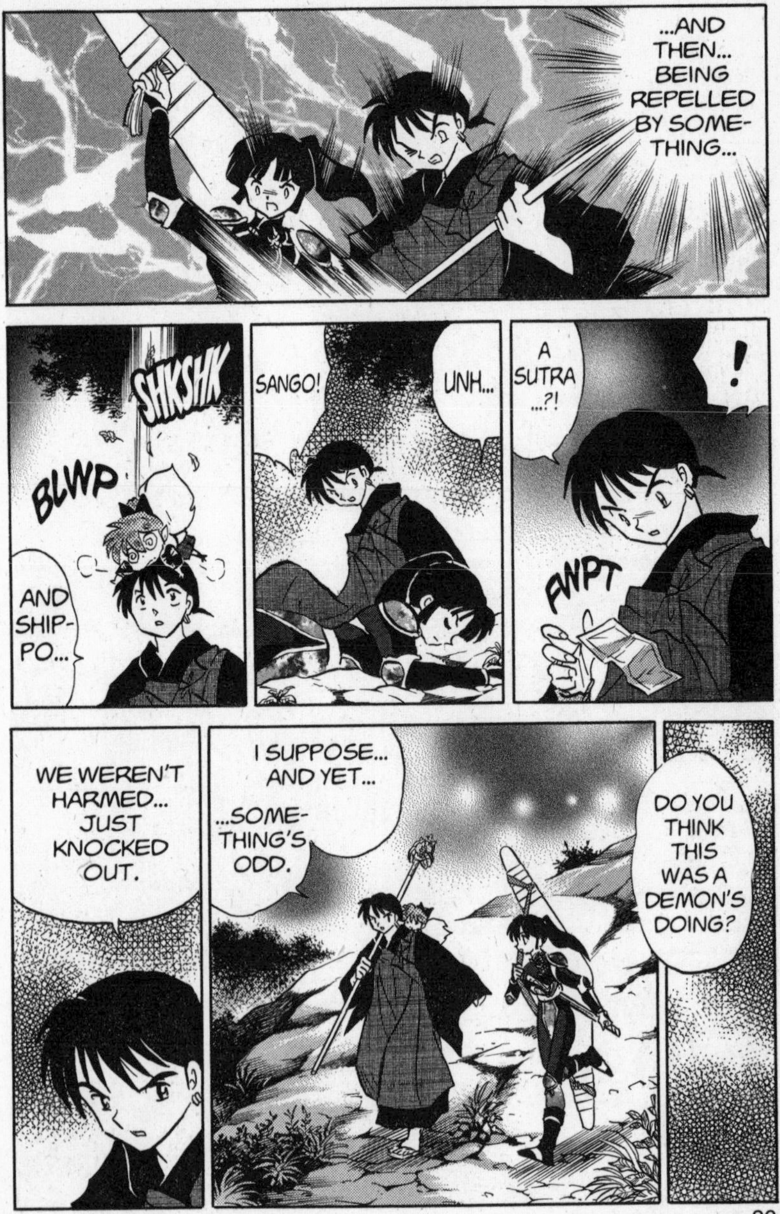
...AND THEN... BEING REPELLED BY SOME-THING...
SHKSHK
BLWP
AND SHIP-PO...
SANGO!
UNH...
A SUTRA ...?!
!
FWPT
WE WEREN'T HARMED... JUST KNOCKED OUT.
I SUPPOSE... AND YET...
...SOME-THING'S ODD.
DO YOU THINK THIS WAS A DEMON'S DOING?

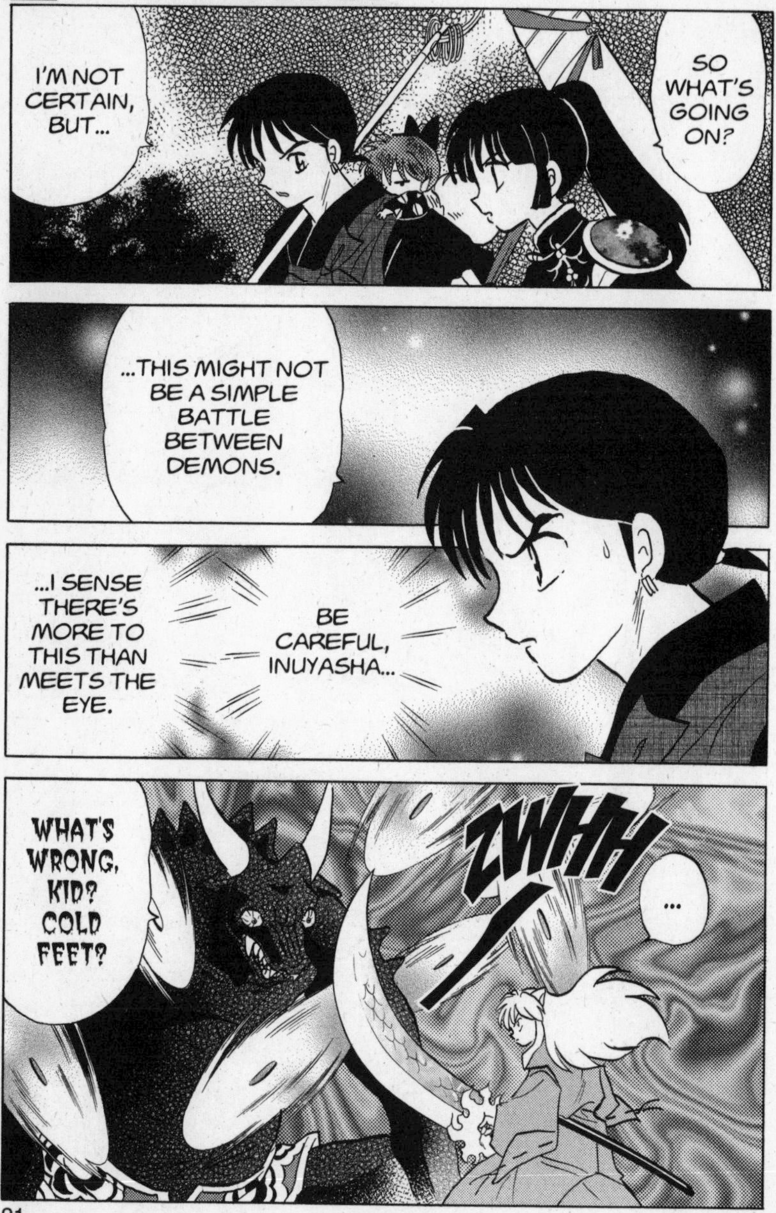
SO WHAT'S GOING ON?
I'M NOT CERTAIN, BUT...
...THIS MIGHT NOT BE A SIMPLE BATTLE BETWEEN DEMONS.
BE CAREFUL, INUYASHA...
...I SENSE THERE'S MORE TO THIS THAN MEETS THE EYE.
ZWHH
...
WHAT'S WRONG, KID? COLD FEET?

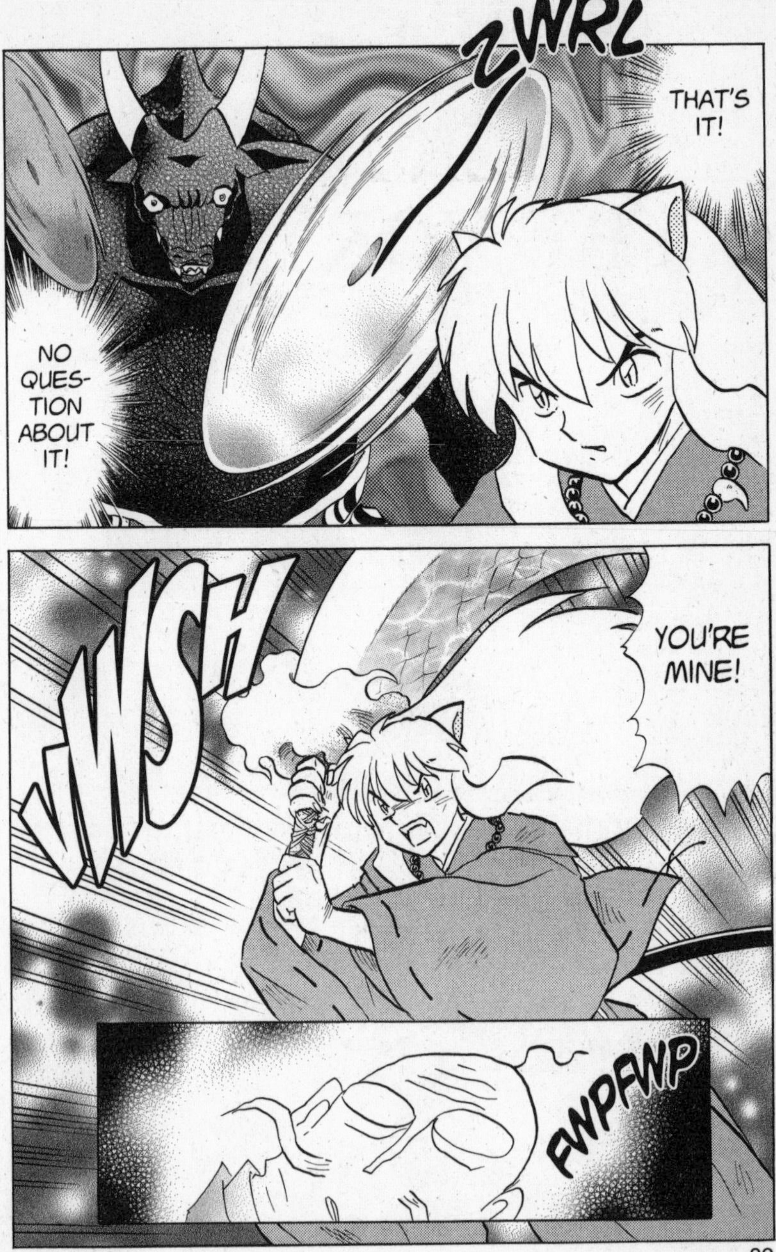
ZWRL
THAT'S IT!
NO QUES-TION ABOUT IT!
YOU'RE MINE!
WSH
FWPFWP

SCROLL 2
SCENT OF THE VORTEX

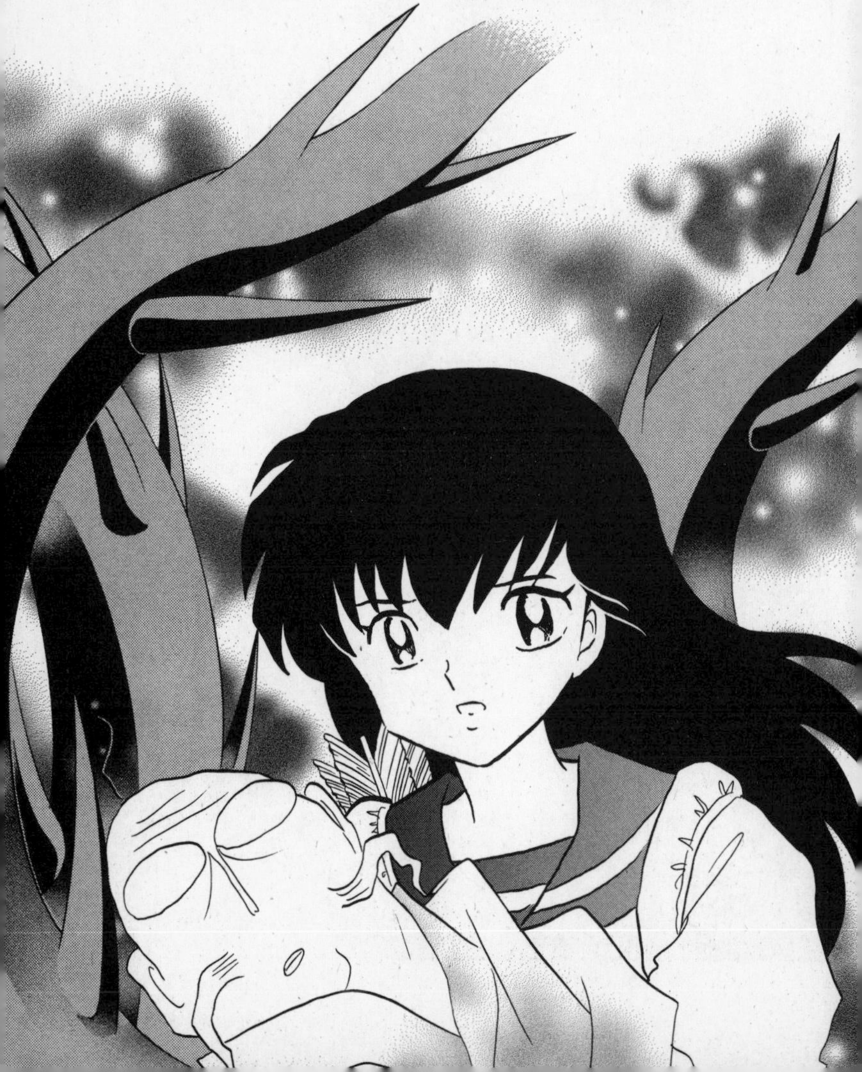

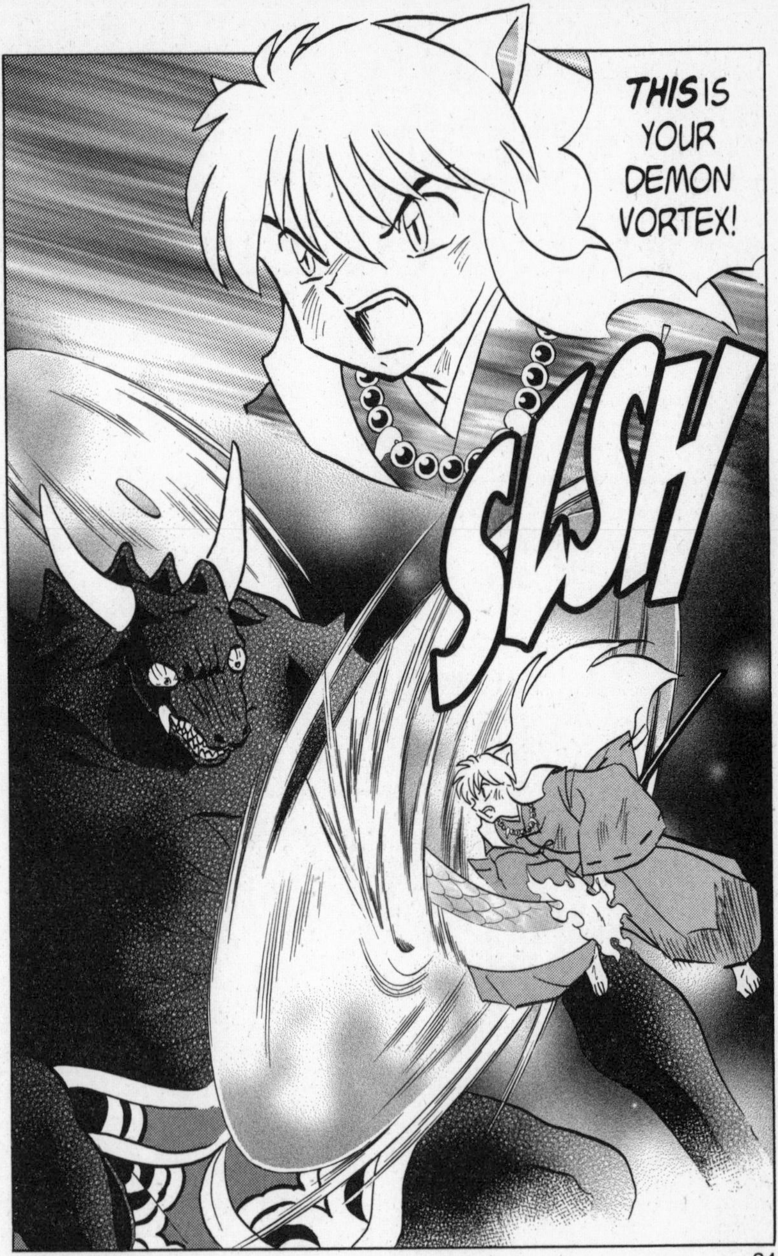
THIS IS YOUR DEMON VORTEX!
SLASH

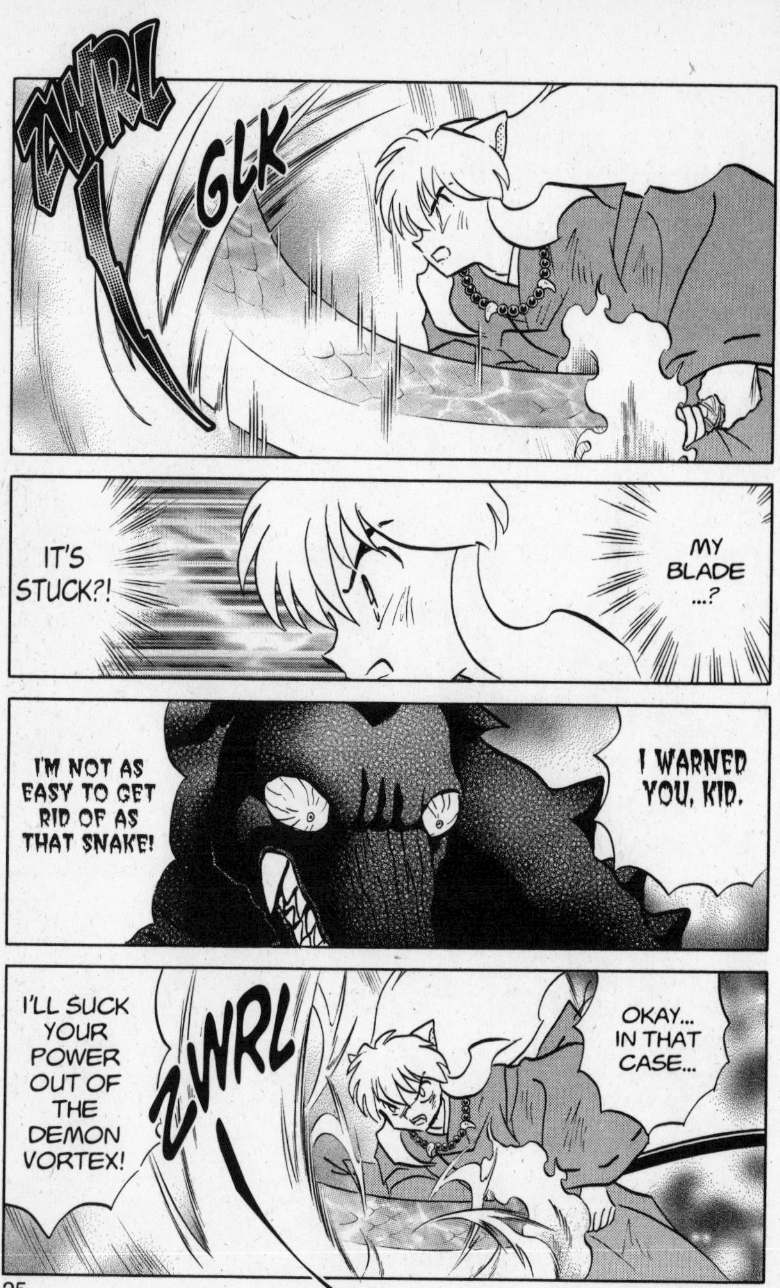
GLK
ZWRL
MY BLADE ...?
IT'S STUCK?!
I WARNED YOU, KID.
I'M NOT AS EASY TO GET RID OF AS THAT SNAKE!
OKAY... IN THAT CASE...
ZWRL
I'LL SUCK YOUR POWER OUT OF THE DEMON VORTEX!

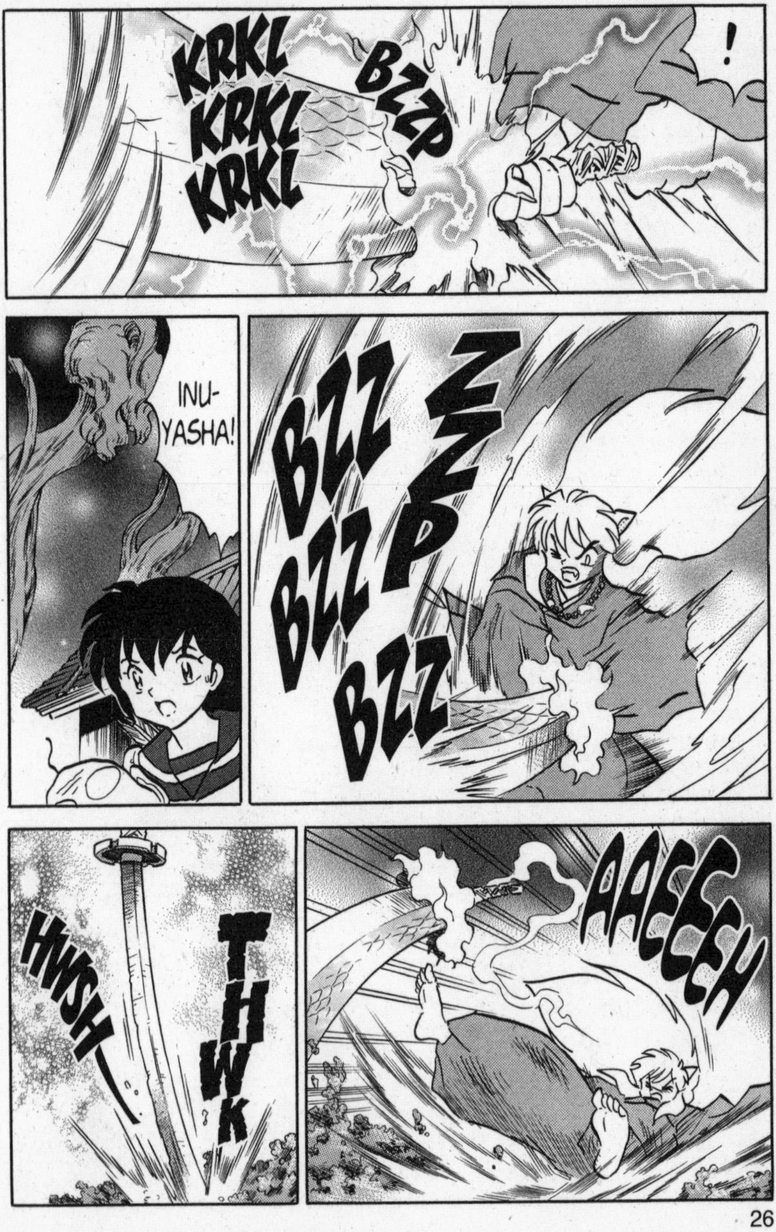
!
BZZZP
KRKL KRKL KRKL
BZZ BZZ BZZ BZZ BZZ
INU-
YASHA!
AAEEEH
THWK
HWSH—

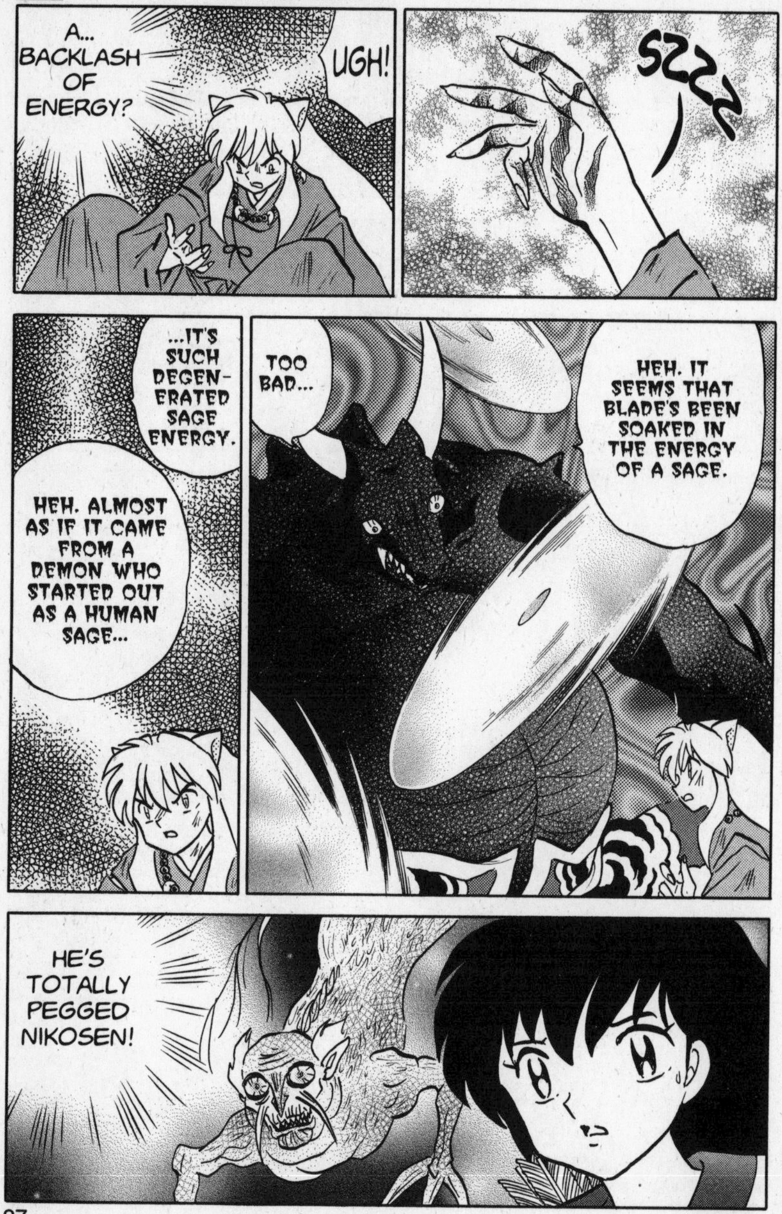
SZZZ
UGH!
A... BACKLASH OF ENERGY?
HEH. IT SEEMS THAT BLADE'S BEEN SOAKED IN THE ENERGY OF A SAGE.
TOO BAD...
...IT'S SUCH DEGEN-ERATED SAGE ENERGY.
HEH. ALMOST AS IF IT CAME FROM A DEMON WHO STARTED OUT AS A HUMAN SAGE...
HE'S TOTALLY PEGGED NIKOSEN!

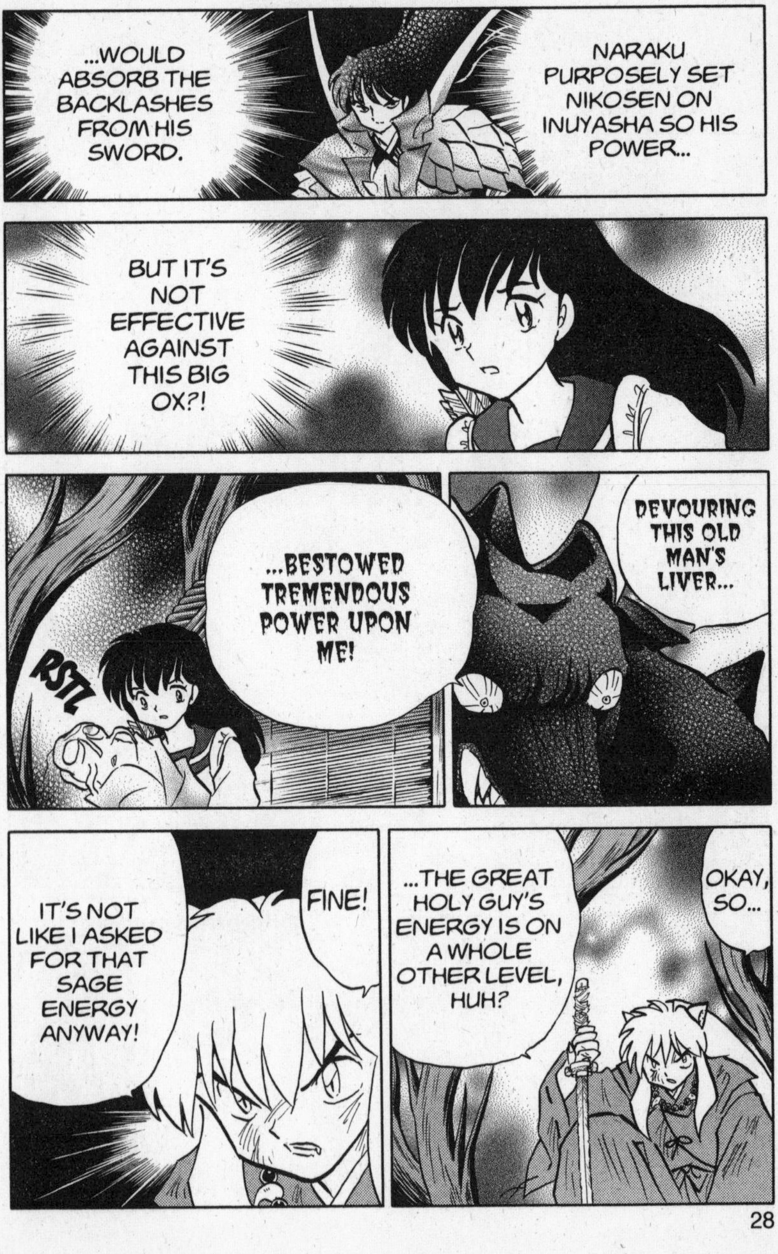
NARAKU PURPOSELY SET NIKOSEN ON INUYASHA SO HIS POWER...
...WOULD ABSORB THE BACKLASHES FROM HIS SWORD.
BUT IT'S NOT EFFECTIVE AGAINST THIS BIG OX?!
DEVOURING THIS OLD MAN'S LIVER...
...BESTOWED TREMENDOUS POWER UPON ME!
RSTL
OKAY, SO...
...THE GREAT HOLY GUY'S ENERGY IS ON A WHOLE OTHER LEVEL, HUH?
FINE!
IT'S NOT LIKE I ASKED FOR THAT SAGE ENERGY ANYWAY!

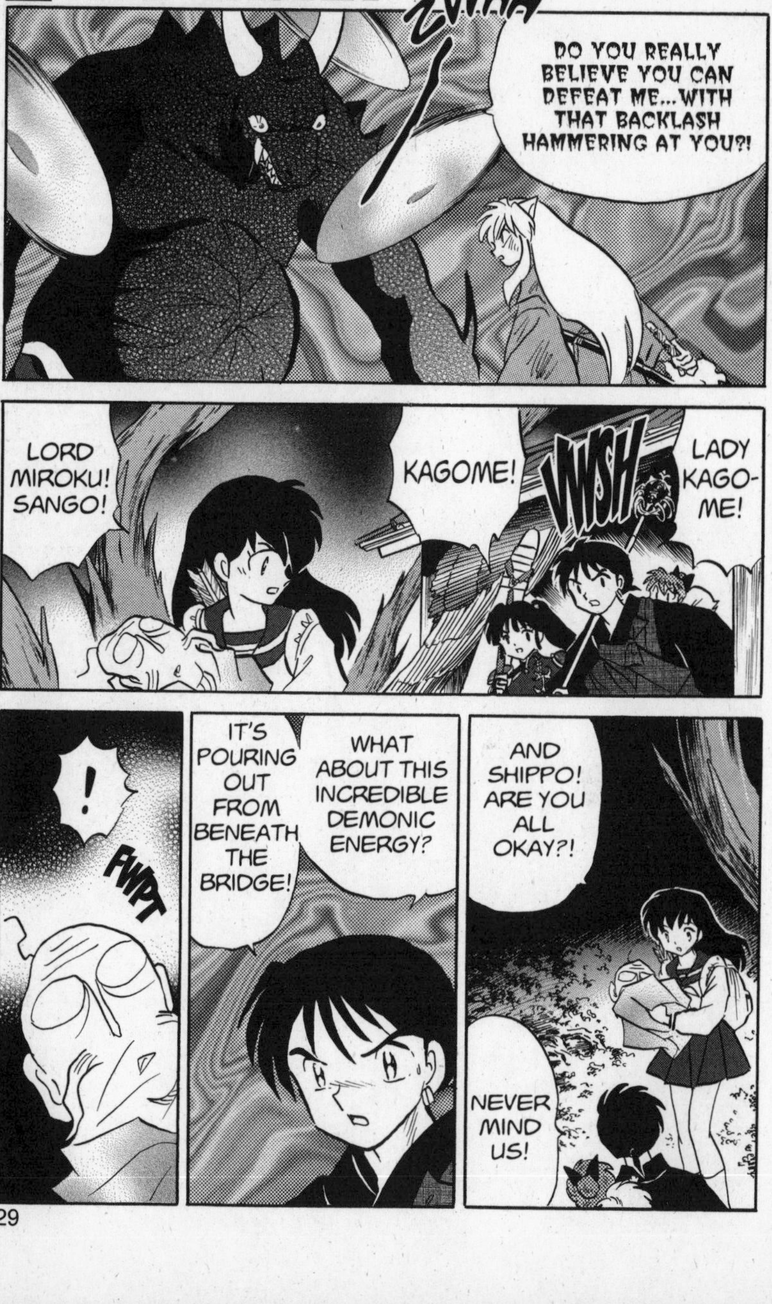
ZWHH
DO YOU REALLY BELIEVE YOU CAN DEFEAT ME...WITH THAT BACKLASH HAMMERING AT YOU?!
LADY KAGO-ME!
VWISH
KAGOME!
LORD MIROKU! SANGO!
AND SHIPPO! ARE YOU ALL OKAY?!
NEVER MIND US!
WHAT ABOUT THIS INCREDIBLE DEMONIC ENERGY?
IT'S POURING OUT FROM BENEATH THE BRIDGE!
!
FWPT

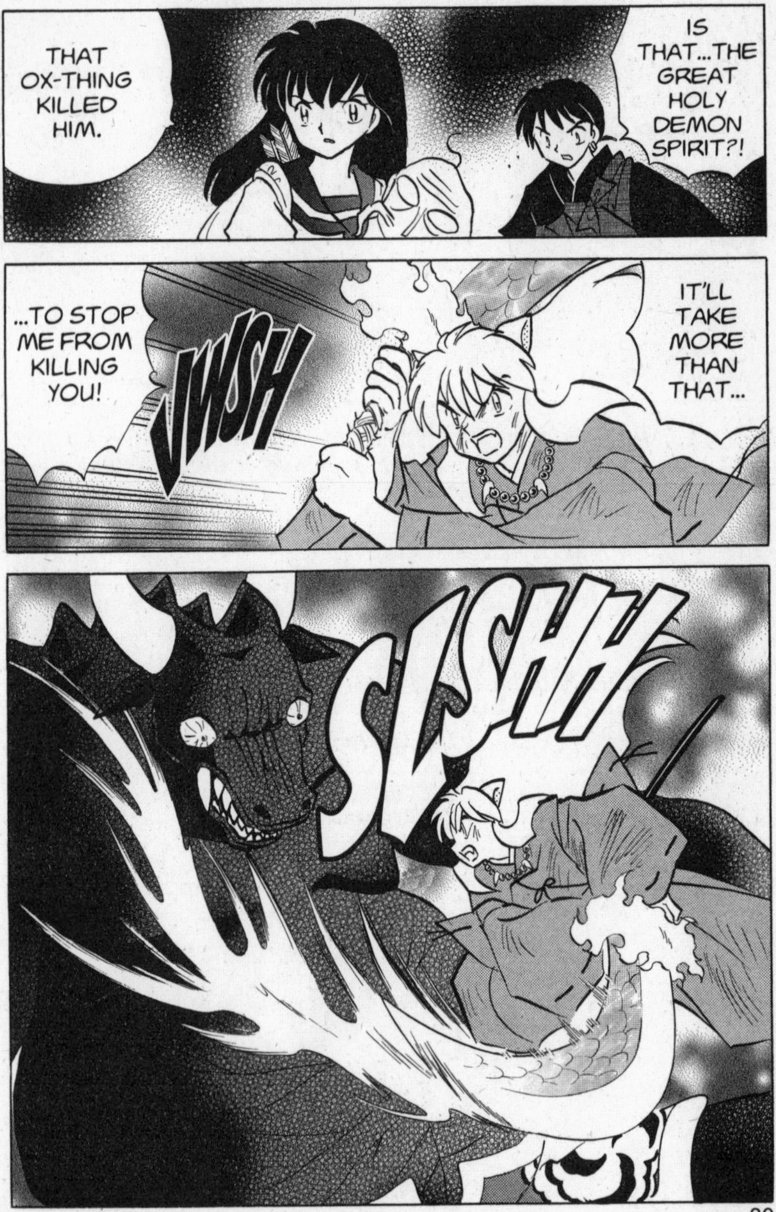
IS THAT...THE GREAT HOLY DEMON SPIRIT?!
THAT OX-THING KILLED HIM.
IT'LL TAKE MORE THAN THAT...
JWISH
...TO STOP ME FROM KILLING YOU!
SLSHH

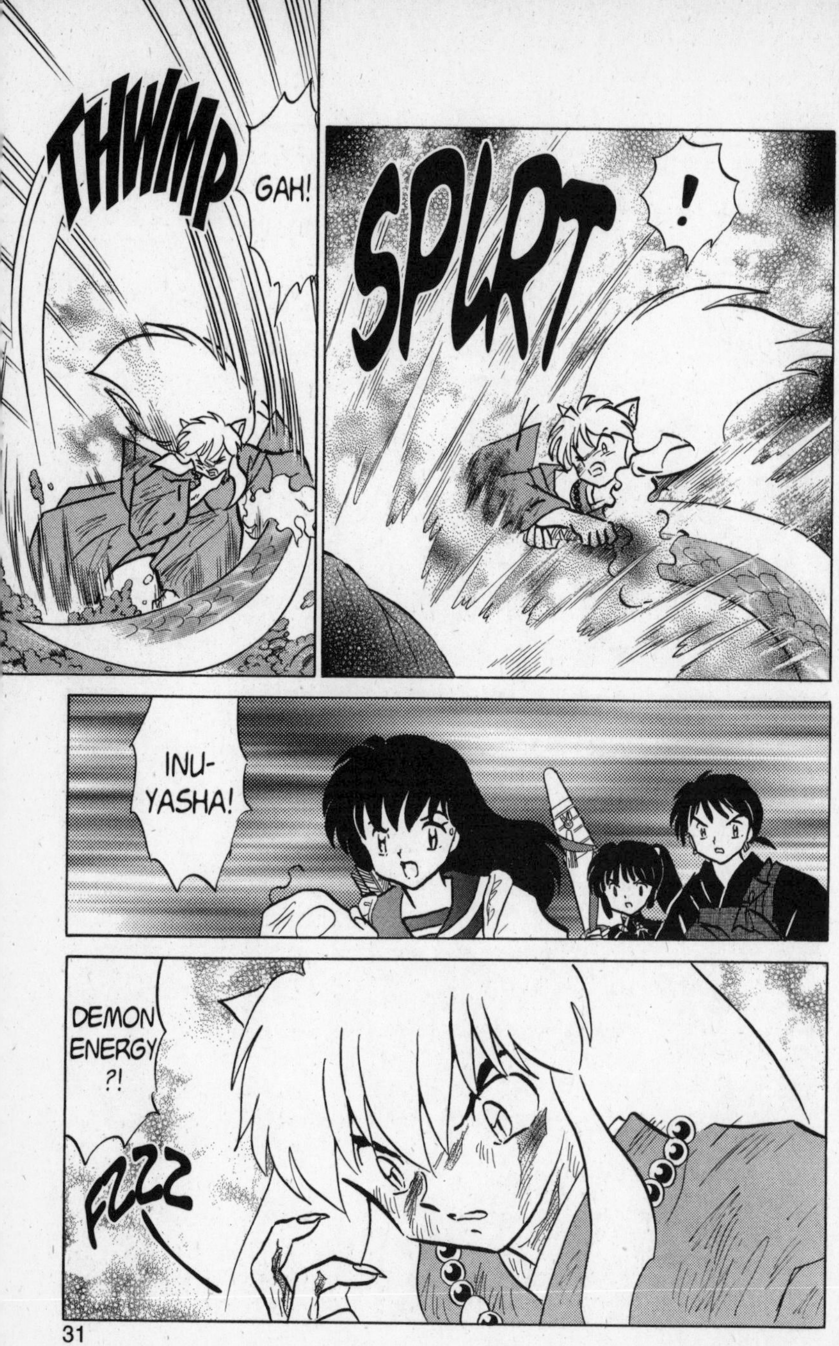
SPLRT
!
THWMP
GAH!
INU-YASHA!
DEMON ENERGY ?!
FZZZ

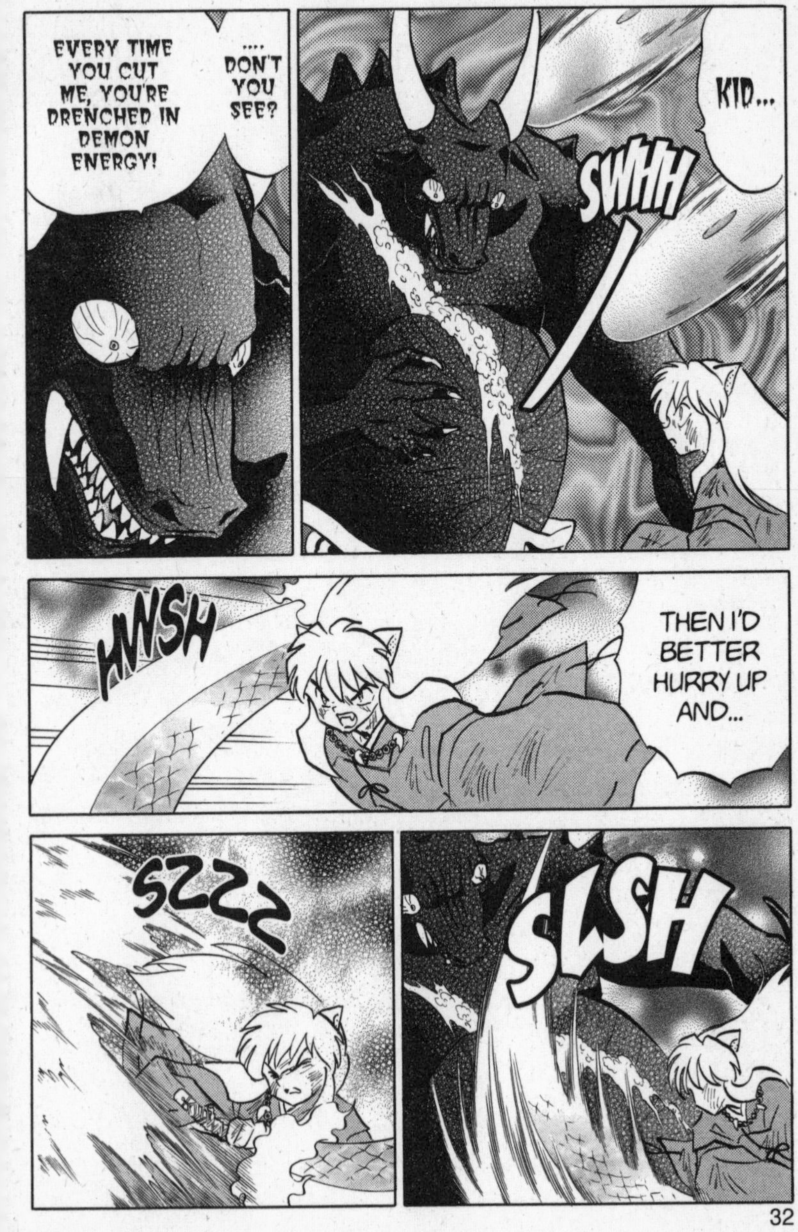
KID...
SWHH
.... DON'T YOU SEE?
EVERY TIME YOU CUT ME, YOU'RE DRENCHED IN DEMON ENERGY!
THEN I'D BETTER HURRY UP AND...
HWSH
SLSH
SZZZ

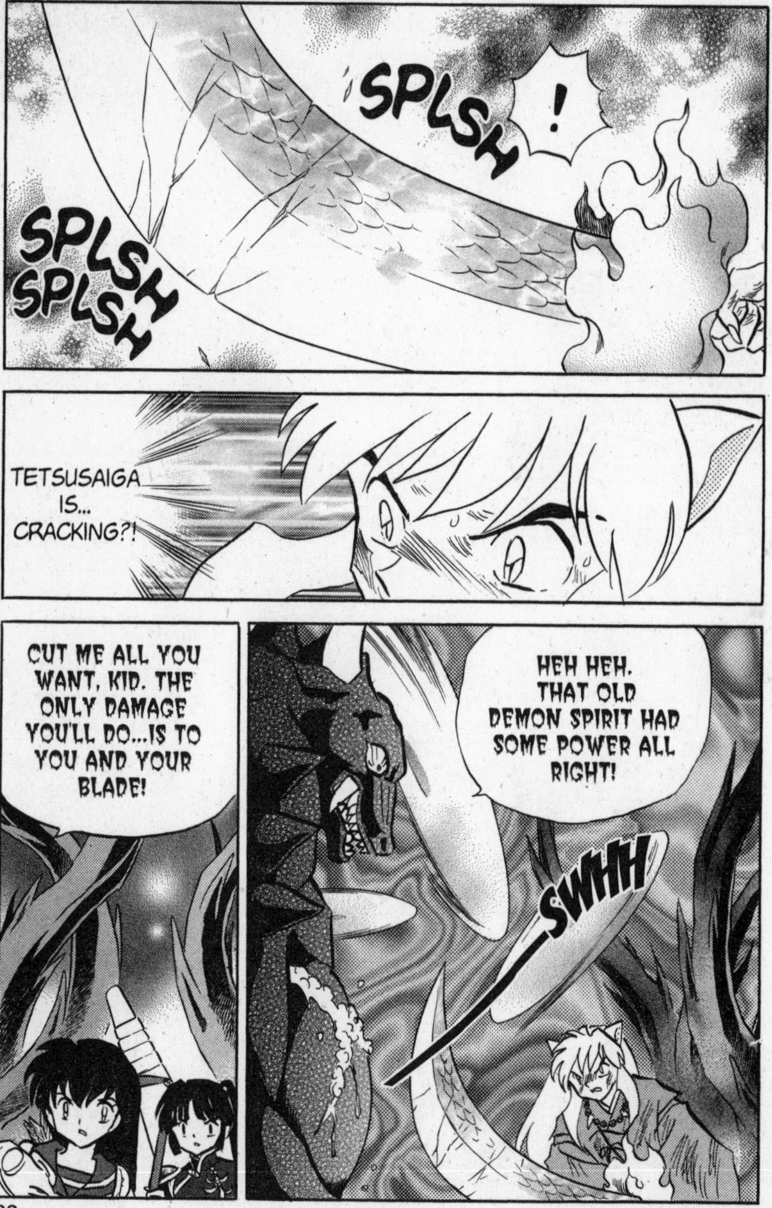
!
SPLSH
SPLSH SPLSH
TETSUSAIGA IS... CRACKING?!
HEH HEH. THAT OLD DEMON SPIRIT HAD SOME POWER ALL RIGHT!
SWHH
CUT ME ALL YOU WANT, KID. THE ONLY DAMAGE YOU'LL DO...IS TO YOU AND YOUR BLADE!

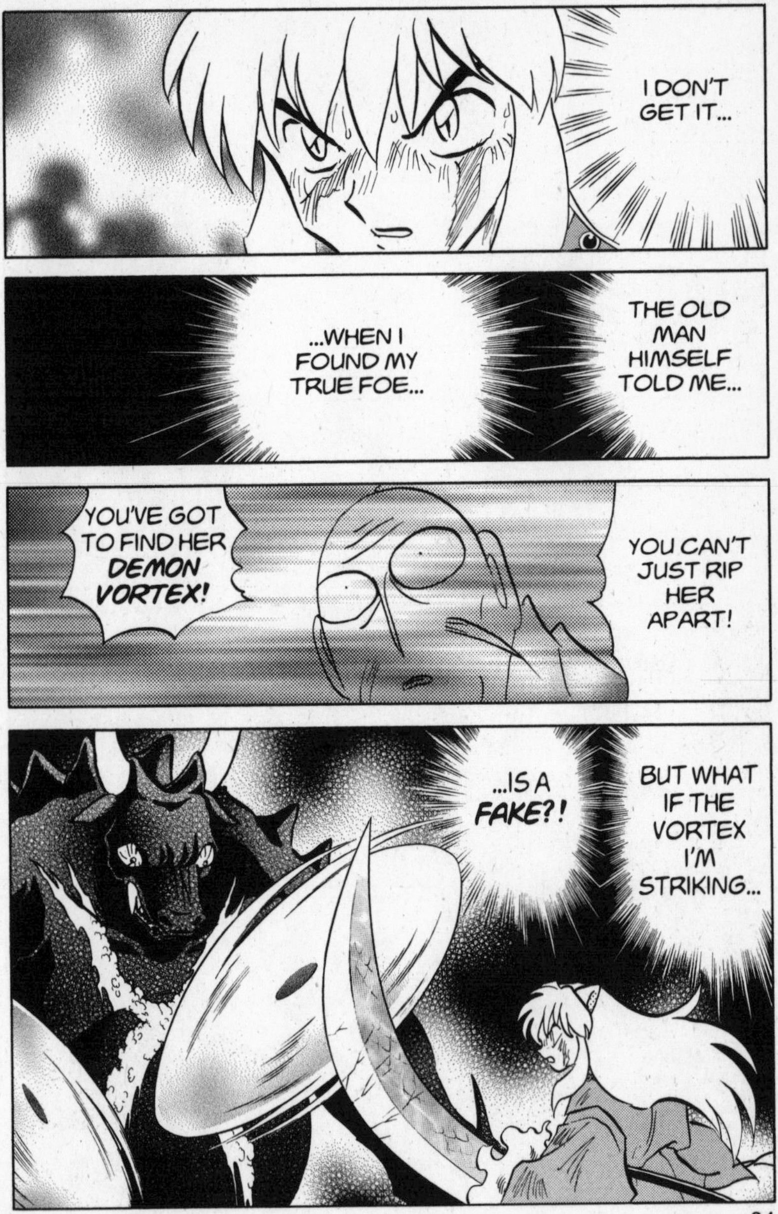
I DON'T GET IT...
THE OLD MAN HIMSELF TOLD ME...
...WHEN I FOUND MY TRUE FOE...
YOU CAN'T JUST RIP HER APART!
YOU'VE GOT TO FIND HER *DEMON VORTEX!*
BUT WHAT IF THE VORTEX I'M STRIKING...
...IS A *FAKE?!*

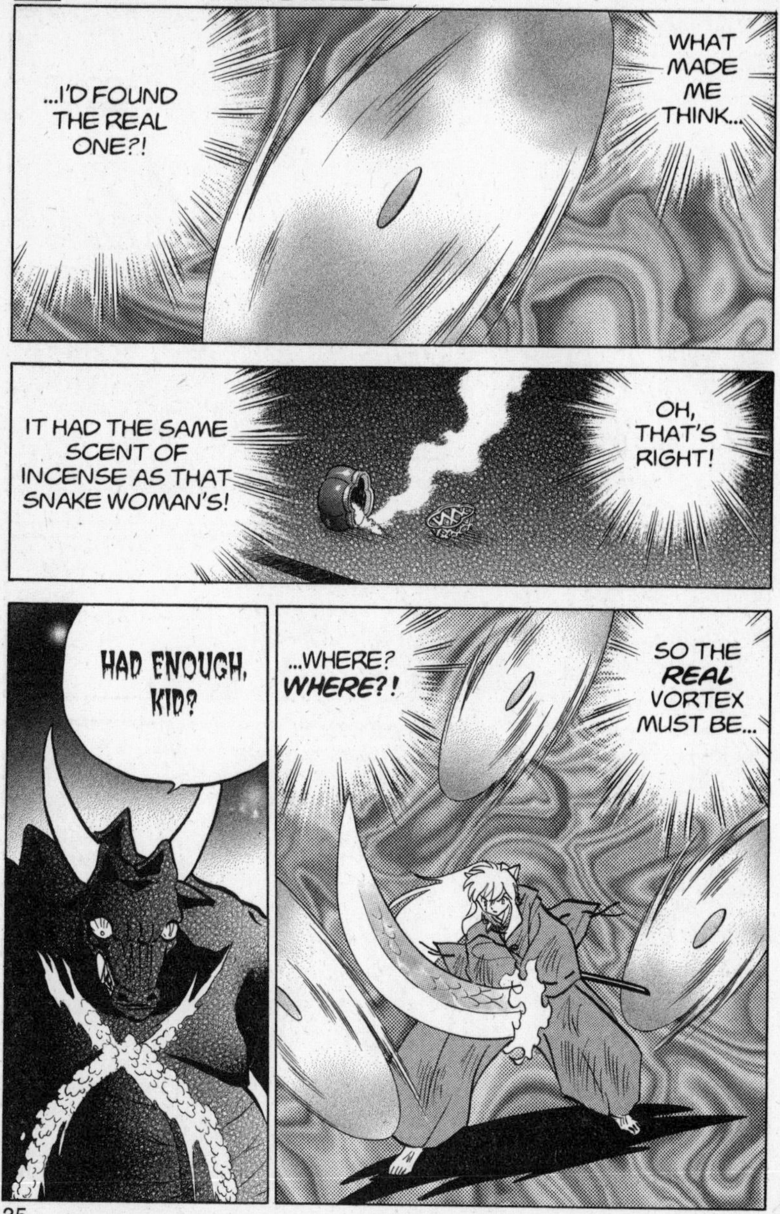
WHAT MADE ME THINK...
...I'D FOUND THE REAL ONE?!
OH, THAT'S RIGHT!
IT HAD THE SAME SCENT OF INCENSE AS THAT SNAKE WOMAN'S!
SO THE REAL VORTEX MUST BE...
...WHERE? WHERE?!
HAD ENOUGH, KID?

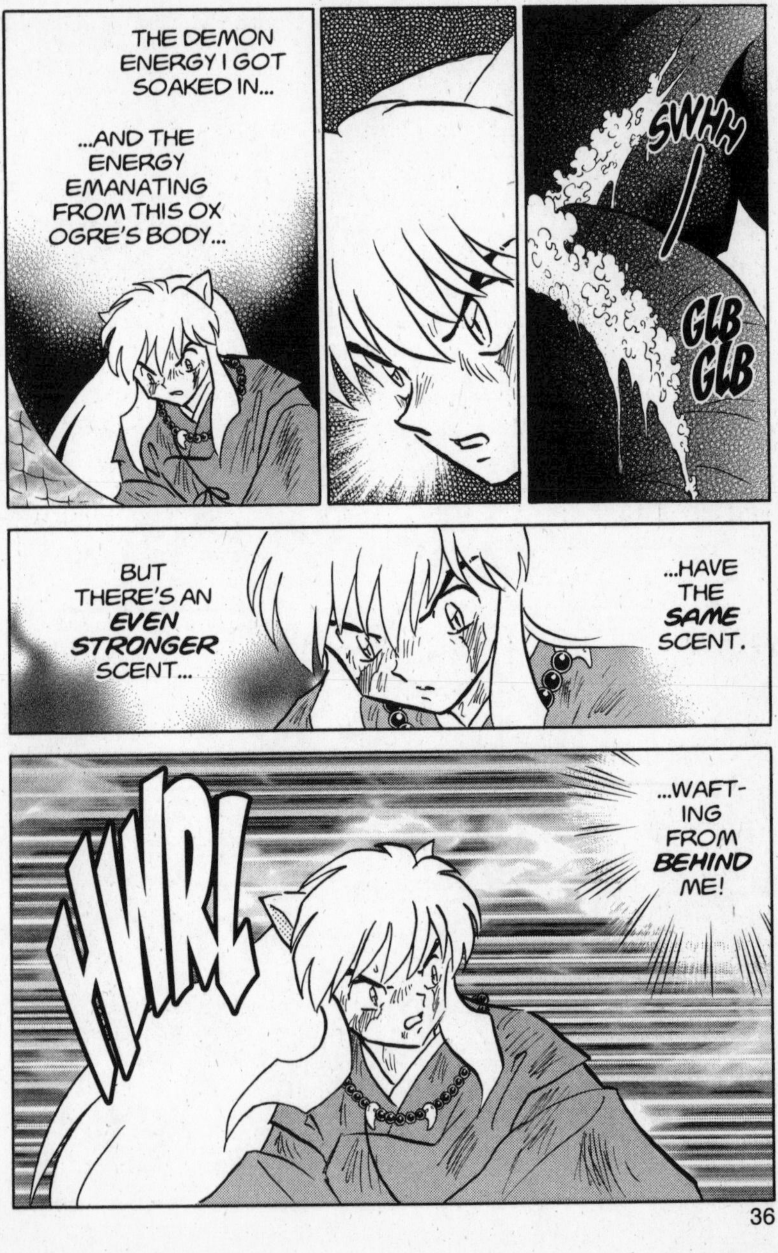
SWHH
GLB GLB
THE DEMON ENERGY I GOT SOAKED IN...
...AND THE ENERGY EMANATING FROM THIS OX OGRE'S BODY...
...HAVE THE SAME SCENT.
BUT THERE'S AN EVEN STRONGER SCENT...
...WAFT-ING FROM BEHIND ME!
HWIRL

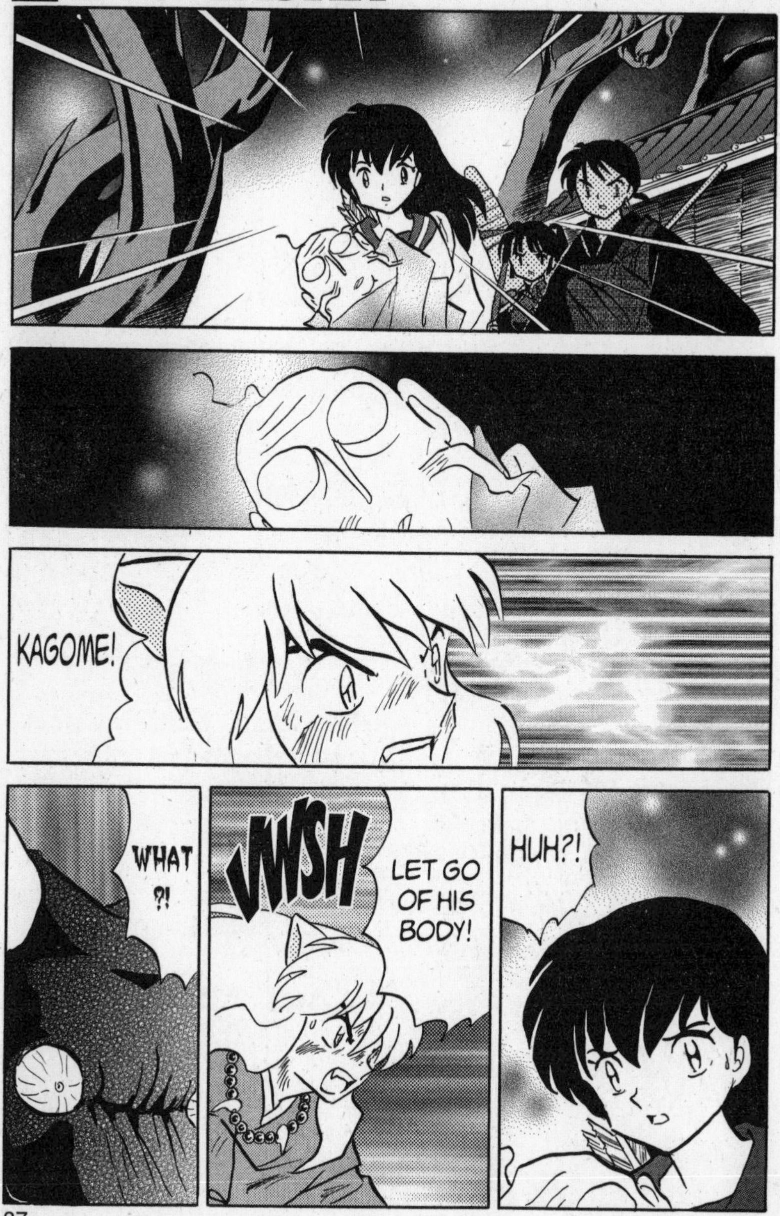
KAGOME!
HUH?!
WHSH
LET GO OF HIS BODY!
WHAT ?!

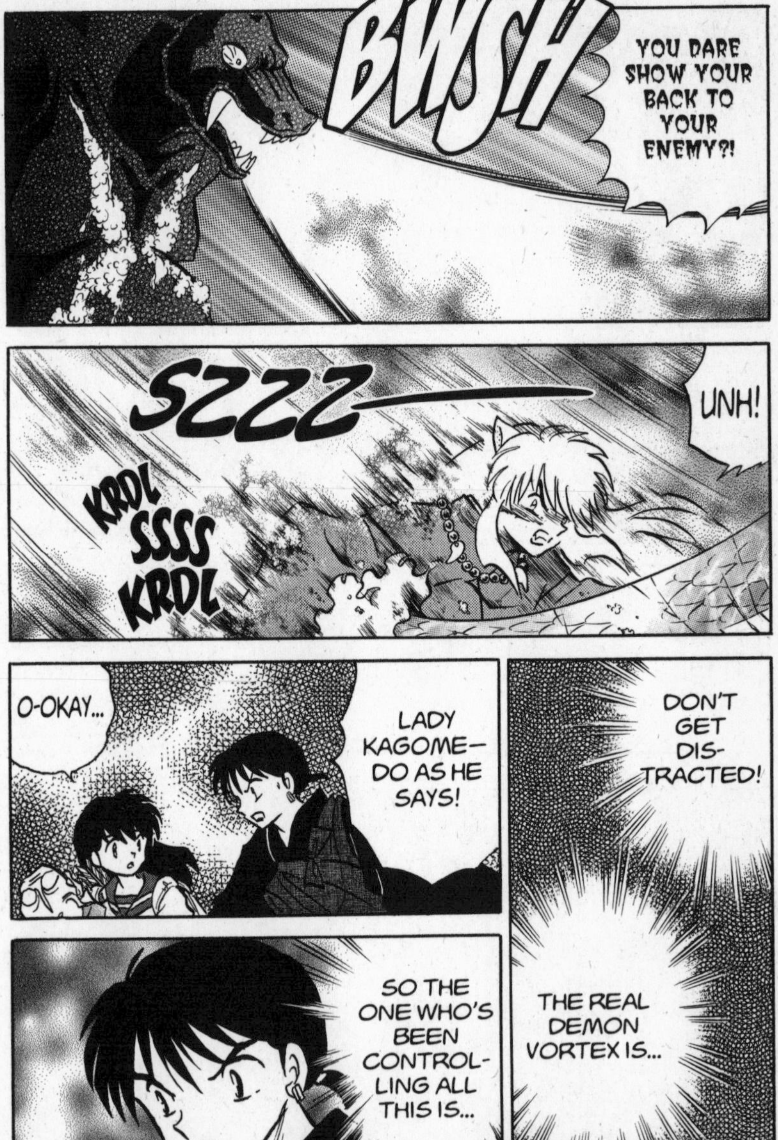
BWSH
YOU DARE SHOW YOUR BACK TO YOUR ENEMY?!
SZZZ
UNH!
KRDL SSSS KRDL
DON'T GET DIS-TRACTED!
THE REAL DEMON VORTEX IS...
LADY KAGOME—DO AS HE SAYS!
O-OKAY...
SO THE ONE WHO'S BEEN CONTROL-LING ALL THIS IS...

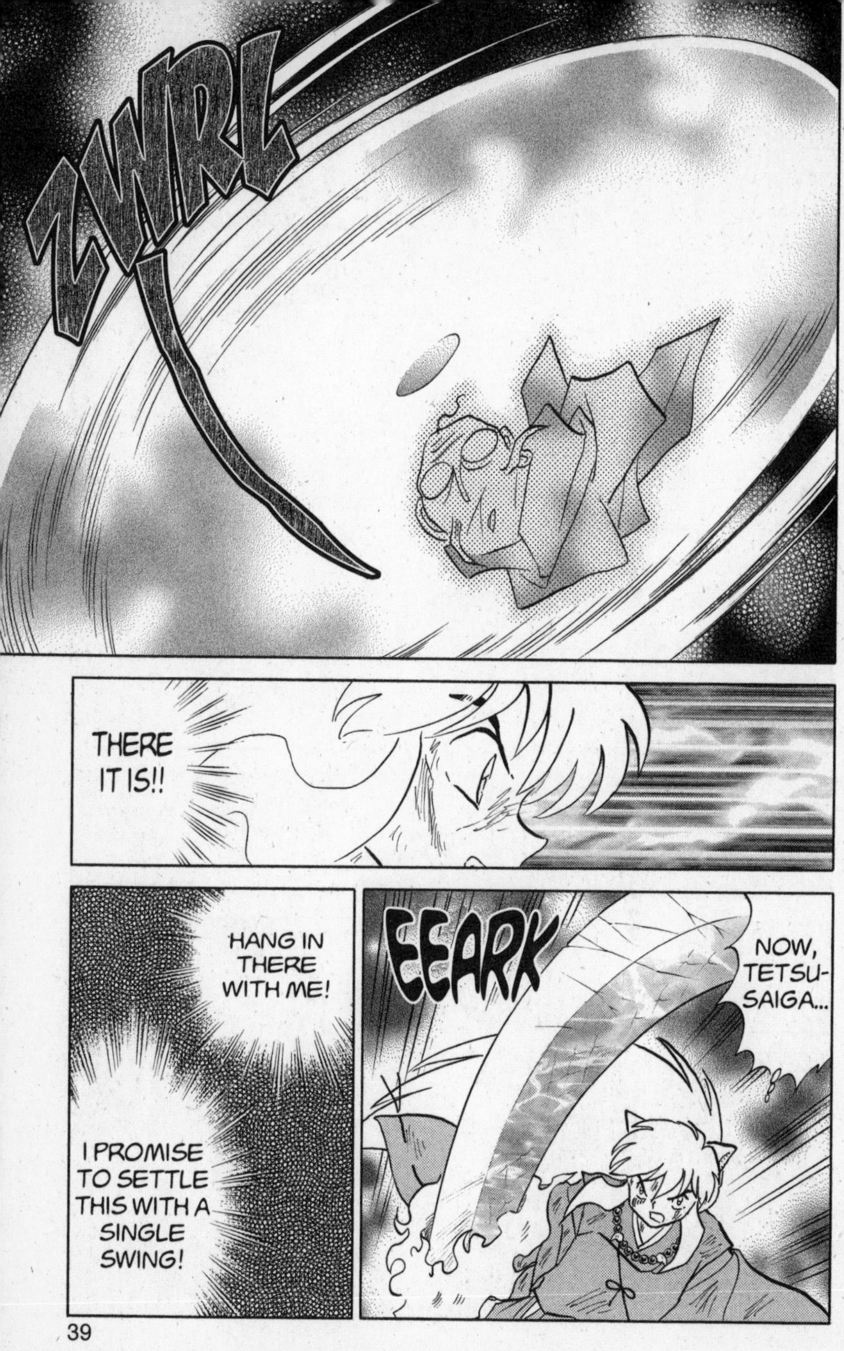
ZWRL
THERE IT IS!!
EEARK
NOW, TETSU-SAIGA...
HANG IN THERE WITH ME!
I PROMISE TO SETTLE THIS WITH A SINGLE SWING!

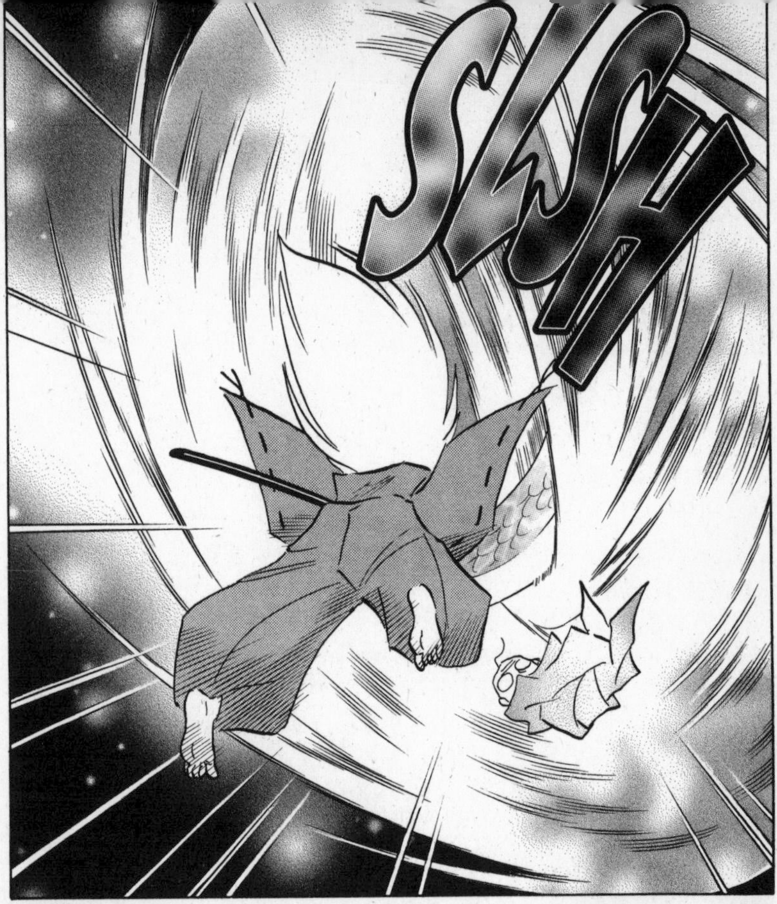
SLASH
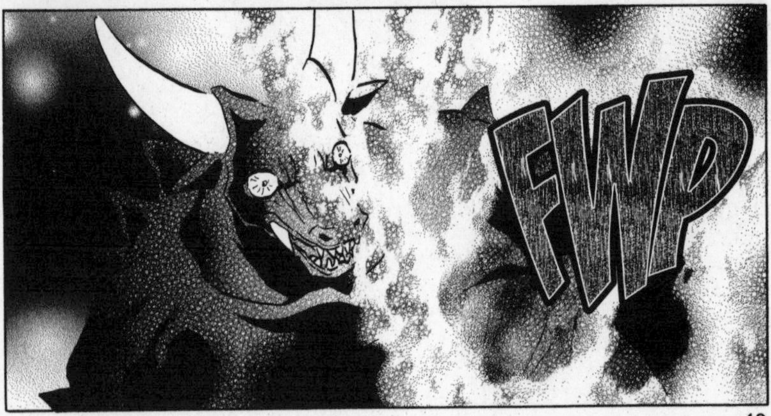
FWP

SCROLL 3
TRAINING

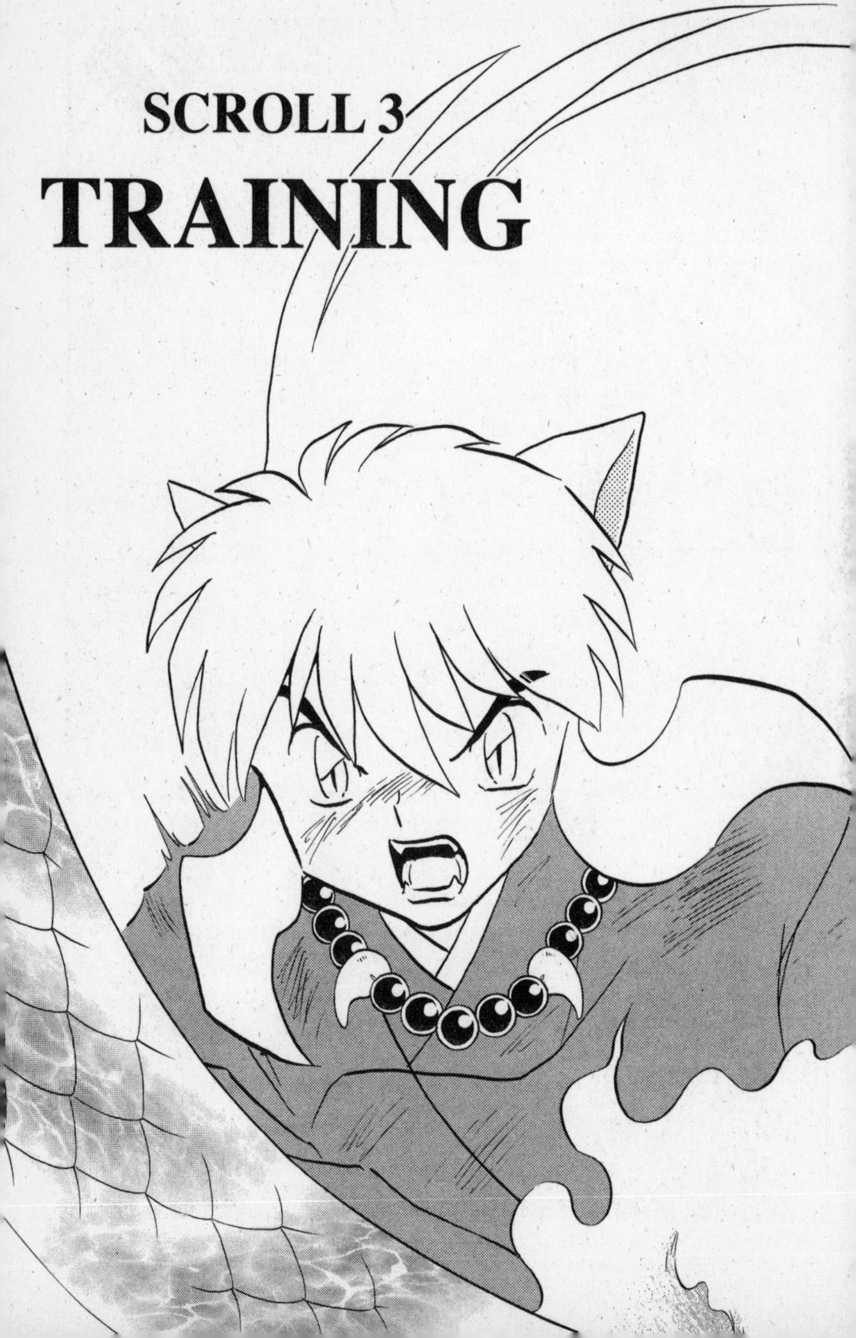

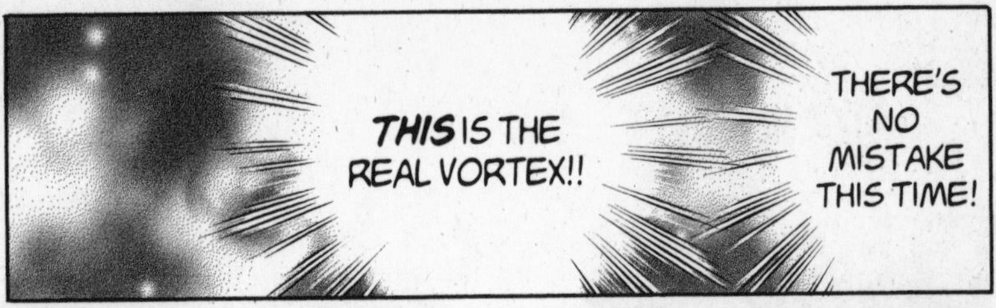
THERE'S NO MISTAKE THIS TIME!
THIS IS THE REAL VORTEX!!
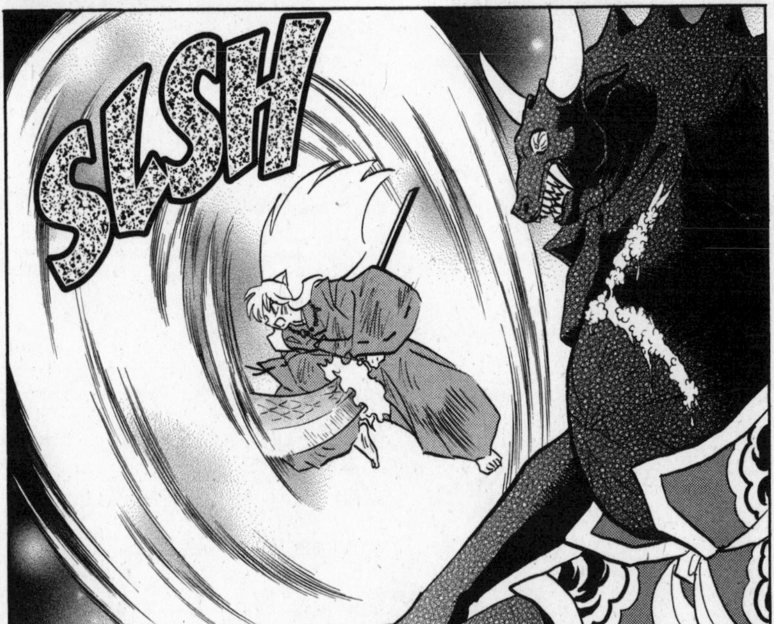
SLSH
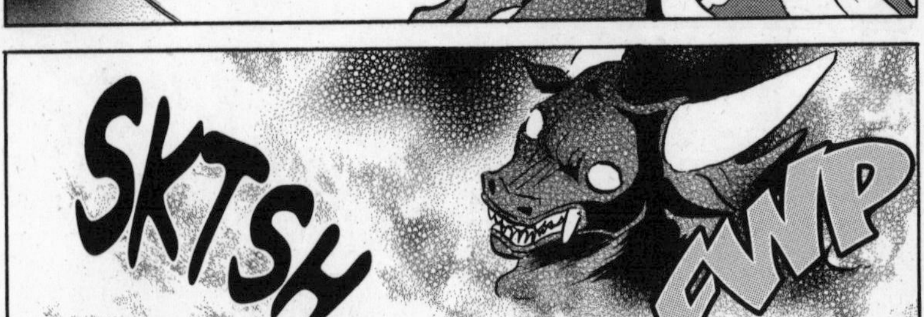
FWP
SKTSH

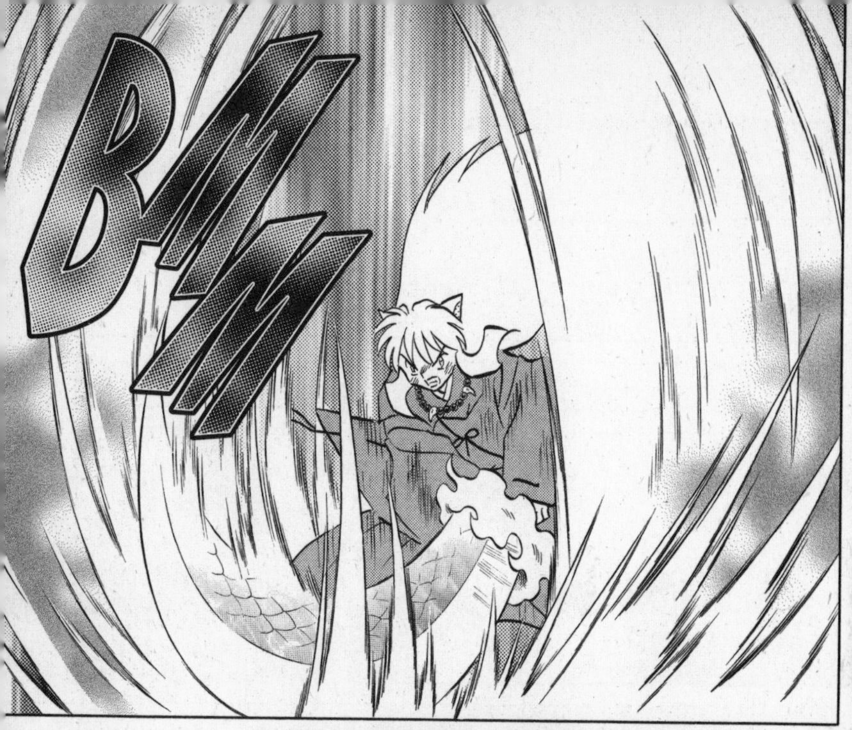
BAMM
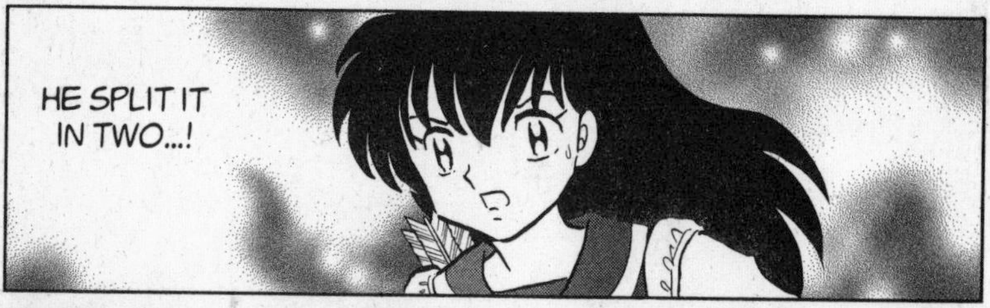
HE SPLIT IT IN TWO...!
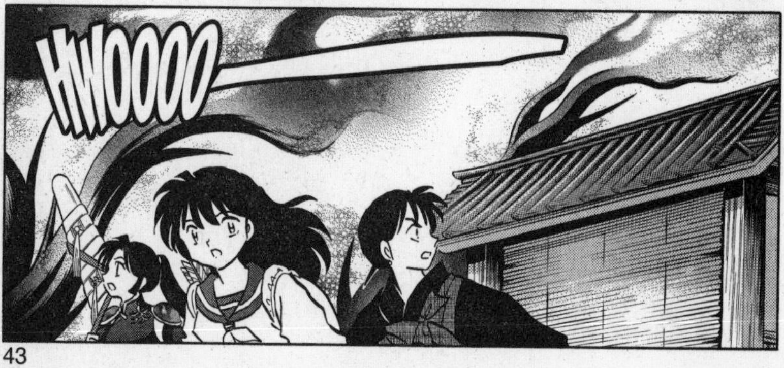
HWOOOO

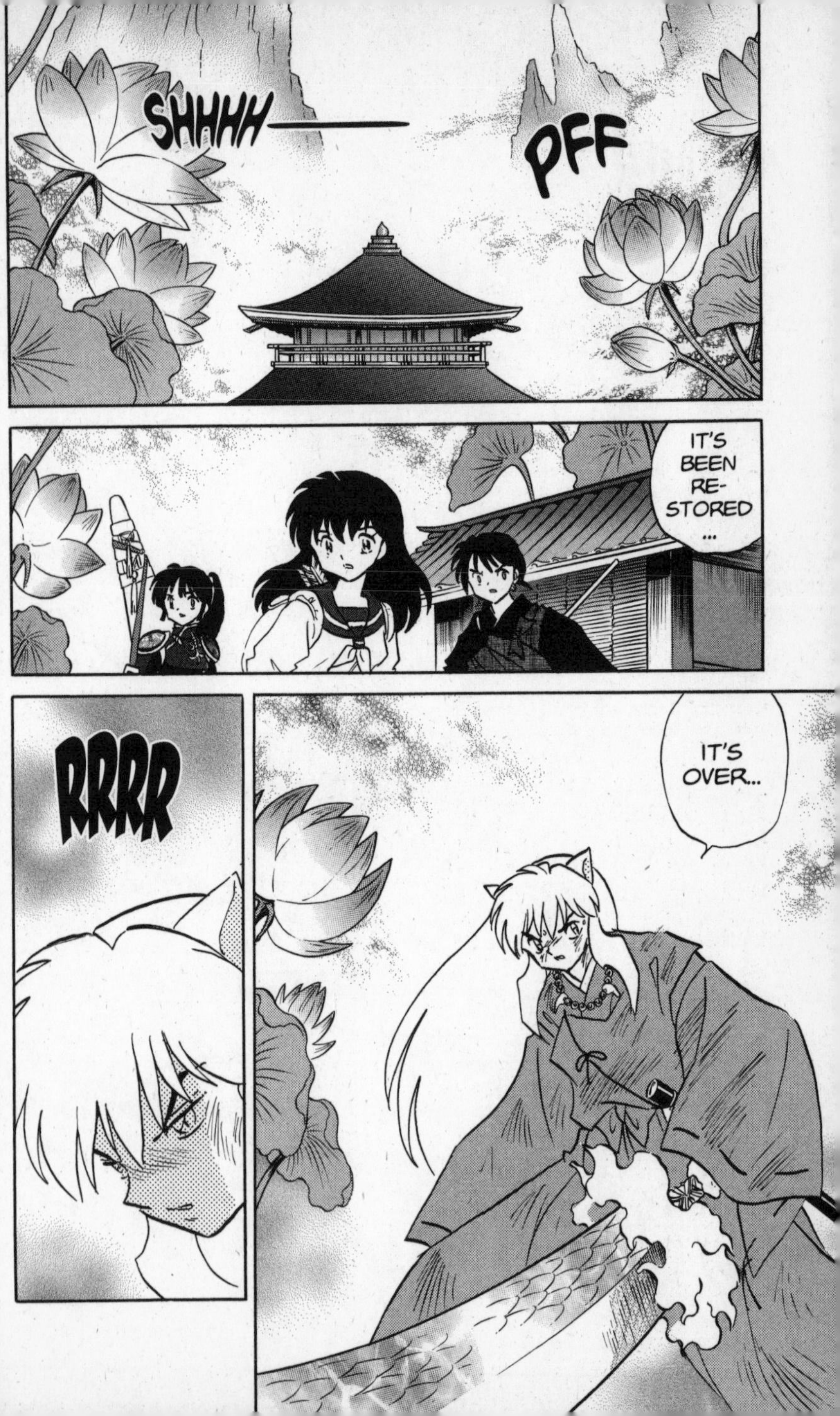
PFF
SHHHH—
IT'S BEEN RE-STORED...
IT'S OVER...
RRRR

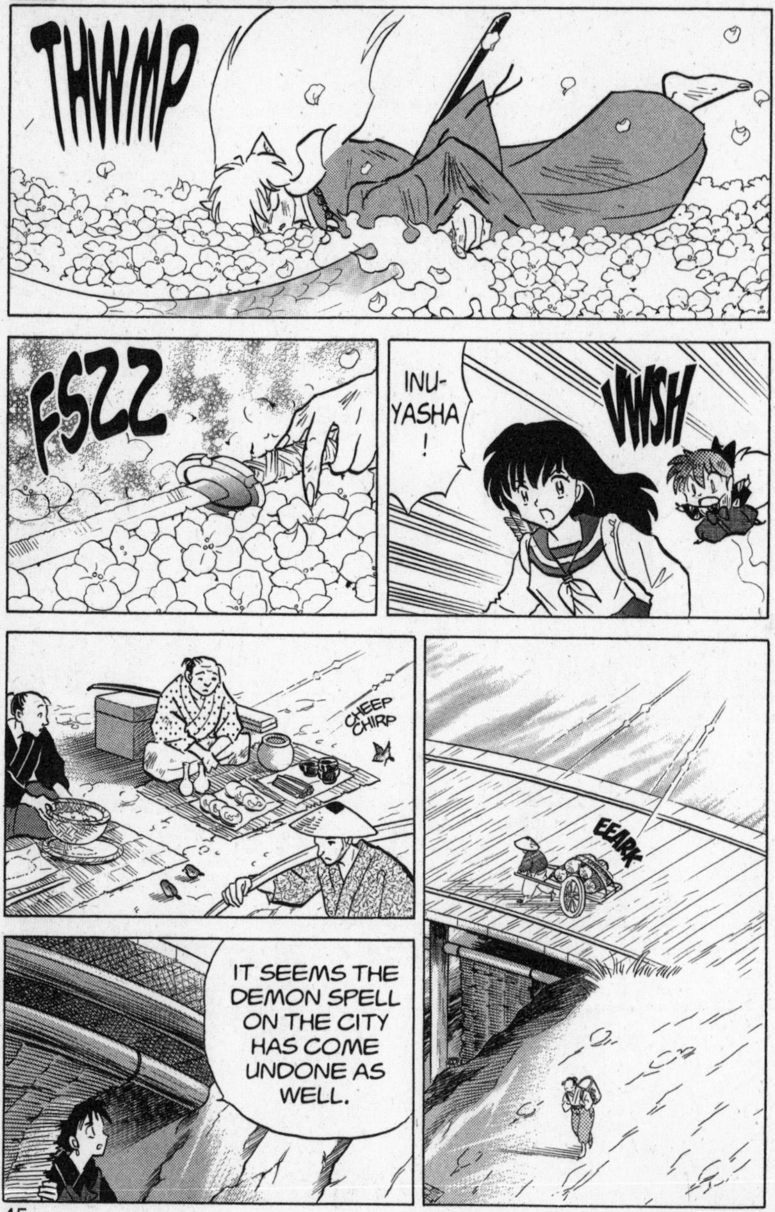
THWMP
INU-YASHA!
VWSH
FSZZ
EEARK
CHEEP CHIRP
IT SEEMS THE DEMON SPELL ON THE CITY HAS COME UNDONE AS WELL.

FWF

...YOU'RE **ALIVE?!**

OLD MAN...

FWRTW

YOU DID IT, MY BOY. CONGRATU-LATIONS.

...

THE DEMON SPIRIT ...!

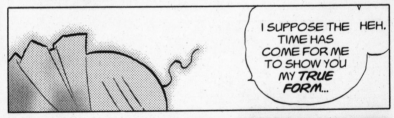

I SUPPOSE THE TIME HAS COME FOR ME TO SHOW YOU MY *TRUE FORM*...

HEH.

TRUE FORM...?!

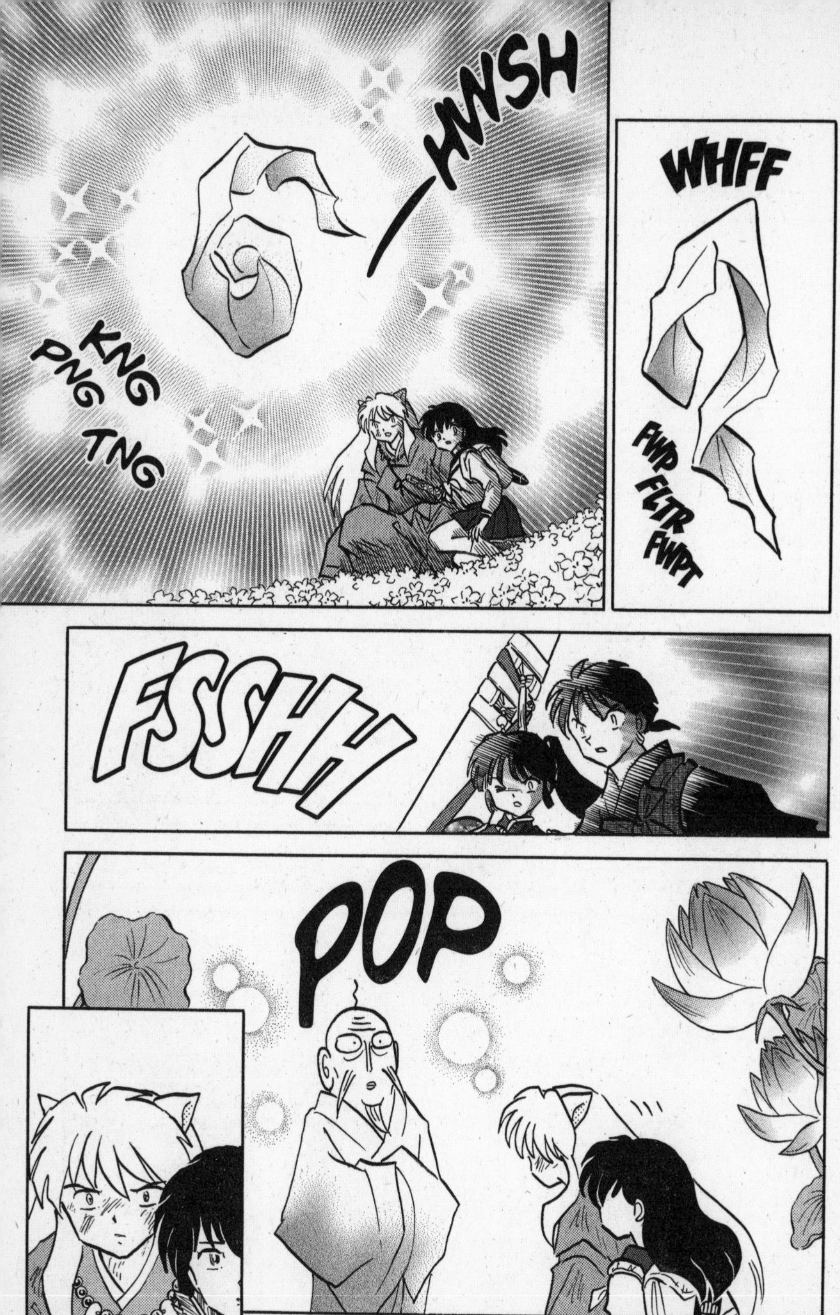
WHFF
FWP FLTR FWPT
—HWSH
KNG PNG TNG
FSSHH
POP

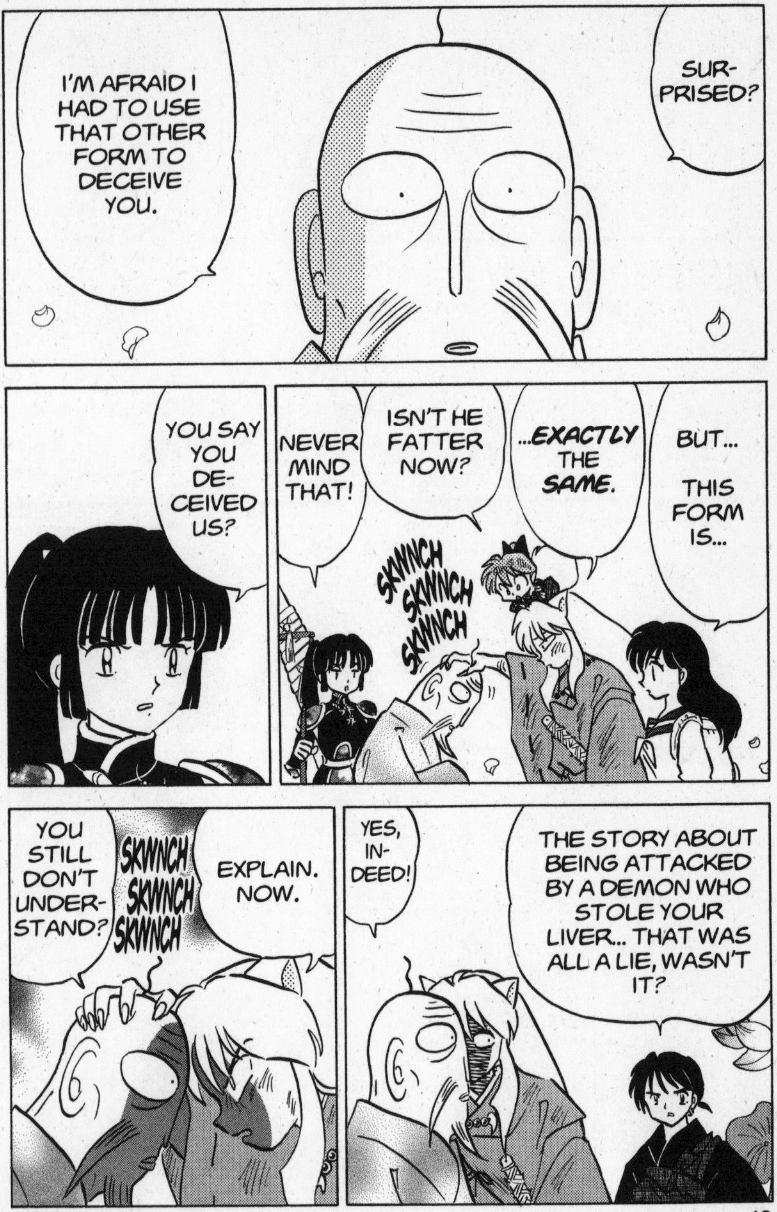
SUR-PRISED?
I'M AFRAID I HAD TO USE THAT OTHER FORM TO DECEIVE YOU.
BUT... THIS FORM IS...
...EXACTLY THE SAME.
ISN'T HE FATTER NOW?
NEVER MIND THAT!
SKWNCH SKWNCH SKWNCH
YOU SAY YOU DE-CEIVED US?
THE STORY ABOUT BEING ATTACKED BY A DEMON WHO STOLE YOUR LIVER... THAT WAS ALL A LIE, WASN'T IT?
YES, IN-DEED!
EXPLAIN. NOW.
SKWNCH SKWNCH SKWNCH
YOU STILL DON'T UNDER-STAND?

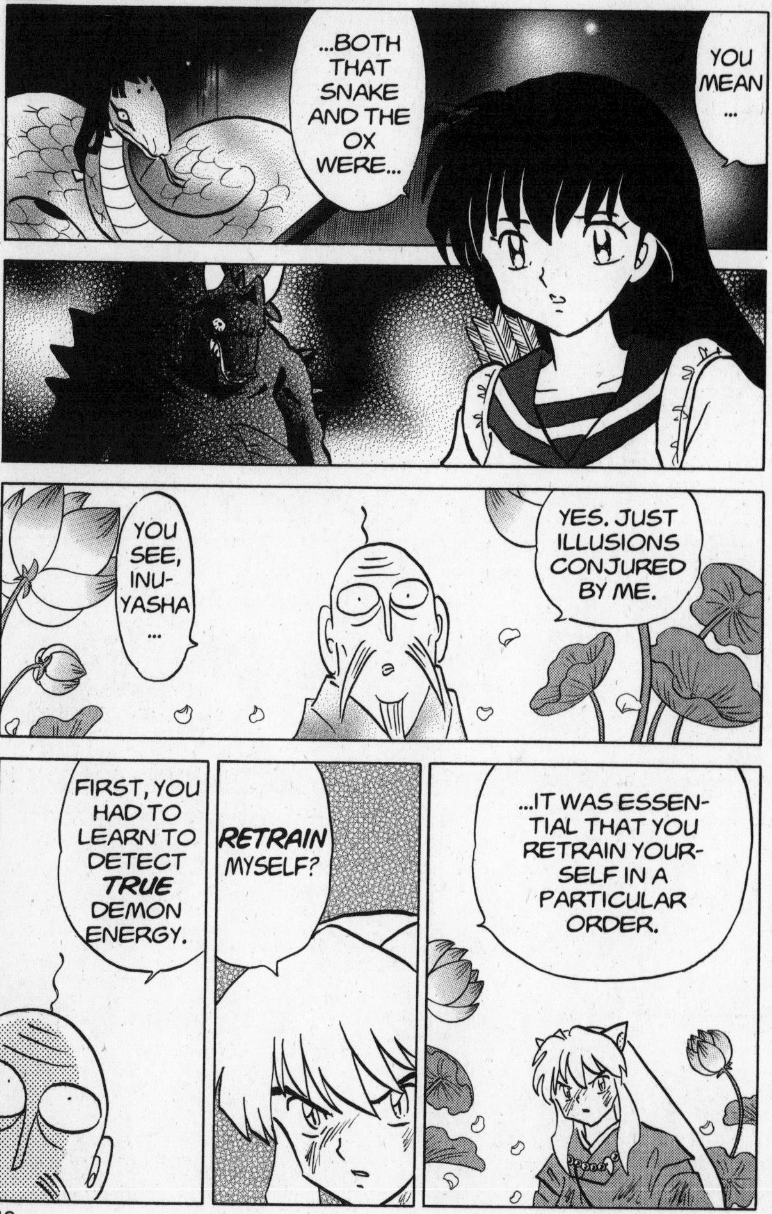
YOU MEAN ...
...BOTH THAT SNAKE AND THE OX WERE...
YES. JUST ILLUSIONS CONJURED BY ME.
YOU SEE, INU-YASHA ...
...IT WAS ESSENTIAL THAT YOU RETRAIN YOURSELF IN A PARTICULAR ORDER.
RETRAIN MYSELF?
FIRST, YOU HAD TO LEARN TO DETECT TRUE DEMON ENERGY.

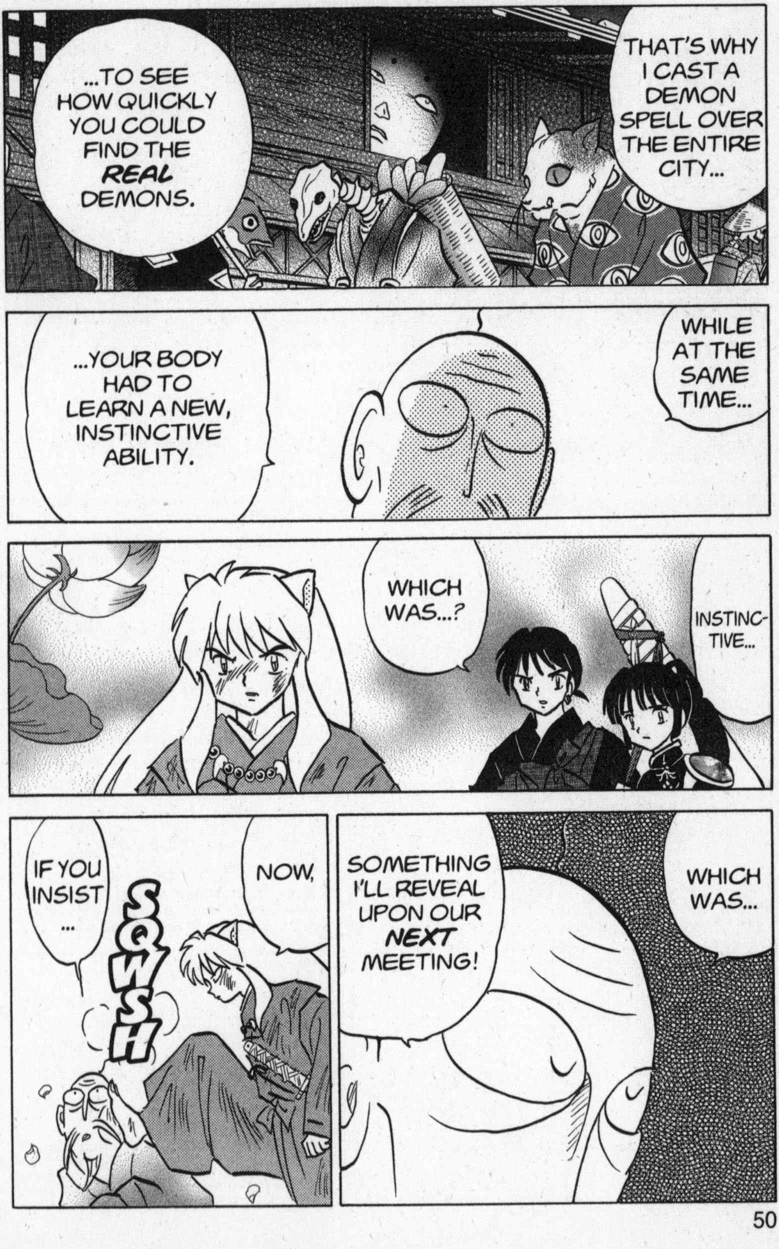
THAT'S WHY I CAST A DEMON SPELL OVER THE ENTIRE CITY...
...TO SEE HOW QUICKLY YOU COULD FIND THE REAL DEMONS.
WHILE AT THE SAME TIME...
...YOUR BODY HAD TO LEARN A NEW, INSTINCTIVE ABILITY.
INSTINC-TIVE...
WHICH WAS...?
WHICH WAS...
SOMETHING I'LL REVEAL UPON OUR NEXT MEETING!
NOW,
SQWSH
IF YOU INSIST ...

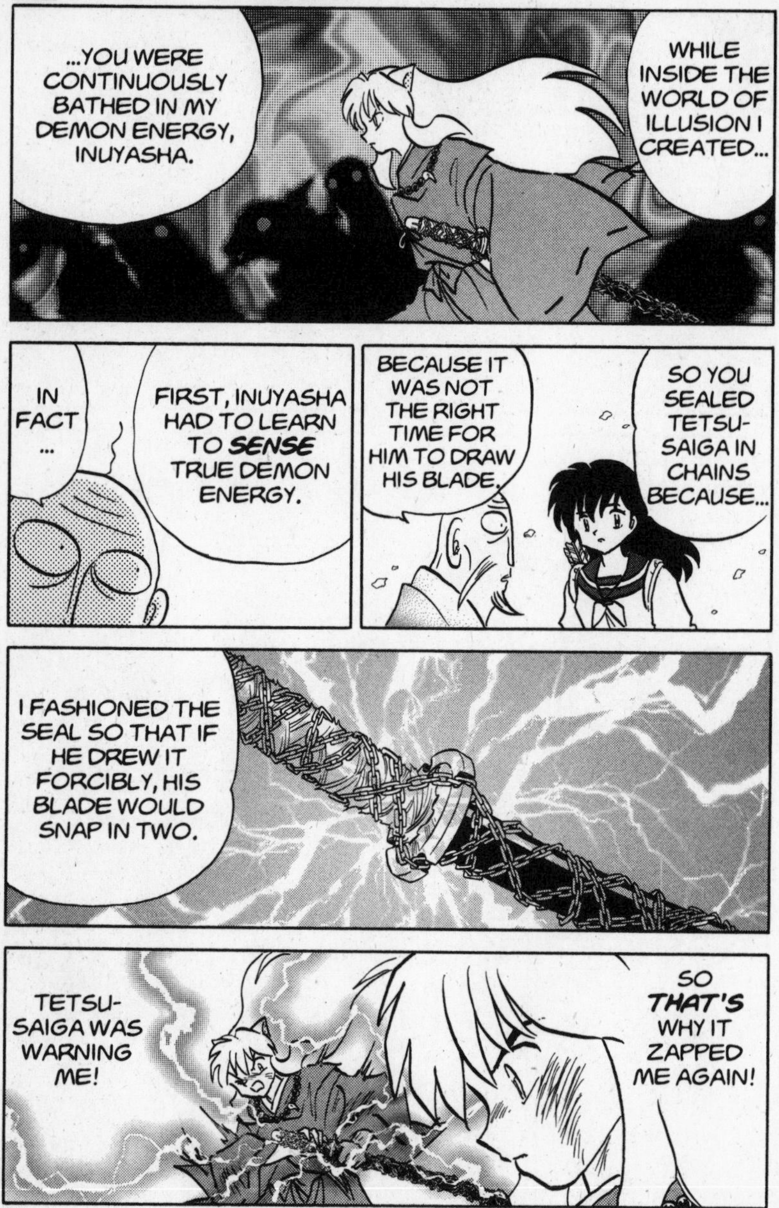
WHILE INSIDE THE WORLD OF ILLUSION I CREATED...
...YOU WERE CONTINUOUSLY BATHED IN MY DEMON ENERGY, INUYASHA.
SO YOU SEALED TETSU-SAIGA IN CHAINS BECAUSE...
BECAUSE IT WAS NOT THE RIGHT TIME FOR HIM TO DRAW HIS BLADE.
FIRST, INUYASHA HAD TO LEARN TO SENSE TRUE DEMON ENERGY.
IN FACT ...
I FASHIONED THE SEAL SO THAT IF HE DREW IT FORCIBLY, HIS BLADE WOULD SNAP IN TWO.
SO THAT'S WHY IT ZAPPED ME AGAIN!
TETSU-SAIGA WAS WARNING ME!

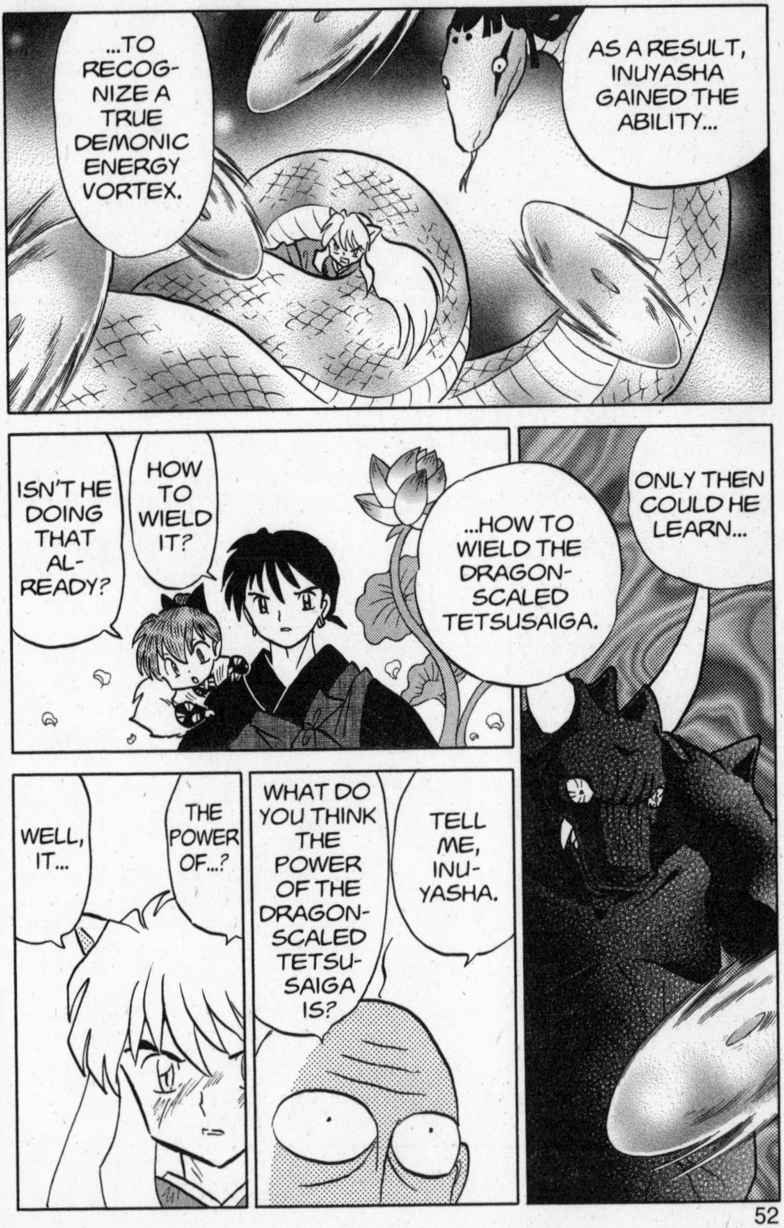
AS A RESULT, INUYASHA GAINED THE ABILITY...
...TO RECOGNIZE A TRUE DEMONIC ENERGY VORTEX.
ONLY THEN COULD HE LEARN...
...HOW TO WIELD THE DRAGON-SCALED TETSUSAIGA.
HOW TO WIELD IT?
ISN'T HE DOING THAT ALREADY?
TELL ME, INUYASHA.
WHAT DO YOU THINK THE POWER OF THE DRAGON-SCALED TETSUSAIGA IS?
THE POWER OF...?
WELL, IT...

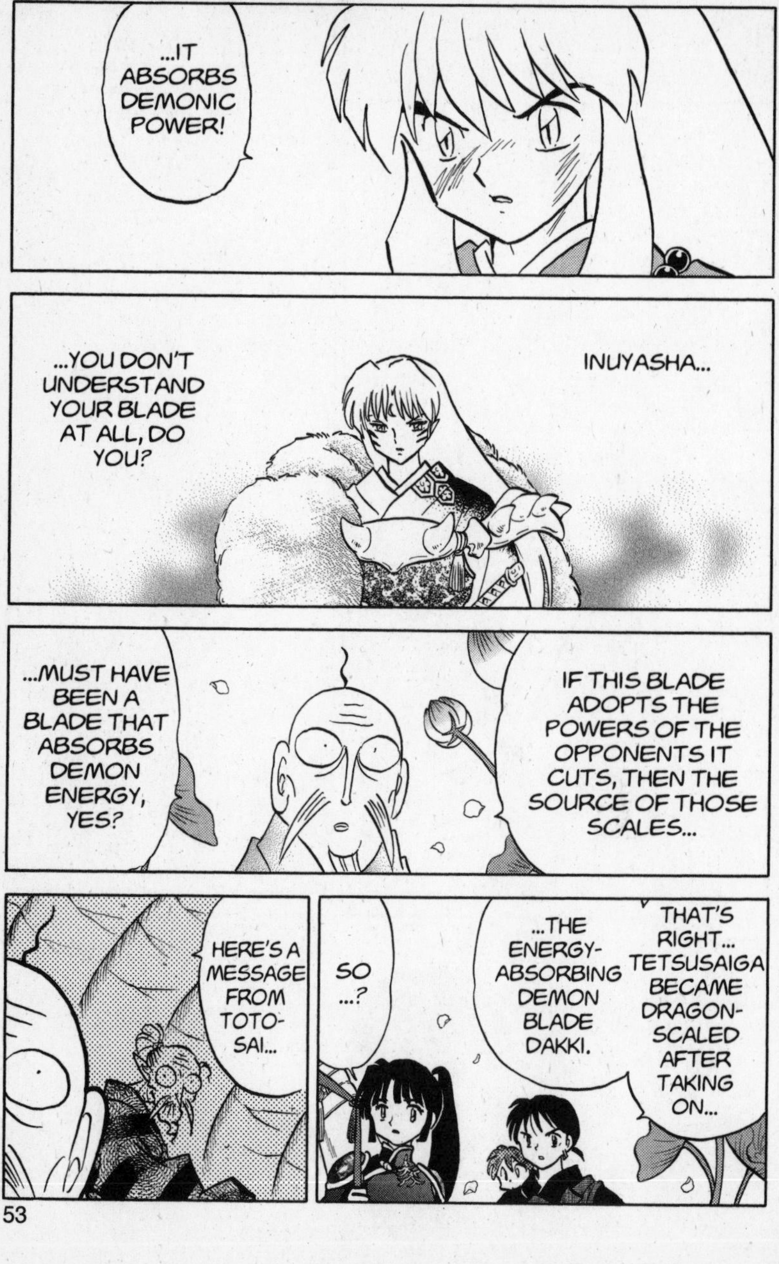
...IT ABSORBS DEMONIC POWER!
INUYASHA...
...YOU DON'T UNDERSTAND YOUR BLADE AT ALL, DO YOU?
IF THIS BLADE ADOPTS THE POWERS OF THE OPPONENTS IT CUTS, THEN THE SOURCE OF THOSE SCALES...
...MUST HAVE BEEN A BLADE THAT ABSORBS DEMON ENERGY, YES?
THAT'S RIGHT... TETSUSAIGA BECAME DRAGON-SCALED AFTER TAKING ON...
...THE ENERGY-ABSORBING DEMON BLADE DAKKI.
SO ...?
HERE'S A MESSAGE FROM TOTO-SAI...

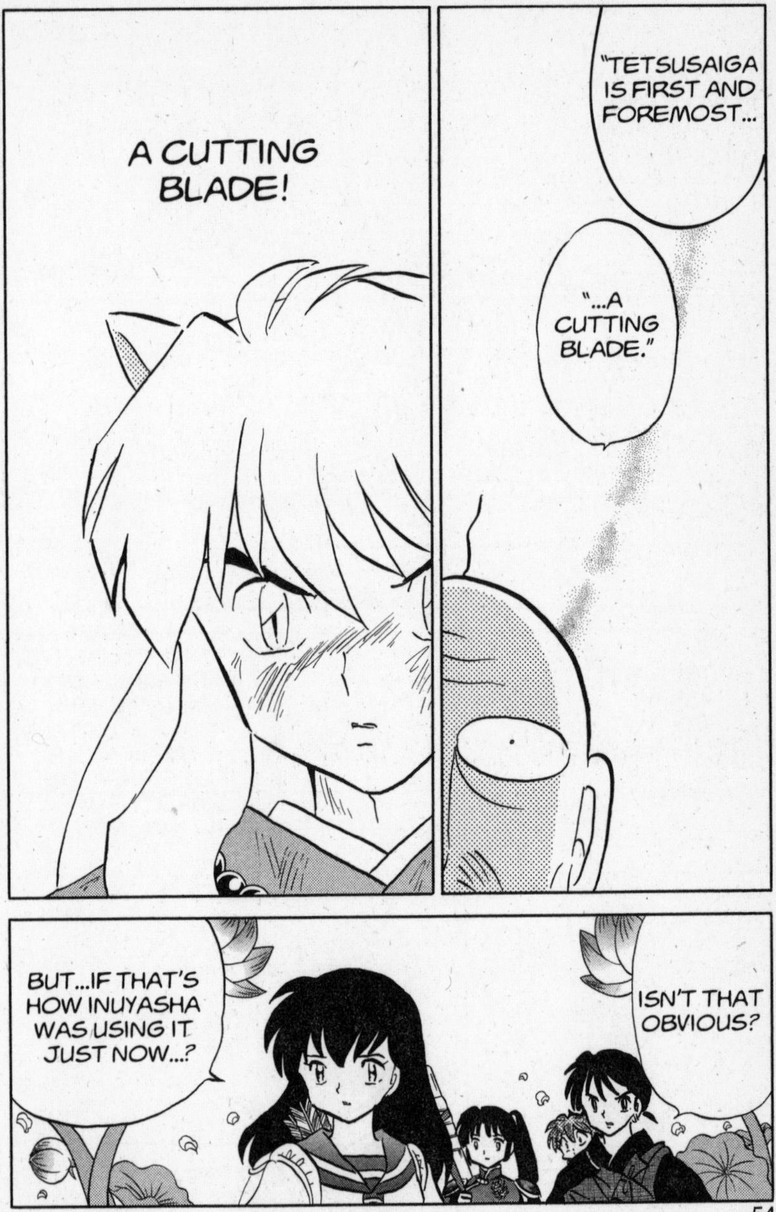
"TETSUSAIGA IS FIRST AND FOREMOST...
"...A CUTTING BLADE."
A CUTTING BLADE!
ISN'T THAT OBVIOUS?
BUT...IF THAT'S HOW INUYASHA WAS USING IT JUST NOW...?

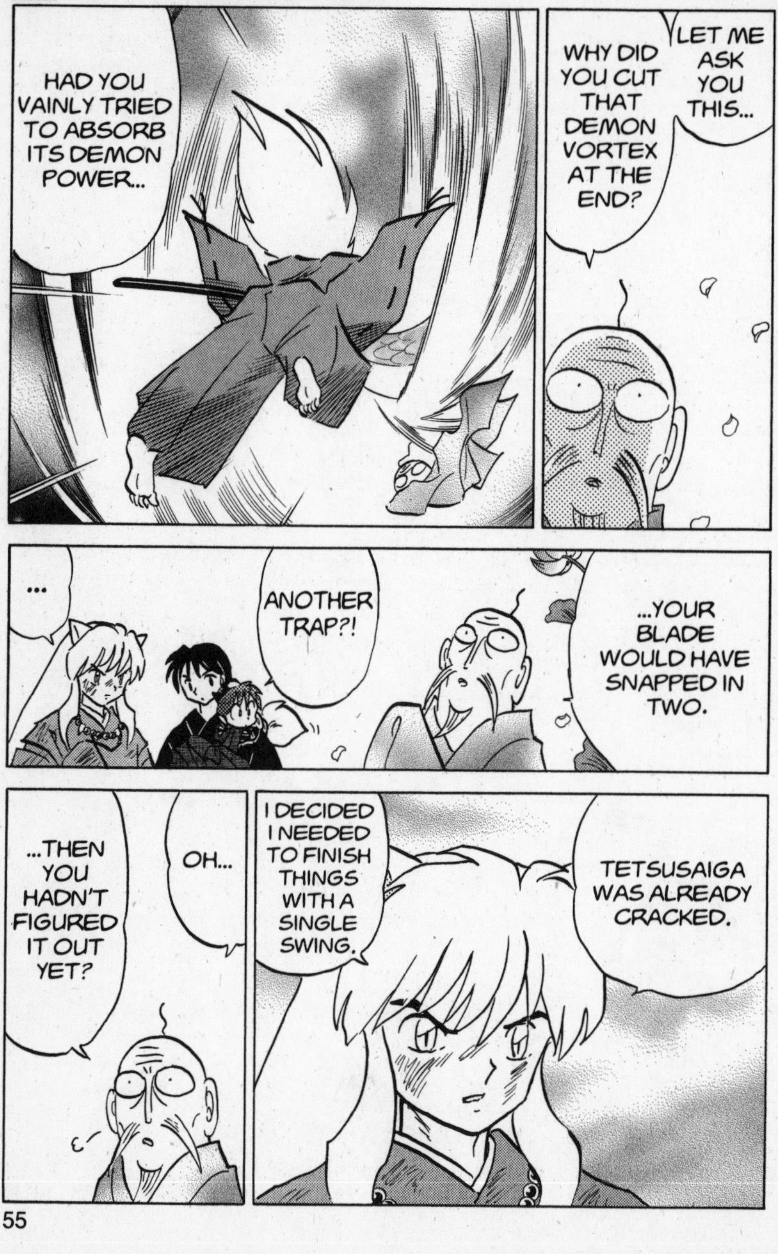
LET ME ASK YOU THIS...
WHY DID YOU CUT THAT DEMON VORTEX AT THE END?
HAD YOU VAINLY TRIED TO ABSORB ITS DEMON POWER...
...YOUR BLADE WOULD HAVE SNAPPED IN TWO.
ANOTHER TRAP?!
...
TETSUSAIGA WAS ALREADY CRACKED.
I DECIDED I NEEDED TO FINISH THINGS WITH A SINGLE SWING.
OH...
...THEN YOU HADN'T FIGURED IT OUT YET?

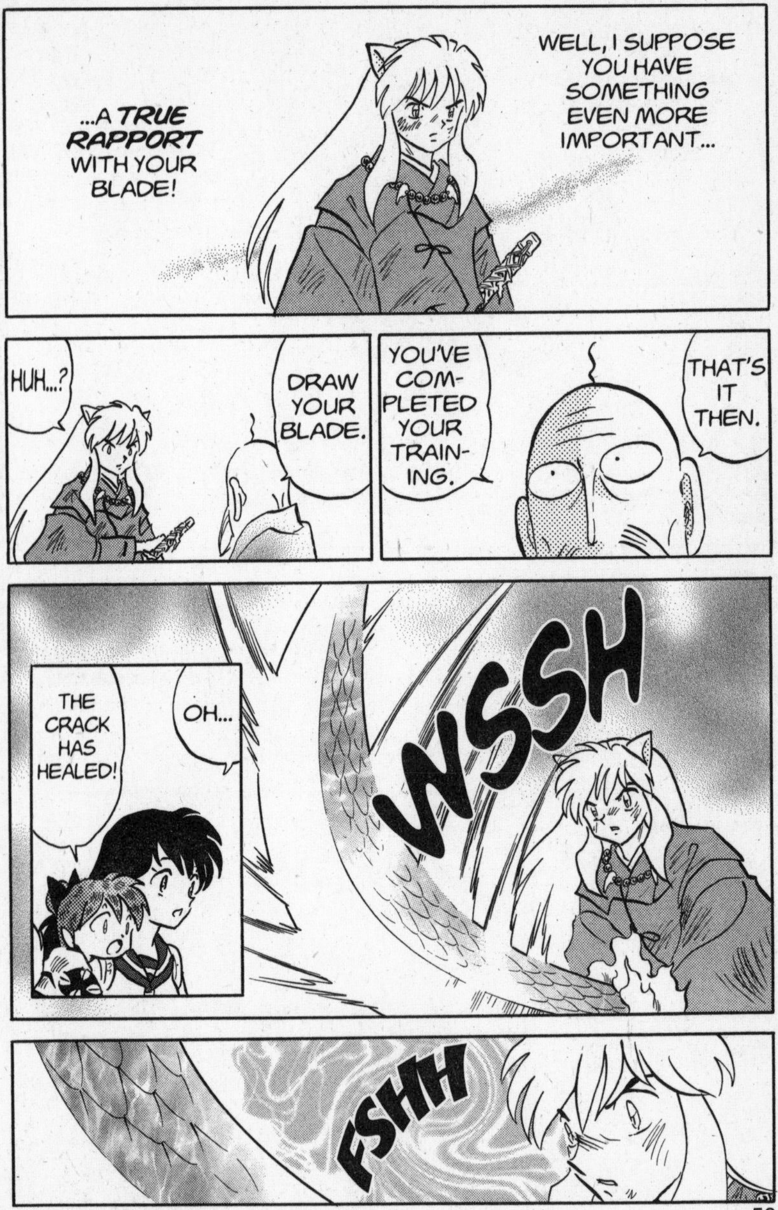
WELL, I SUPPOSE YOU HAVE SOMETHING EVEN MORE IMPORTANT...
...A TRUE RAPPORT WITH YOUR BLADE!
THAT'S IT THEN.
YOU'VE COMPLETED YOUR TRAINING.
DRAW YOUR BLADE.
HUH...?
WSSH
OH...
THE CRACK HAS HEALED!
FSHH

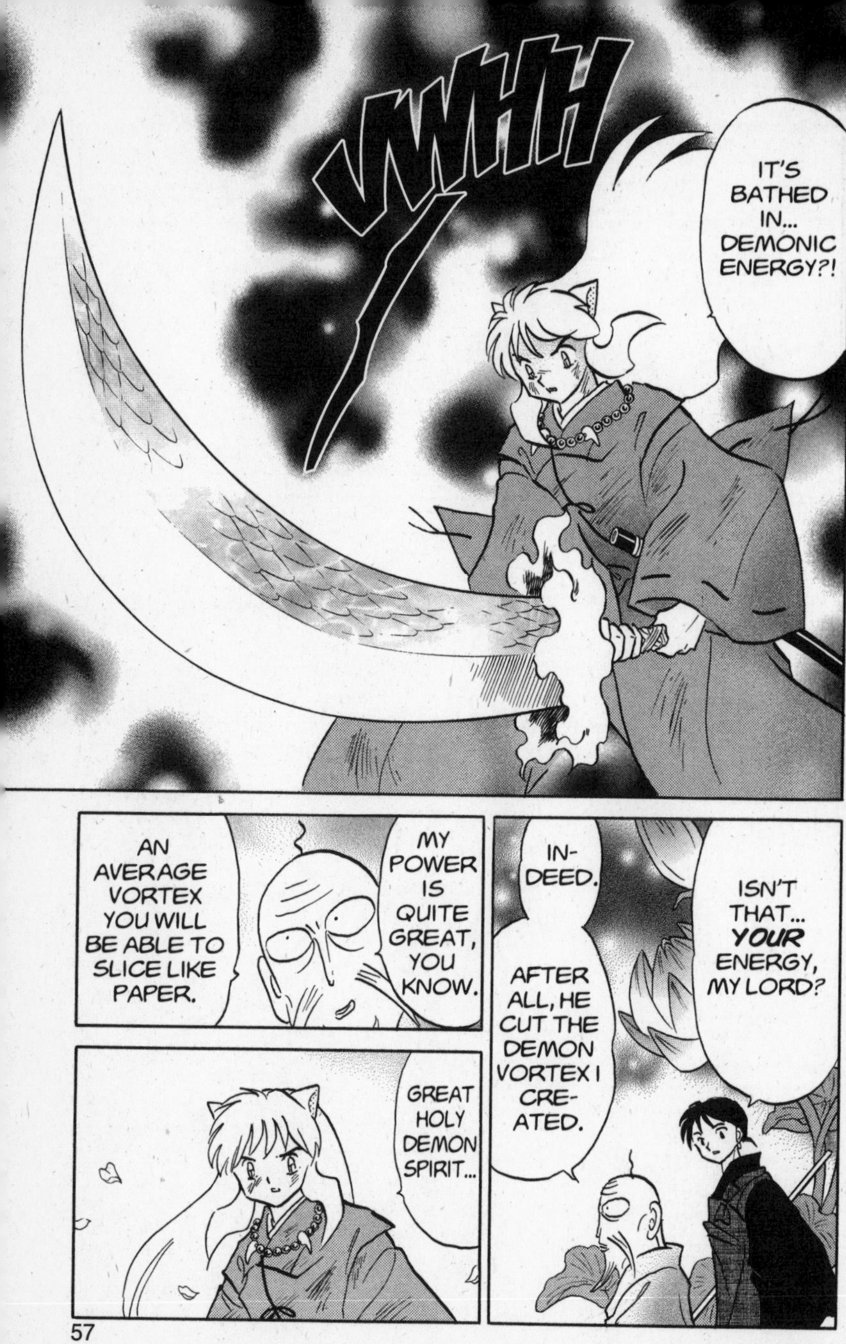
VWHH
IT'S BATHED IN... DEMONIC ENERGY?!
ISN'T THAT... YOUR ENERGY, MY LORD?
IN-DEED.
AFTER ALL, HE CUT THE DEMON VORTEX I CRE-ATED.
MY POWER IS QUITE GREAT, YOU KNOW.
AN AVERAGE VORTEX YOU WILL BE ABLE TO SLICE LIKE PAPER.
GREAT HOLY DEMON SPIRIT...

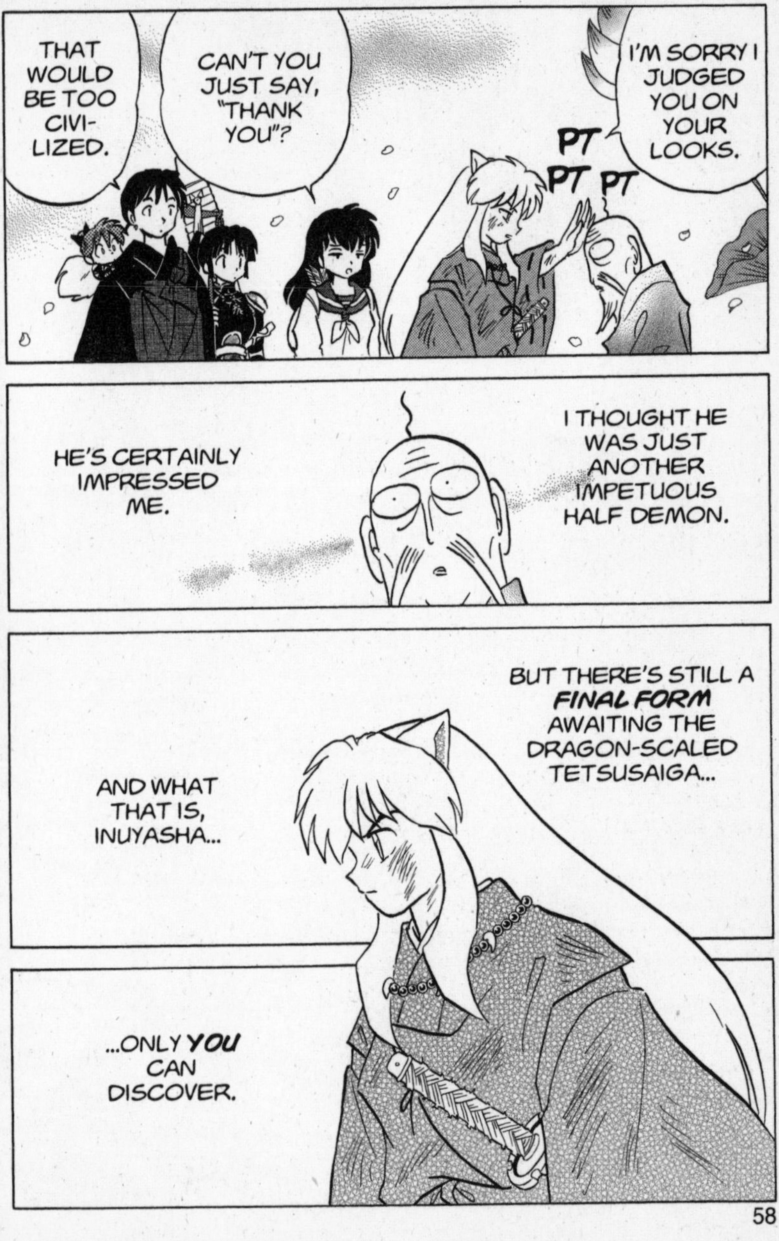
I'M SORRY I JUDGED YOU ON YOUR LOOKS.
PT PT PT
CAN'T YOU JUST SAY, "THANK YOU"?
THAT WOULD BE TOO CIVI-LIZED.
I THOUGHT HE WAS JUST ANOTHER IMPETUOUS HALF DEMON.
HE'S CERTAINLY IMPRESSED ME.
BUT THERE'S STILL A **FINAL FORM** AWAITING THE DRAGON-SCALED TETSUSAIGA...
AND WHAT THAT IS, INUYASHA...
...ONLY **YOU** CAN DISCOVER.

SCROLL 4

KAI

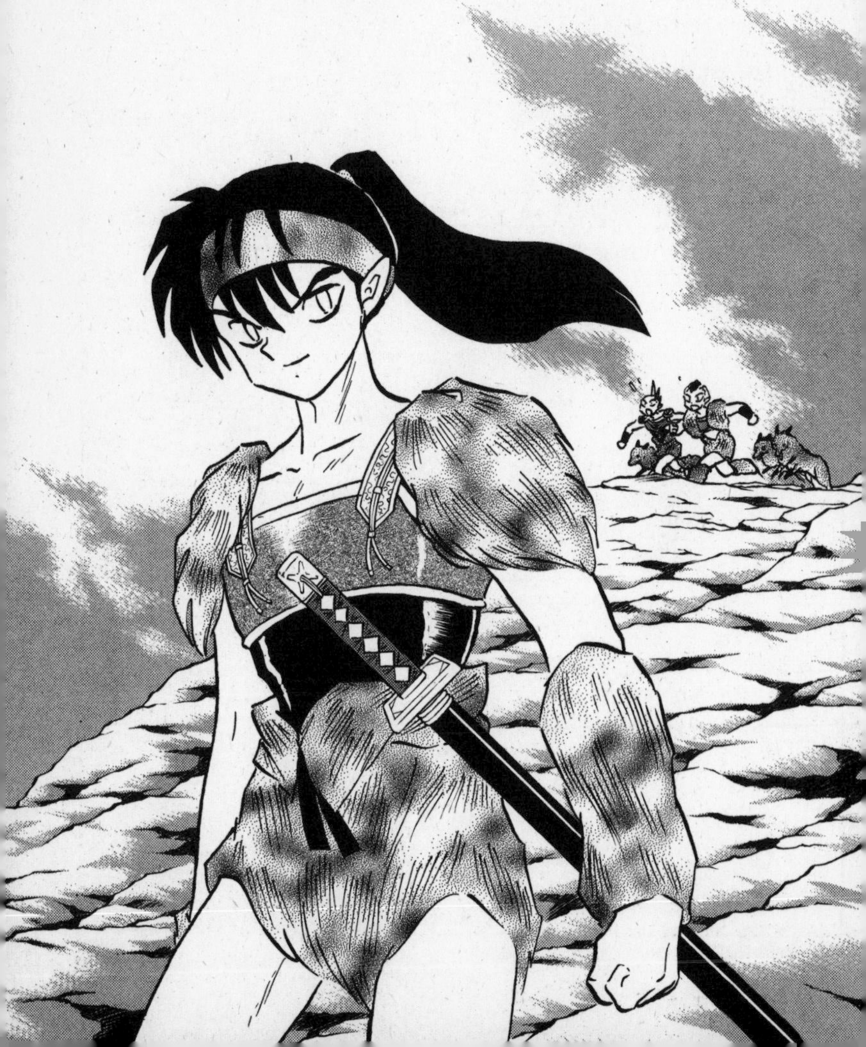

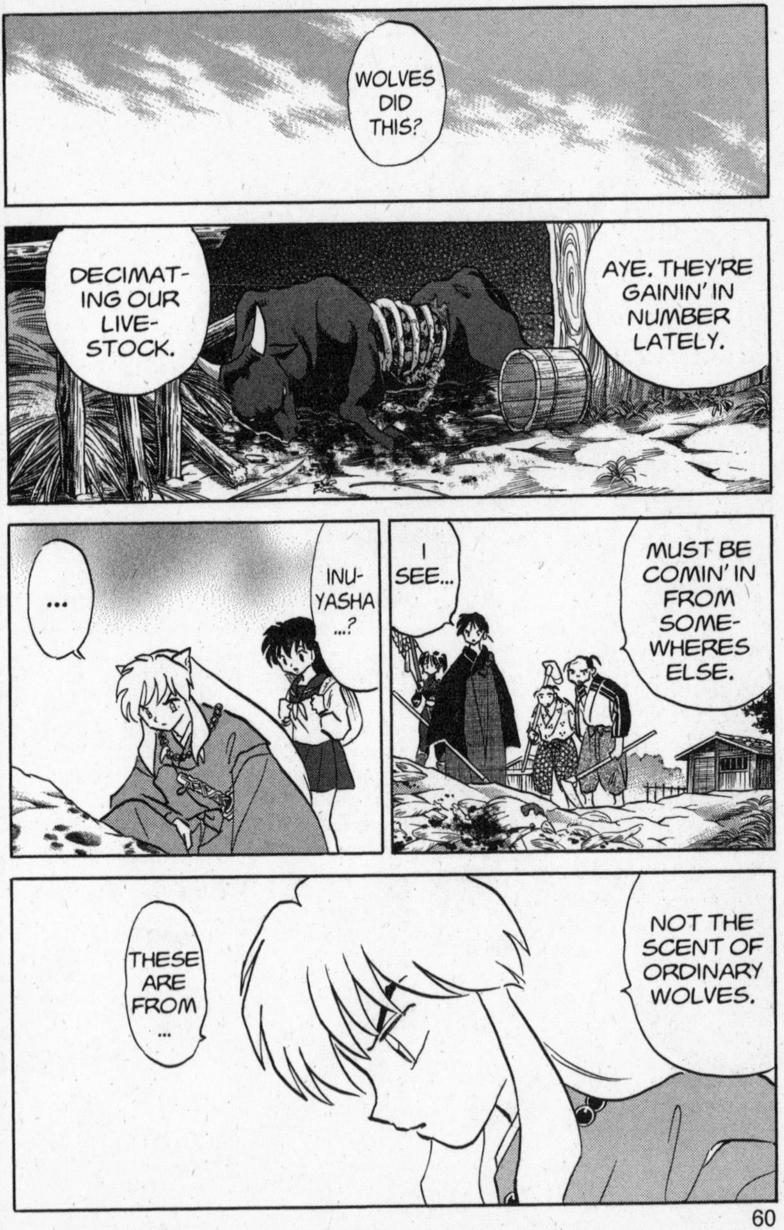
WOLVES DID THIS?
AYE. THEY'RE GAININ' IN NUMBER LATELY.
DECIMATING OUR LIVESTOCK.
MUST BE COMIN' IN FROM SOMEWHERES ELSE.
I SEE...
INUYASHA ...?
...
NOT THE SCENT OF ORDINARY WOLVES.
THESE ARE FROM ...

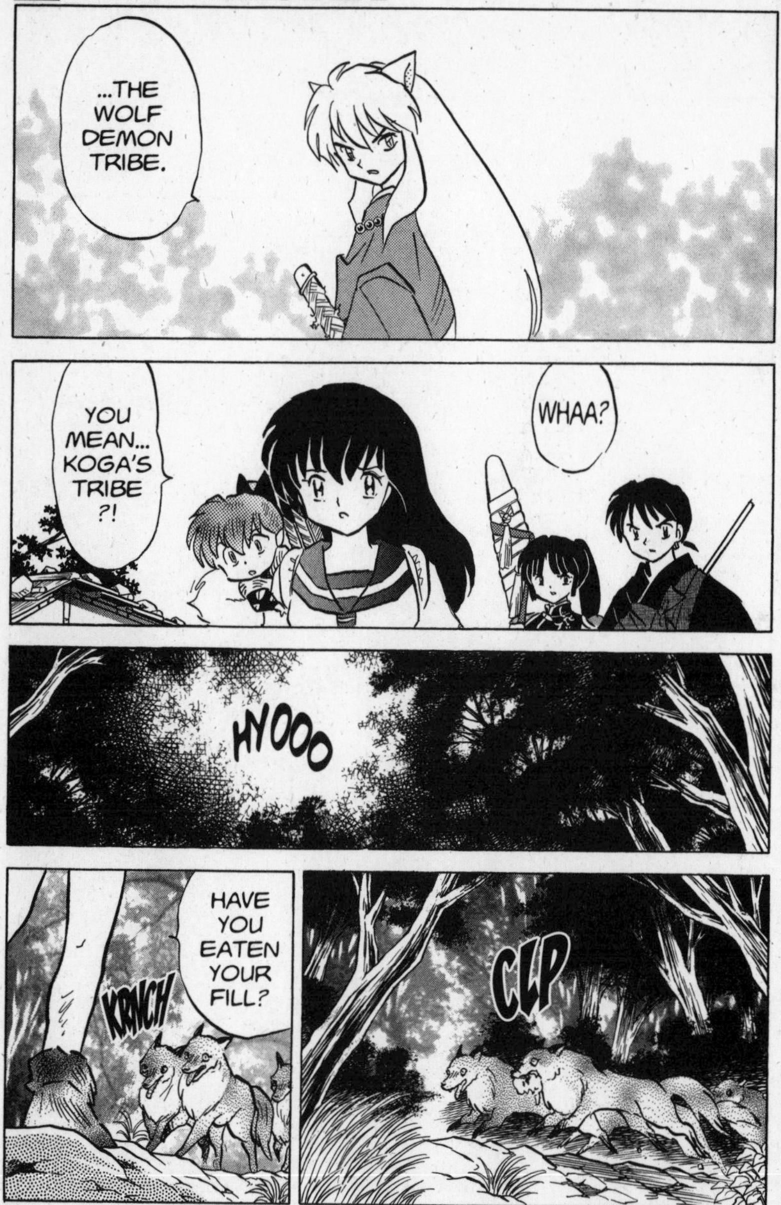
...THE WOLF DEMON TRIBE.
WHAA?
YOU MEAN... KOGA'S TRIBE ?!
HYOOO
CLP
HAVE YOU EATEN YOUR FILL?
KRNCH

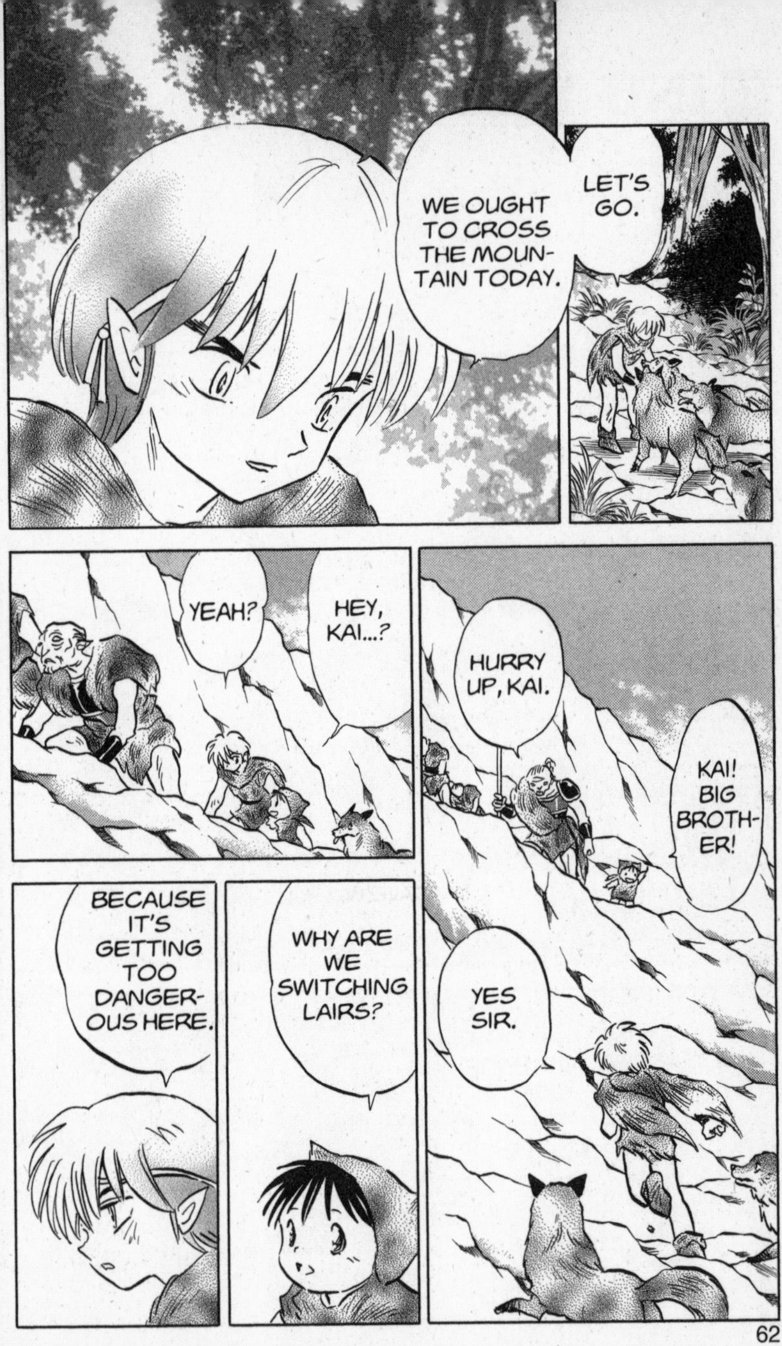
LET'S GO.
WE OUGHT TO CROSS THE MOUN-TAIN TODAY.
KAI! BIG BROTH-ER!
HURRY UP, KAI.
YES SIR.
HEY, KAI...?
YEAH?
WHY ARE WE SWITCHING LAIRS?
BECAUSE IT'S GETTING TOO DANGER-OUS HERE.

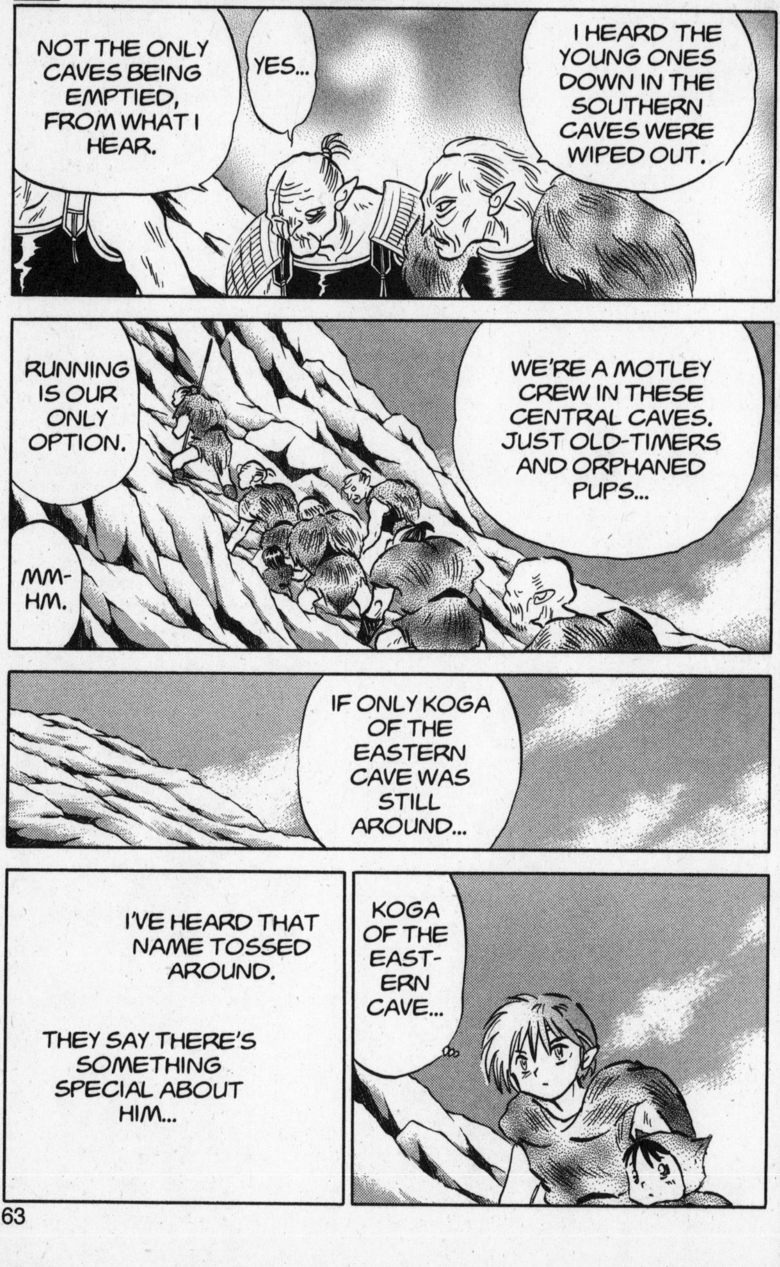
I HEARD THE YOUNG ONES DOWN IN THE SOUTHERN CAVES WERE WIPED OUT.
YES...
NOT THE ONLY CAVES BEING EMPTIED, FROM WHAT I HEAR.
WE'RE A MOTLEY CREW IN THESE CENTRAL CAVES. JUST OLD-TIMERS AND ORPHANED PUPS...
RUNNING IS OUR ONLY OPTION.
MM-HM.
IF ONLY KOGA OF THE EASTERN CAVE WAS STILL AROUND...
KOGA OF THE EAST-ERN CAVE...
I'VE HEARD THAT NAME TOSSED AROUND.
THEY SAY THERE'S SOMETHING SPECIAL ABOUT HIM...

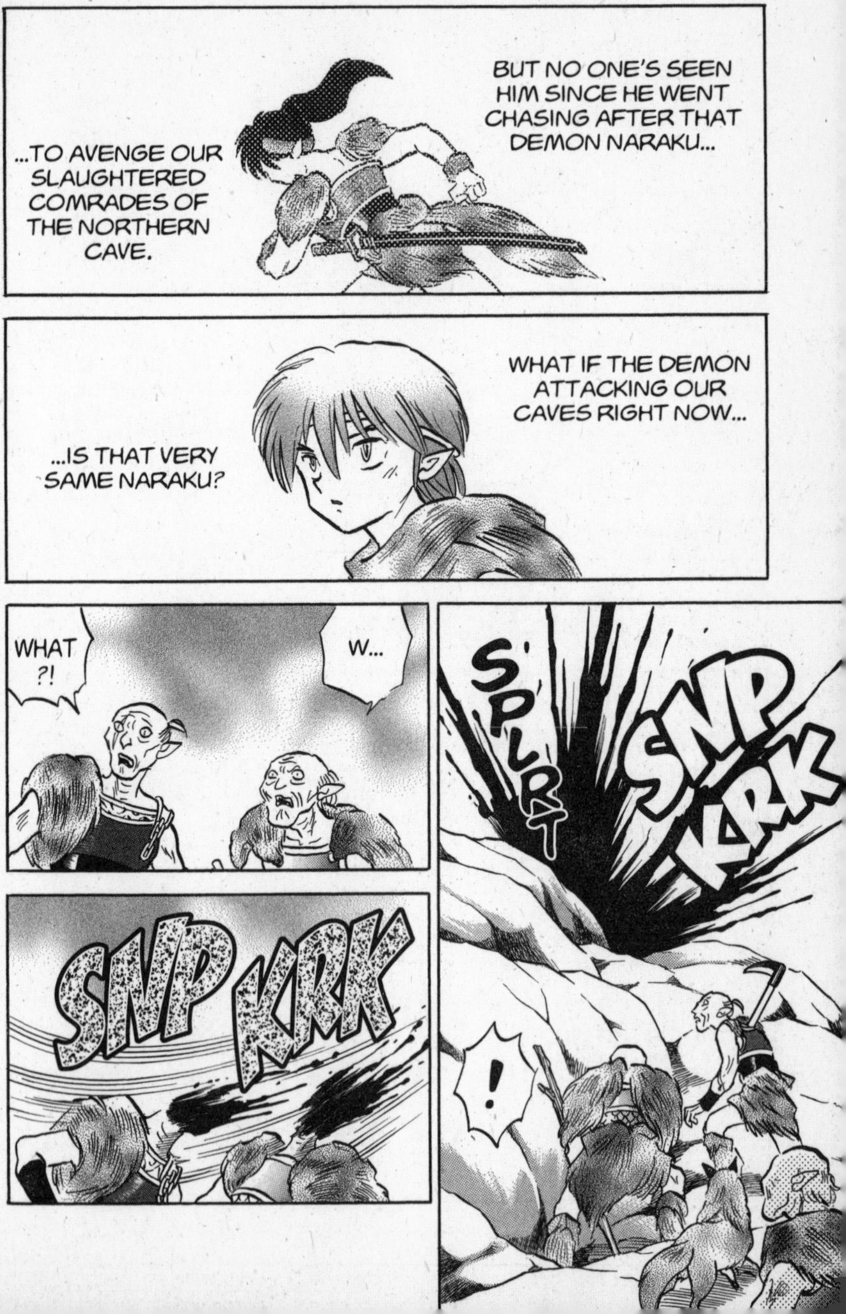

...TO AVENGE OUR SLAUGHTERED COMRADES OF THE NORTHERN CAVE.
BUT NO ONE'S SEEN HIM SINCE HE WENT CHASING AFTER THAT DEMON NARAKU...
WHAT IF THE DEMON ATTACKING OUR CAVES RIGHT NOW...
...IS THAT VERY SAME NARAKU?
SPLURT
SNP KRK
!
W...
WHAT ?!
SNP KRK

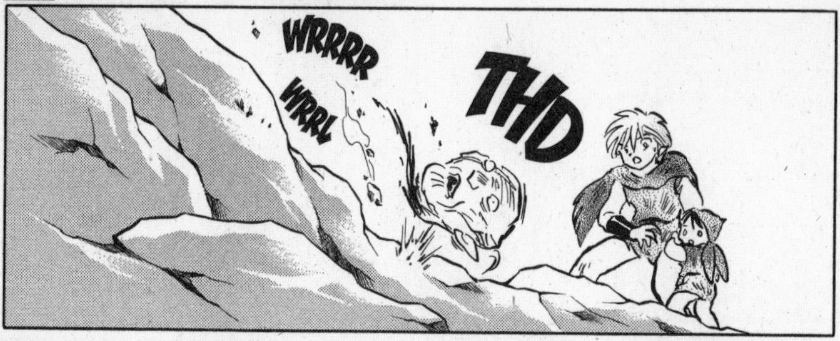
WRRRRR
WRRRL
THD

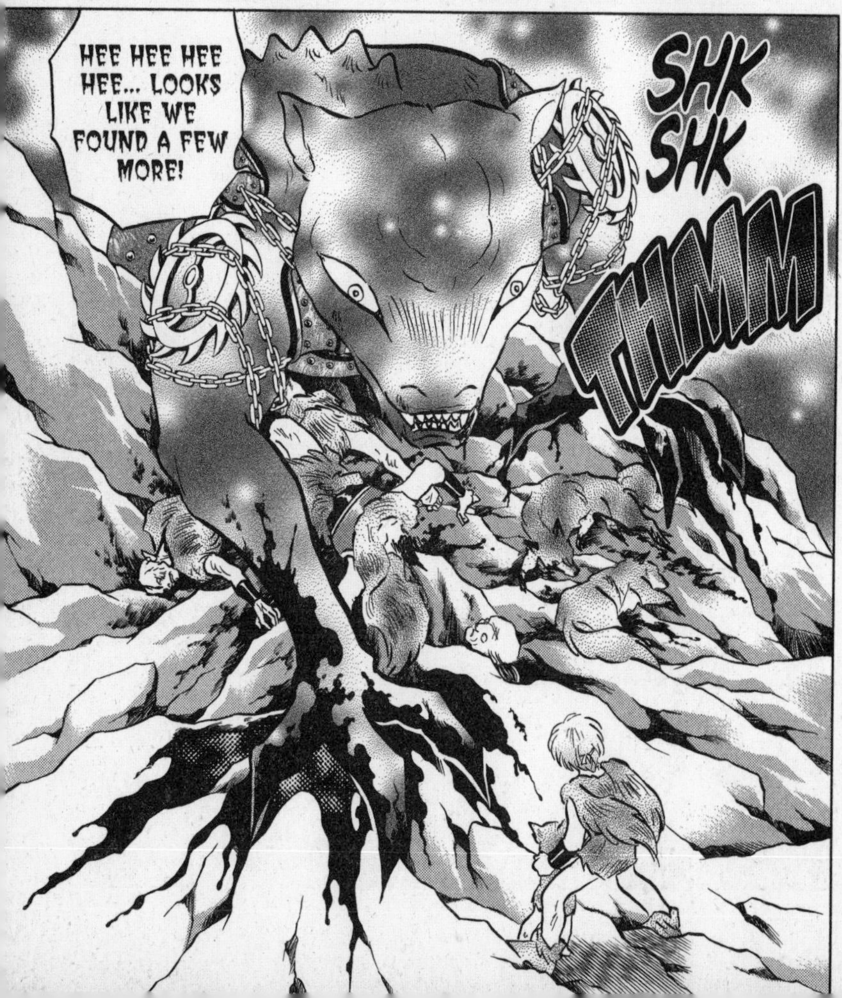
SHK SHK
THMM
HEE HEE HEE HEE... LOOKS LIKE WE FOUND A FEW MORE!

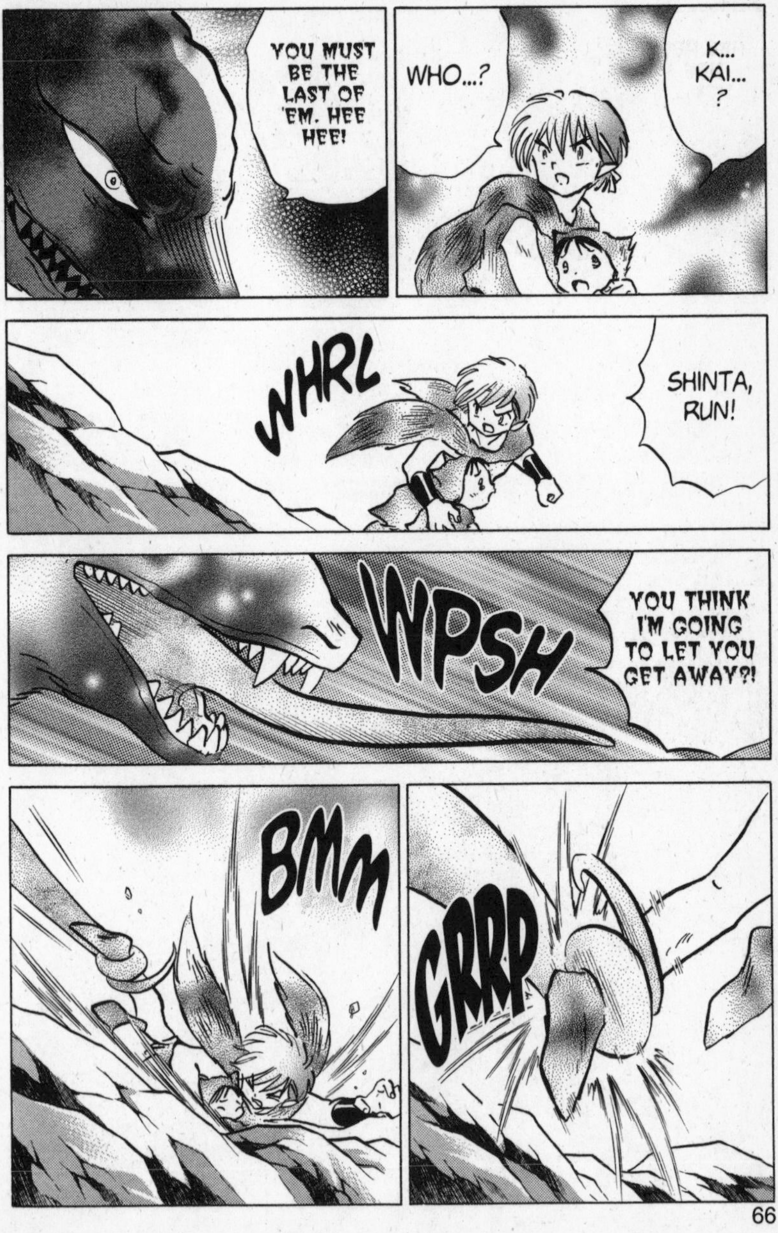
K... KAI... ?
WHO...?
YOU MUST BE THE LAST OF 'EM. HEE HEE!
SHINTA, RUN!
WHRL
YOU THINK I'M GOING TO LET YOU GET AWAY?!
WPSH
GRRP
BMM

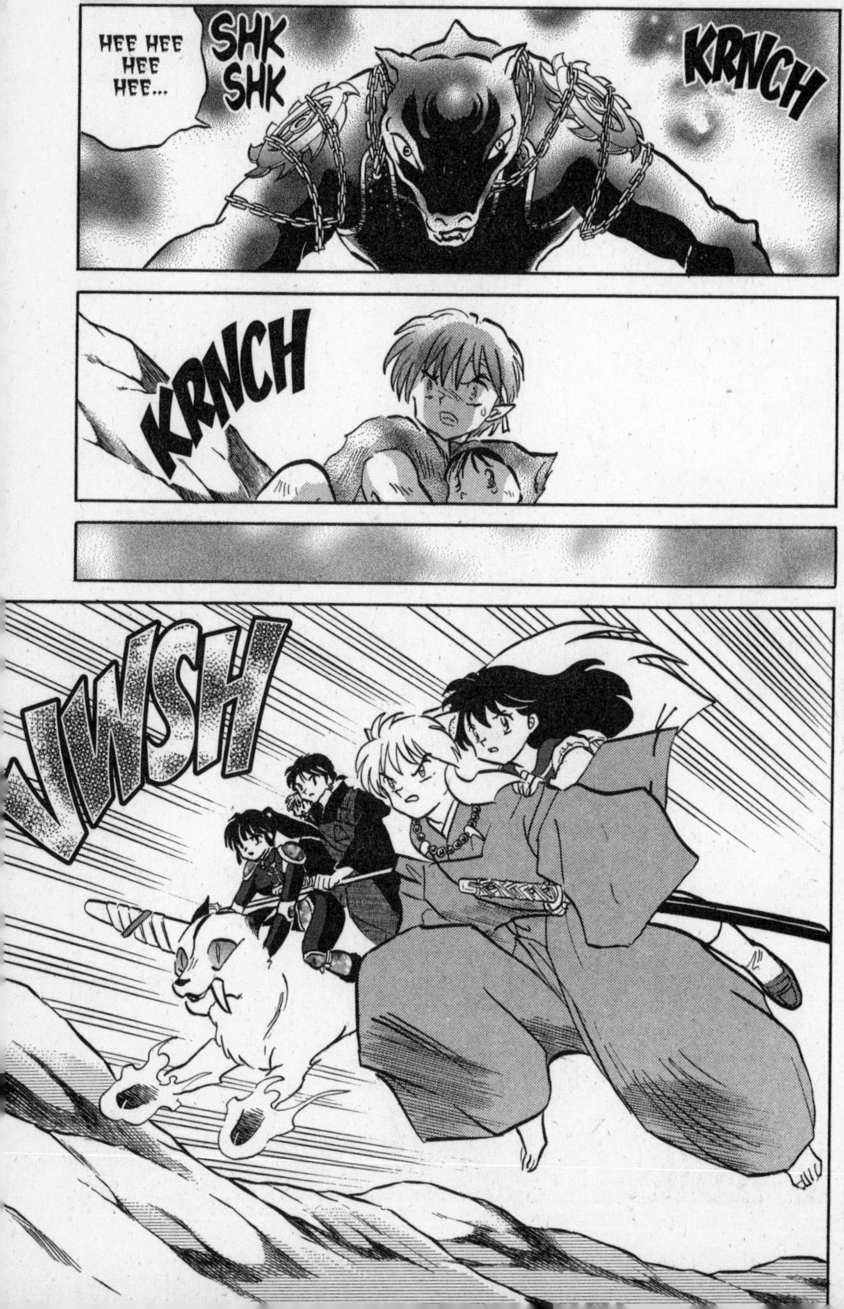
KRNCH
SHK SHK
HEE HEE HEE HEE...
KRNCH
VWSH

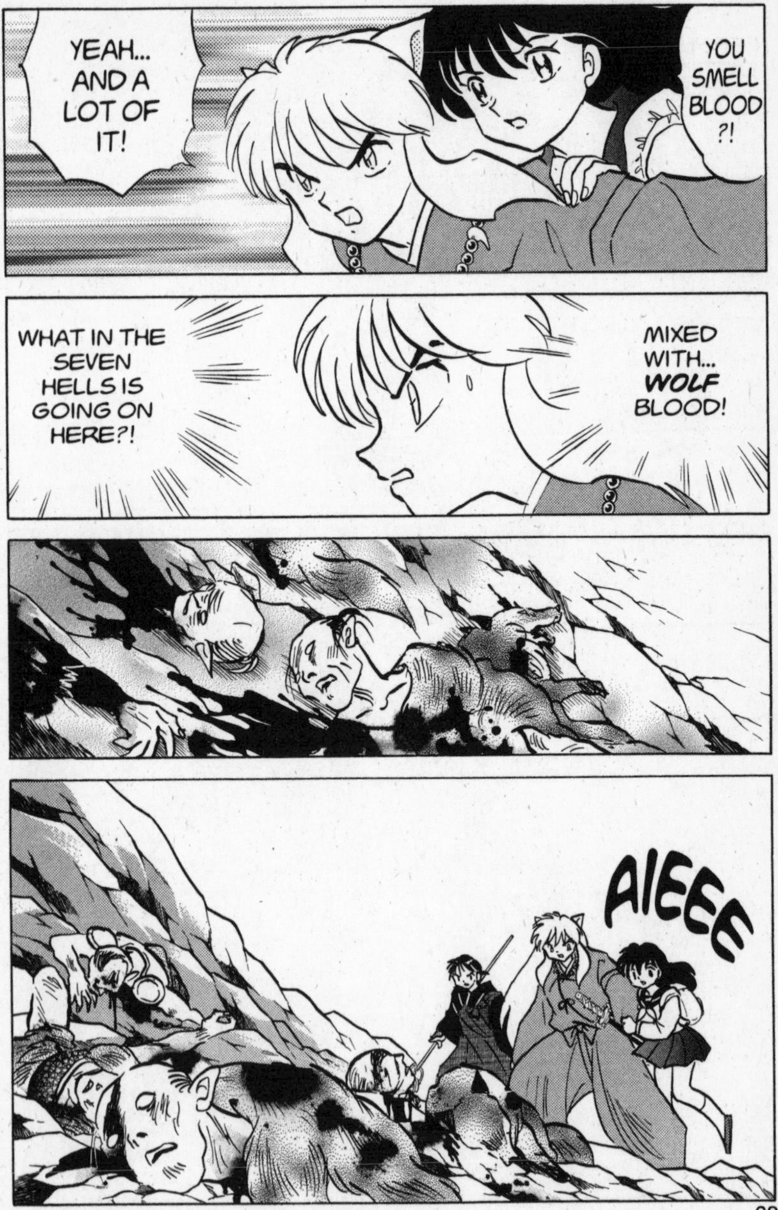
YOU SMELL BLOOD ?!
YEAH... AND A LOT OF IT!
MIXED WITH... **WOLF** BLOOD!
WHAT IN THE SEVEN HELLS IS GOING ON HERE?!
AIEEE

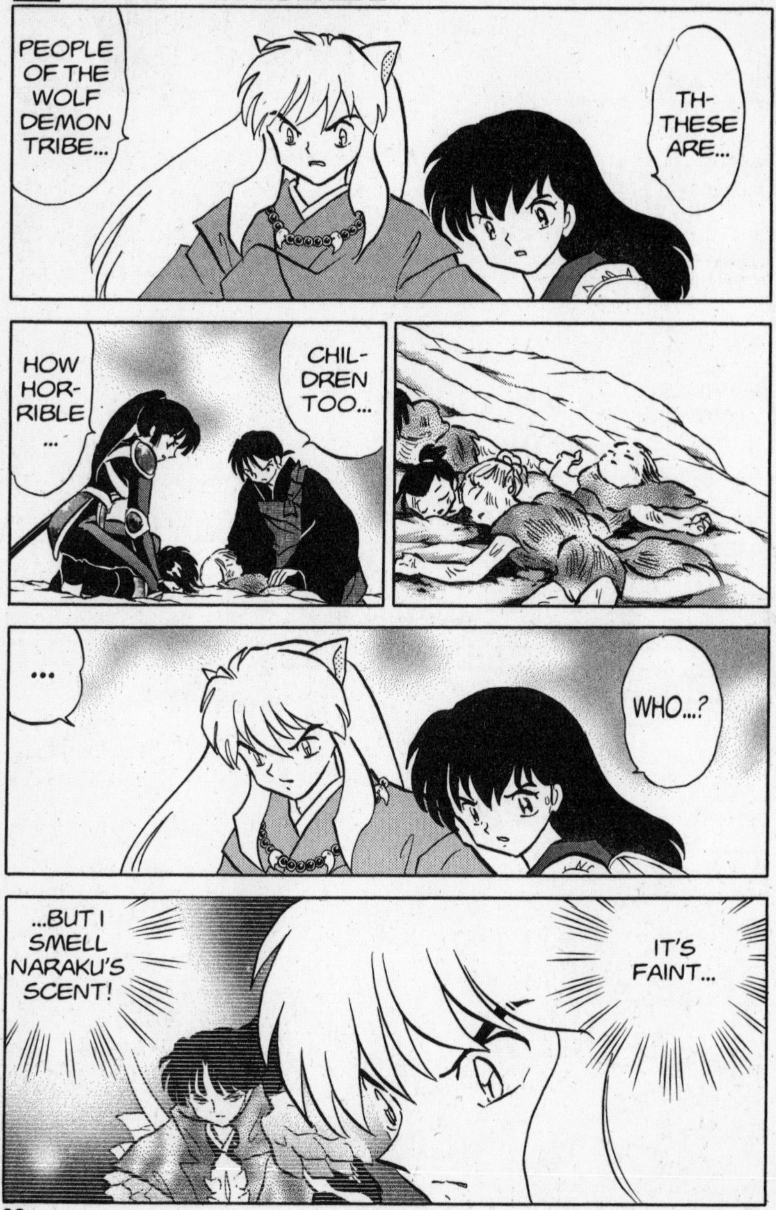
TH-THESE ARE...
PEOPLE OF THE WOLF DEMON TRIBE...
CHIL-DREN TOO...
HOW HOR-RIBLE...
WHO...?
...
IT'S FAINT...
...BUT I SMELL NARAKU'S SCENT!

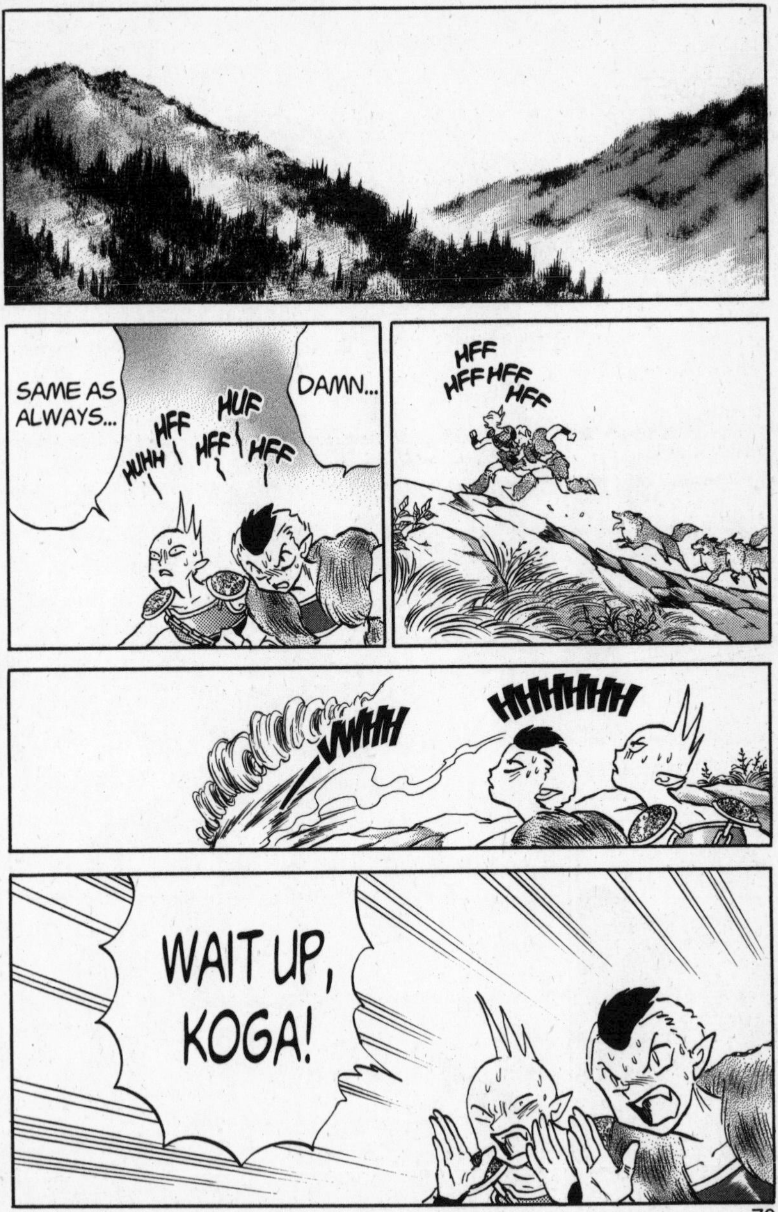
HFF
HFF HFF
HFF
DAMN...
HUF
HFF
HFF
HFF
HUHH
SAME AS ALWAYS...
HHHHHHH
VWHH
WAIT UP, KOGA!

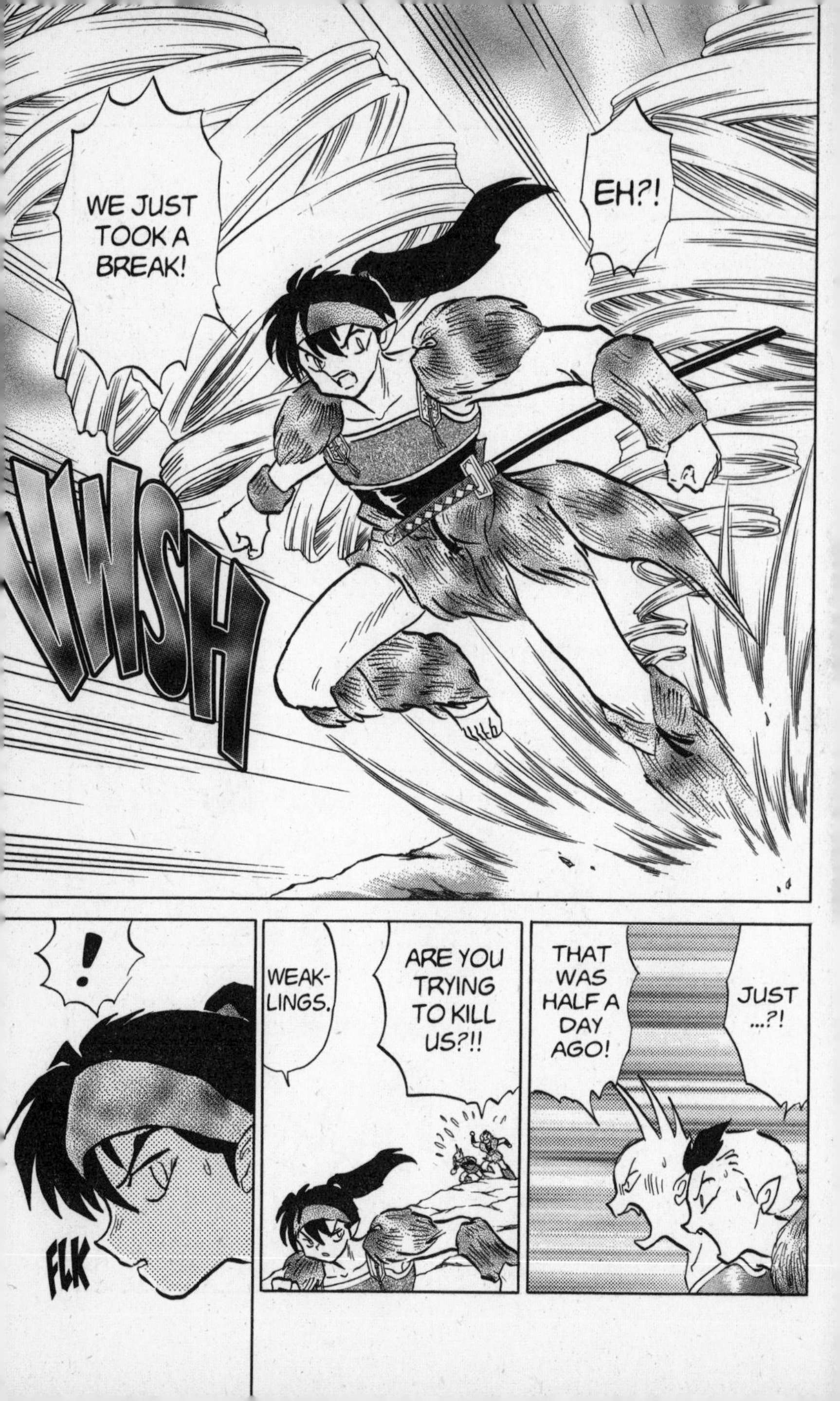
EH?!
WE JUST TOOK A BREAK!
VWSH
JUST ...?!
THAT WAS HALF A DAY AGO!
ARE YOU TRYING TO KILL US?!!
WEAK-LINGS.
!
FLK

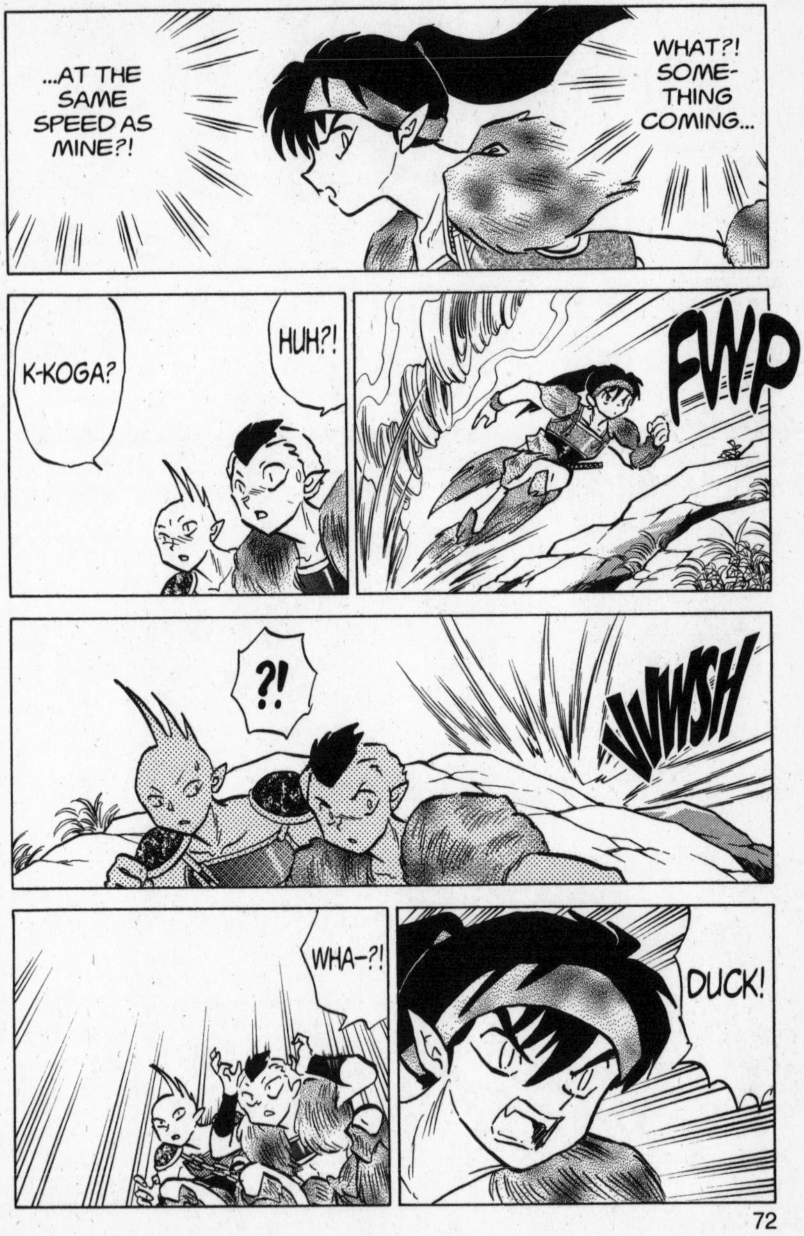
WHAT?! SOME-THING COMING...
...AT THE SAME SPEED AS MINE?!
FWP
HUH?!
K-KOGA?
VVWSH
?!
DUCK!
WHA-?!

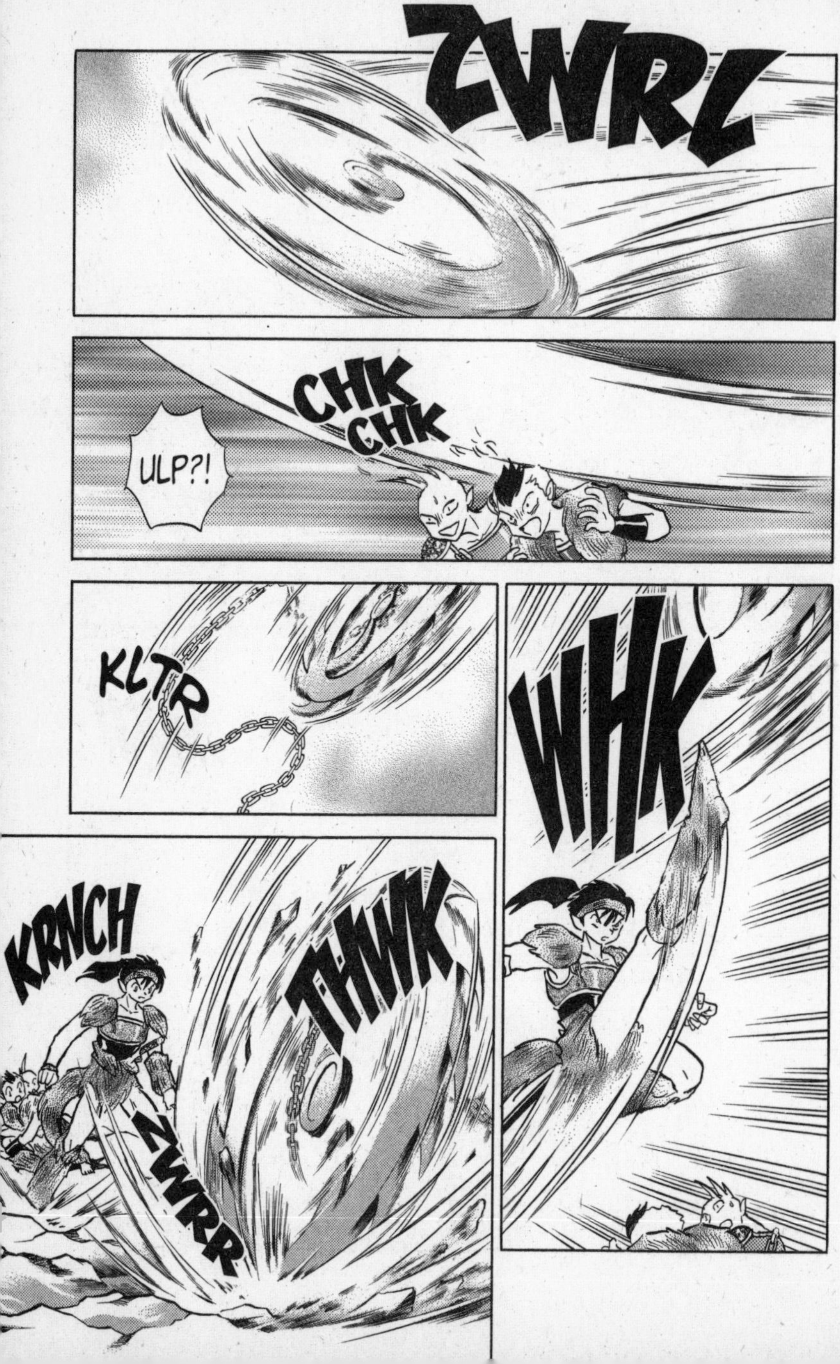
ZWRL
CHK CHK
ULP?!
WHK
KLTR
THWK
ZWRR
KRNCH

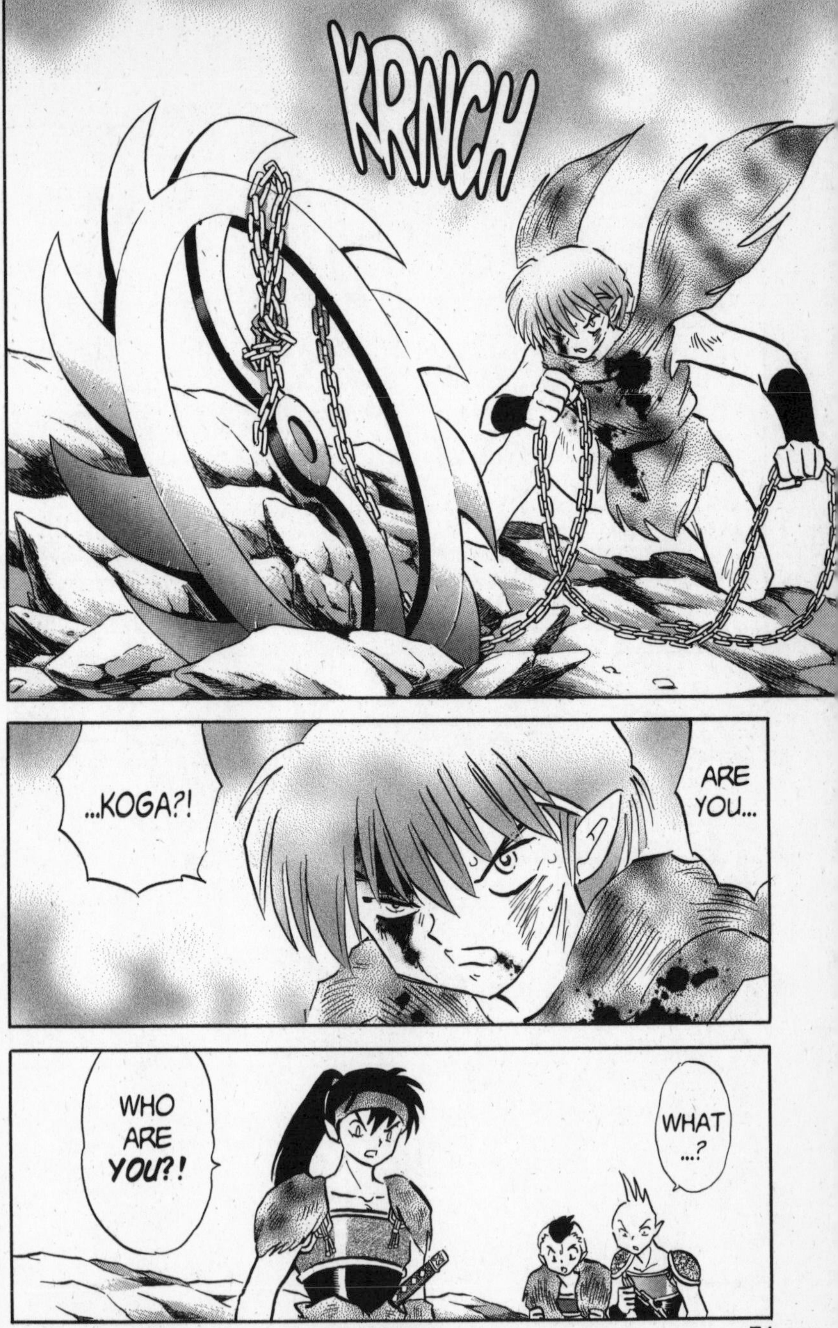
KRNCH
ARE YOU...
...KOGA?!
WHAT ...?
WHO ARE YOU?!

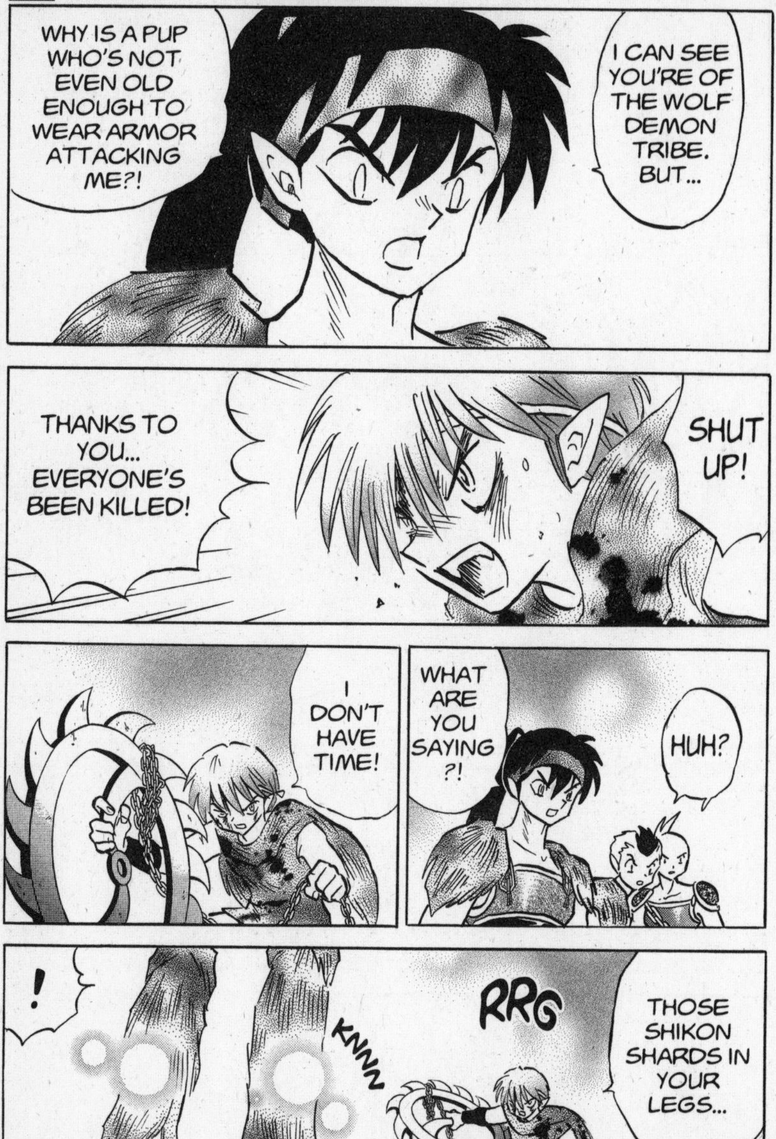
I CAN SEE YOU'RE OF THE WOLF DEMON TRIBE. BUT...
WHY IS A PUP WHO'S NOT EVEN OLD ENOUGH TO WEAR ARMOR ATTACKING ME?!
SHUT UP!
THANKS TO YOU... EVERYONE'S BEEN KILLED!
HUH?
WHAT ARE YOU SAYING ?!
I DON'T HAVE TIME!
THOSE SHIKON SHARDS IN YOUR LEGS...
RRG
KNNN
!

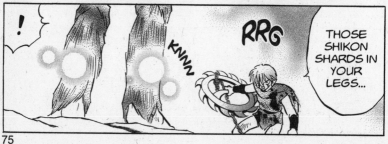

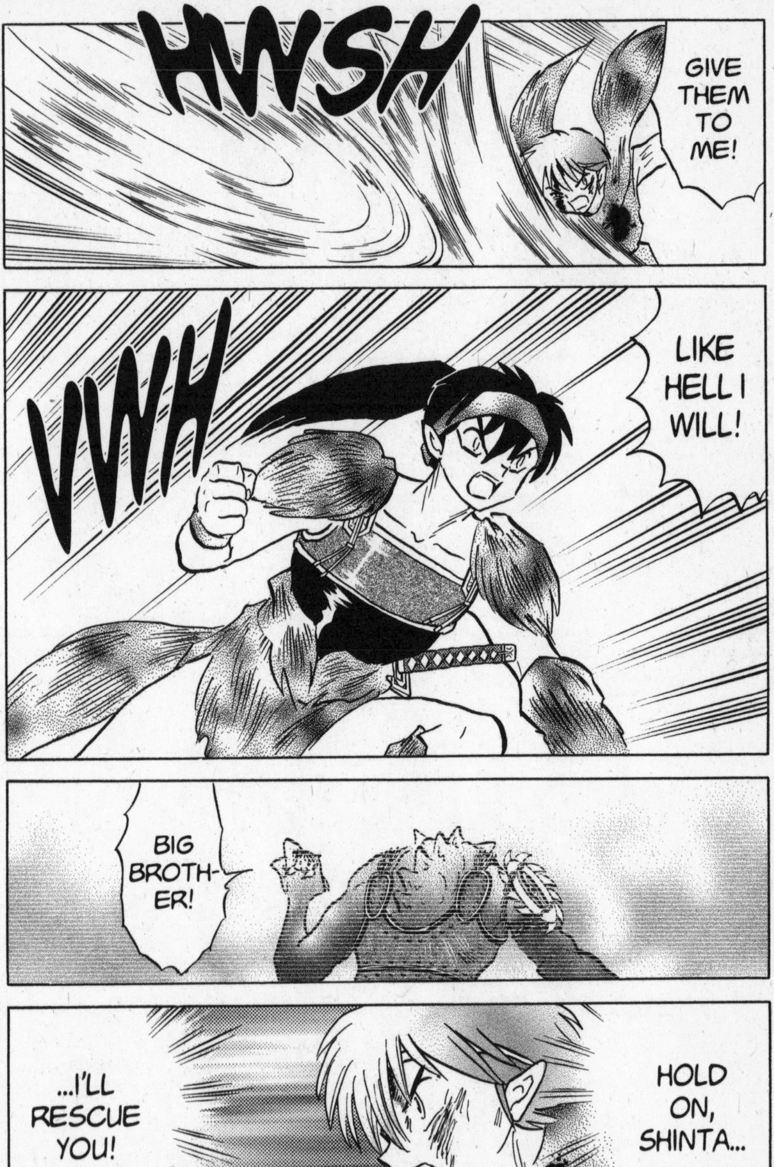
GIVE THEM TO ME!
HWSH
LIKE HELL I WILL!
VWH
BIG BROTH-ER!
HOLD ON, SHINTA...
...I'LL RESCUE YOU!

SCROLL 5
SUNDOWN

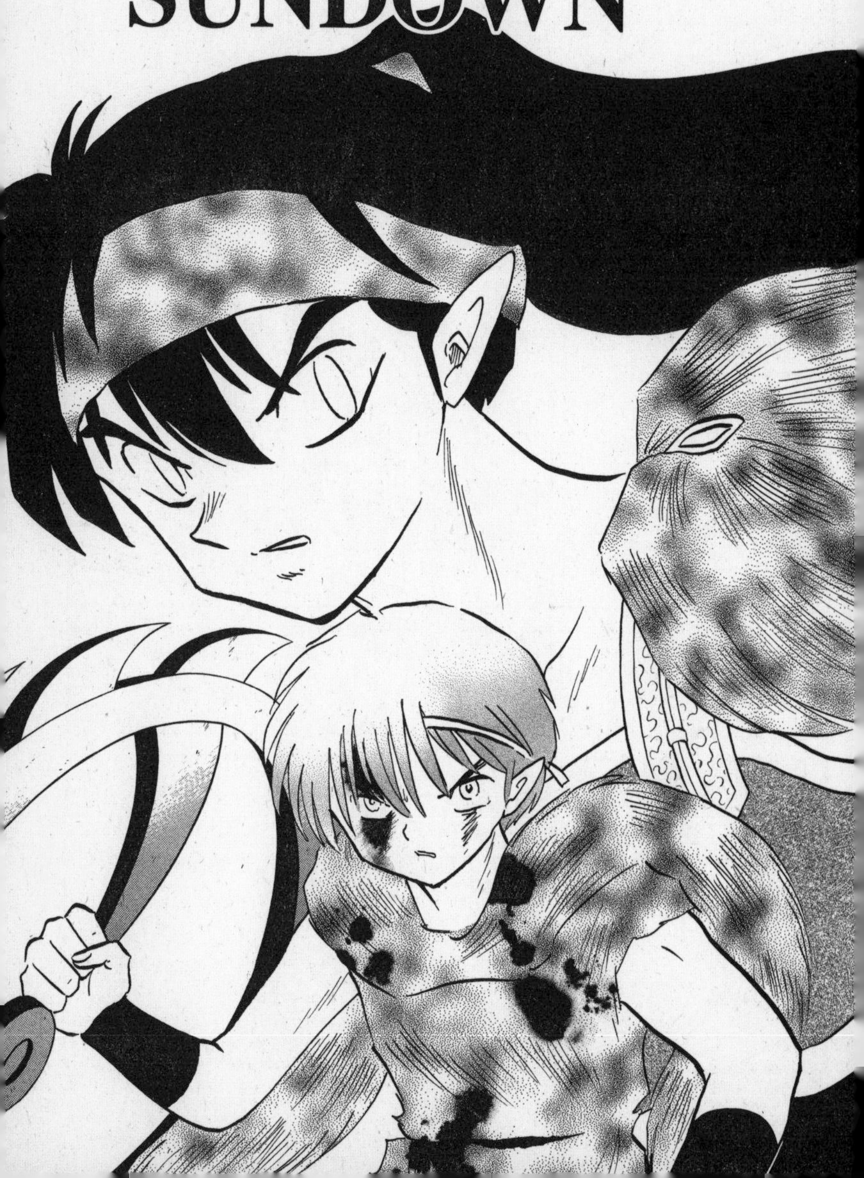

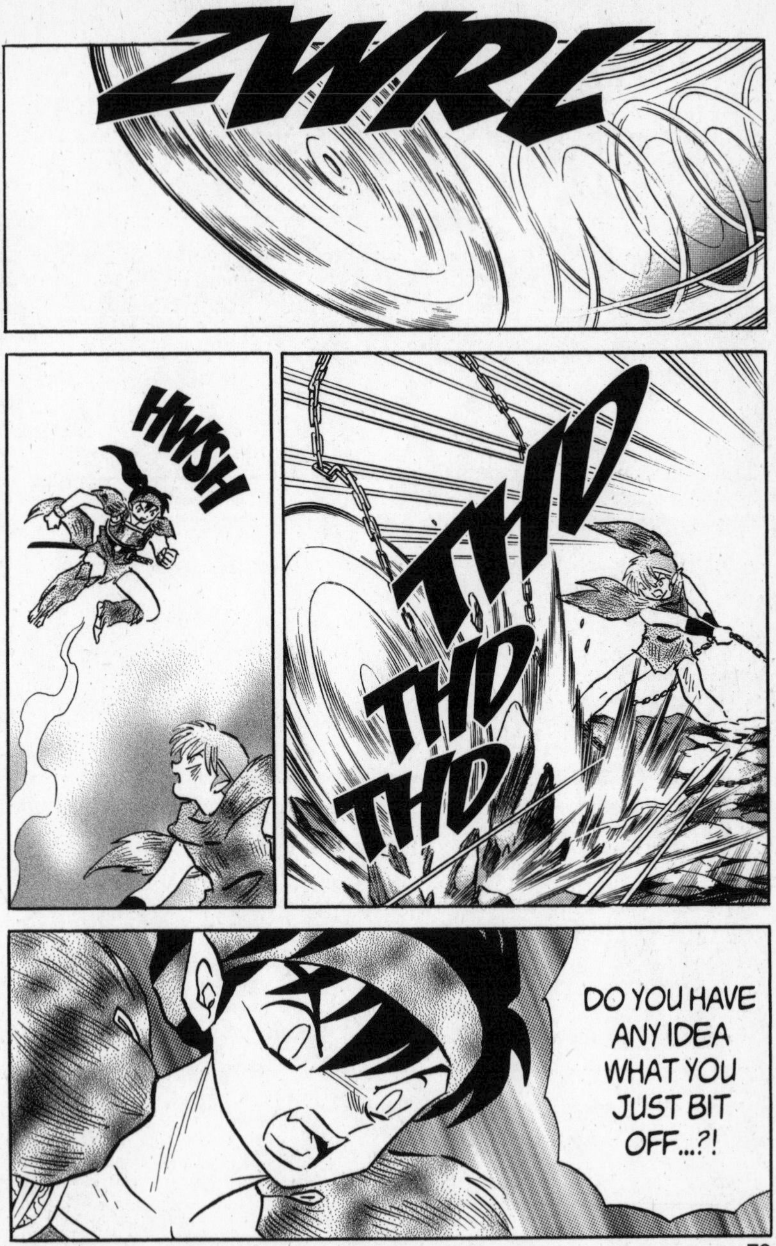
ZWRL
THD
THD
THD
HWSH!
DO YOU HAVE ANY IDEA WHAT YOU JUST BIT OFF...?!

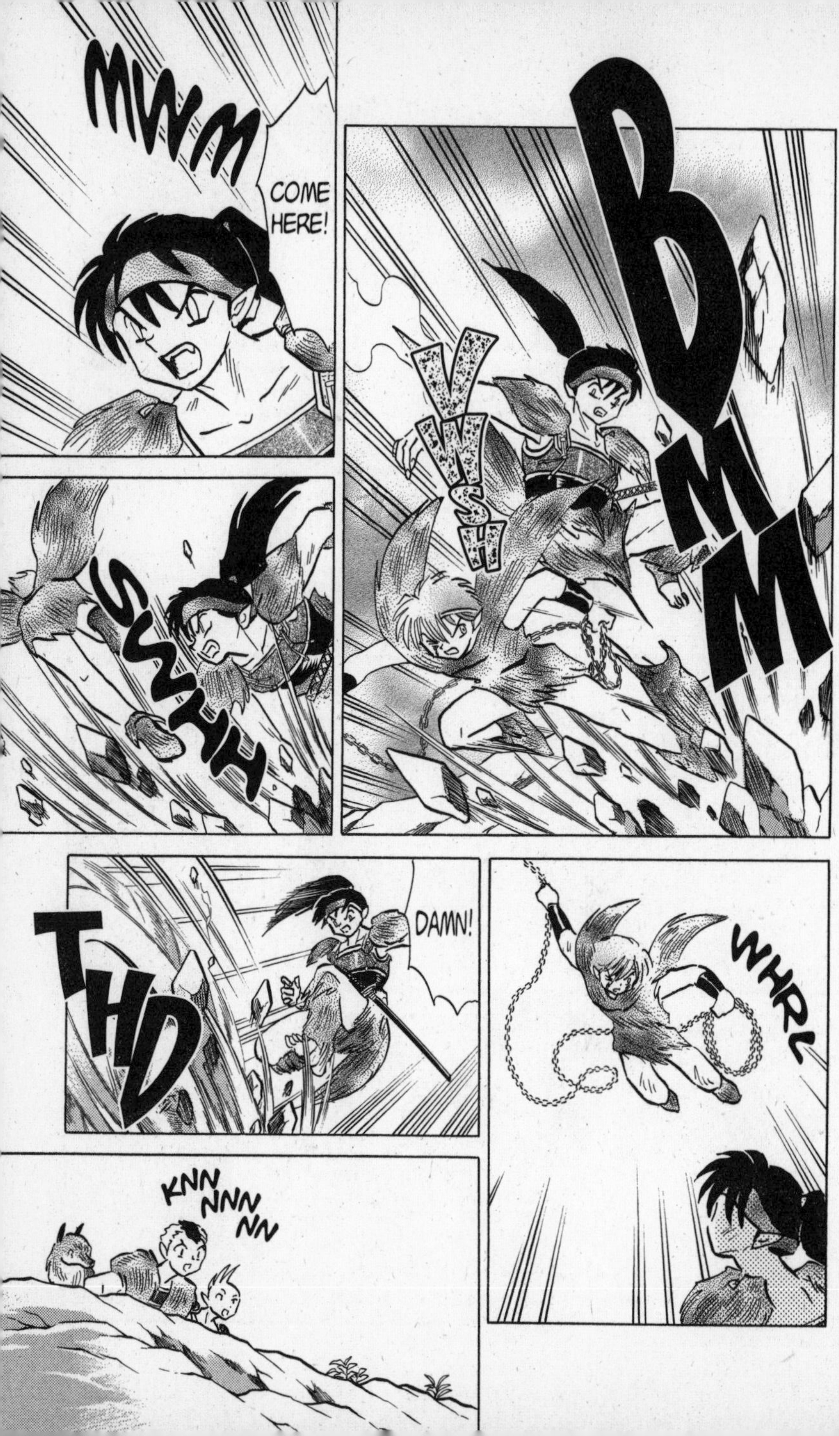
BMMM
VWSH
MWM
COME HERE!
SWHH
WHRL
THD
DAMN!
KNN NNN NN

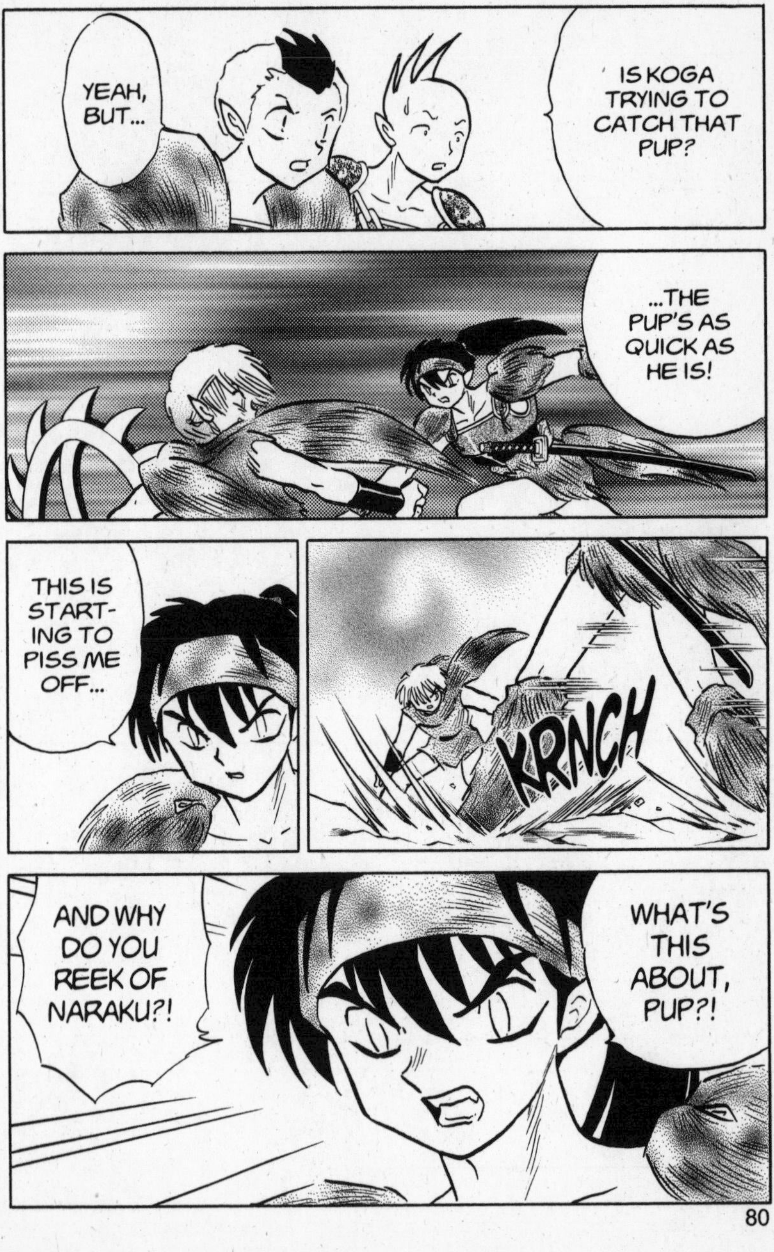
IS KOGA TRYING TO CATCH THAT PUP?
YEAH, BUT...
...THE PUP'S AS QUICK AS HE IS!
KRNCH
THIS IS START-ING TO PISS ME OFF...
WHAT'S THIS ABOUT, PUP?!
AND WHY DO YOU REEK OF NARAKU?!

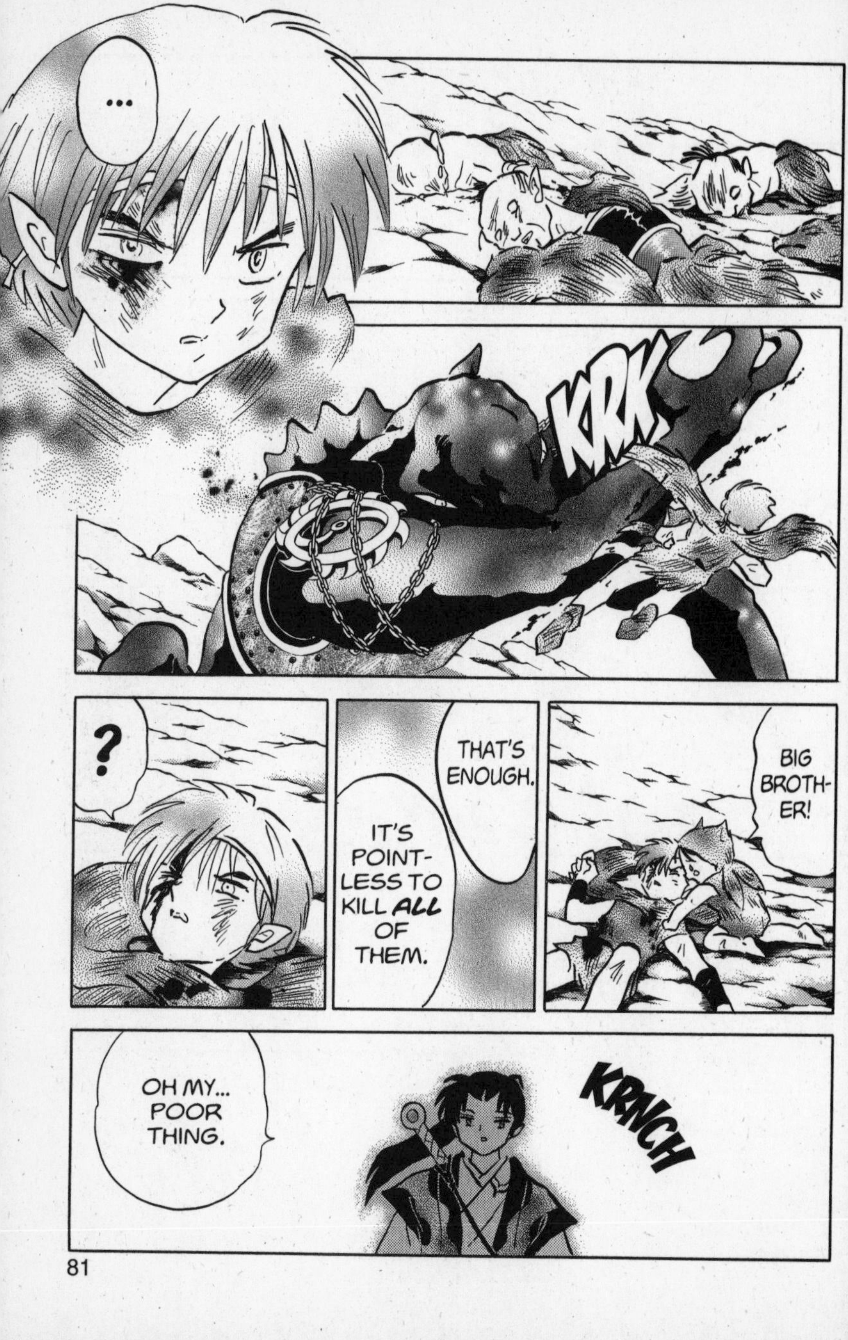
...
KRK
BIG BROTH-ER!
THAT'S ENOUGH.
IT'S POINT-LESS TO KILL ALL OF THEM.
?
KRNCH
OH MY... POOR THING.

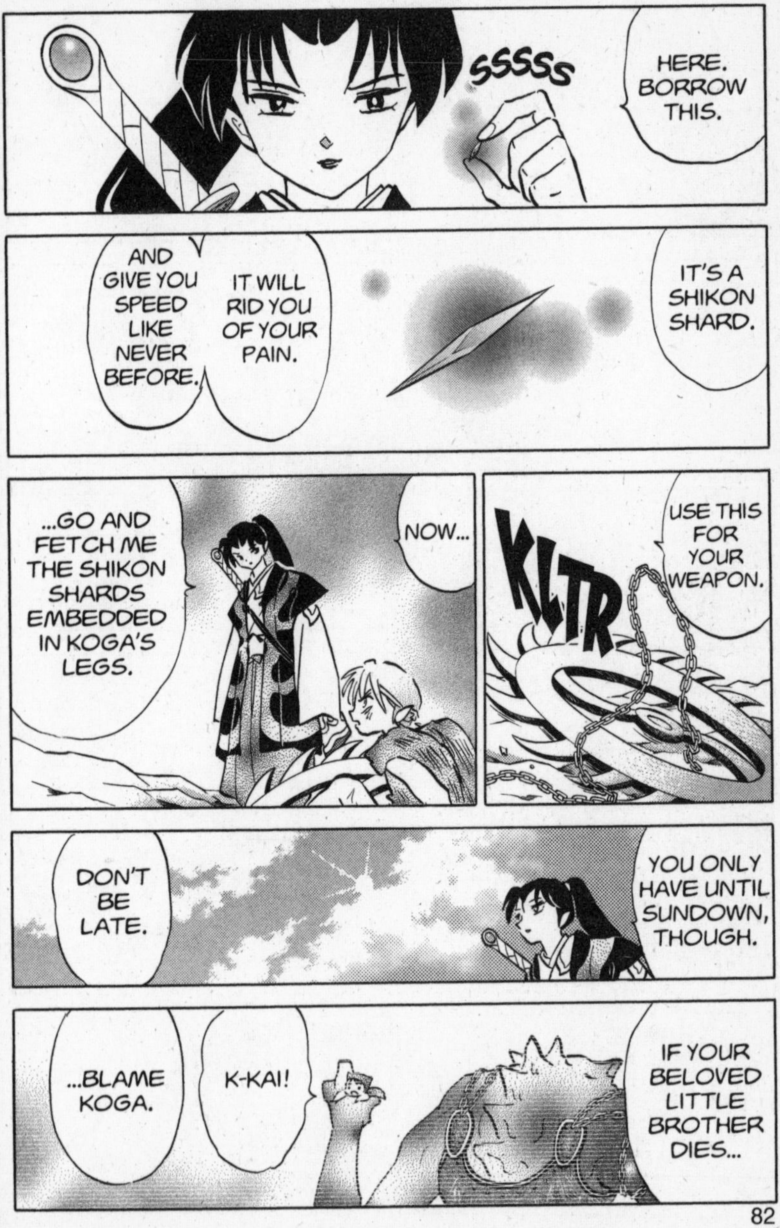
HERE. BORROW THIS.
SSSSS
IT'S A SHIKON SHARD.
IT WILL RID YOU OF YOUR PAIN.
AND GIVE YOU SPEED LIKE NEVER BEFORE.
USE THIS FOR YOUR WEAPON.
KLTR
NOW...
...GO AND FETCH ME THE SHIKON SHARDS EMBEDDED IN KOGA'S LEGS.
YOU ONLY HAVE UNTIL SUNDOWN, THOUGH.
DON'T BE LATE.
IF YOUR BELOVED LITTLE BROTHER DIES...
K-KAI!
...BLAME KOGA.

I'VE GOT TO SAVE SHINTA!

ARE YOU SERVING NARAKU?!

VWSH

ANSWER ME!

HUH?!

NO!!

HWSH

CHK CHK

WHOA!

TA

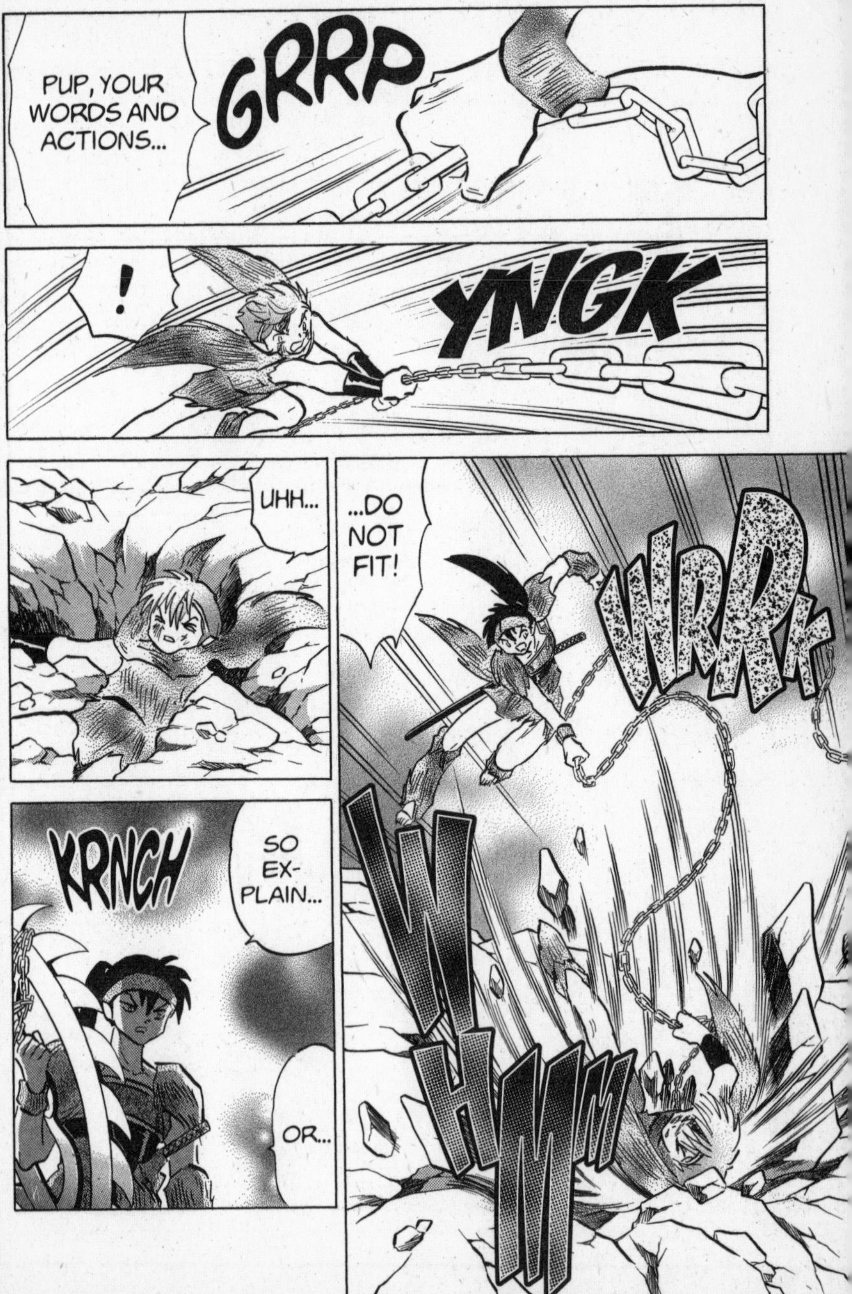
PUP, YOUR WORDS AND ACTIONS...
GRRP
!
YNGK
UHH...
...DO NOT FIT!
WRRRK
WHMMM
KRNCH
SO EX-PLAIN...
OR...

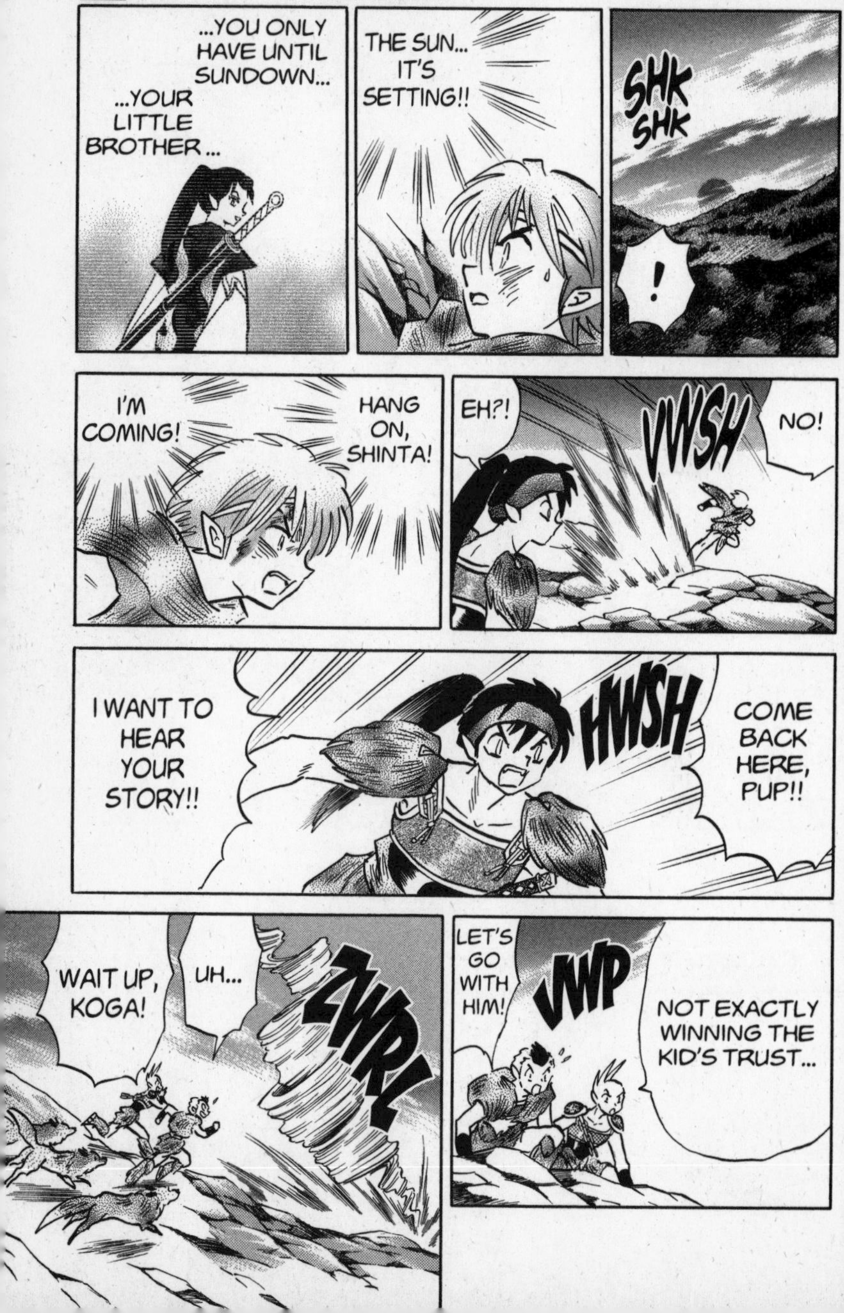
...YOU ONLY HAVE UNTIL SUNDOWN...
...YOUR LITTLE BROTHER...
THE SUN... IT'S SETTING!!
SHK SHK
!
I'M COMING!
HANG ON, SHINTA!
EH?!
VWSH
NO!
I WANT TO HEAR YOUR STORY!!
HWSH
COME BACK HERE, PUP!!
WAIT UP, KOGA!
UH...
ZWRL
LET'S GO WITH HIM!
VWP
NOT EXACTLY WINNING THE KID'S TRUST...

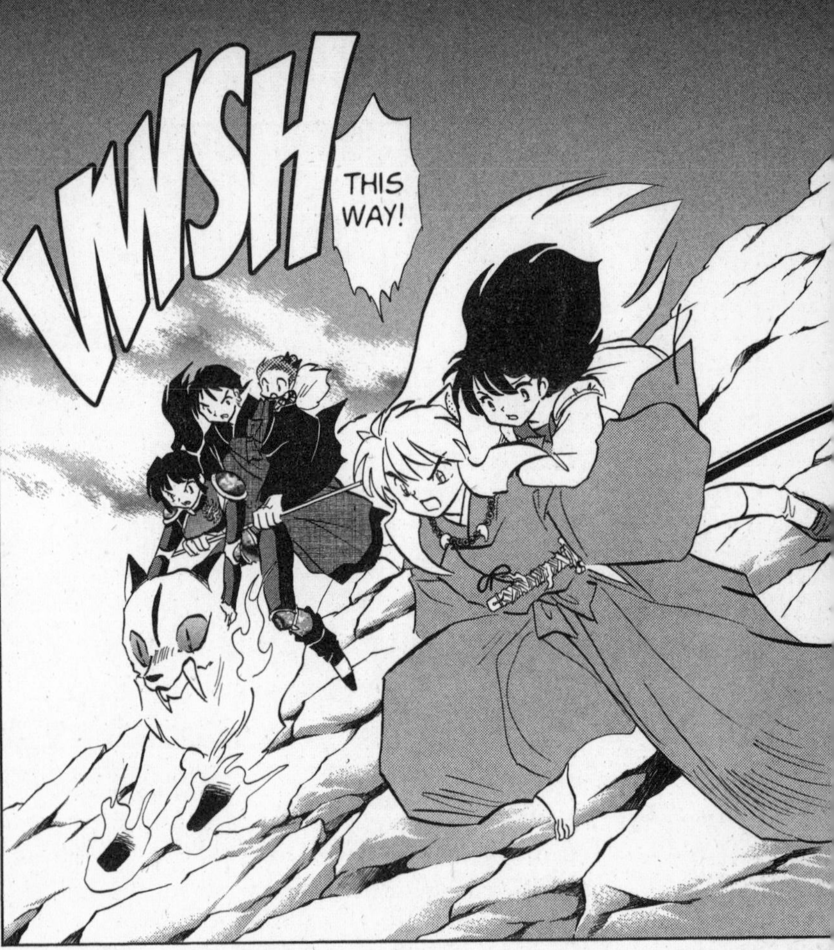
VWSH
THIS WAY!

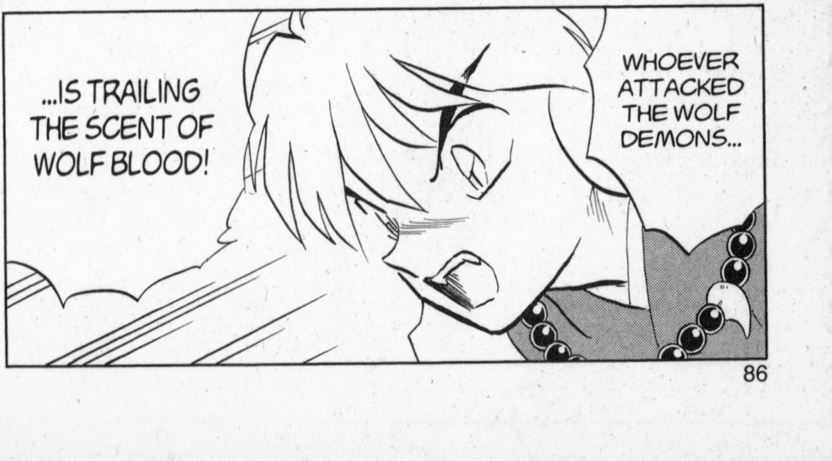
WHOEVER ATTACKED THE WOLF DEMONS...
...IS TRAILING THE SCENT OF WOLF BLOOD!

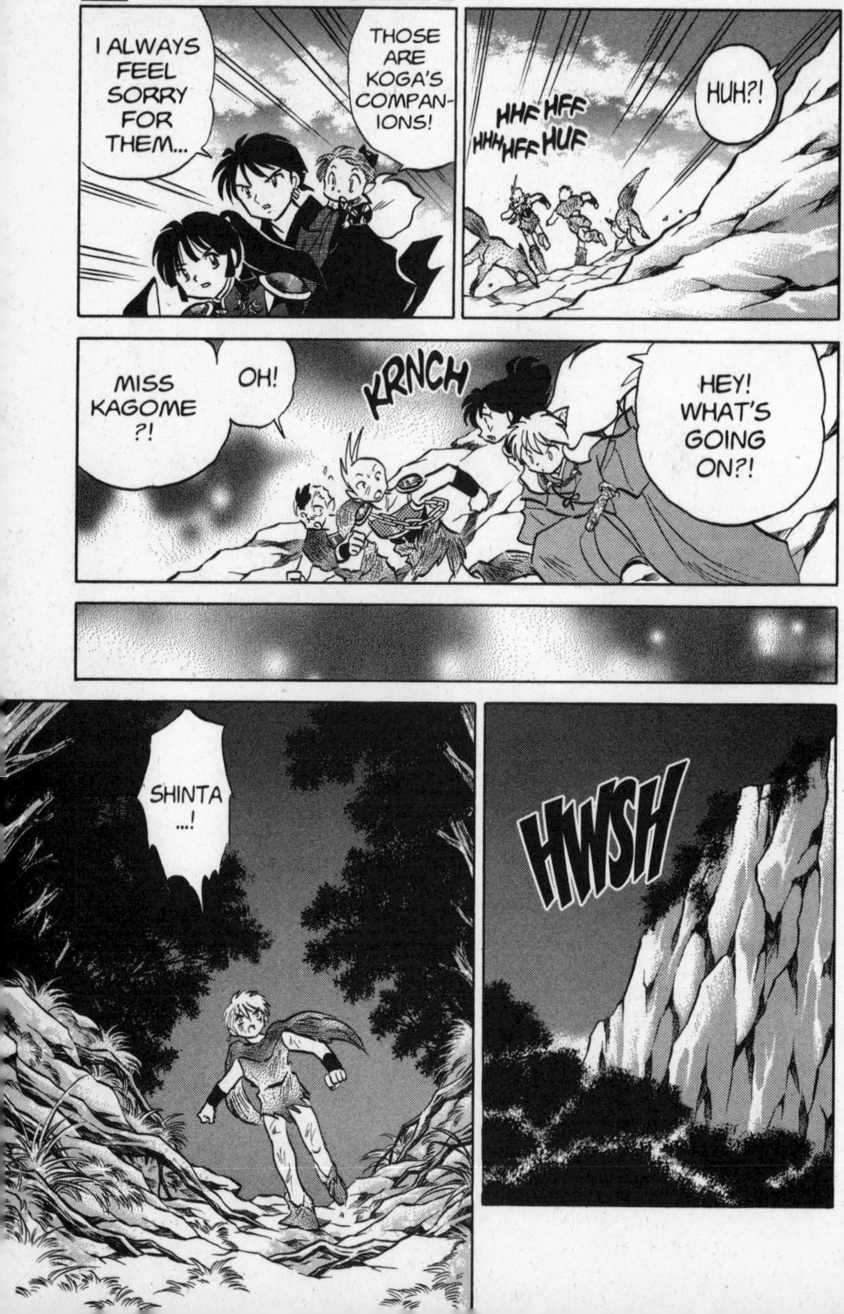
HUH?!
HHF HFF HHH HFF HUF
THOSE ARE KOGA'S COMPAN-IONS!
I ALWAYS FEEL SORRY FOR THEM...
HEY! WHAT'S GOING ON?!
KRNCH
OH!
MISS KAGOME ?!
HWSH
SHINTA ...!

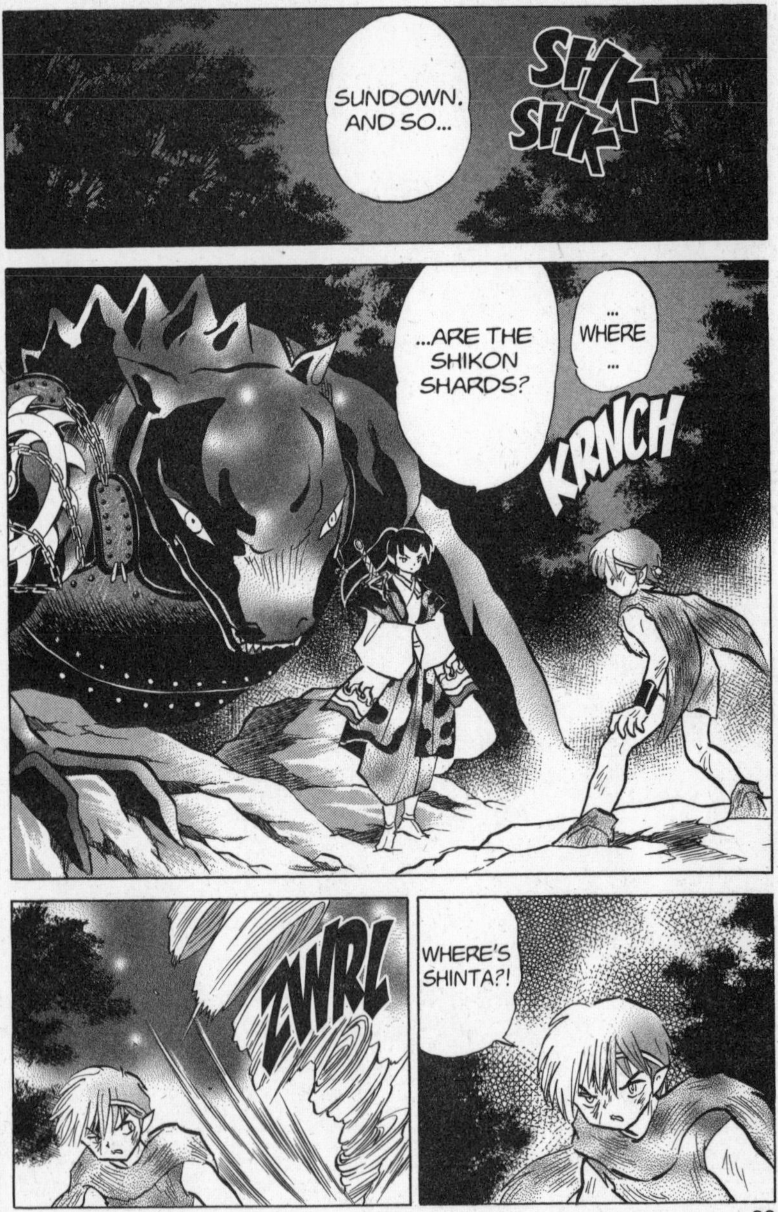
SUNDOWN. AND SO...
SHK SHK
... WHERE ...
...ARE THE SHIKON SHARDS?
KRNCH
WHERE'S SHINTA?!
ZWRL

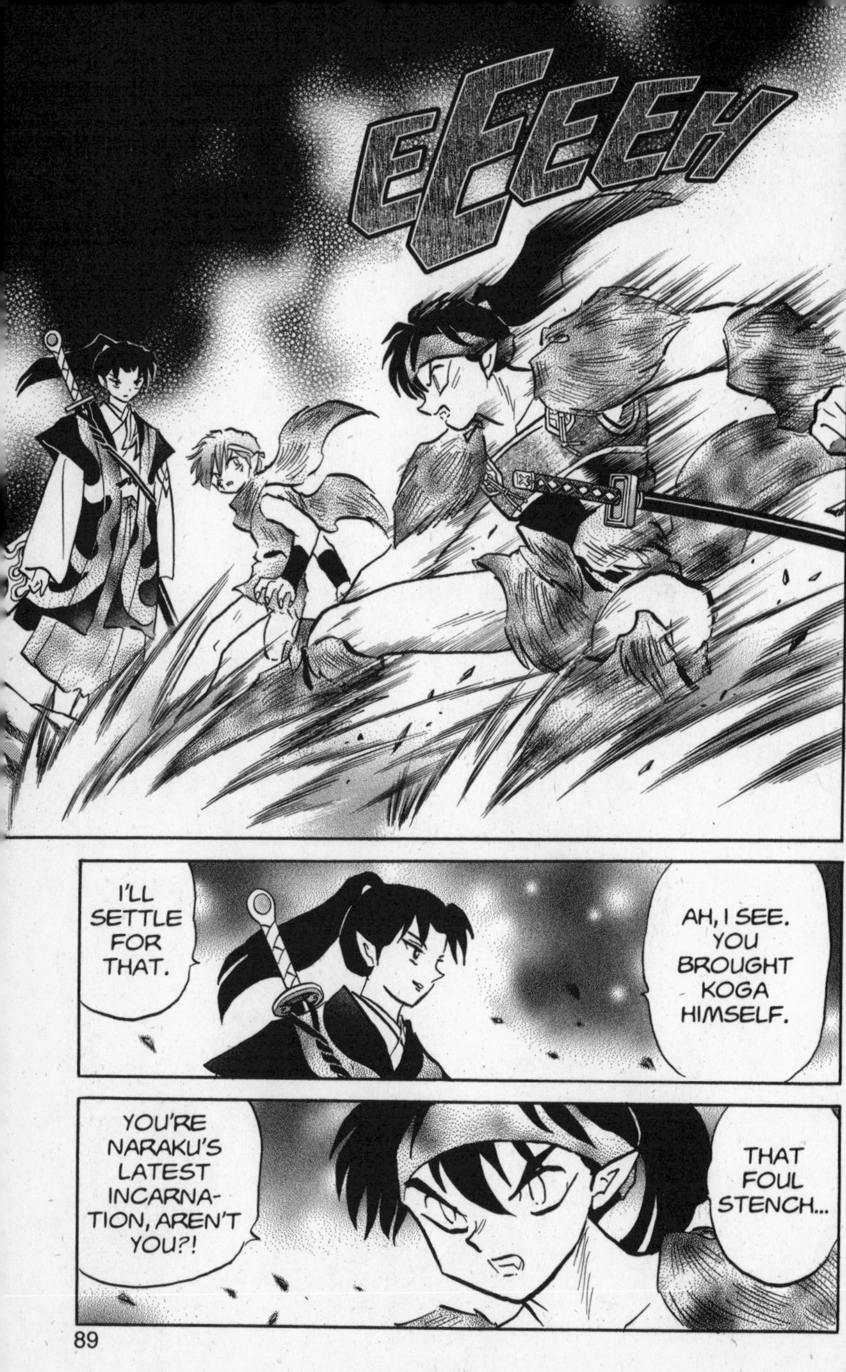
EEEEH
AH, I SEE. YOU BROUGHT KOGA HIMSELF.
I'LL SETTLE FOR THAT.
THAT FOUL STENCH...
YOU'RE NARAKU'S LATEST INCARNATION, AREN'T YOU?!

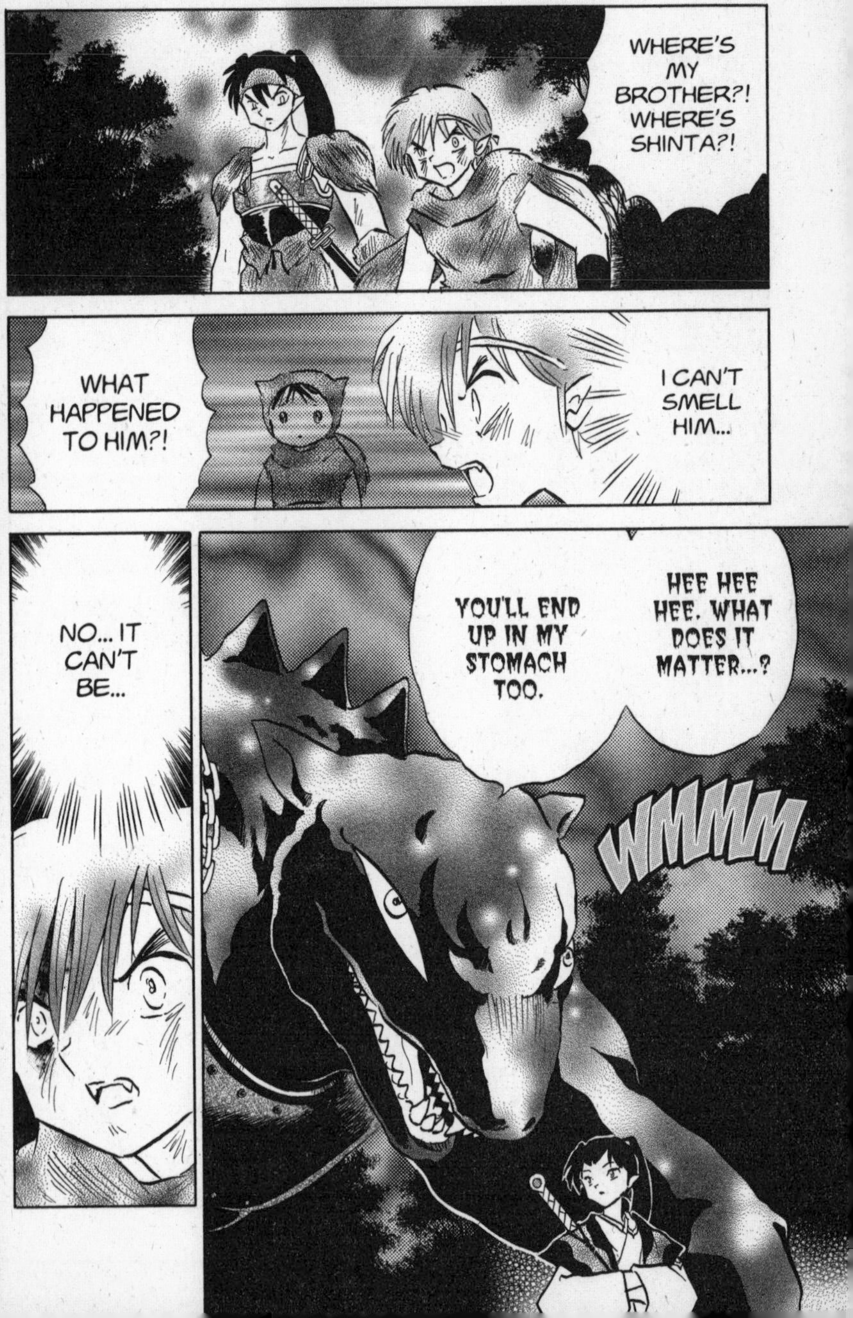
WHERE'S MY BROTHER?! WHERE'S SHINTA?!
I CAN'T SMELL HIM...
WHAT HAPPENED TO HIM?!
HEE HEE HEE. WHAT DOES IT MATTER...?
YOU'LL END UP IN MY STOMACH TOO.
WMMMM
NO... IT CAN'T BE...

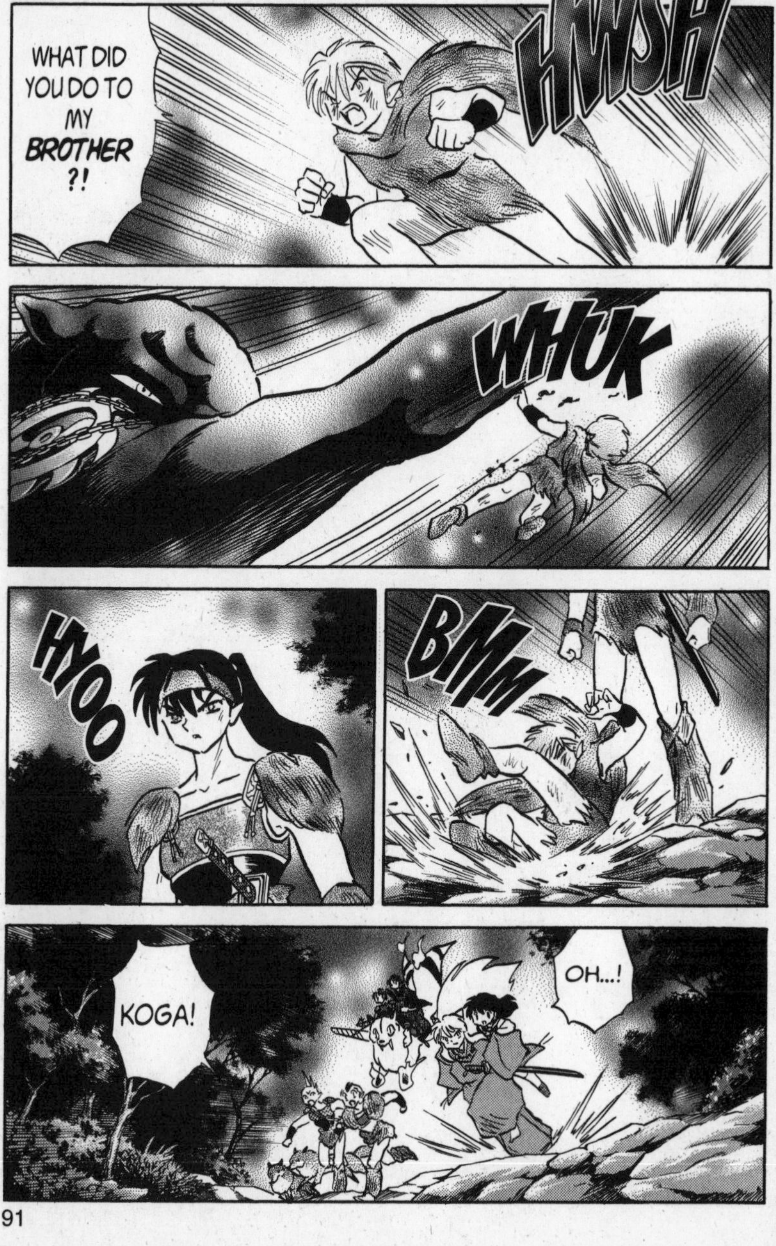
HWSH
WHAT DID YOU DO TO MY BROTHER ?!
WHUK
BMM
HYOO
OH...!
KOGA!

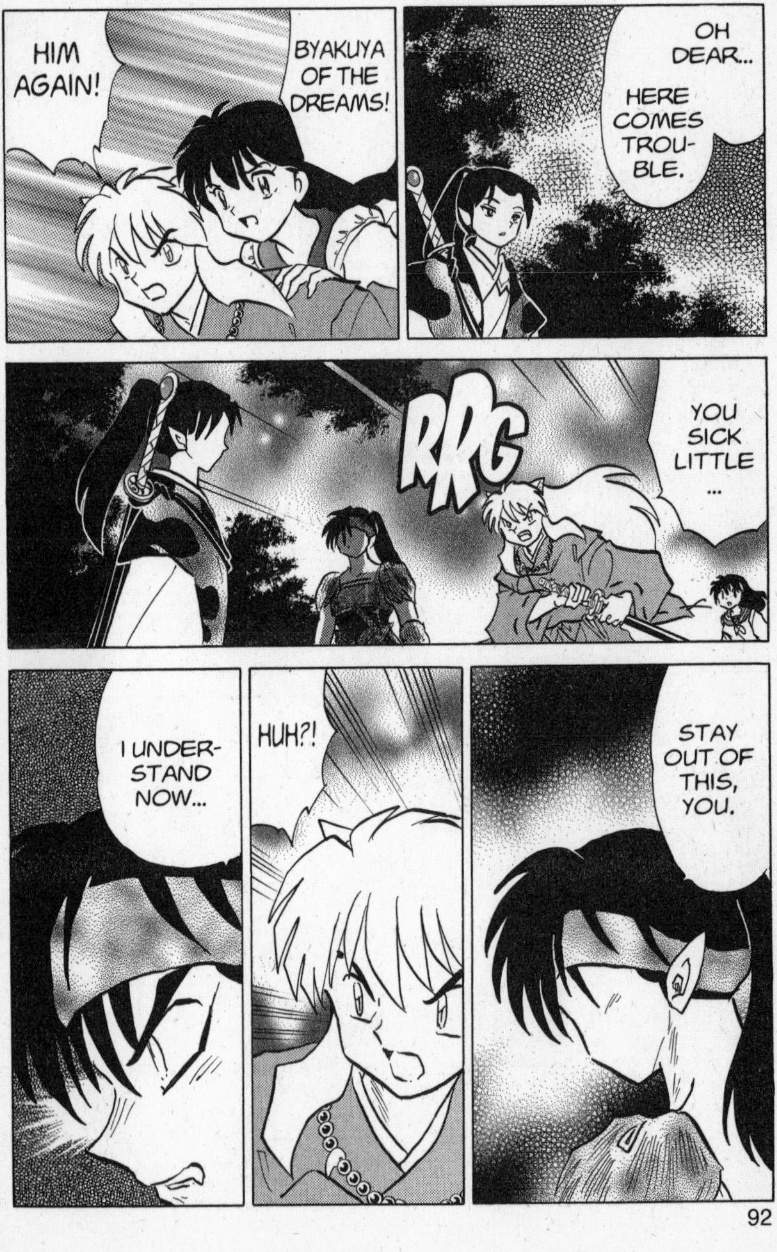
OH DEAR...
HERE COMES TROU-BLE.
BYAKUYA OF THE DREAMS!
HIM AGAIN!
YOU SICK LITTLE ...
RRG
STAY OUT OF THIS, YOU.
HUH?!
I UNDER-STAND NOW...

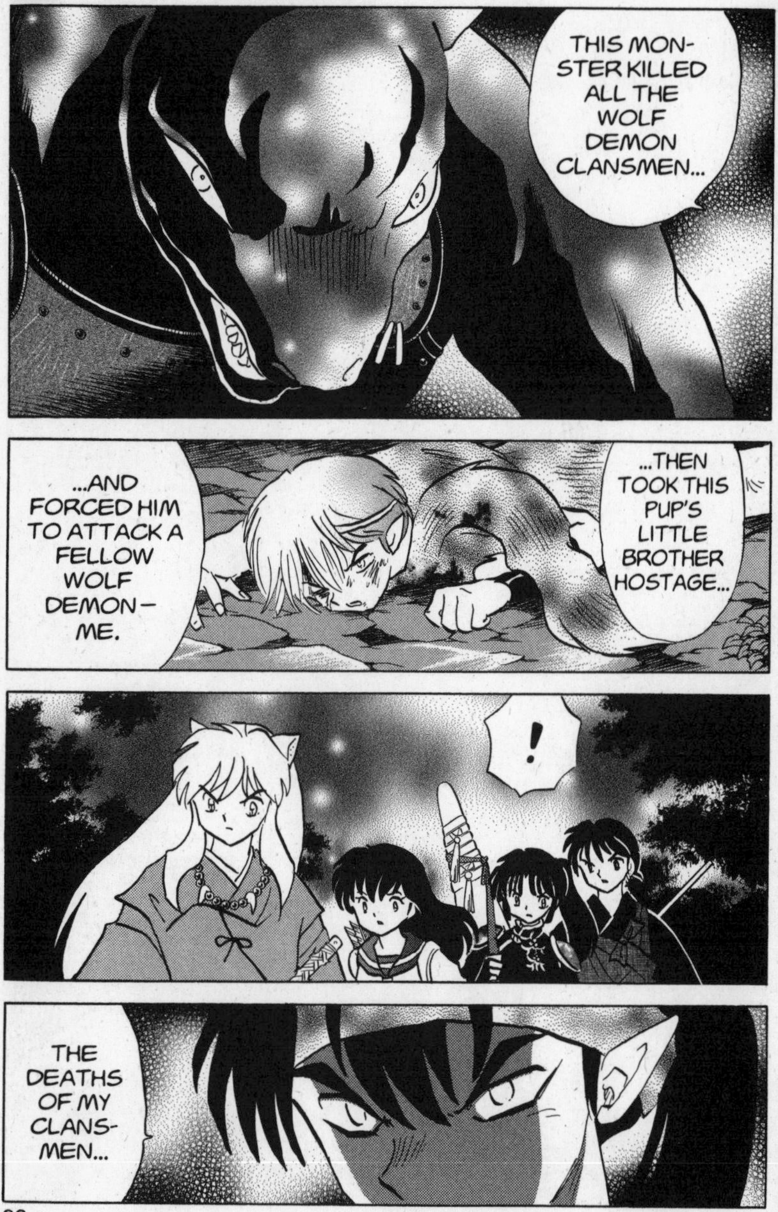
THIS MONSTER KILLED ALL THE WOLF DEMON CLANSMEN...
...THEN TOOK THIS PUP'S LITTLE BROTHER HOSTAGE...
...AND FORCED HIM TO ATTACK A FELLOW WOLF DEMON— ME.
!
THE DEATHS OF MY CLANSMEN...

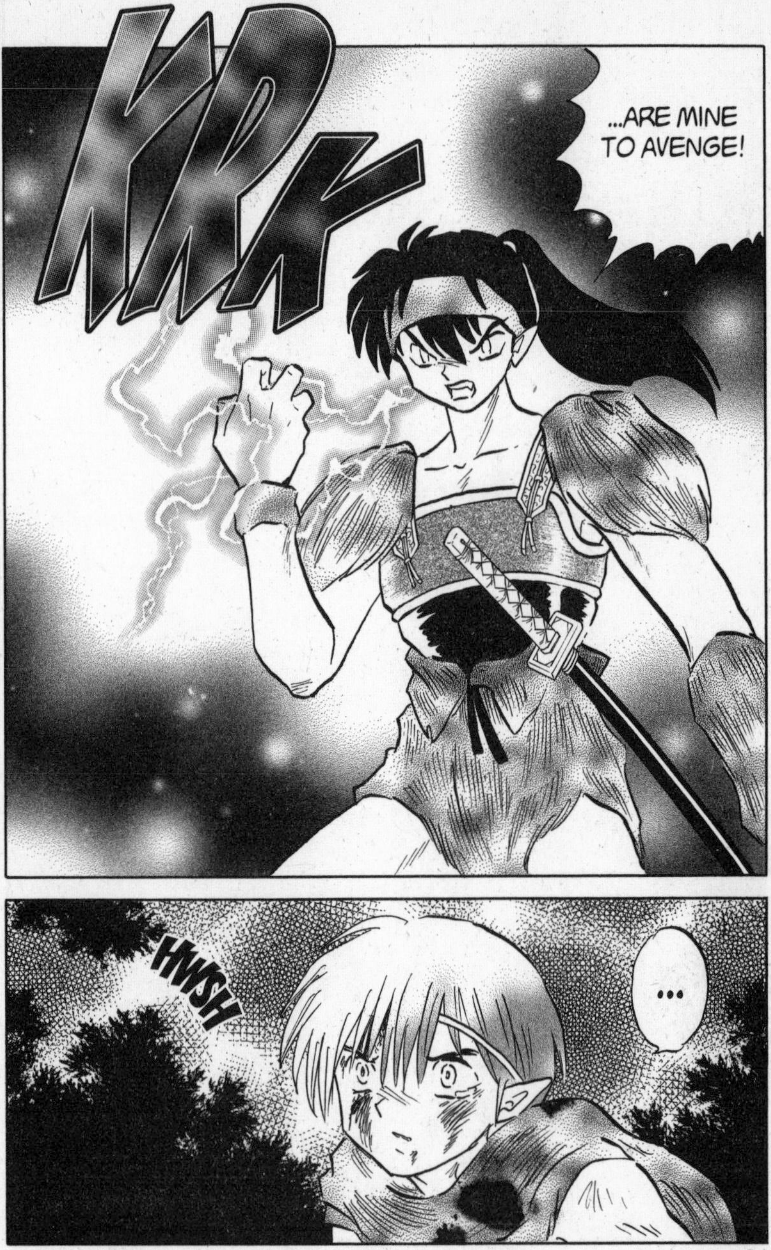
KRRK
...ARE MINE TO AVENGE!
HWSH
...

SCROLL 6

THE GORAISHI'S MIGHT

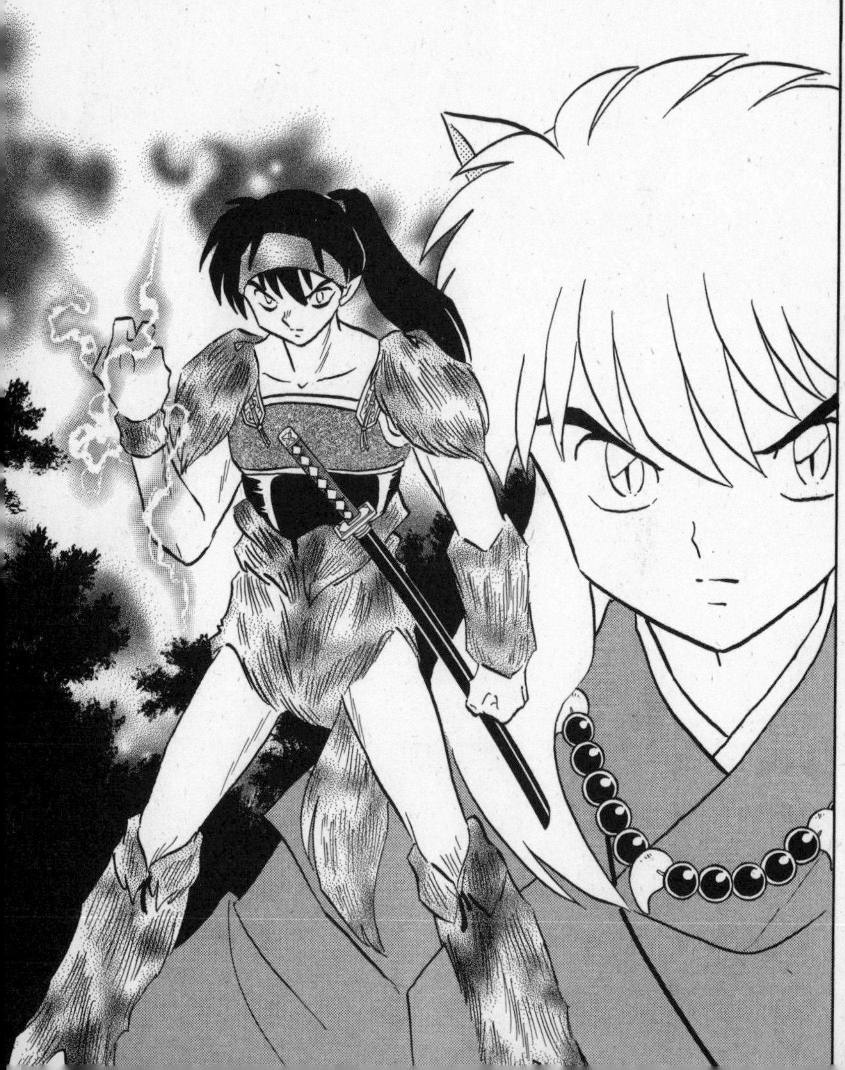

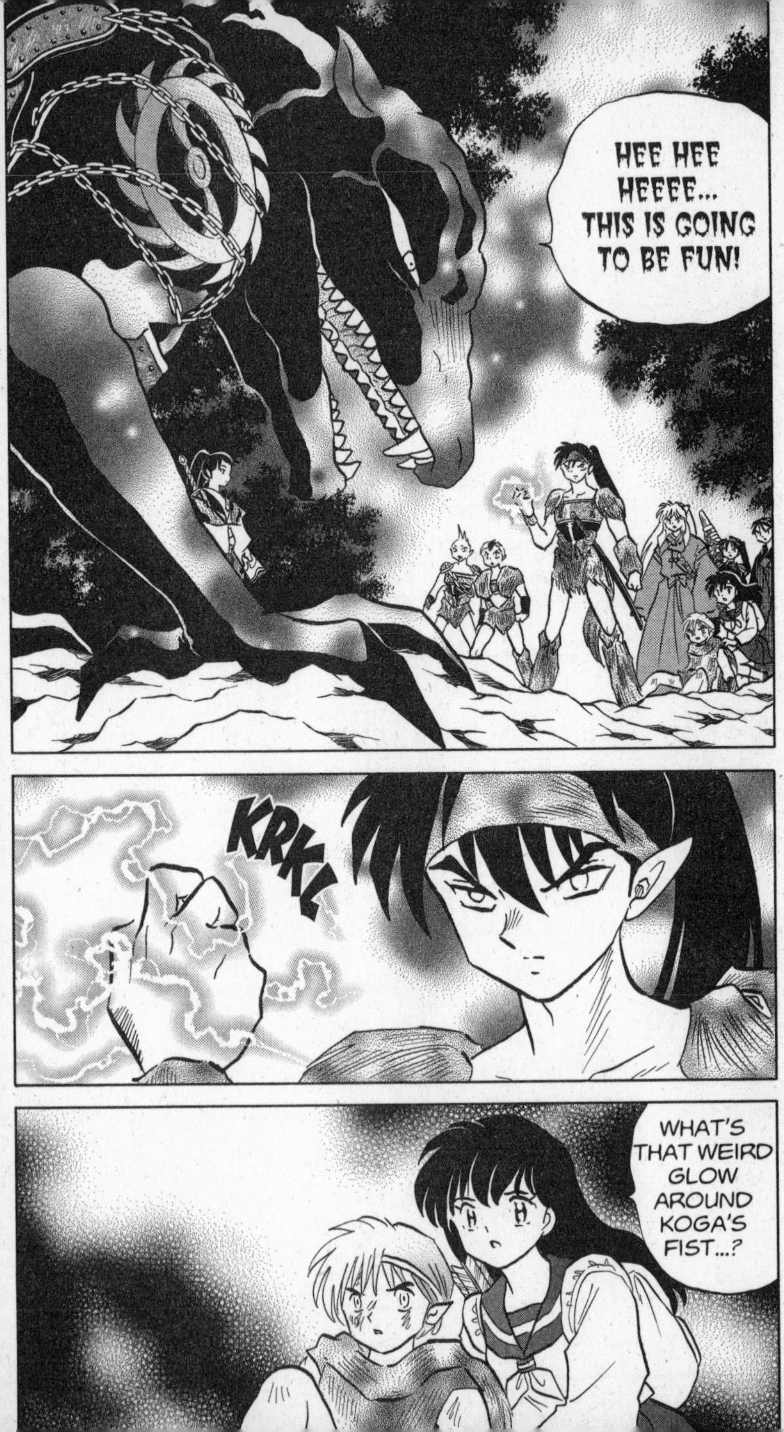
HEE HEE HEEEE... THIS IS GOING TO BE FUN!
KRKL
WHAT'S THAT WEIRD GLOW AROUND KOGA'S FIST...?

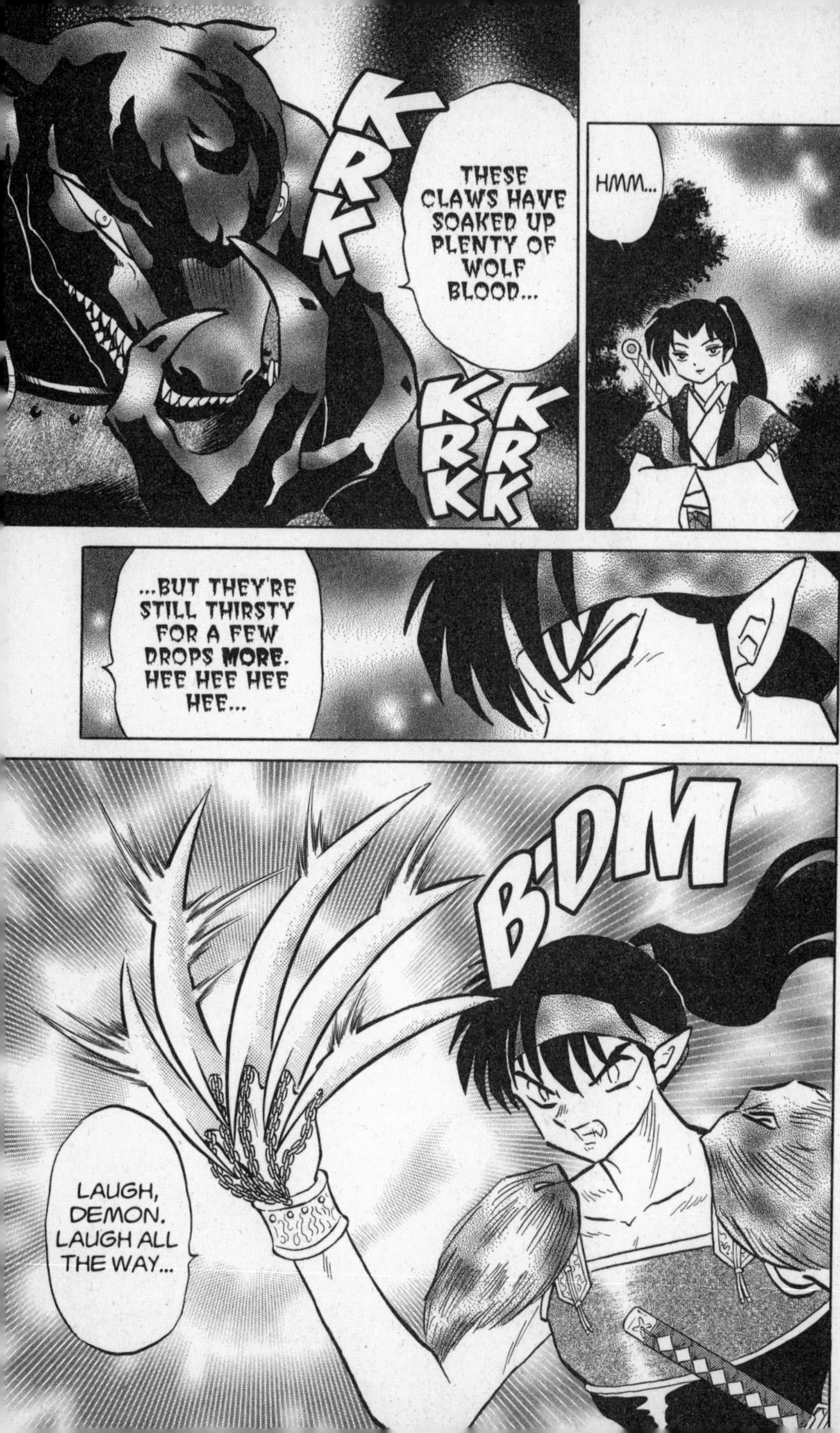
HMM...
THESE CLAWS HAVE SOAKED UP PLENTY OF WOLF BLOOD...
KRK
KRK KRK
...BUT THEY'RE STILL THIRSTY FOR A FEW DROPS MORE. HEE HEE HEE HEE...
B-DM
LAUGH, DEMON. LAUGH ALL THE WAY...

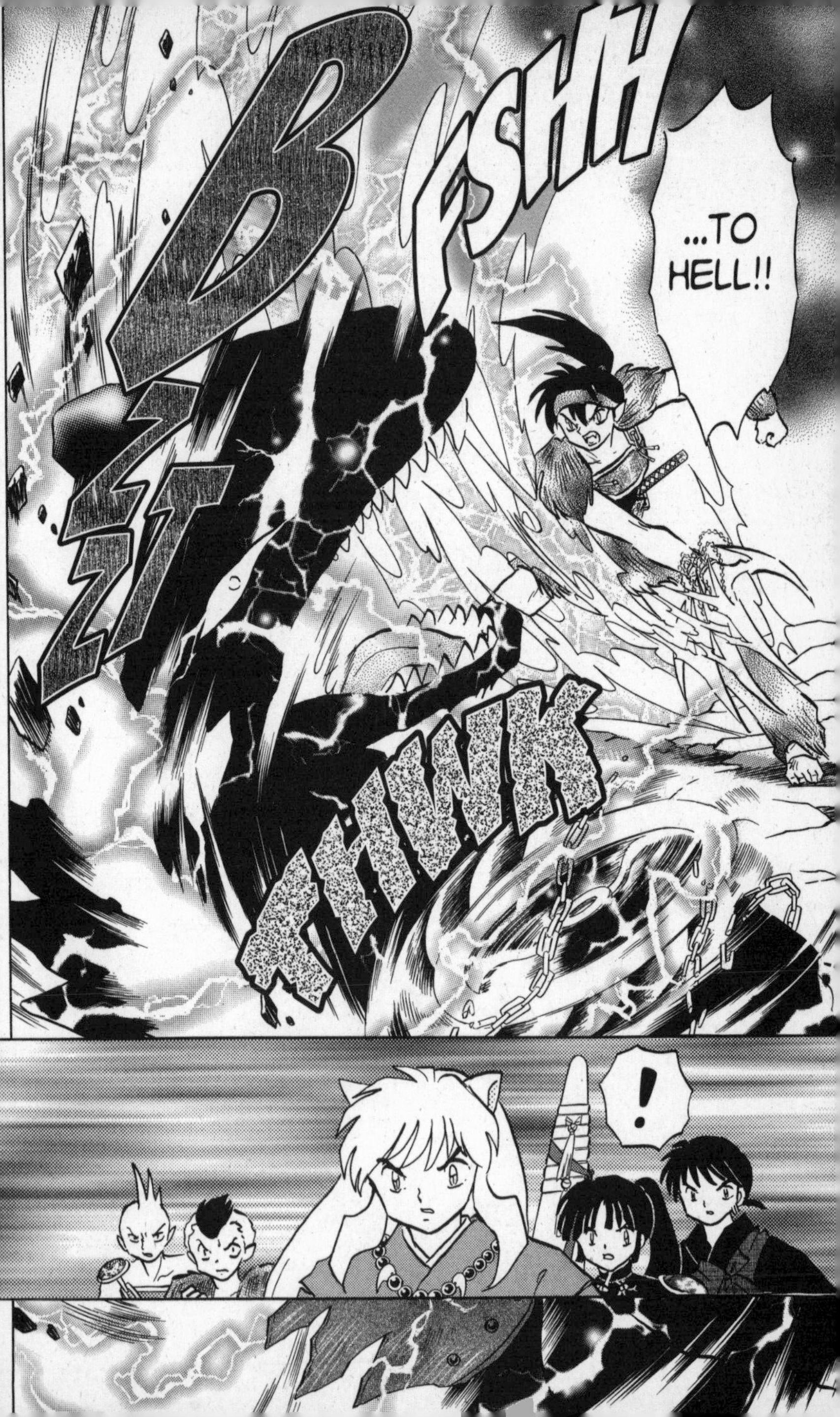
...TO HELL!!
BASHHH
ZZT
THWK
!

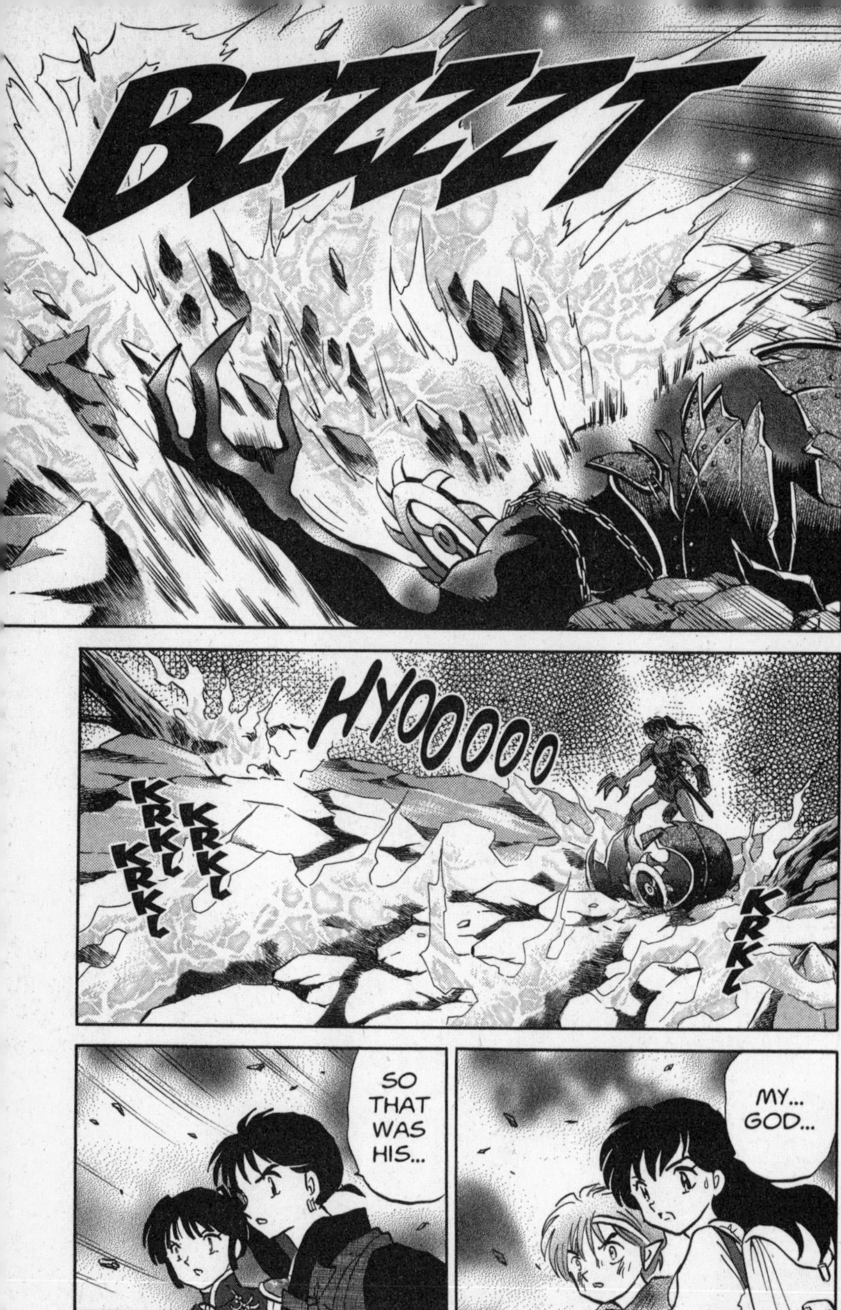
BZZZT
HYOOOOO
KRKL
KRKL
KRKL
KRKL
MY... GOD...
SO THAT WAS HIS...

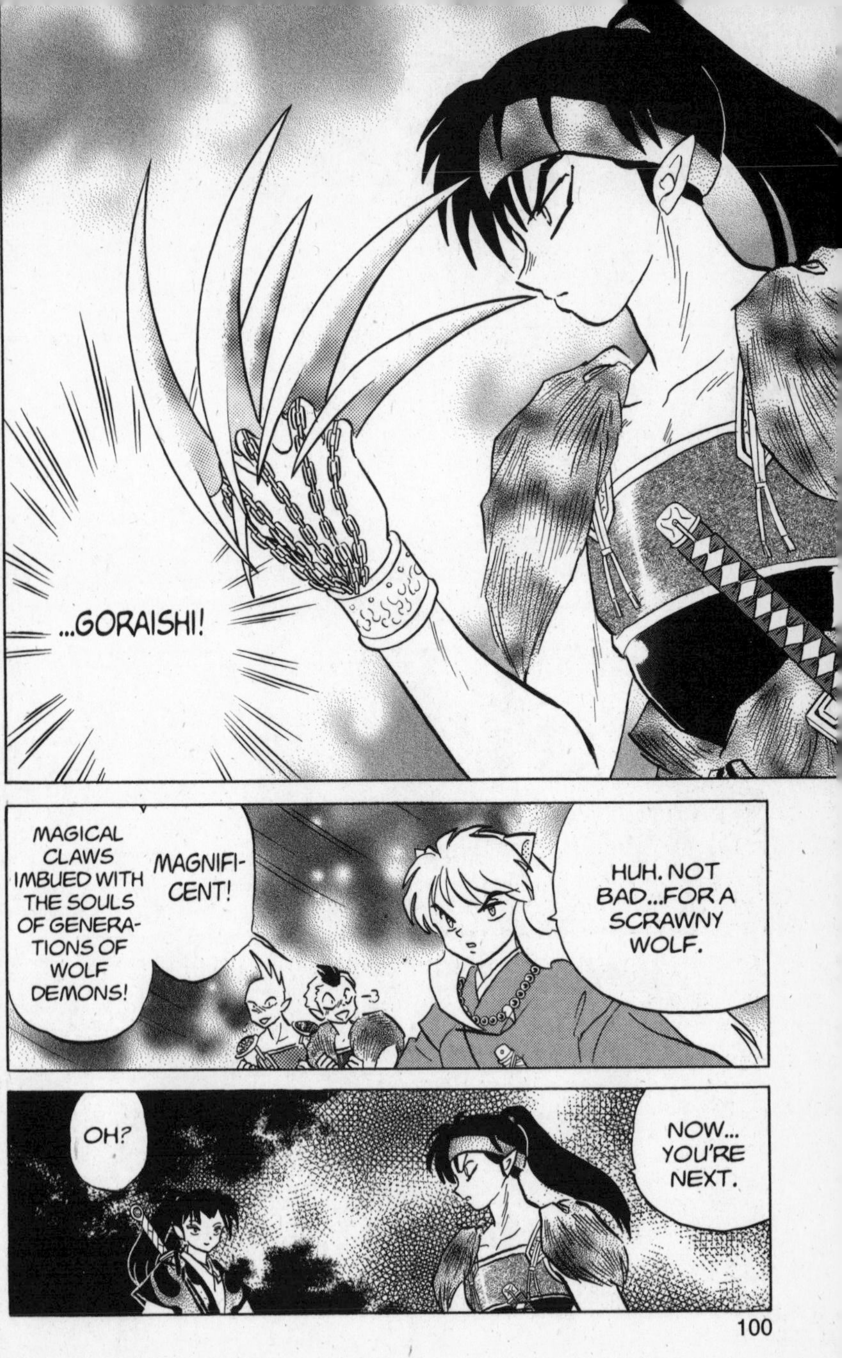
...GORAISHI!
HUH. NOT BAD...FOR A SCRAWNY WOLF.
MAGNIFI-CENT!
MAGICAL CLAWS IMBUED WITH THE SOULS OF GENERA-TIONS OF WOLF DEMONS!
NOW... YOU'RE NEXT.
OH?

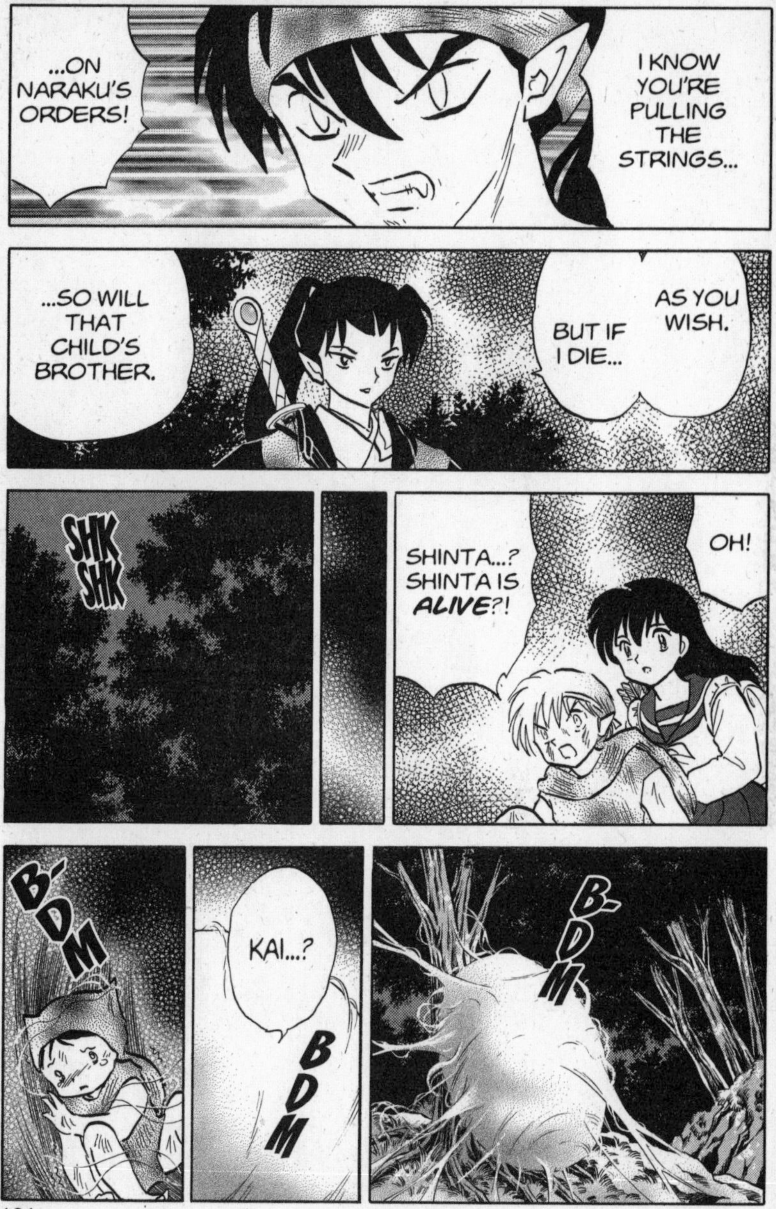
I KNOW YOU'RE PULLING THE STRINGS...
...ON NARAKU'S ORDERS!
AS YOU WISH.
BUT IF I DIE...
...SO WILL THAT CHILD'S BROTHER.
OH!
SHINTA...? SHINTA IS *ALIVE*?!
SHK SHK
B-DM
KAI...?
BDM
B-DM

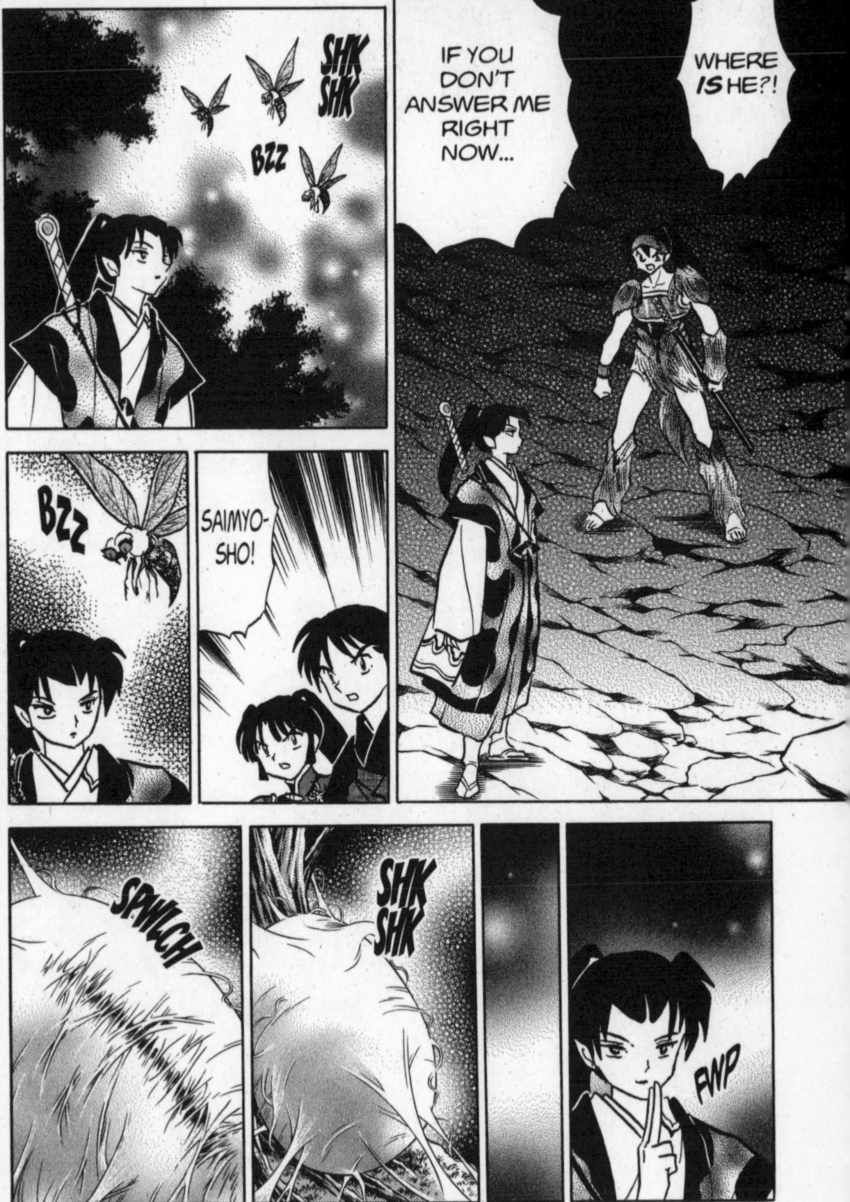
WHERE IS HE?!
IF YOU DON'T ANSWER ME RIGHT NOW...
SHK SHK
BZZ
SAIMYO-SHO!
BZZ
FWP
SHK SHK
SPWLCH

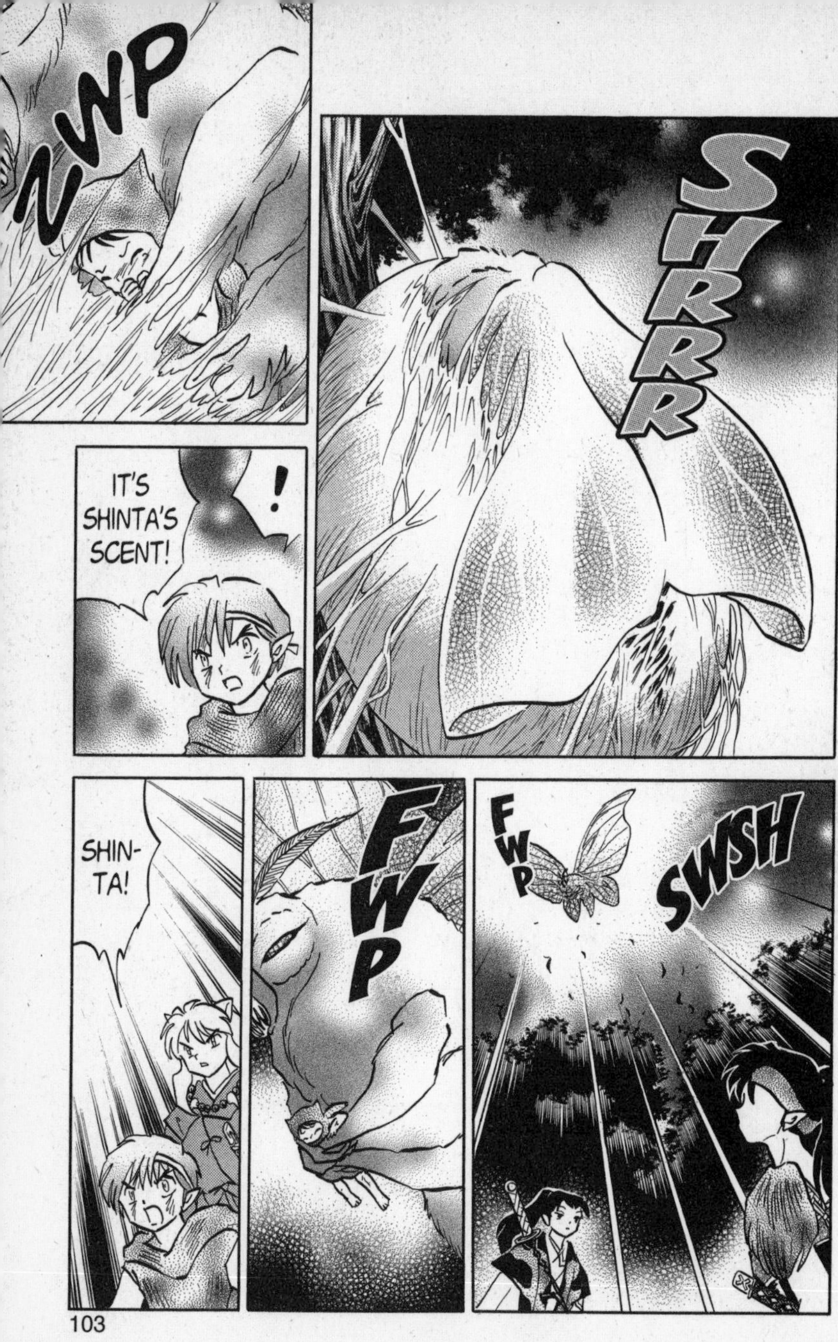
SHRRR
ZWP
!
IT'S SHINTA'S SCENT!
SWSH
FWP
FWP
SHIN-TA!

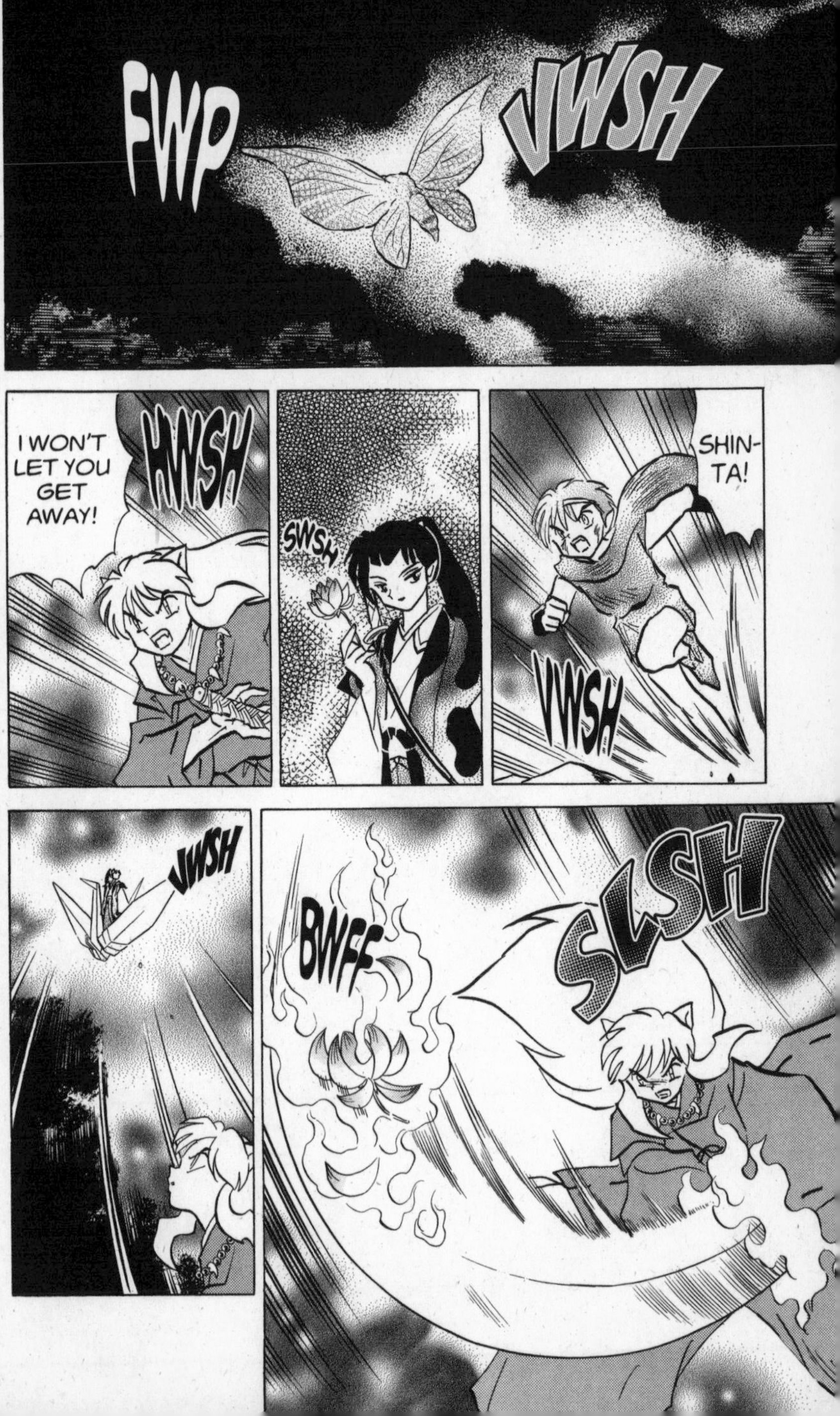
JWSH
FWP
SHIN-TA!
VWSH
SWSH
I WON'T LET YOU GET AWAY!
HWSH
SLSH
BWFF
JWSH

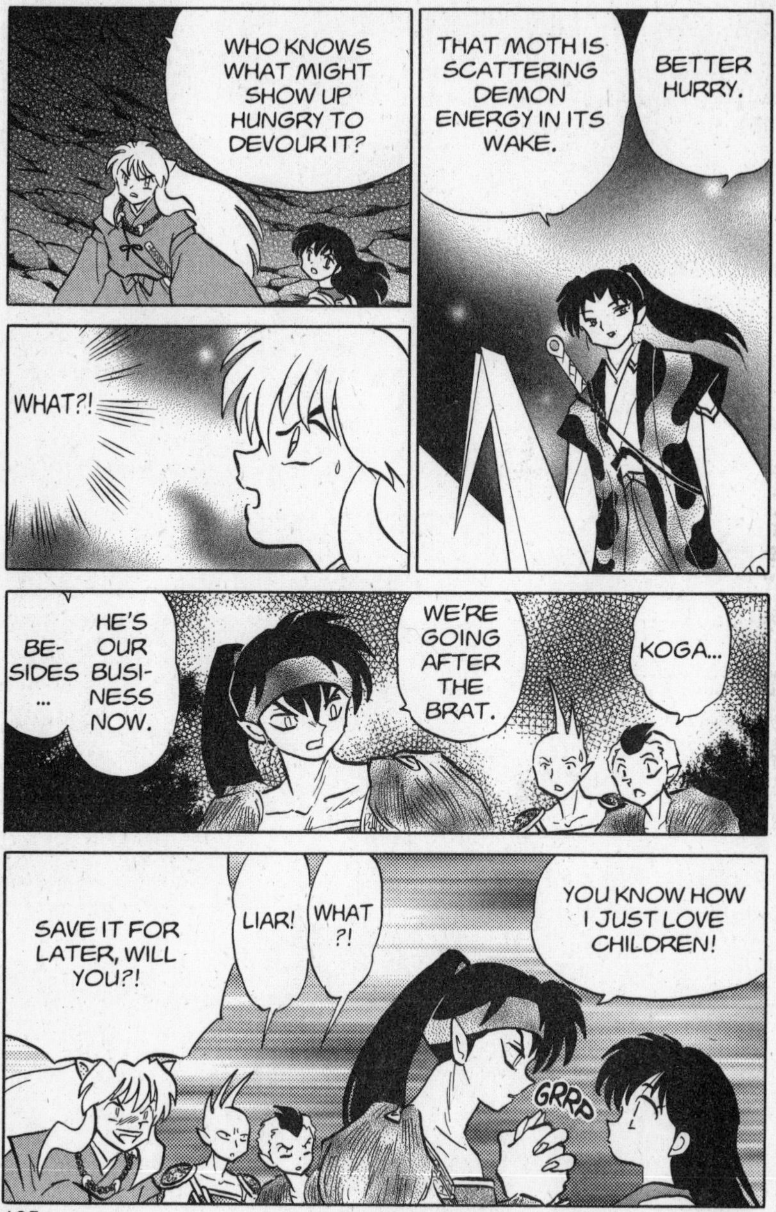
BETTER HURRY.
THAT MOTH IS SCATTERING DEMON ENERGY IN ITS WAKE.
WHO KNOWS WHAT MIGHT SHOW UP HUNGRY TO DEVOUR IT?
WHAT?!
KOGA...
WE'RE GOING AFTER THE BRAT.
HE'S OUR BUSINESS NOW.
BESIDES...
YOU KNOW HOW I JUST LOVE CHILDREN!
GRRP
WHAT?!
LIAR!
SAVE IT FOR LATER, WILL YOU?!

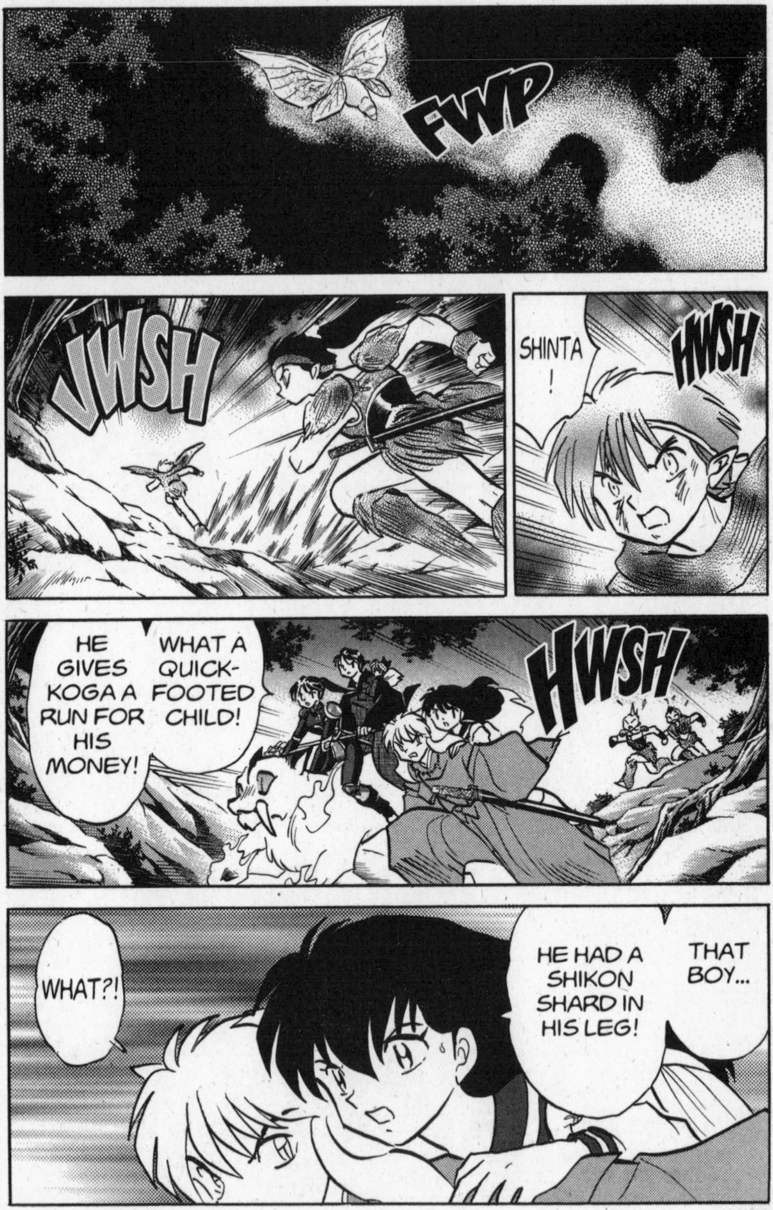
FWP
HWSH
SHINTA!
JWSH
HWSH
WHAT A QUICK-FOOTED CHILD!
HE GIVES KOGA A RUN FOR HIS MONEY!
THAT BOY...
HE HAD A SHIKON SHARD IN HIS LEG!
WHAT?!

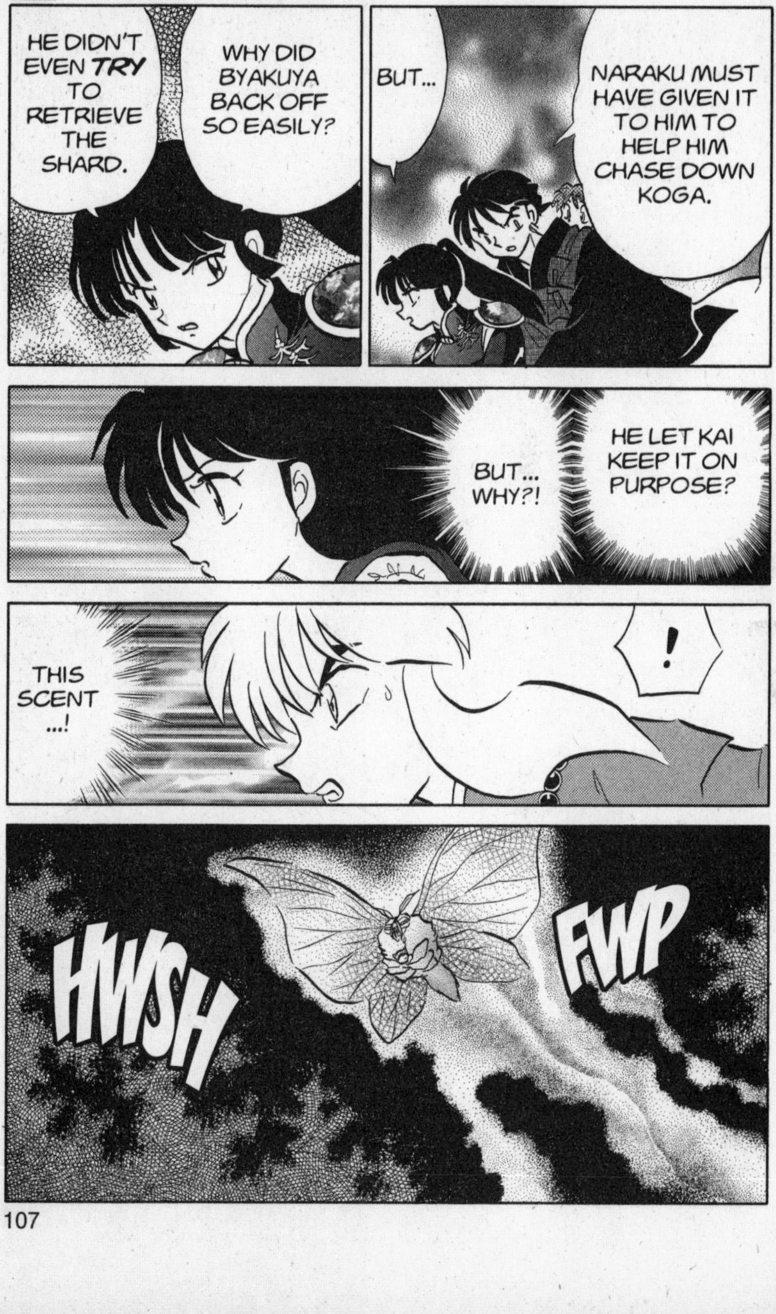
NARAKU MUST HAVE GIVEN IT TO HIM TO HELP HIM CHASE DOWN KOGA.
BUT...
WHY DID BYAKUYA BACK OFF SO EASILY?
HE DIDN'T EVEN *TRY* TO RETRIEVE THE SHARD.
HE LET KAI KEEP IT ON PURPOSE?
BUT... WHY?!
!
THIS SCENT ...!
FWP
HWSH

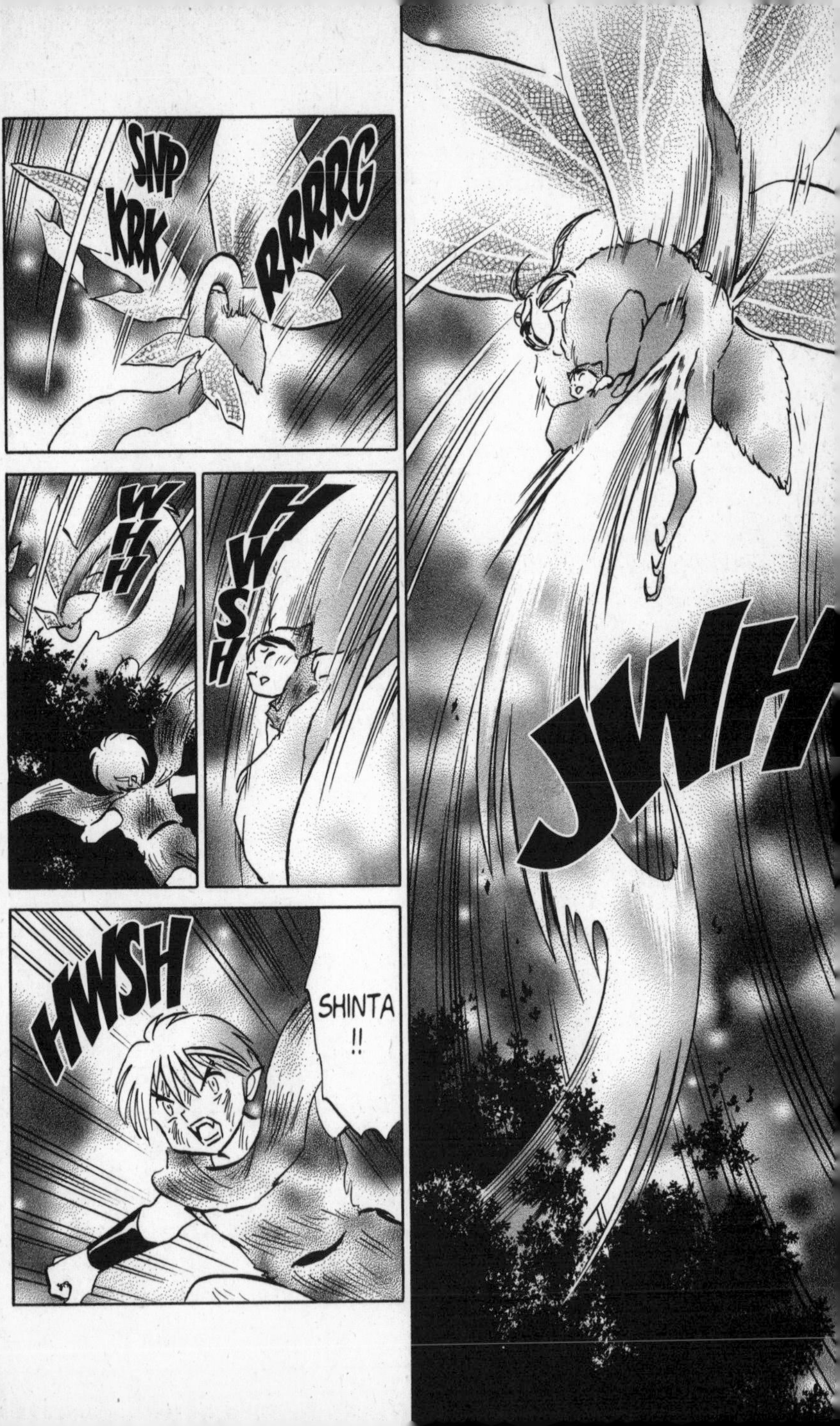
JWH
SNP
KRK
RRRRG
FWSH
WHH
HWSH
SHINTA
!!

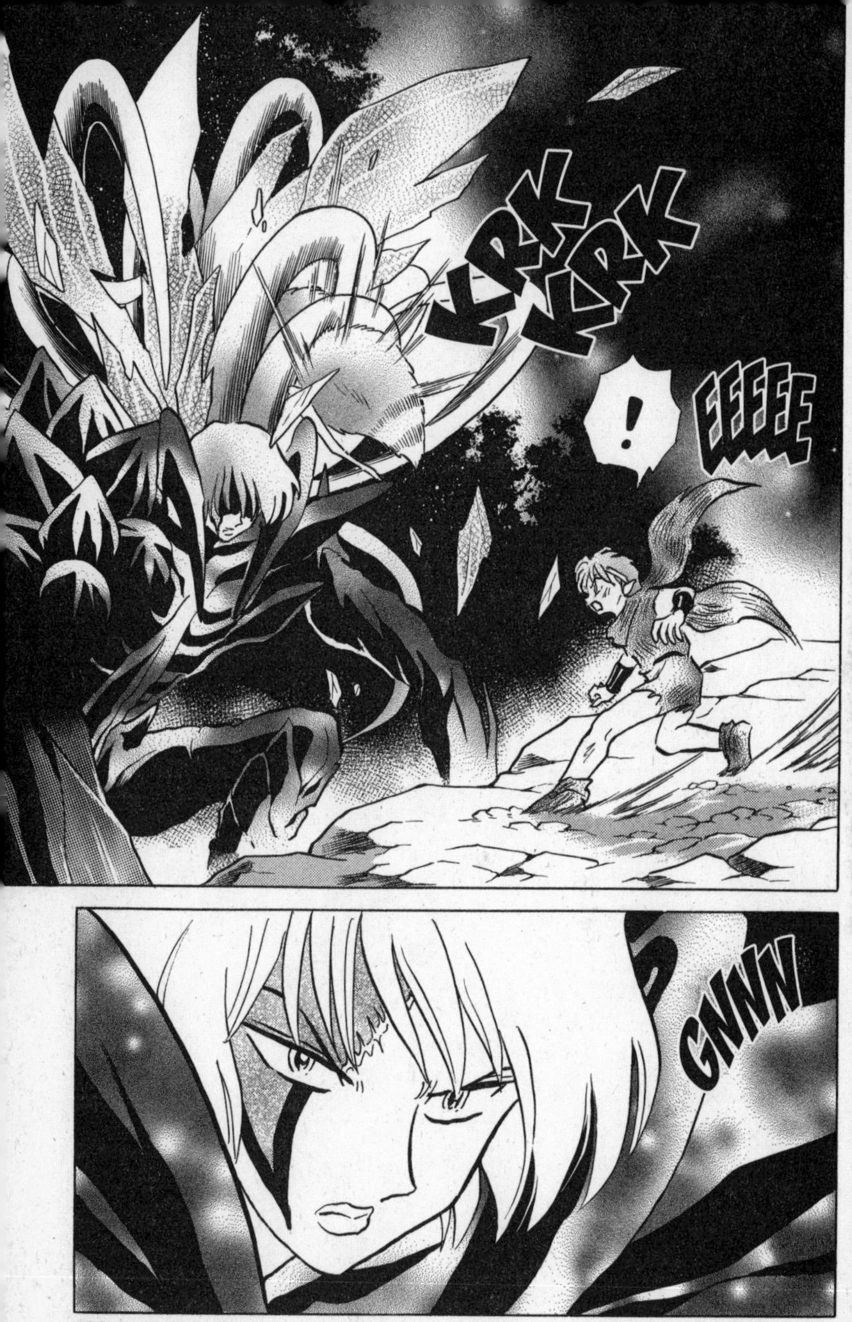
KRK KRK
EEEEE
!
GNNN

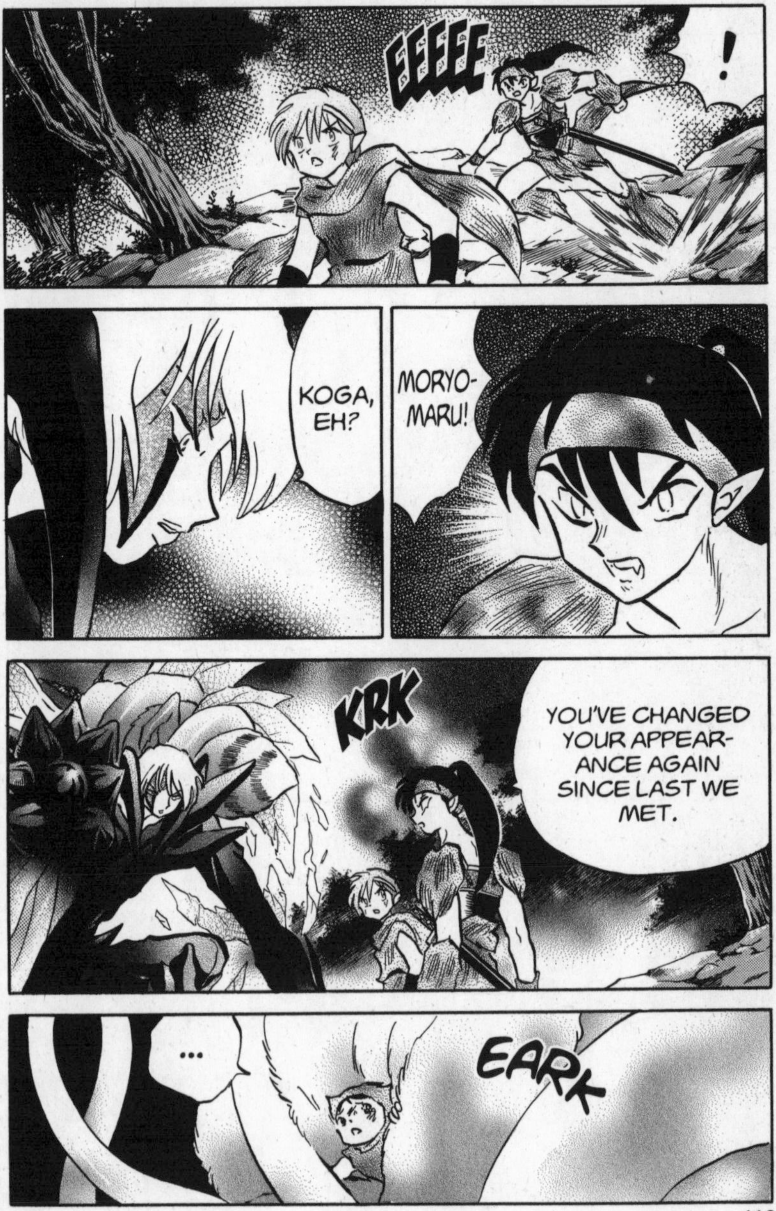
EEEEE
!
MORYO-MARU!
KOGA, EH?
KRK
YOU'VE CHANGED YOUR APPEARANCE AGAIN SINCE LAST WE MET.
EARK
...

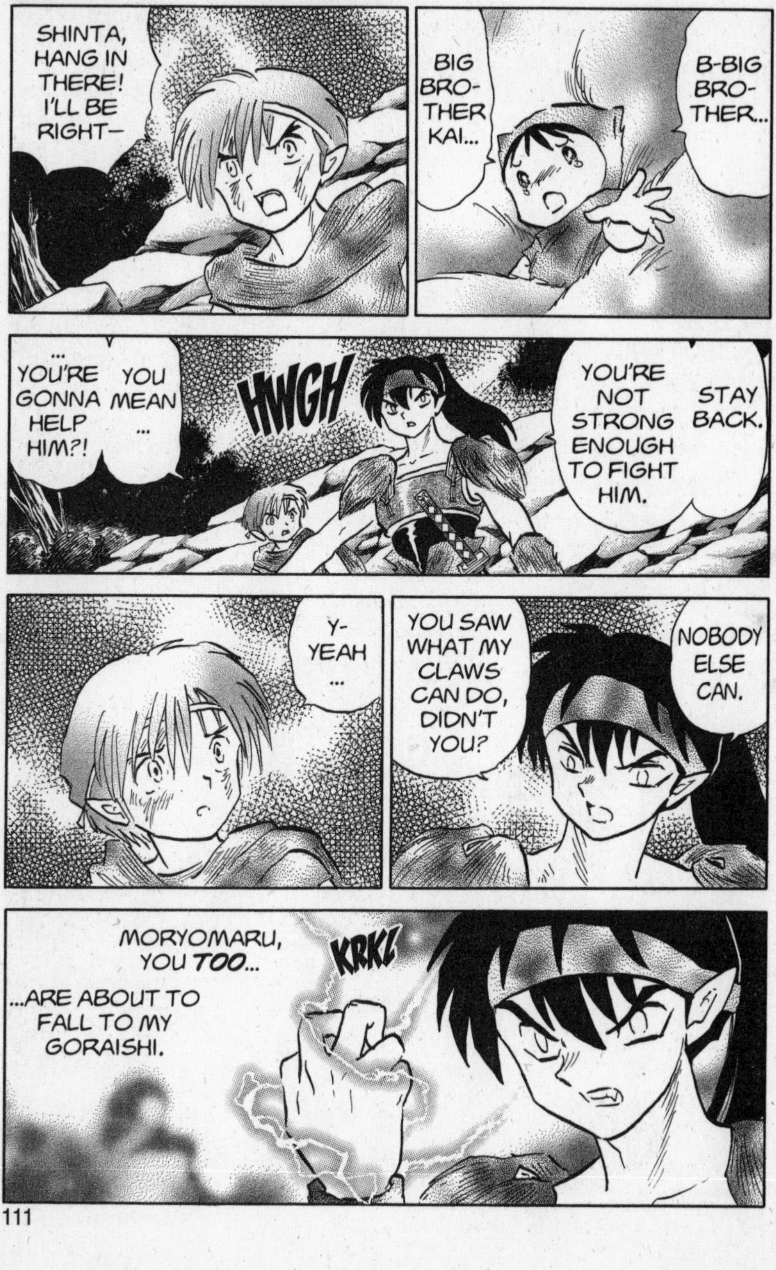
B-BIG BROTHER...
BIG BROTHER KAI...
SHINTA, HANG IN THERE! I'LL BE RIGHT—
STAY BACK.
YOU'RE NOT STRONG ENOUGH TO FIGHT HIM.
HWGH
YOU MEAN...
...YOU'RE GONNA HELP HIM?!
NOBODY ELSE CAN.
YOU SAW WHAT MY CLAWS CAN DO, DIDN'T YOU?
Y-YEAH...
MORYOMARU, YOU TOO...
KRKL
...ARE ABOUT TO FALL TO MY GORAISHI.

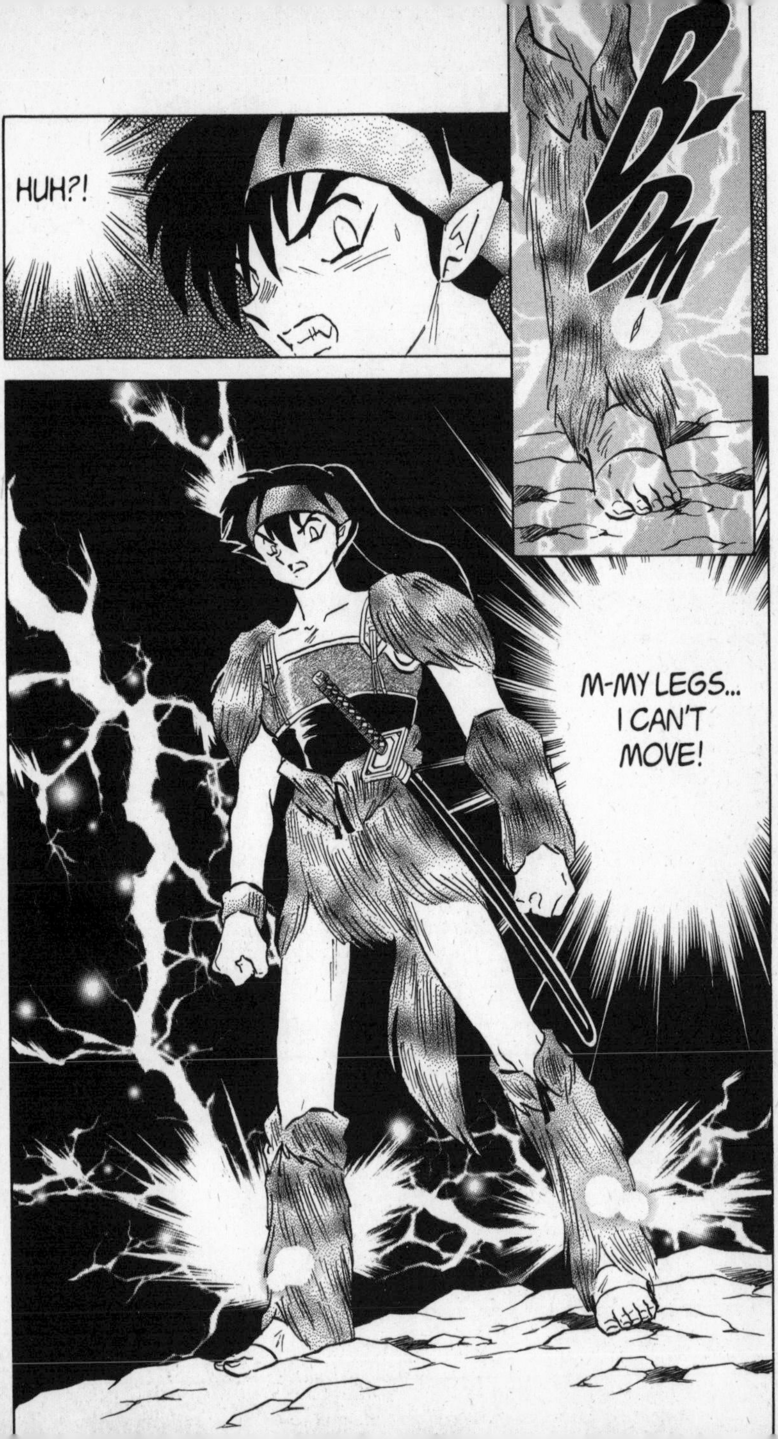
HUH?!
M-MY LEGS... I CAN'T MOVE!

SCROLL 7
MIDORIKO'S WILL

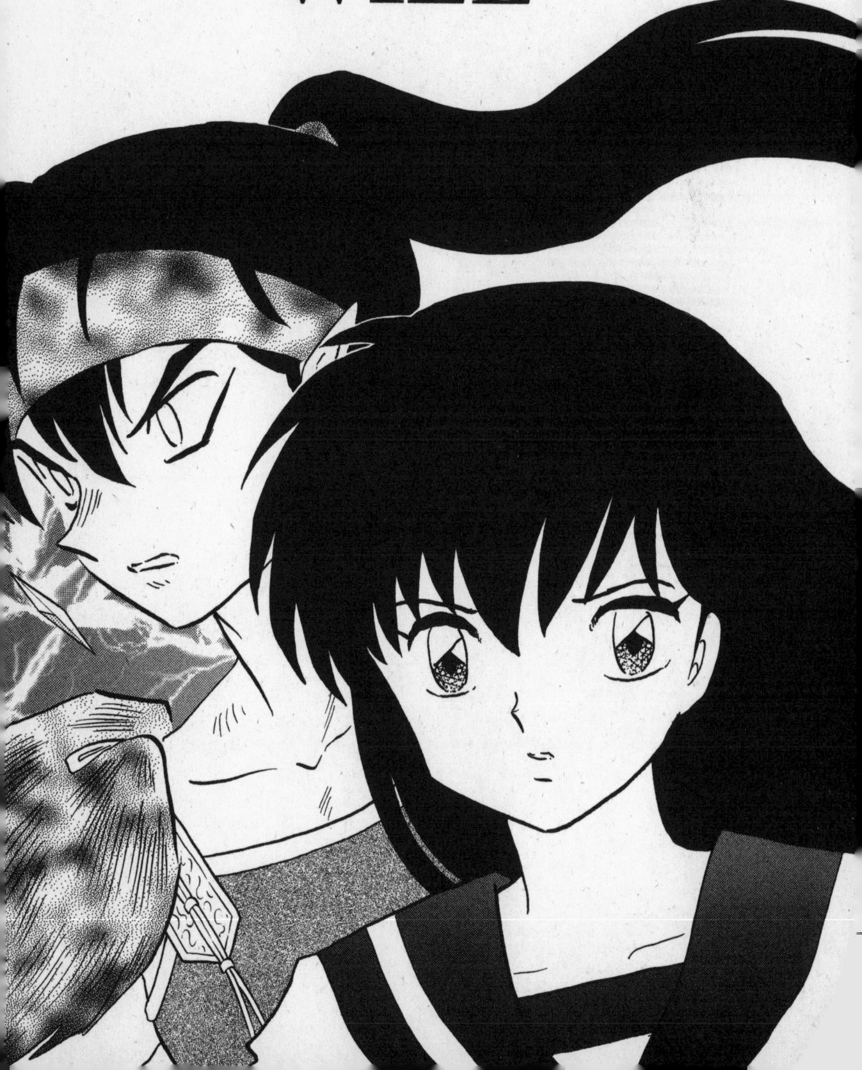

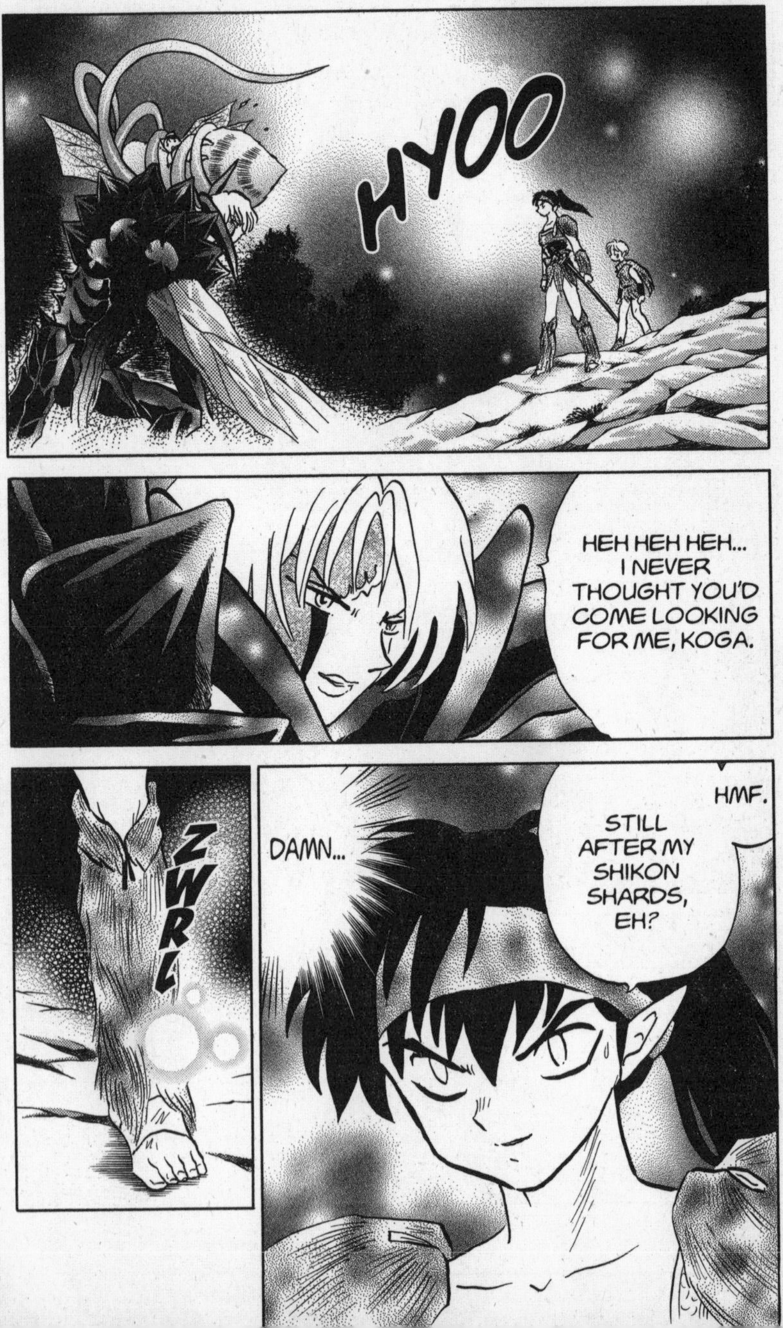
HYOO
HEH HEH HEH... I NEVER THOUGHT YOU'D COME LOOKING FOR ME, KOGA.
HMF. STILL AFTER MY SHIKON SHARDS, EH?
DAMN...
ZWRL

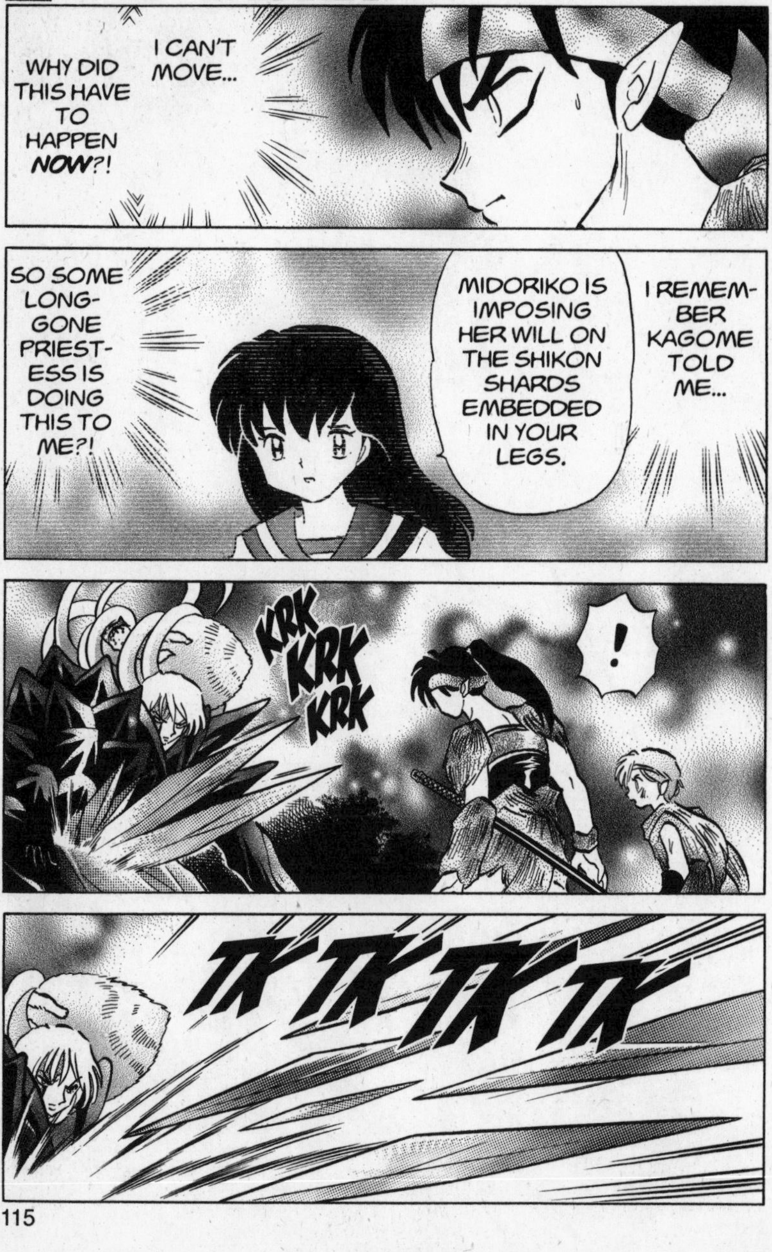
I CAN'T MOVE...
WHY DID THIS HAVE TO HAPPEN *NOW*?!
I REMEMBER KAGOME TOLD ME...
MIDORIKO IS IMPOSING HER WILL ON THE SHIKON SHARDS EMBEDDED IN YOUR LEGS.
SO SOME LONG-GONE PRIESTESS IS DOING THIS TO ME?!
!
KRK KRK KRK

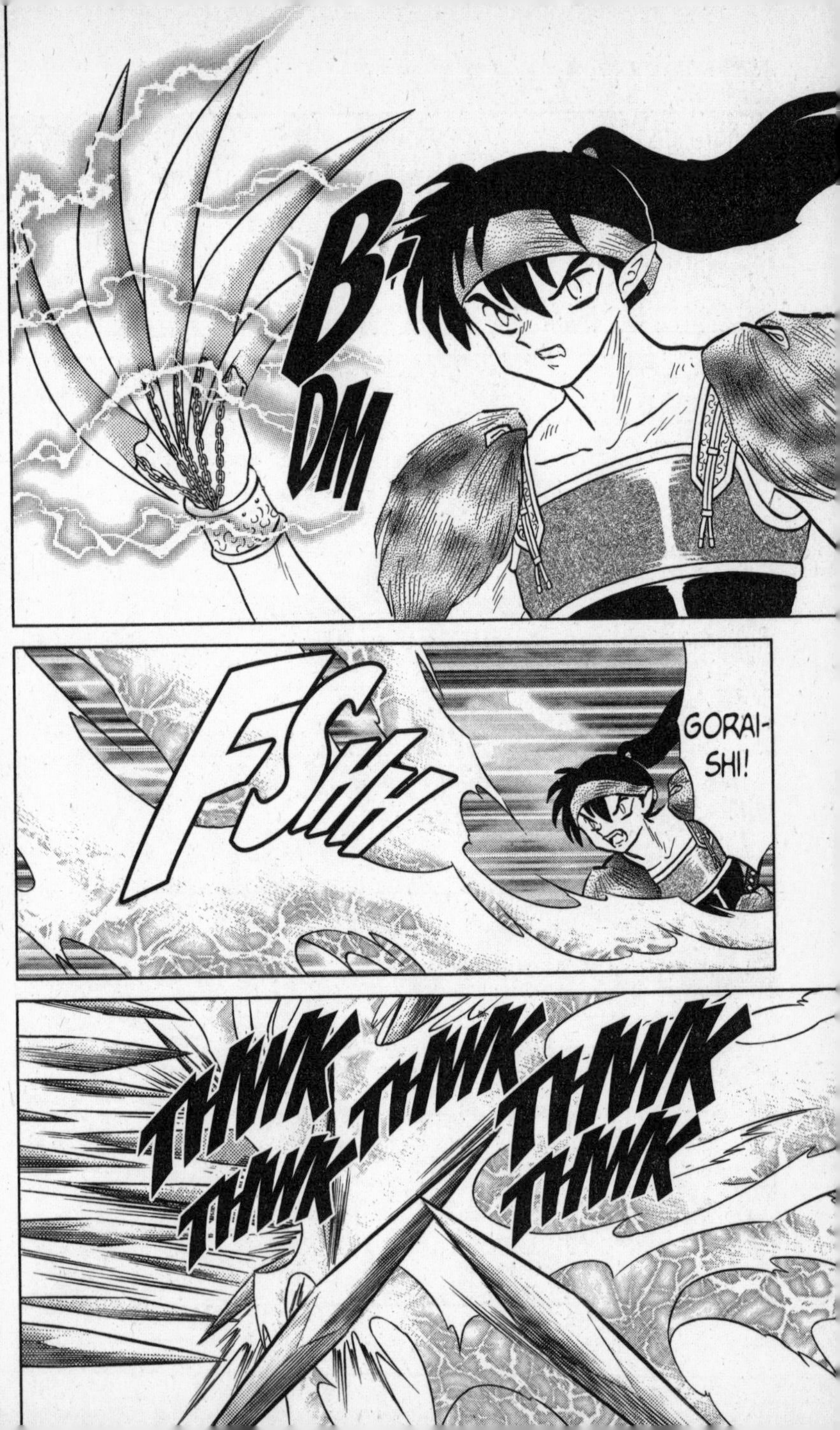
B-DM
FSHH
GORAI-SHI!
THWK THWK THWK THWK THWK THWK

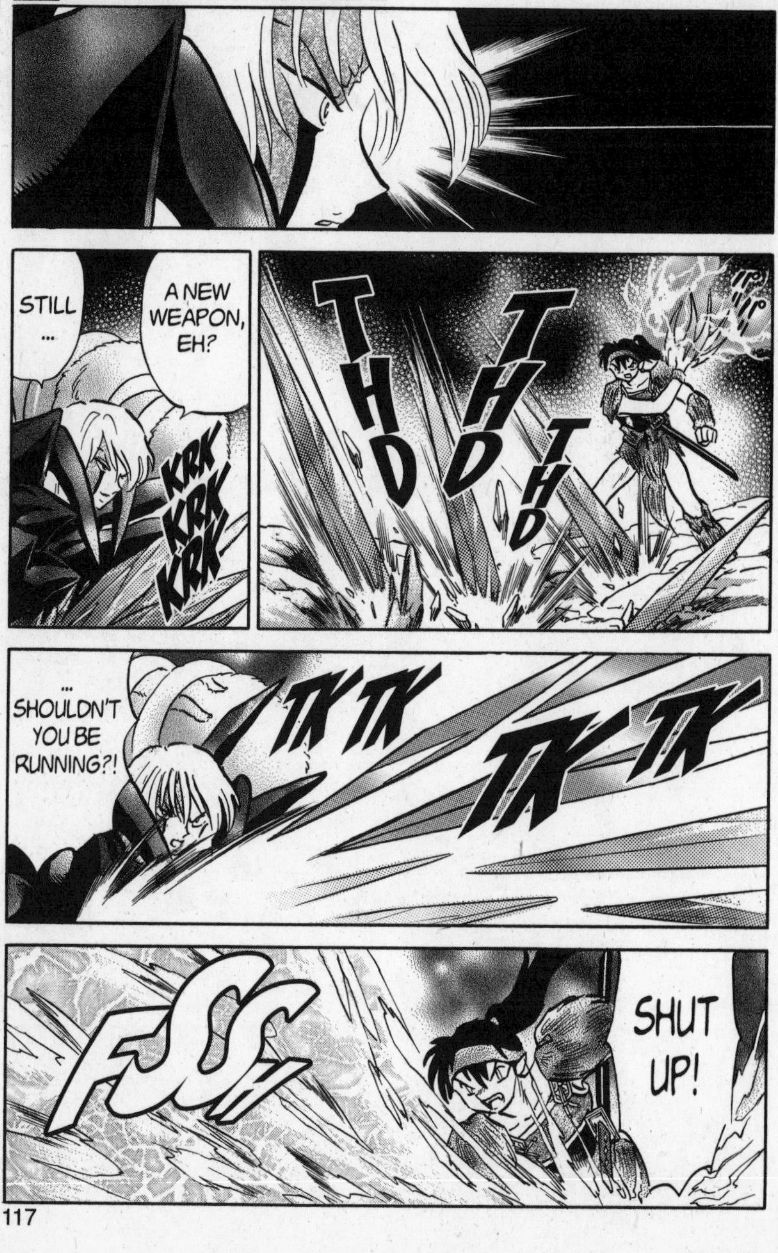
THD
THD
THD
A NEW WEAPON, EH?
STILL ...
KRK KRK KRK
TK TK
TK TK
... SHOULDN'T YOU BE RUNNING?!
SHUT UP!
FSSH

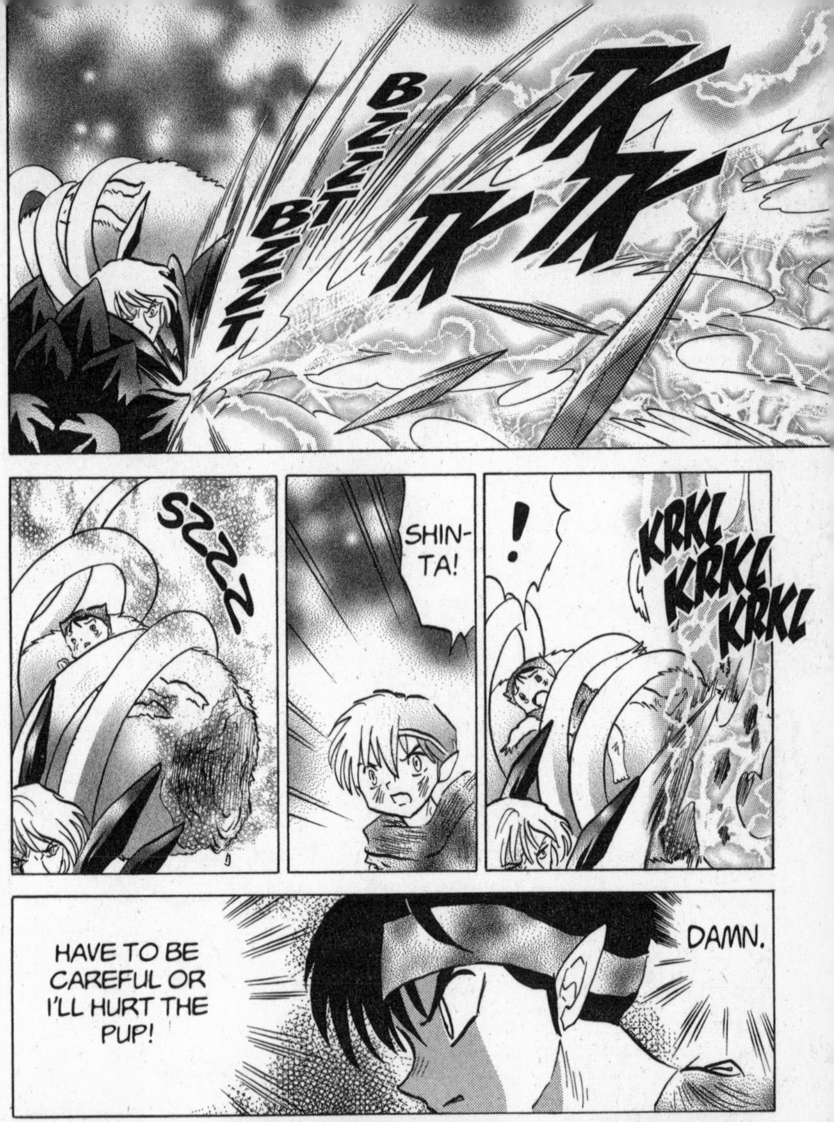
BZZZT
BT
BZZZT
!
KRKL KRKL KRKL
SHIN-TA!
SZZZ
DAMN.
HAVE TO BE CAREFUL OR I'LL HURT THE PUP!
KOGA ...?

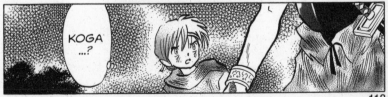

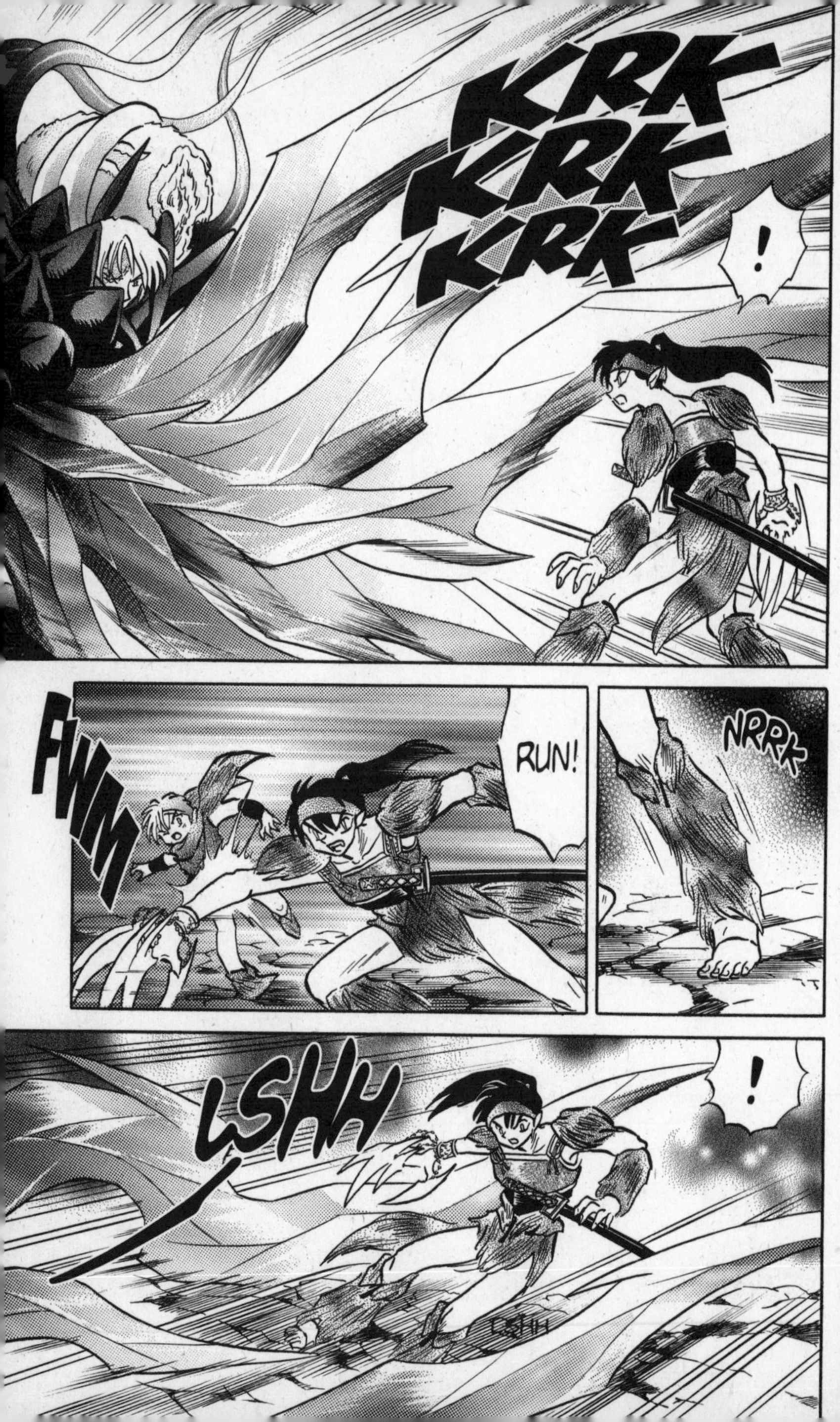
KRK KRK KRK
!
RUN!
FWM
NRRK
!
LSHH
LSHH

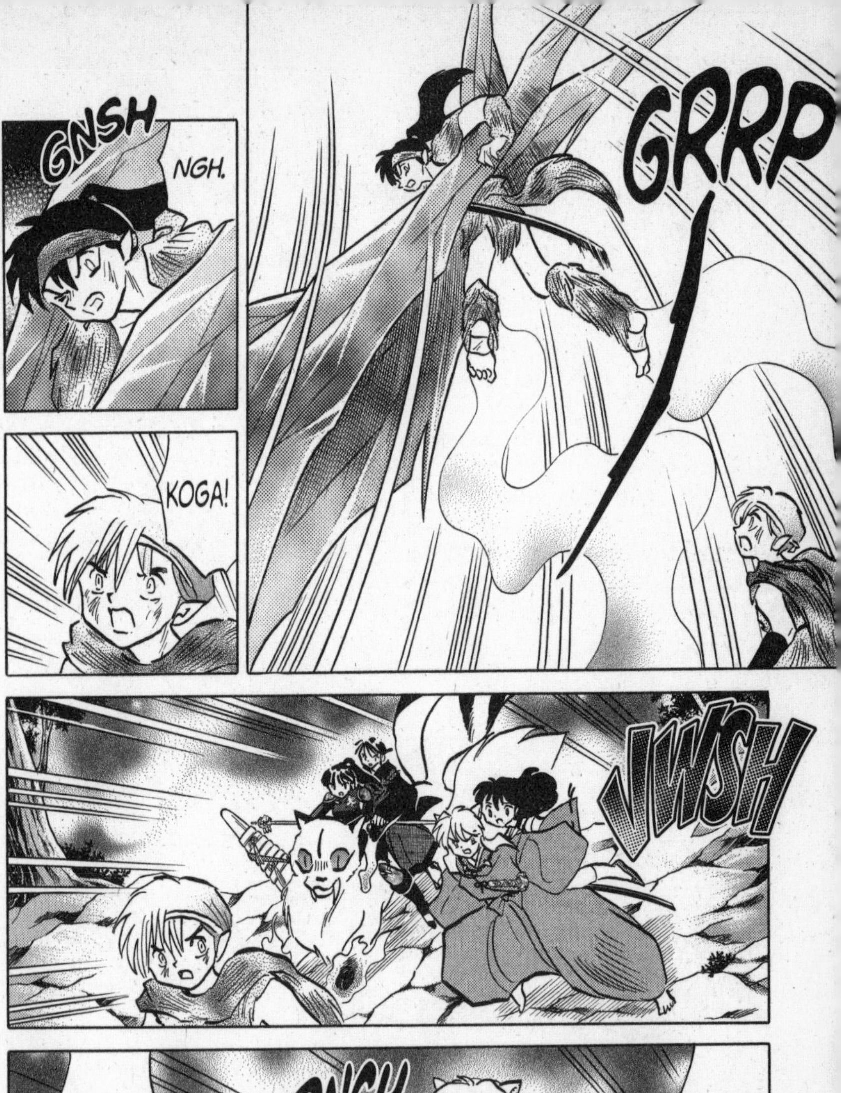
GRRP
GNSH
NGH.
KOGA!
JWSH
KOGA!
KRNCH
KOGA!

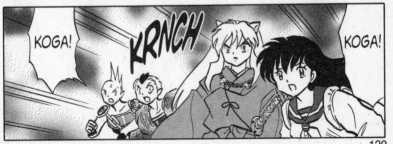

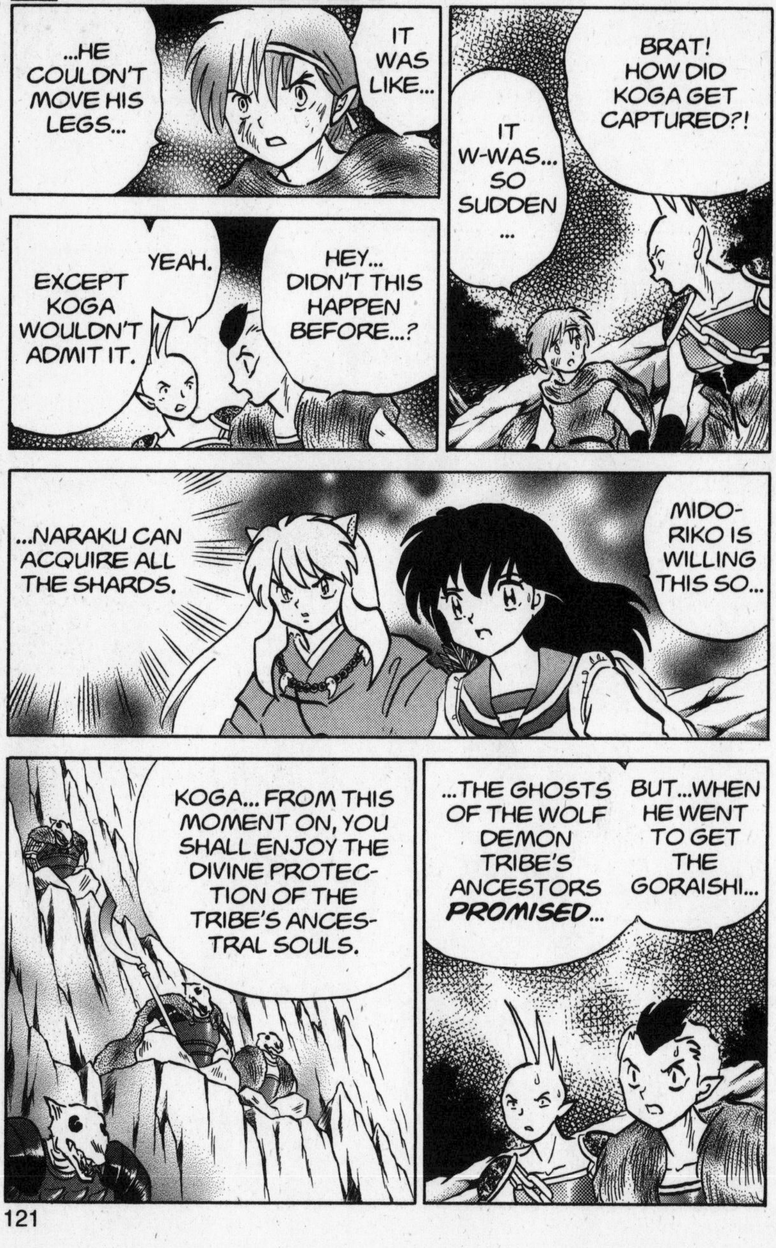
BRAT! HOW DID KOGA GET CAPTURED?!
IT W-WAS... SO SUDDEN ...
IT WAS LIKE...
...HE COULDN'T MOVE HIS LEGS...
HEY... DIDN'T THIS HAPPEN BEFORE...?
YEAH.
EXCEPT KOGA WOULDN'T ADMIT IT.
MIDO-RIKO IS WILLING THIS SO...
...NARAKU CAN ACQUIRE ALL THE SHARDS.
BUT...WHEN HE WENT TO GET THE GORAISHI...
...THE GHOSTS OF THE WOLF DEMON TRIBE'S ANCESTORS **PROMISED**...
KOGA... FROM THIS MOMENT ON, YOU SHALL ENJOY THE DIVINE PROTEC-TION OF THE TRIBE'S ANCES-TRAL SOULS.

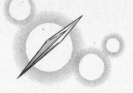

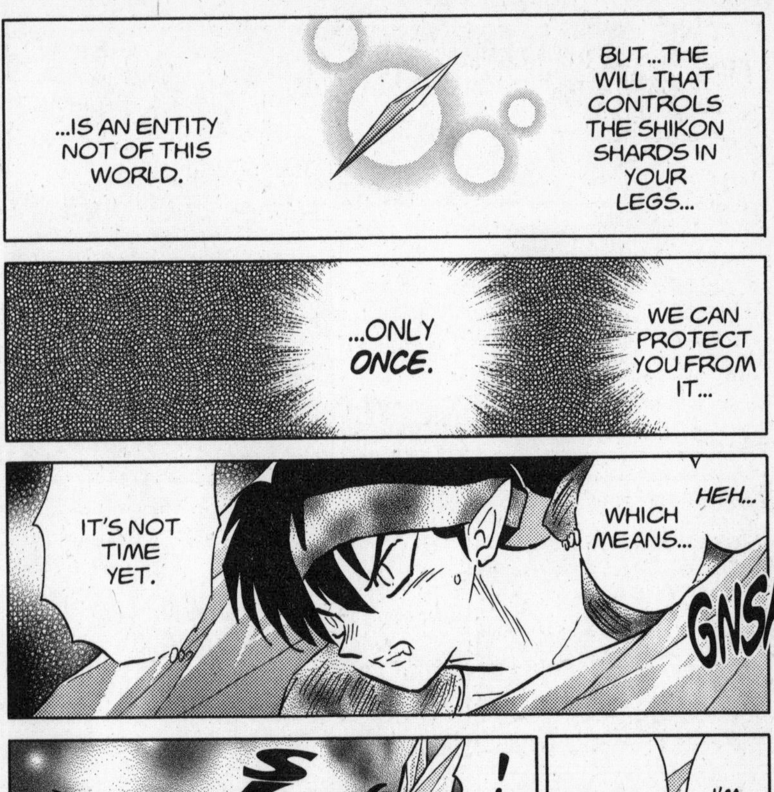

BUT...THE WILL THAT CONTROLS THE SHIKON SHARDS IN YOUR LEGS...
...IS AN ENTITY NOT OF THIS WORLD.
WE CAN PROTECT YOU FROM IT...
...ONLY ONCE.
HEH...
WHICH MEANS...
GNSH
IT'S NOT TIME YET.
I'M TAKING THEM...
...YOUR SHIKON SHARDS.
!
SLTHR SLTHR

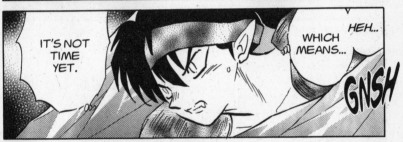

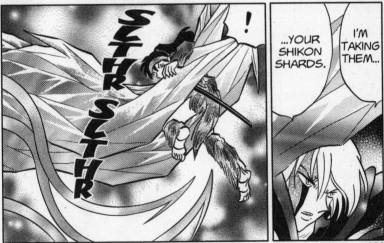

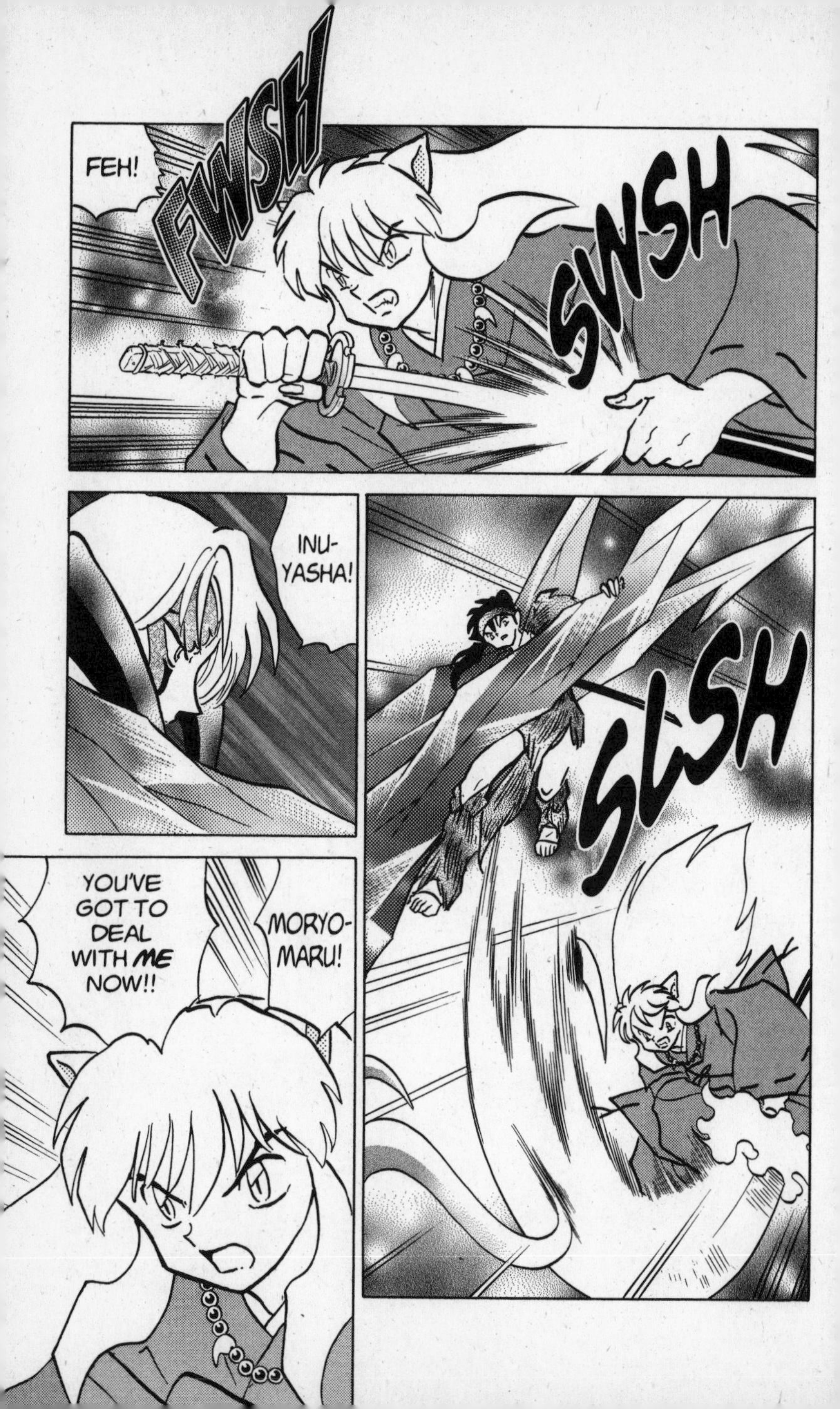
SWSH
FWSH
FEH!
SLSH
INU-YASHA!
MORYO-MARU!
YOU'VE GOT TO DEAL WITH *ME* NOW!!

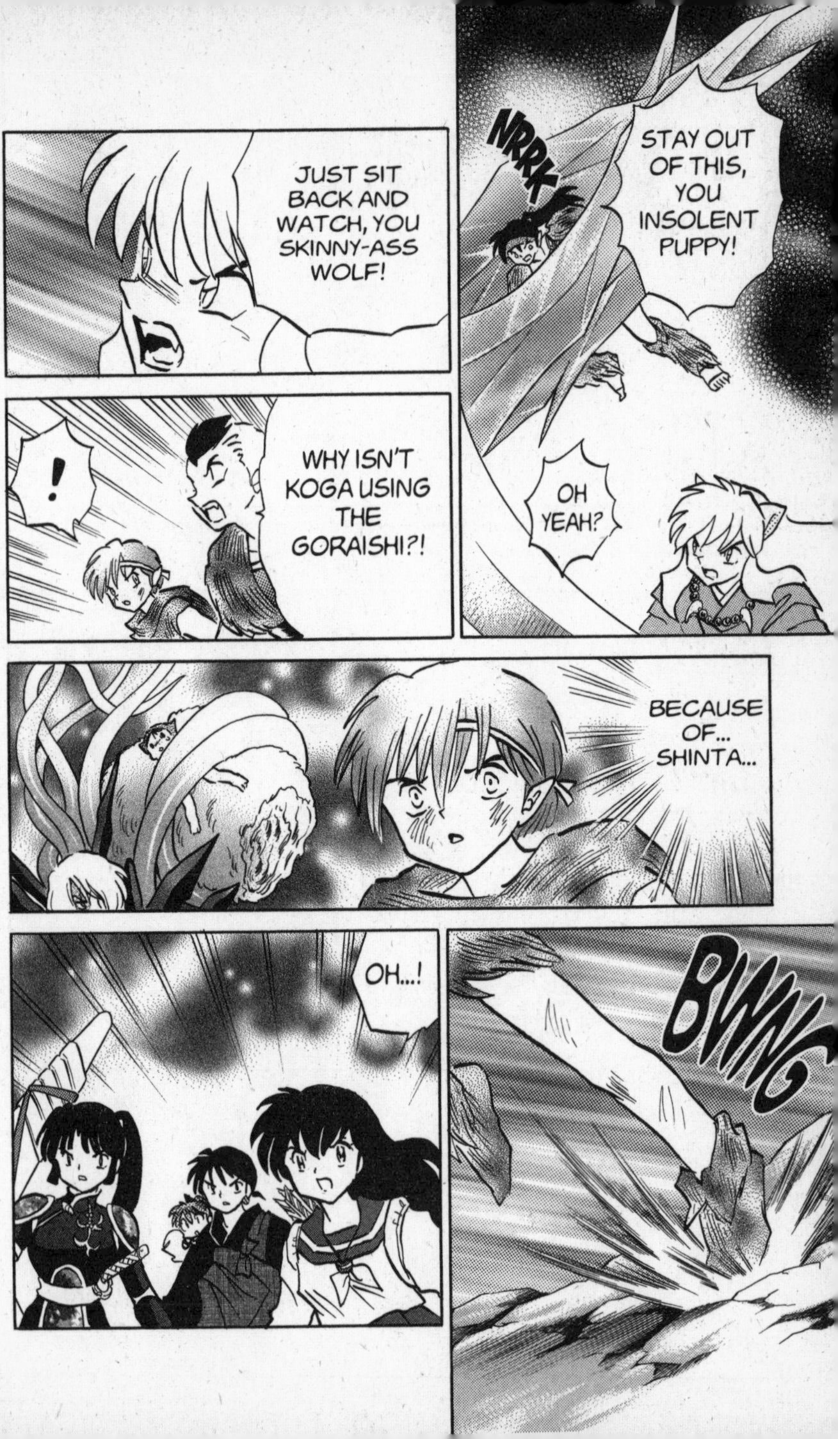
NRRK
STAY OUT OF THIS, YOU INSOLENT PUPPY!
OH YEAH?
JUST SIT BACK AND WATCH, YOU SKINNY-ASS WOLF!
!
WHY ISN'T KOGA USING THE GORAISHI?!
BECAUSE OF... SHINTA...
BWNG
OH...!

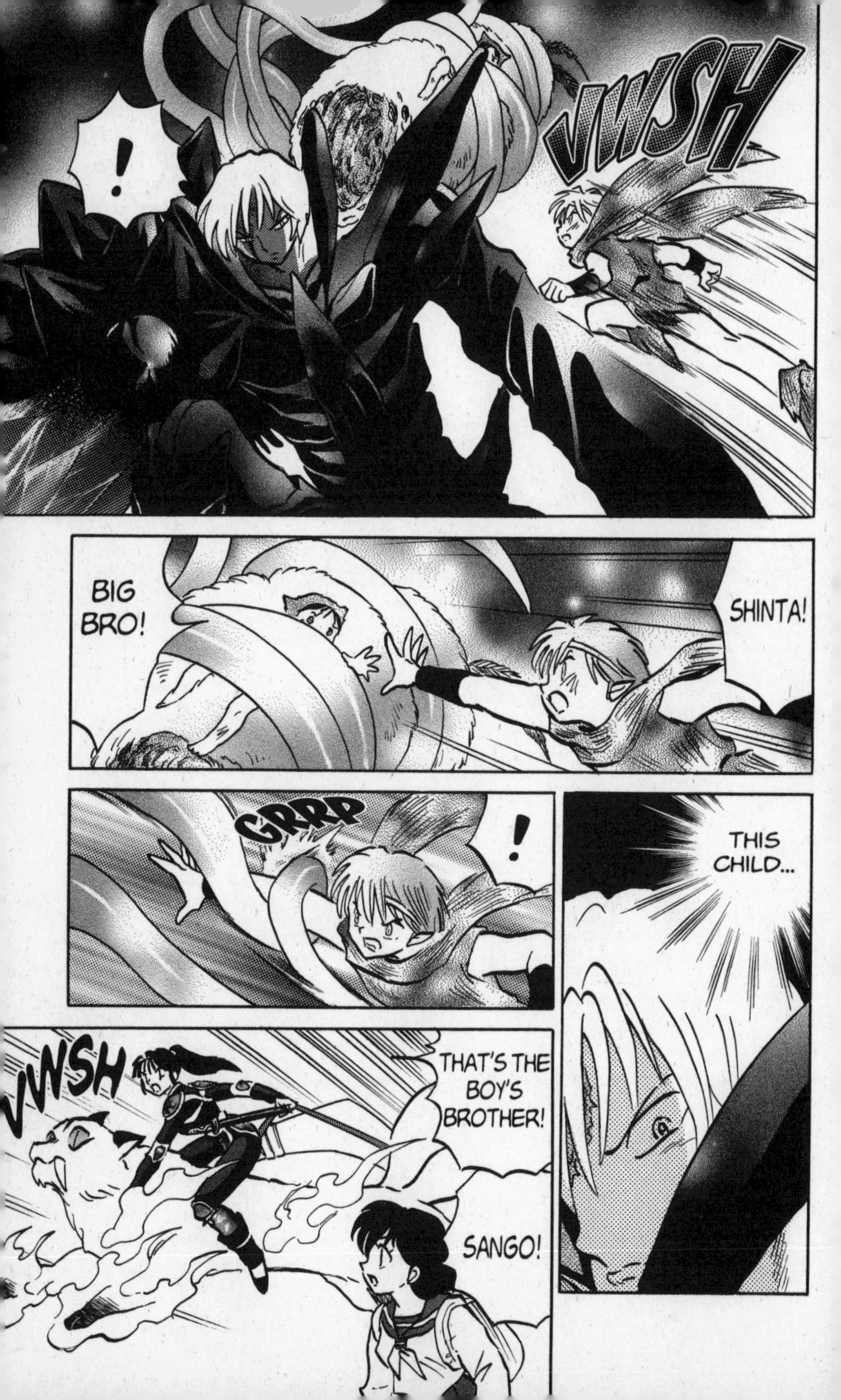
JWSH
!
SHINTA!
BIG BRO!
THIS CHILD...
!
GRRP
THAT'S THE BOY'S BROTHER!
VWSH
SANGO!

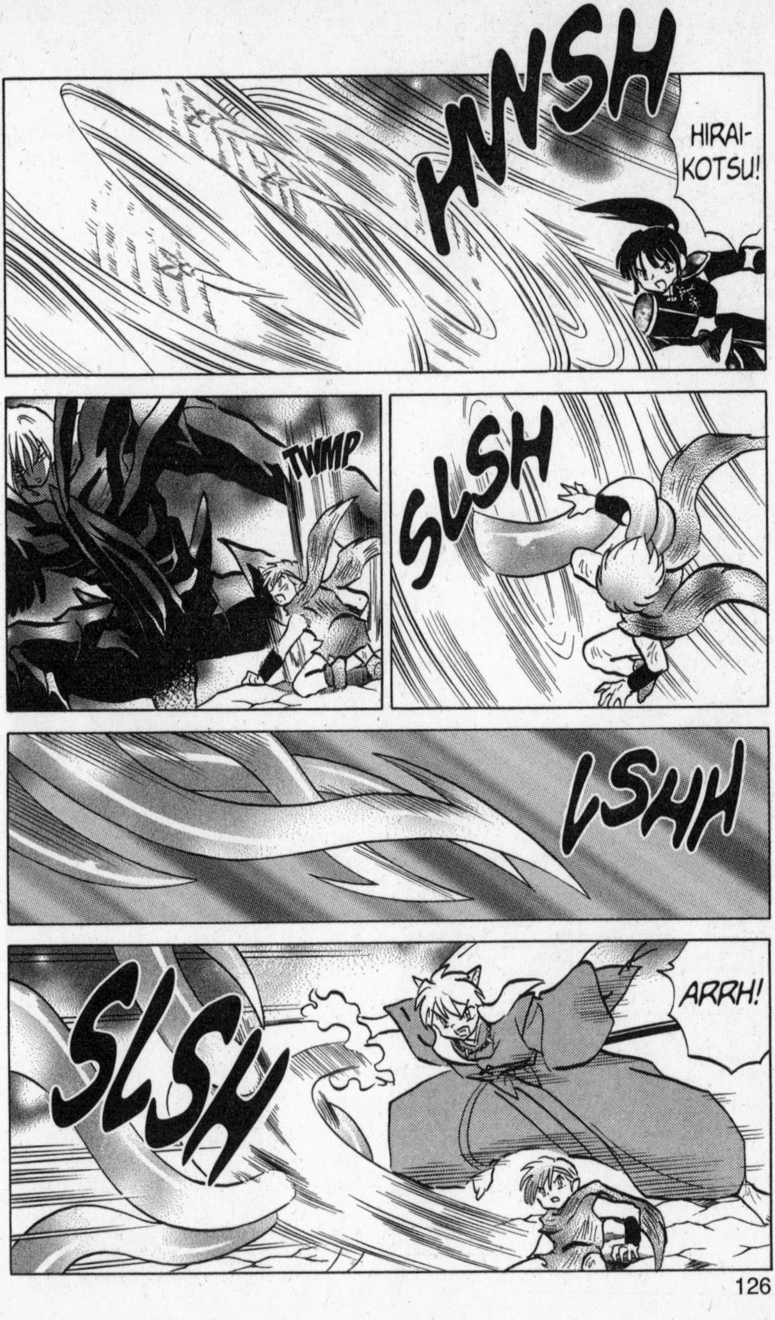
HIRAI-
KOTSU!
WWSH
SLSH
TWMP
WSHH
ARRH!
SLSH

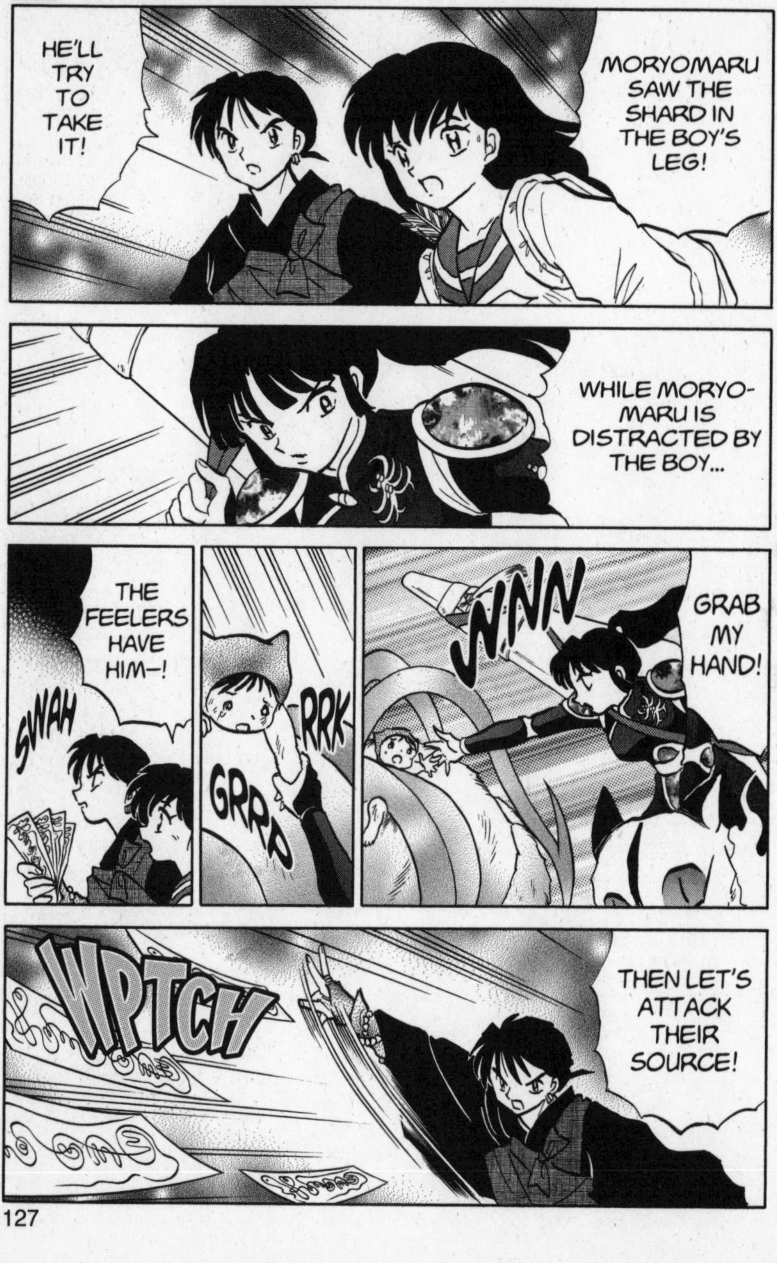
MORYOMARU SAW THE SHARD IN THE BOY'S LEG!
HE'LL TRY TO TAKE IT!
WHILE MORYOMARU IS DISTRACTED BY THE BOY...
GRAB MY HAND!
WNN
RRK
GRRP
THE FEELERS HAVE HIM—!
SWAH
THEN LET'S ATTACK THEIR SOURCE!
WPTCH

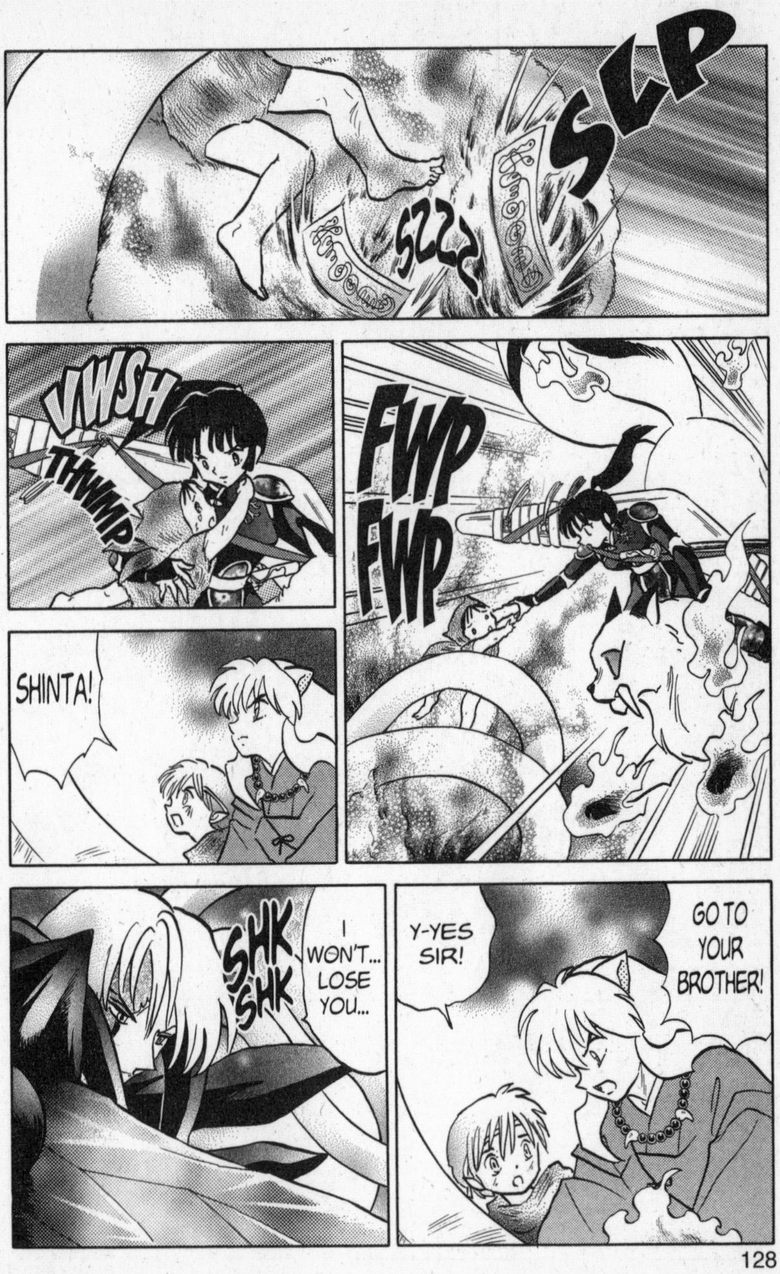
SCLP
SZZZ
FWP FWP
VWSH
THWMP
SHINTA!
GO TO YOUR BROTHER!
Y-YES SIR!
I WON'T... LOSE YOU...
SHK SHK

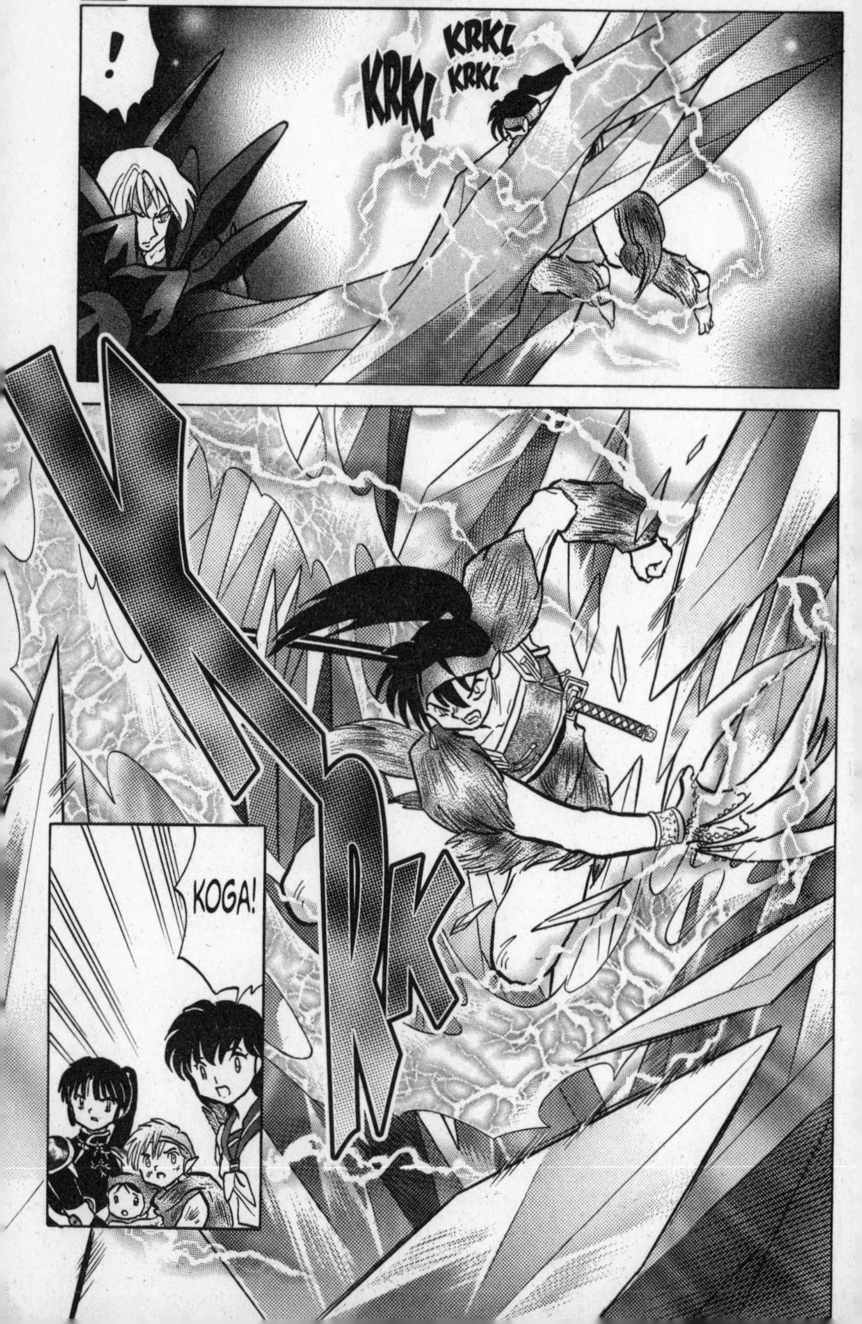
KRKL
KRKL
KRKL
!
KRK
KOGA!

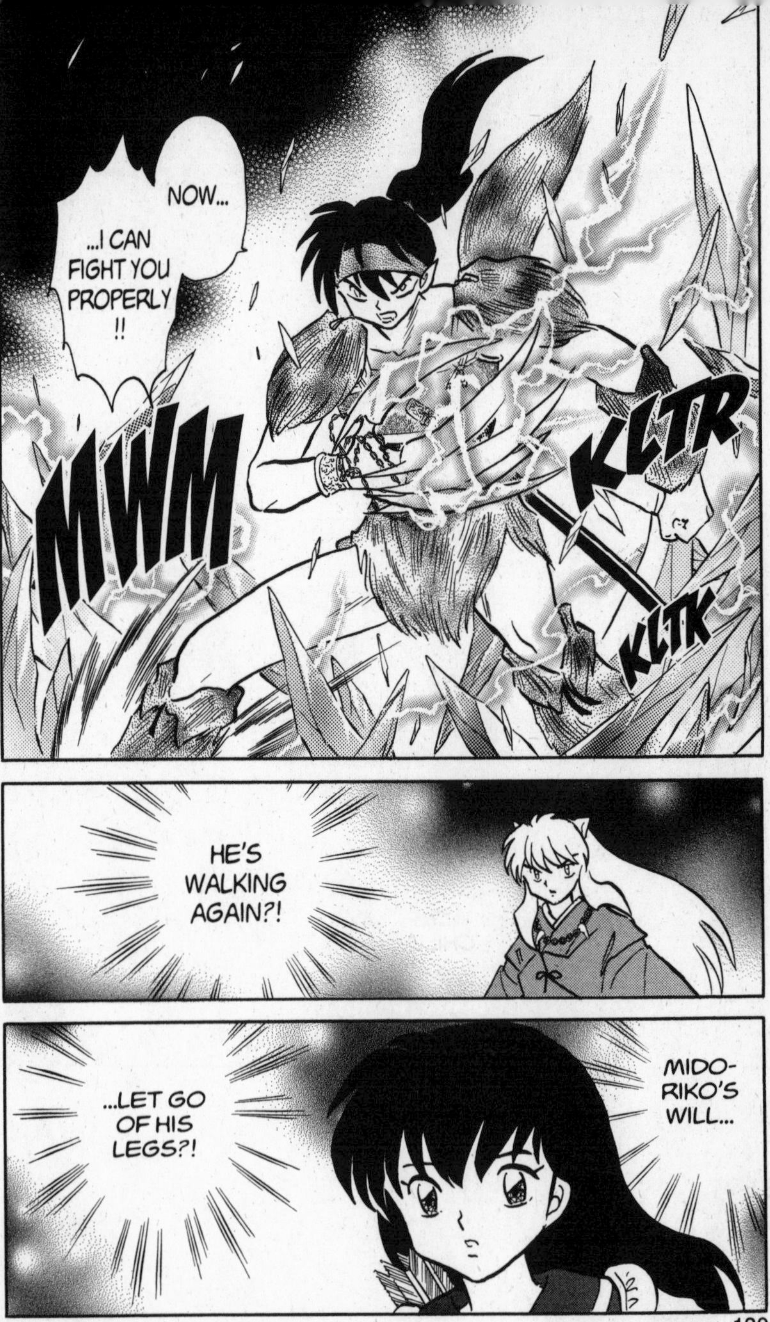
NOW...
...I CAN FIGHT YOU PROPERLY !!
KLTR
MWM
KLTK
HE'S WALKING AGAIN?!
MIDO-RIKO'S WILL...
...LET GO OF HIS LEGS?!

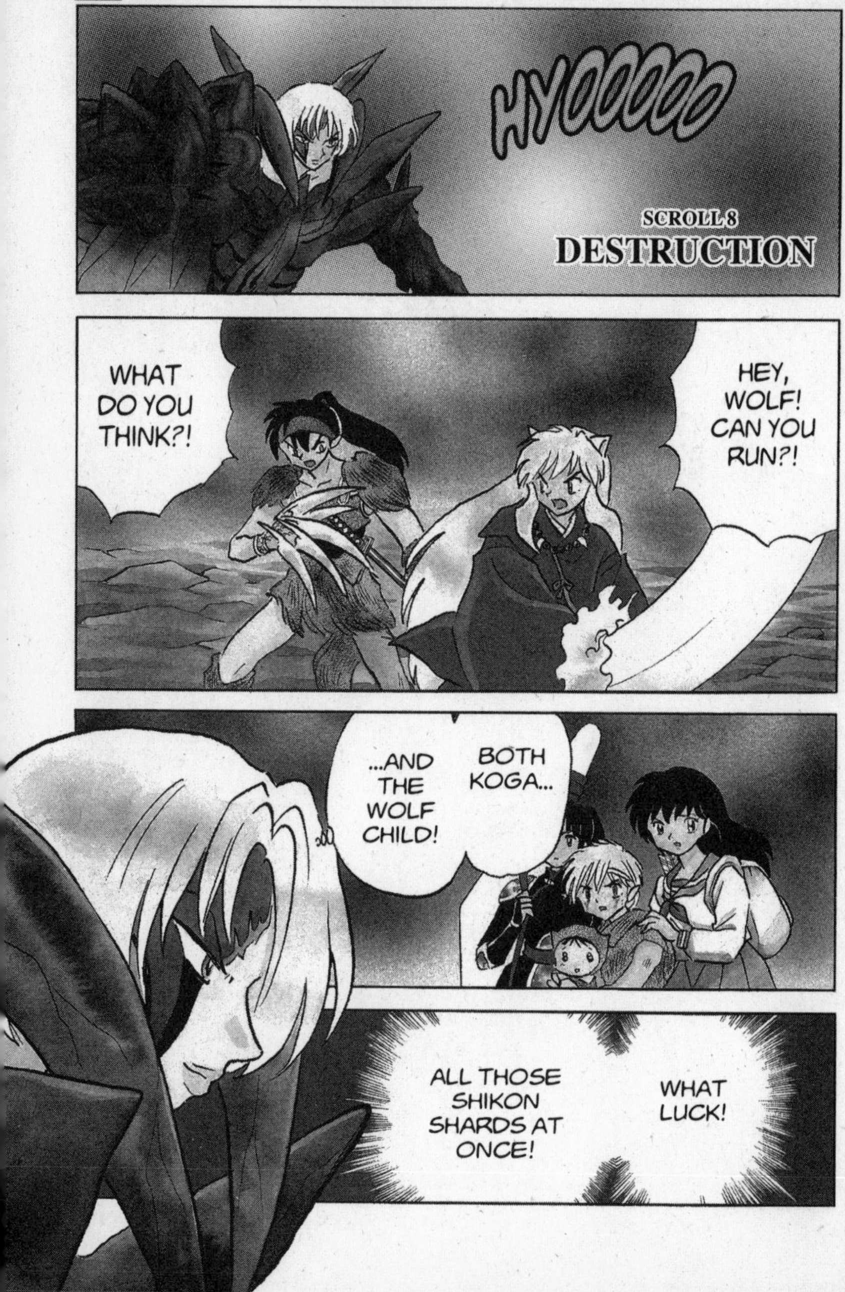
HYOOOOO
SCROLL 8
DESTRUCTION
HEY, WOLF! CAN YOU RUN?!
WHAT DO YOU THINK?!
BOTH KOGA...
...AND THE WOLF CHILD!
WHAT LUCK!
ALL THOSE SHIKON SHARDS AT ONCE!

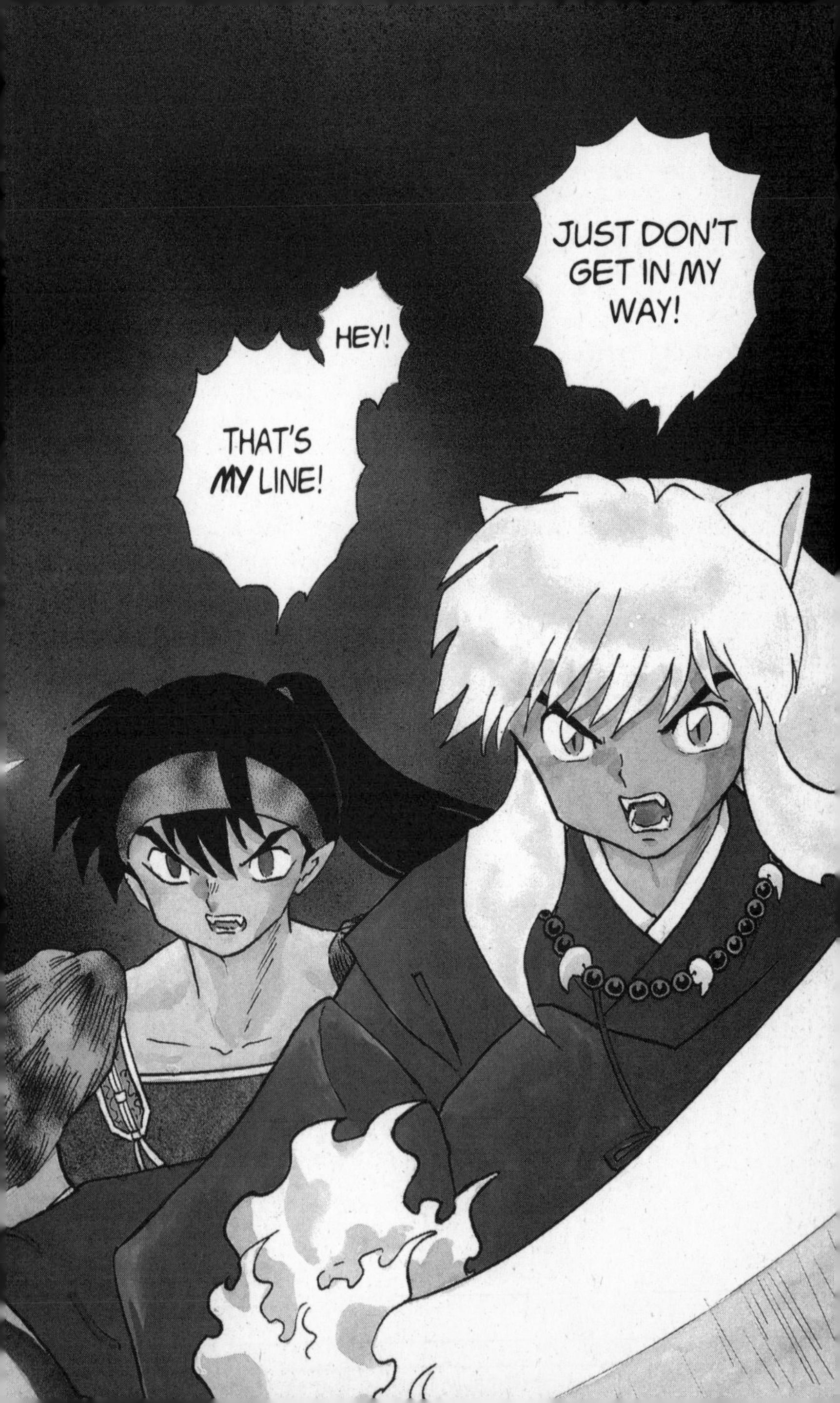
JUST DON'T GET IN MY WAY!
HEY!
THAT'S ***MY*** LINE!

SCROLL 8
DESTRUCTION

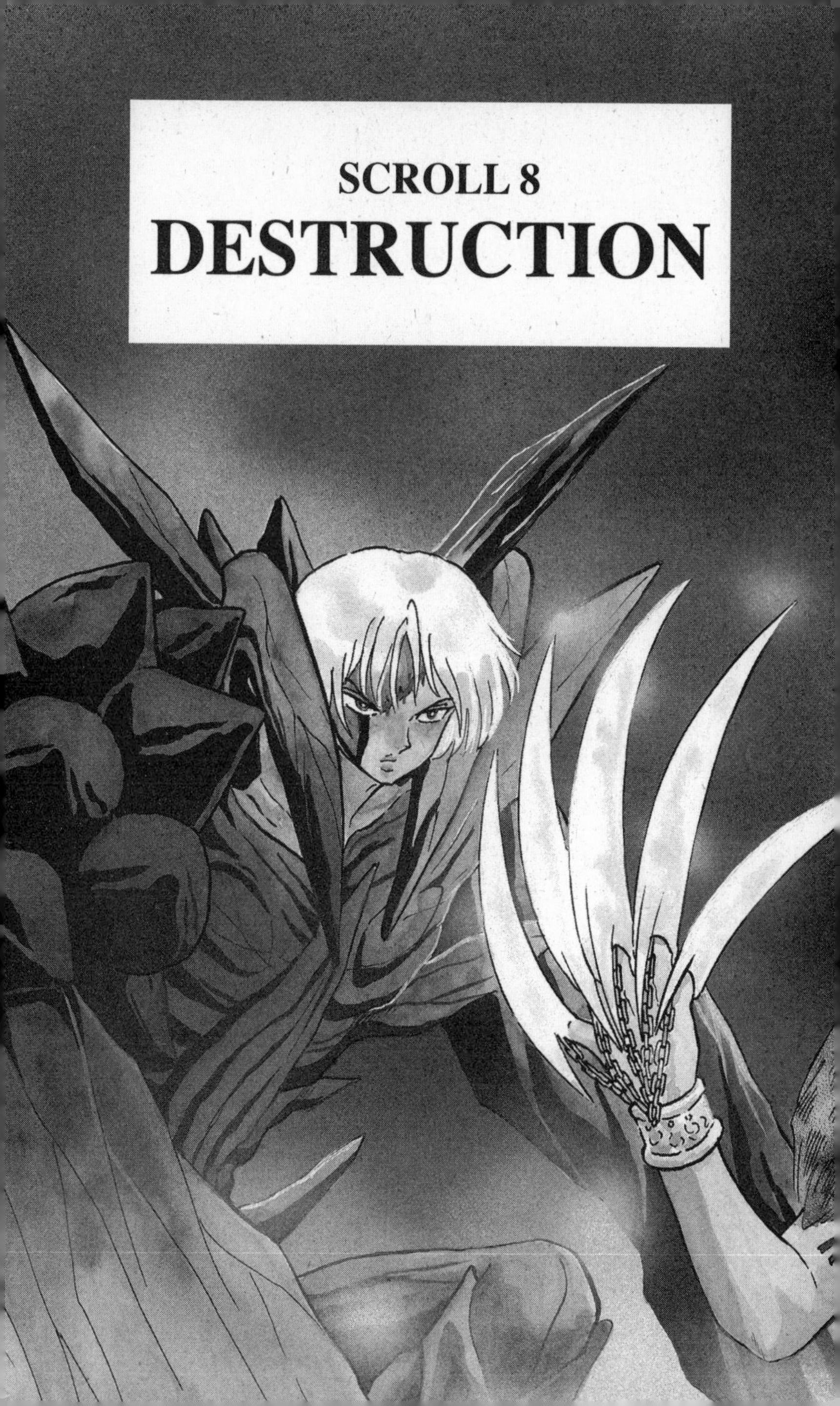

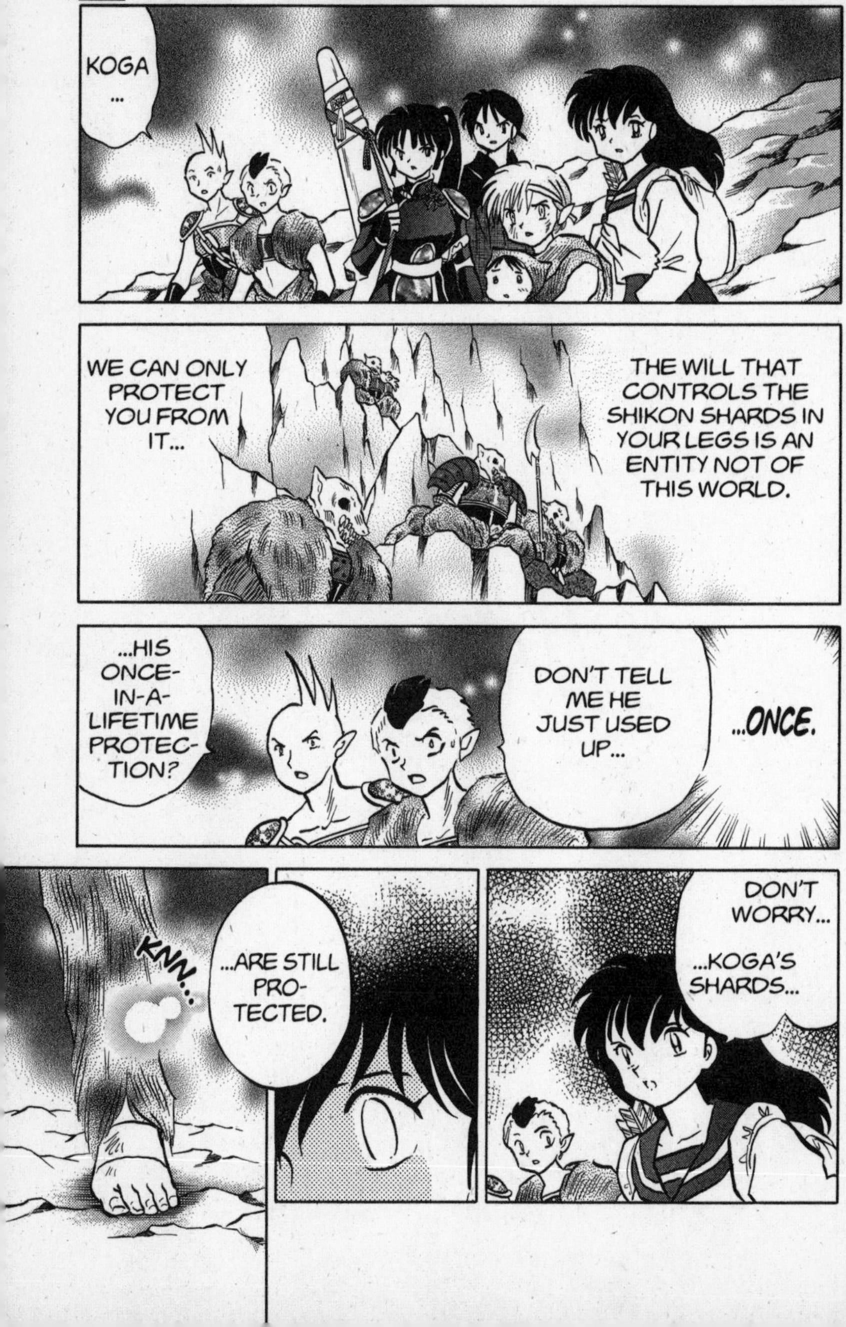
KOGA ...
THE WILL THAT CONTROLS THE SHIKON SHARDS IN YOUR LEGS IS AN ENTITY NOT OF THIS WORLD.
WE CAN ONLY PROTECT YOU FROM IT...
...ONCE.
DON'T TELL ME HE JUST USED UP...
...HIS ONCE-IN-A-LIFETIME PROTECTION?
DON'T WORRY...
...KOGA'S SHARDS...
...ARE STILL PROTECTED.
KNN...

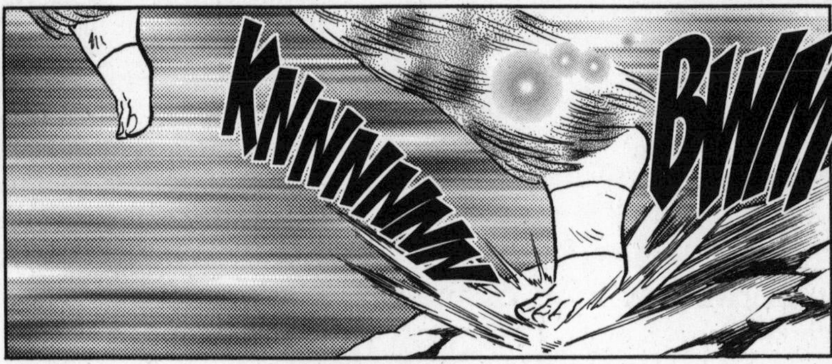
BWM
KNNNNNN
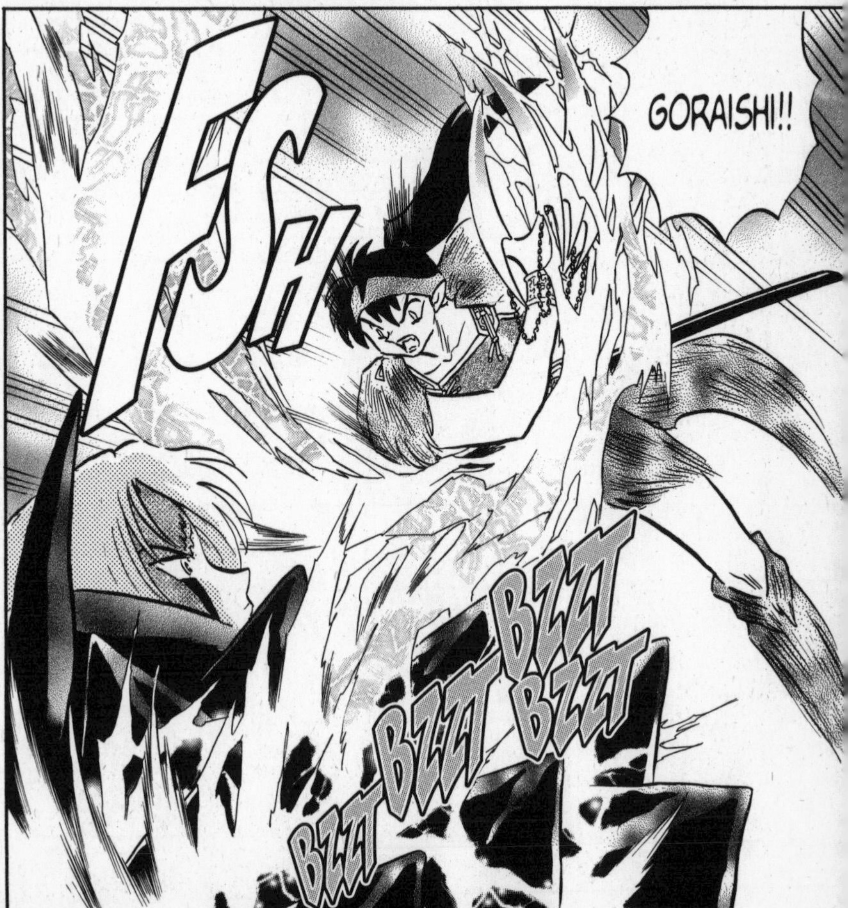
GORAISHI!!
FSH
BZZT
BZZT
BZZT
BZZT

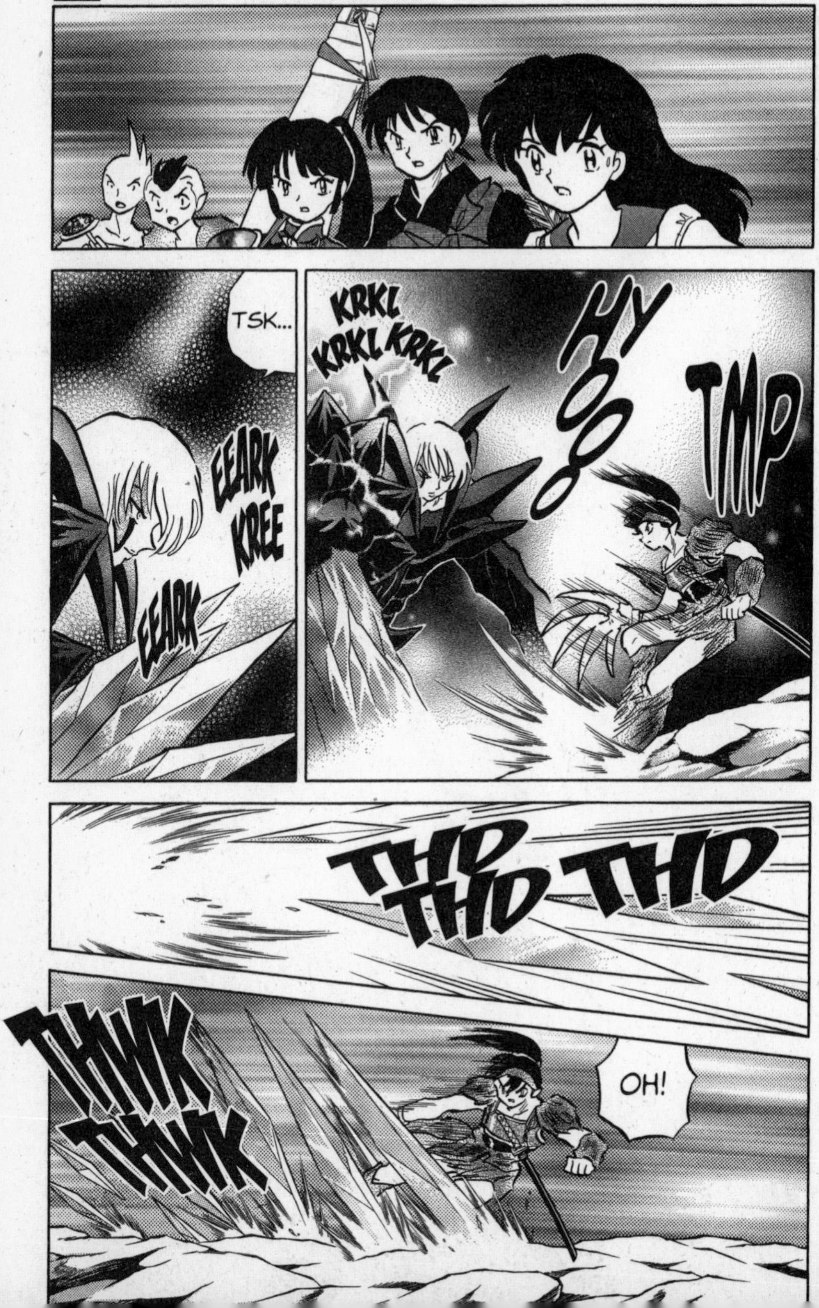
KRKL
KRKL KRKL KRKL
HYOOO
TMP
TSK...
EEARK KREE
EEARK
THD THD THD
THNK THNK
OH!

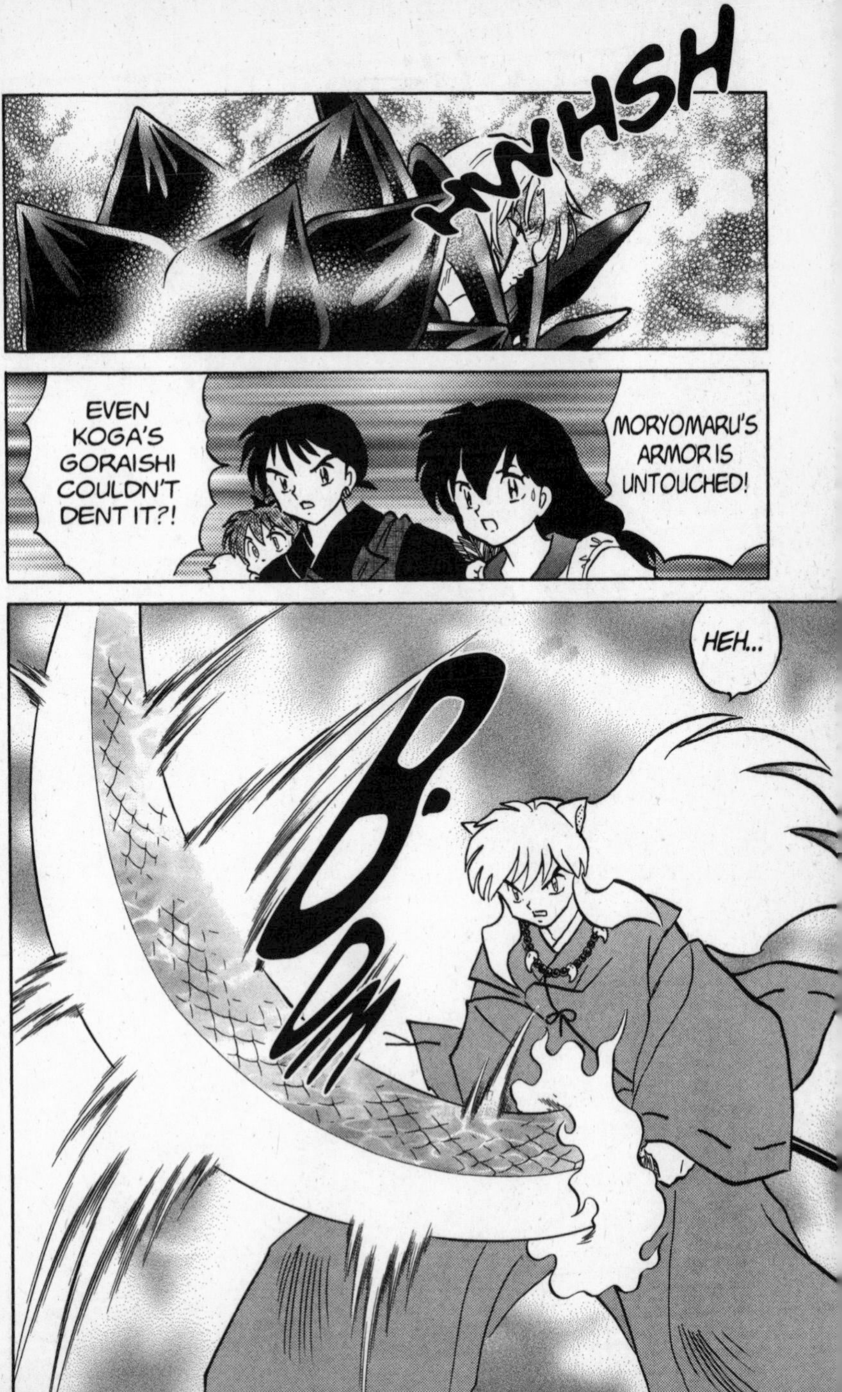
WHSH
MORYOMARU'S ARMOR IS UNTOUCHED!
EVEN KOGA'S GORAISHI COULDN'T DENT IT?!
HEH...

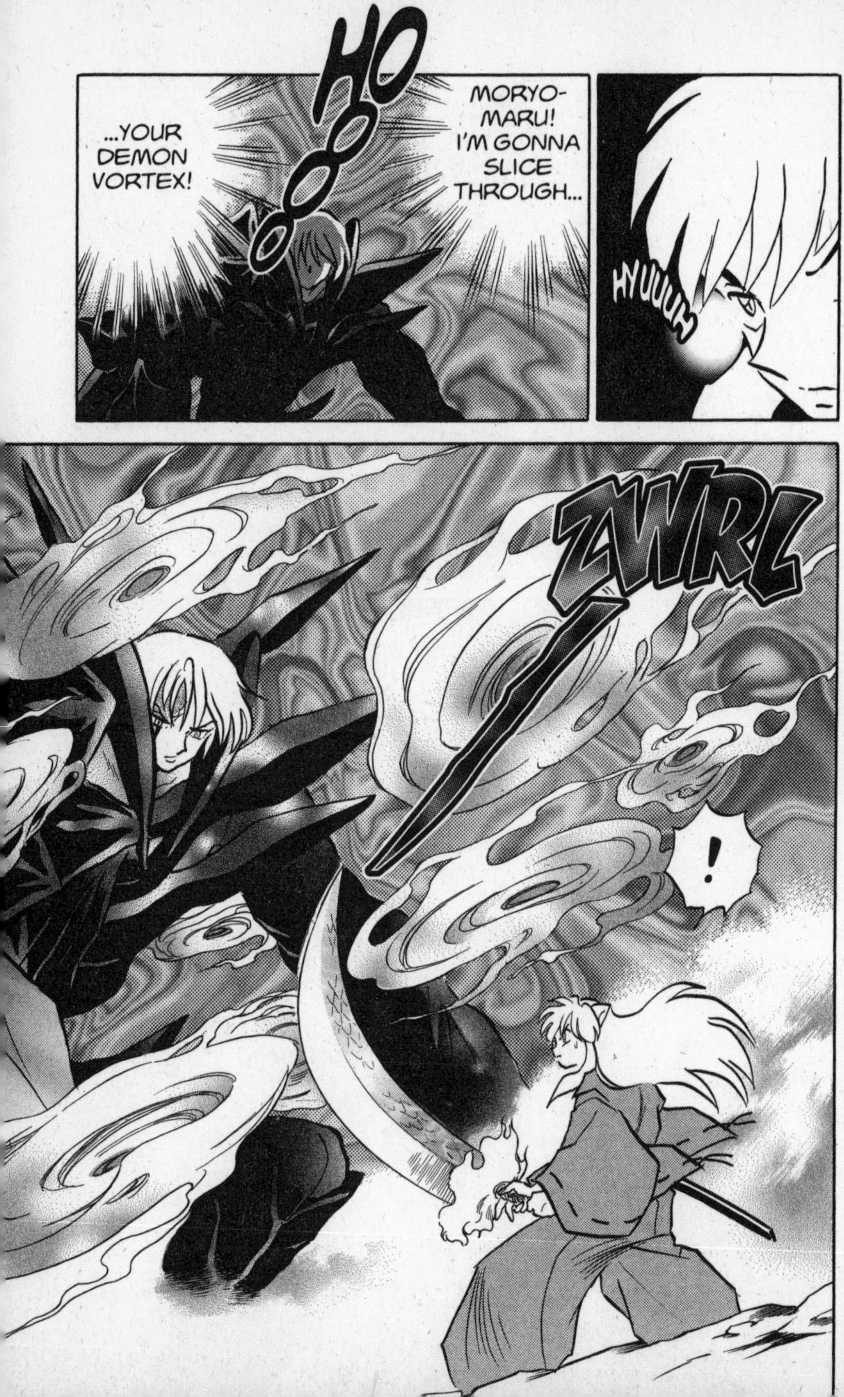
HYUUUH
MORYO-MARU! I'M GONNA SLICE THROUGH...
HOOOOO
...YOUR DEMON VORTEX!
ZWRL
!

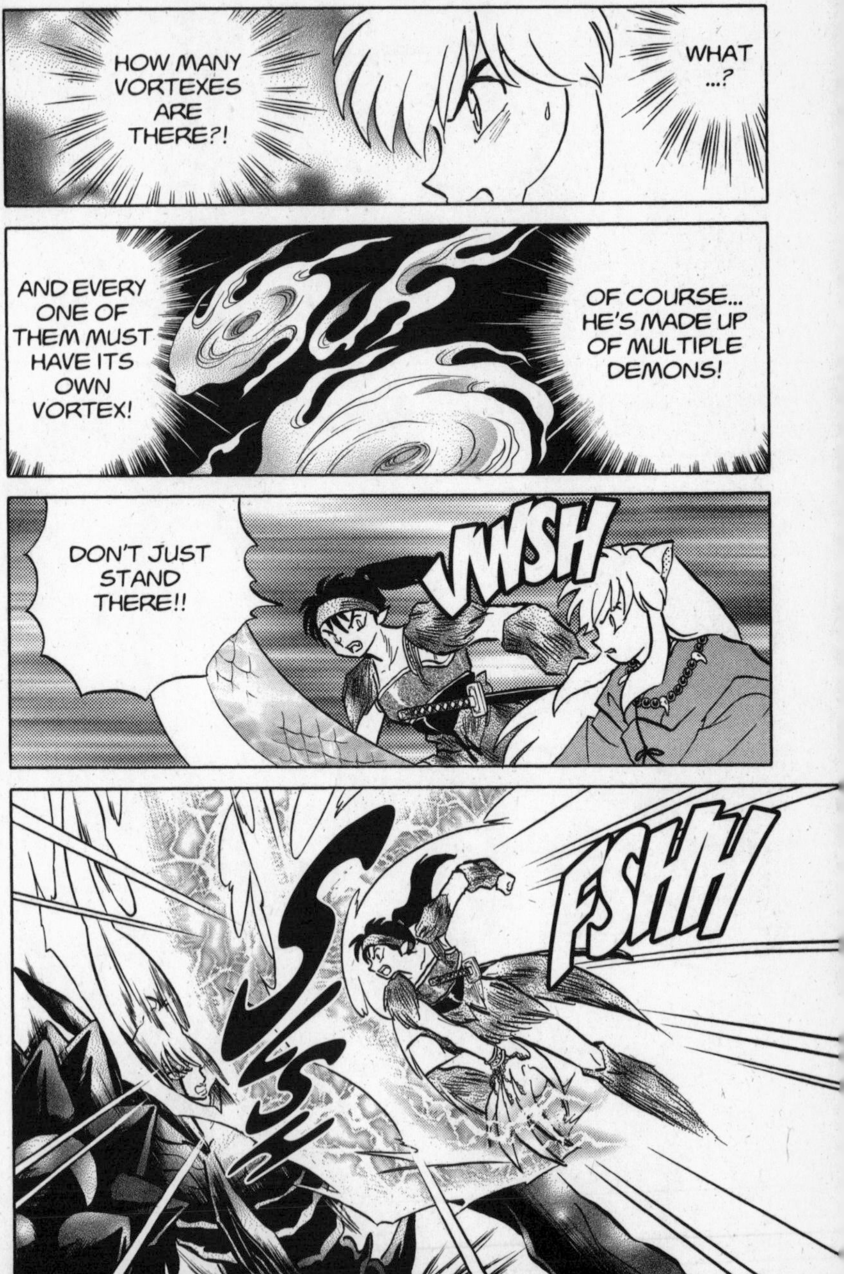
WHAT ...?
HOW MANY VORTEXES ARE THERE?!
OF COURSE... HE'S MADE UP OF MULTIPLE DEMONS!
AND EVERY ONE OF THEM MUST HAVE ITS OWN VORTEX!
VWSH
DON'T JUST STAND THERE!!
FSHH
SWSH

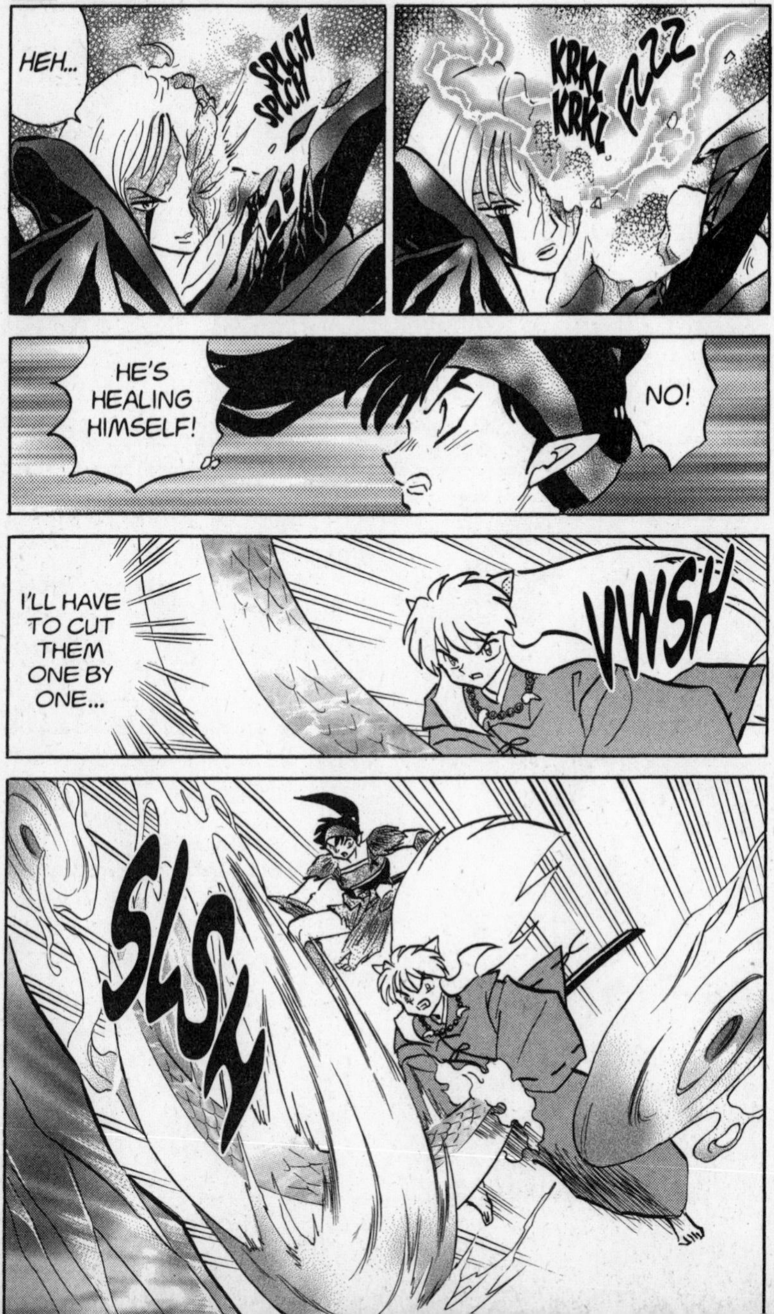
KRKL
KRKL
FZZZ
HEH...
SPLCH
SPLCH
NO!
HE'S HEALING HIMSELF!
VWSH
I'LL HAVE TO CUT THEM ONE BY ONE...
SLSH

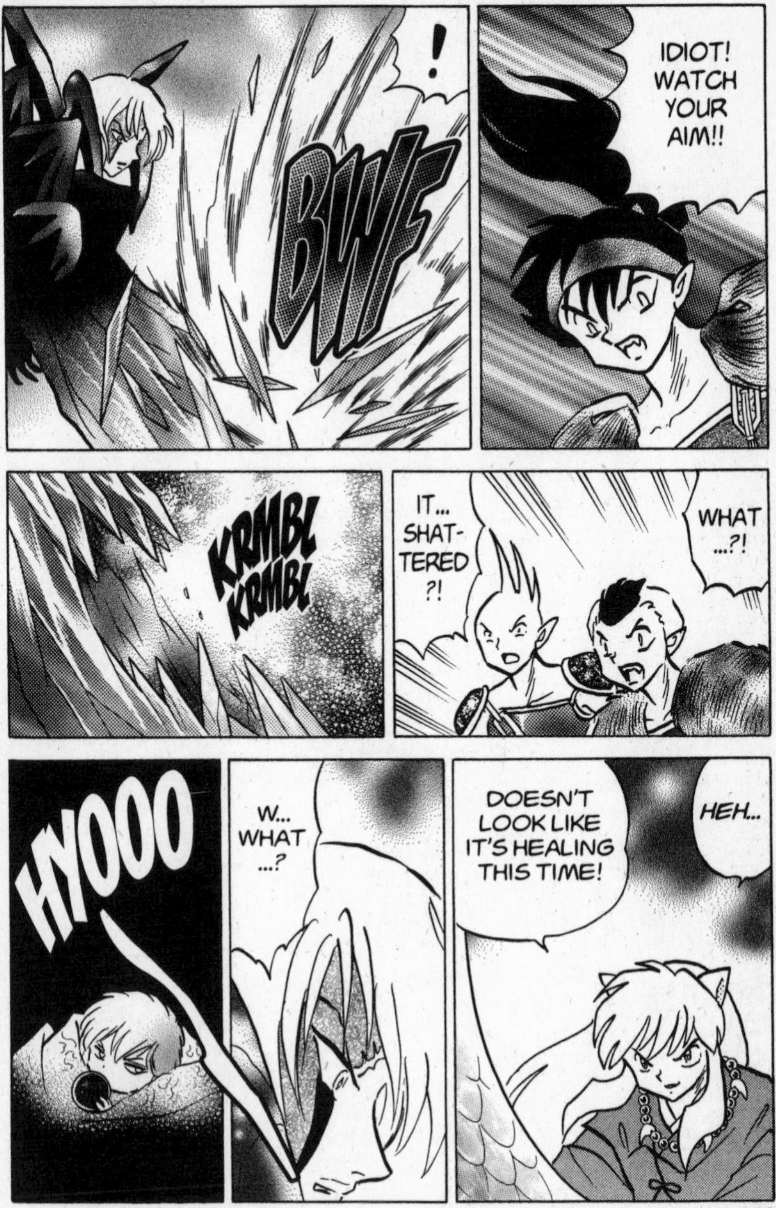
IDIOT! WATCH YOUR AIM!!
!
BWF
WHAT ...?!
IT... SHAT- TERED ?!
KRMBL KRMBL
HEH...
DOESN'T LOOK LIKE IT'S HEALING THIS TIME!
W... WHAT ...?
HYOOO

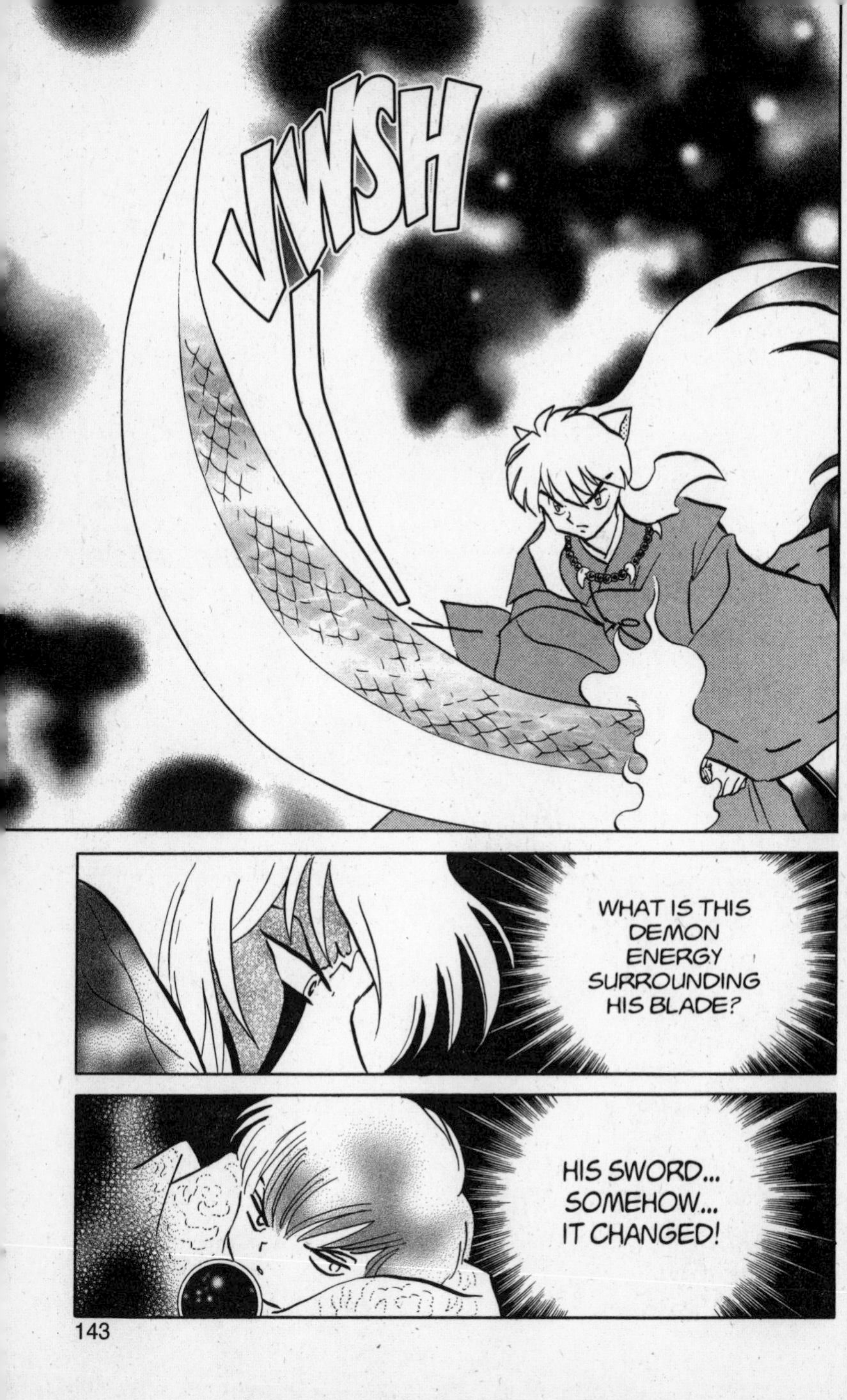
VWSH
WHAT IS THIS DEMON ENERGY SURROUNDING HIS BLADE?
HIS SWORD... SOMEHOW... IT CHANGED!

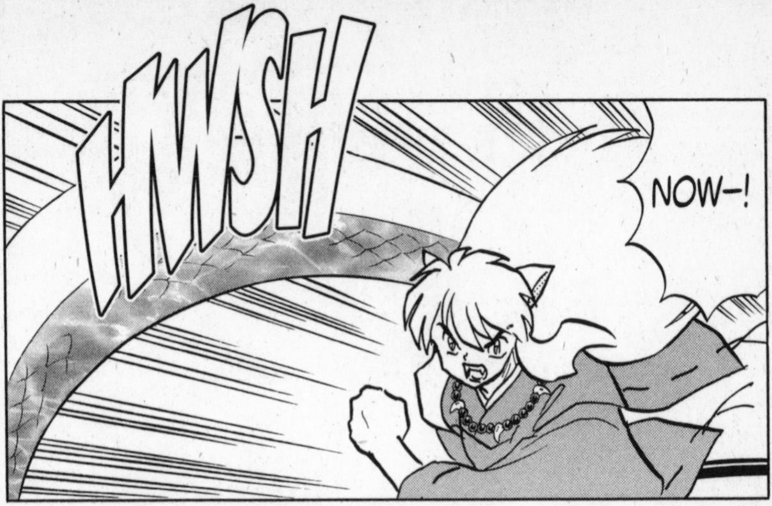
HWSH
NOW-!
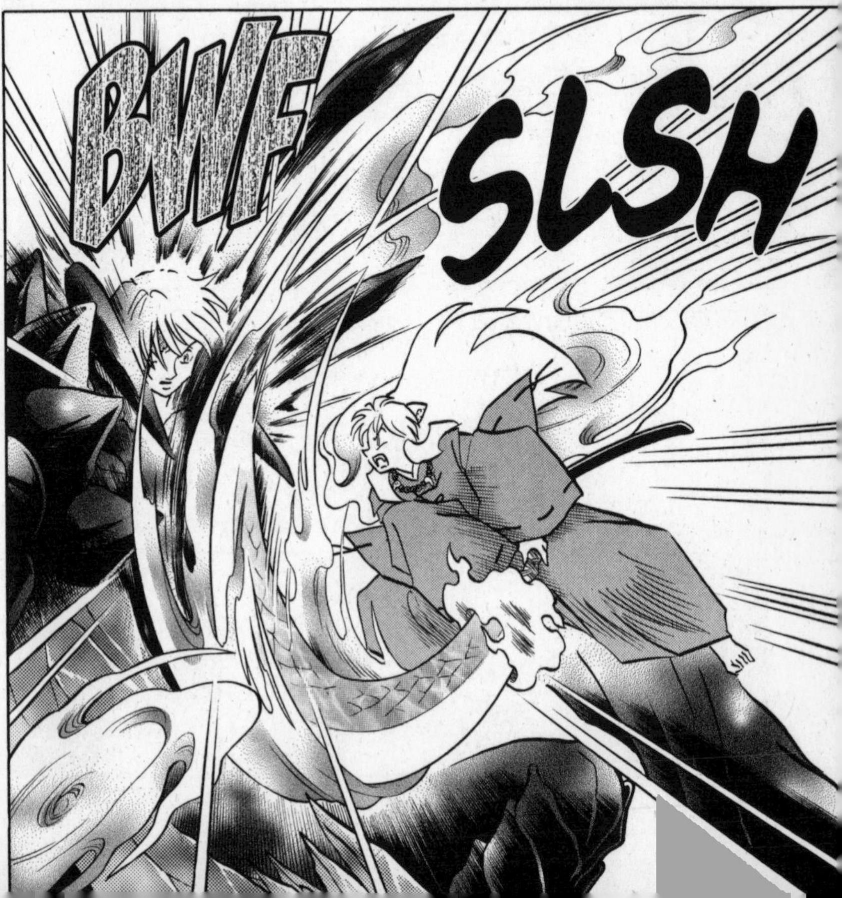
SLSH
BWF

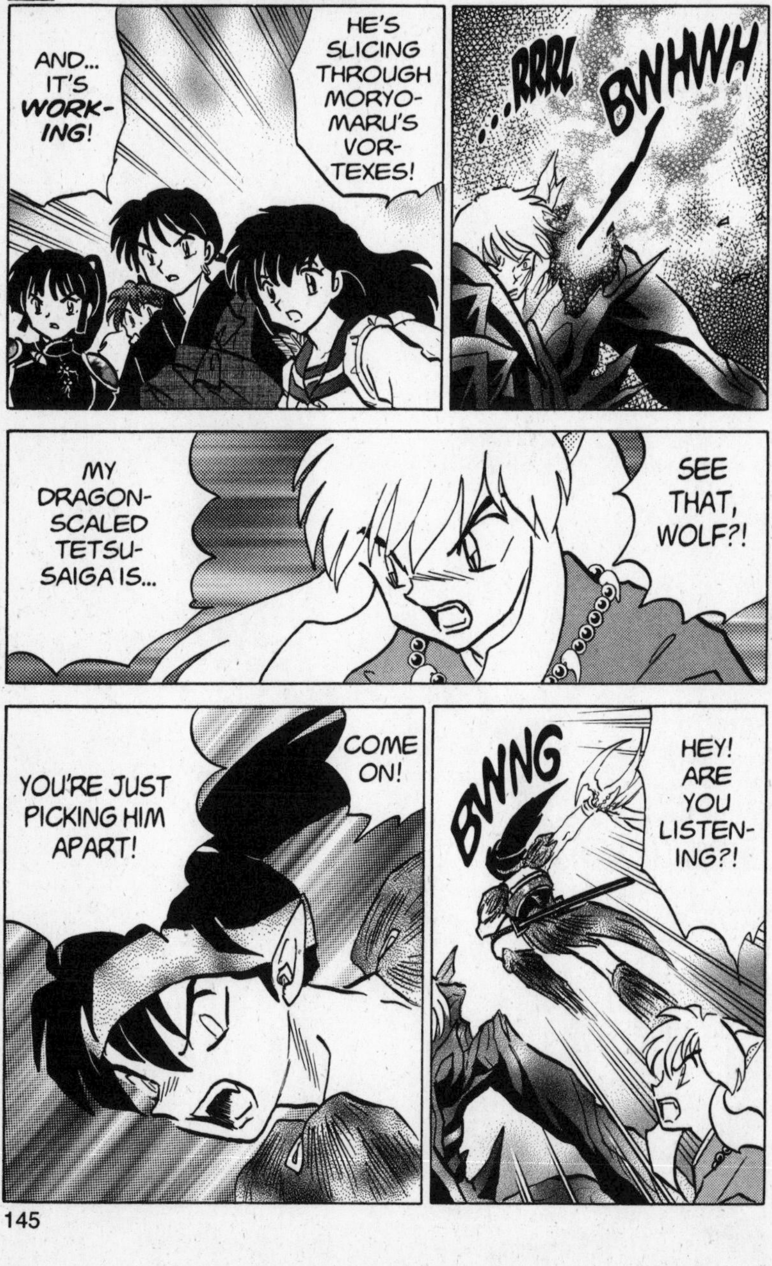
...RRRL
BWHWH
HE'S SLICING THROUGH MORYOMARU'S VORTEXES!
AND... IT'S WORKING!
SEE THAT, WOLF?!
MY DRAGON-SCALED TETSUSAIGA IS...
HEY! ARE YOU LISTENING?!
BWNG
COME ON!
YOU'RE JUST PICKING HIM APART!

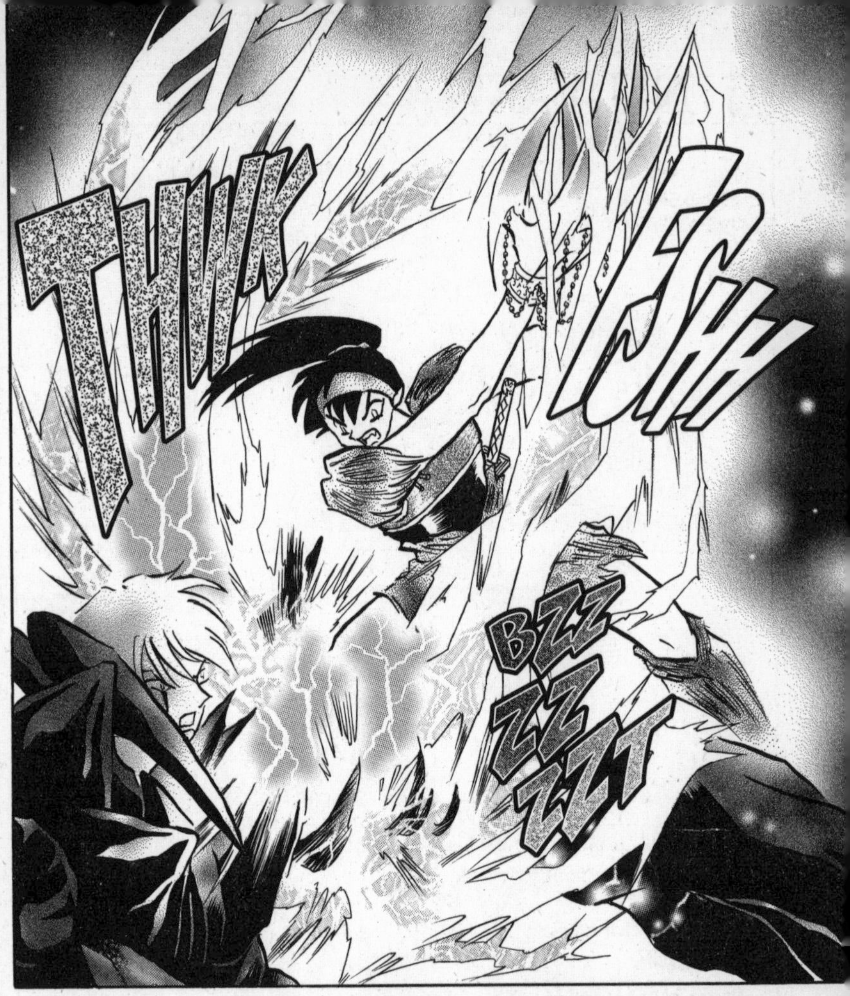
FSHH
THWK
BZZZZZZZT
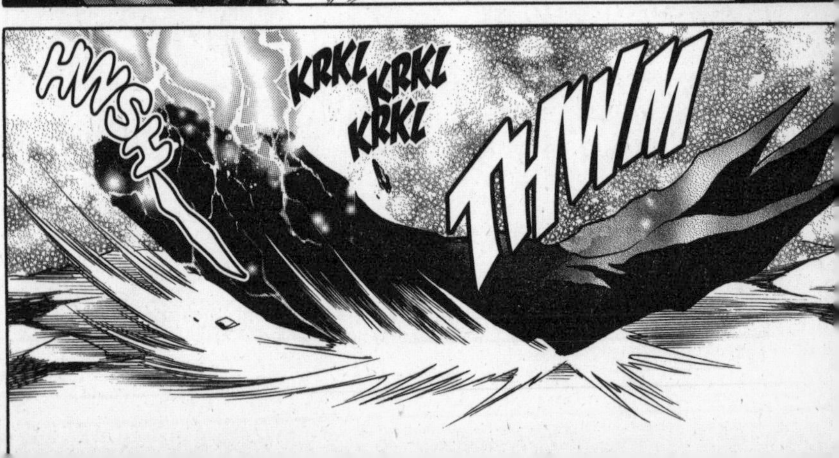
THWM
KRKL KRKL KRKL
HWSH

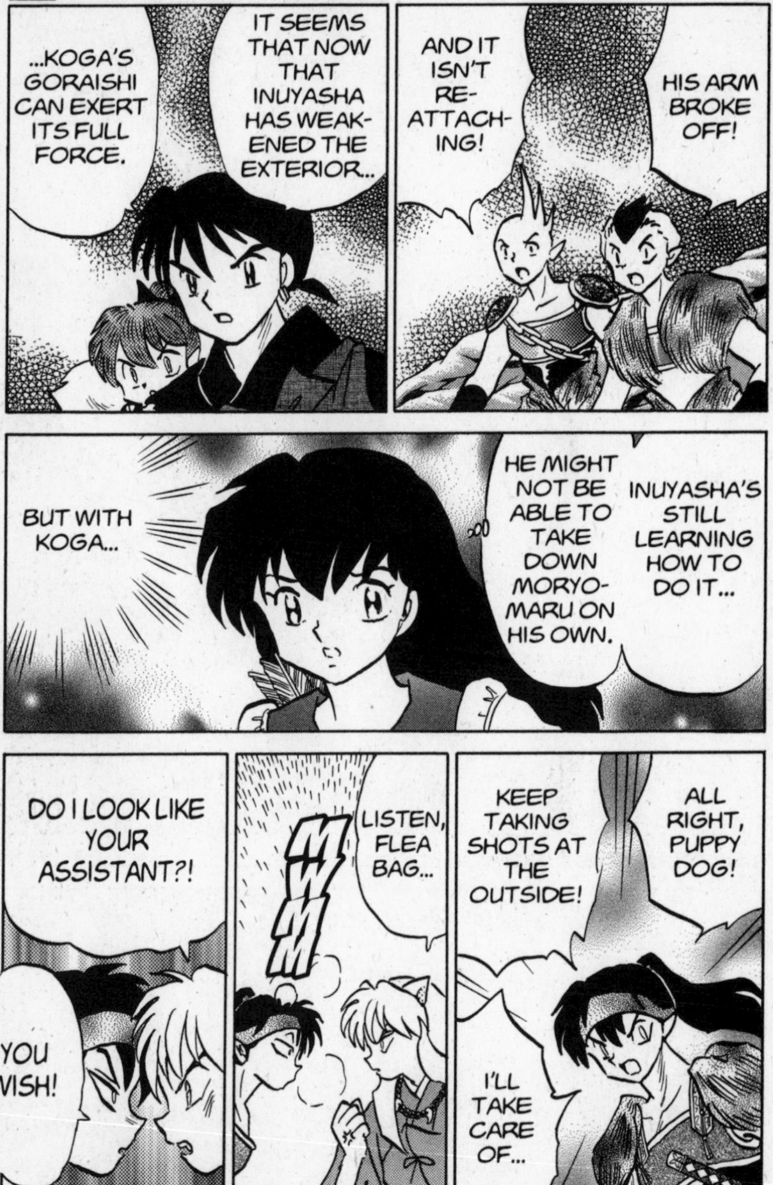
HIS ARM BROKE OFF!
AND IT ISN'T RE-ATTACHING!
IT SEEMS THAT NOW THAT INUYASHA HAS WEAKENED THE EXTERIOR...
...KOGA'S GORAISHI CAN EXERT ITS FULL FORCE.
INUYASHA'S STILL LEARNING HOW TO DO IT...
HE MIGHT NOT BE ABLE TO TAKE DOWN MORYOMARU ON HIS OWN.
BUT WITH KOGA...
ALL RIGHT, PUPPY DOG!
KEEP TAKING SHOTS AT THE OUTSIDE!
I'LL TAKE CARE OF...
LISTEN, FLEA BAG...
DO I LOOK LIKE YOUR ASSISTANT?!
YOU WISH!

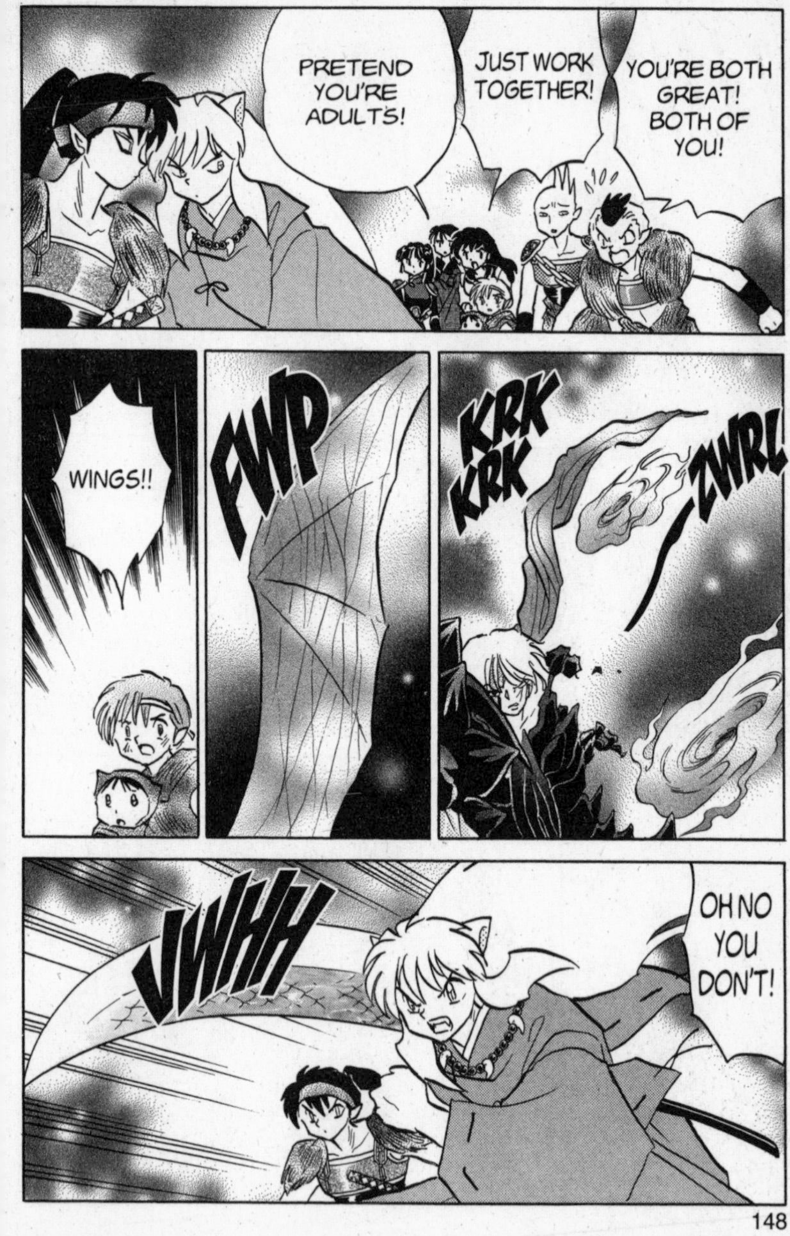
YOU'RE BOTH GREAT! BOTH OF YOU!
JUST WORK TOGETHER!
PRETEND YOU'RE ADULTS!
KRK KRK
ZWRL
FWP
WINGS!!
OH NO YOU DON'T!
JWHH

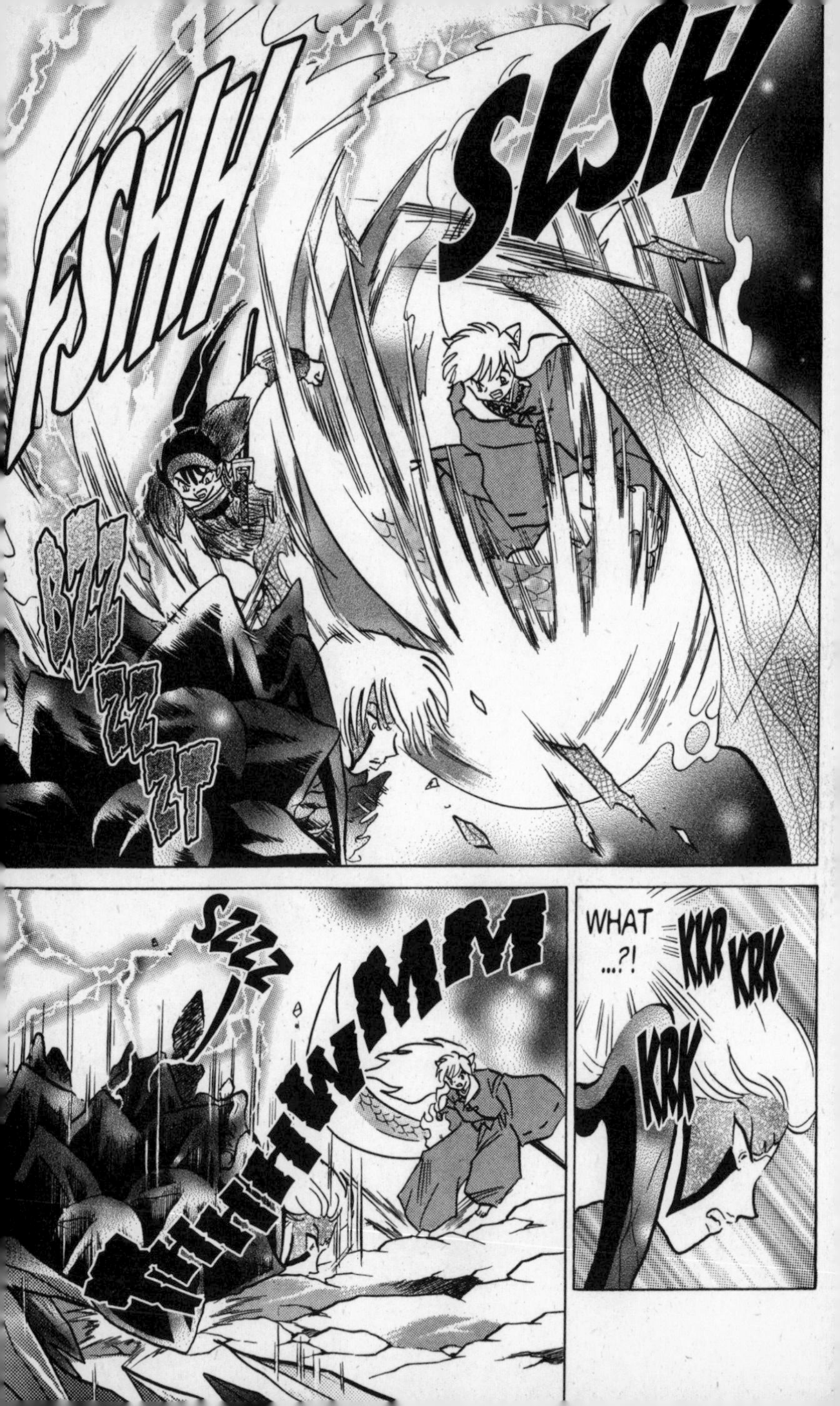
SLSH
FSHH
BZZZZZT
WHAT ...?!
KKR KRK
KRK
SZZZ
THHHHWMM

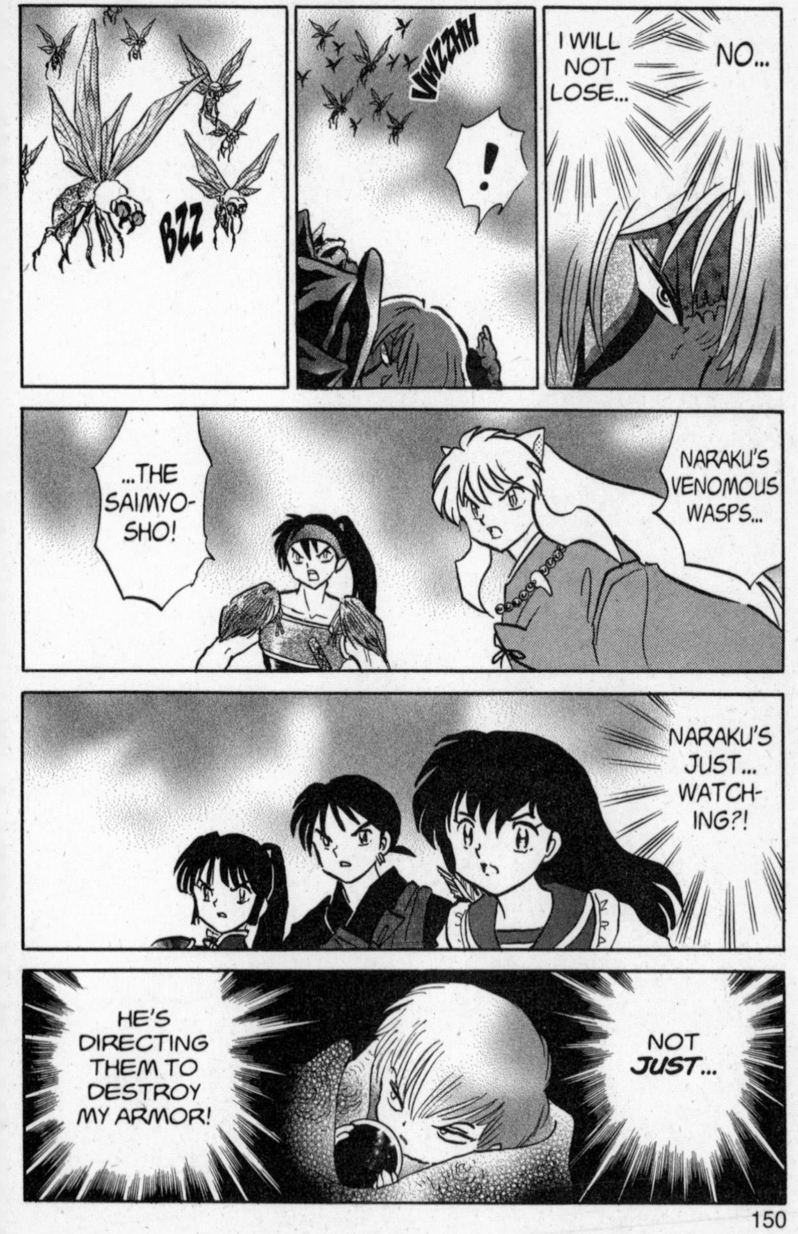
NO...
I WILL NOT LOSE...
VWZZHH
!
BZZ
NARAKU'S VENOMOUS WASPS...
...THE SAIMYO-SHO!
NARAKU'S JUST... WATCHING?!
NOT JUST...
HE'S DIRECTING THEM TO DESTROY MY ARMOR!

SCROLL 9

THE INVISIBLE VORTEX

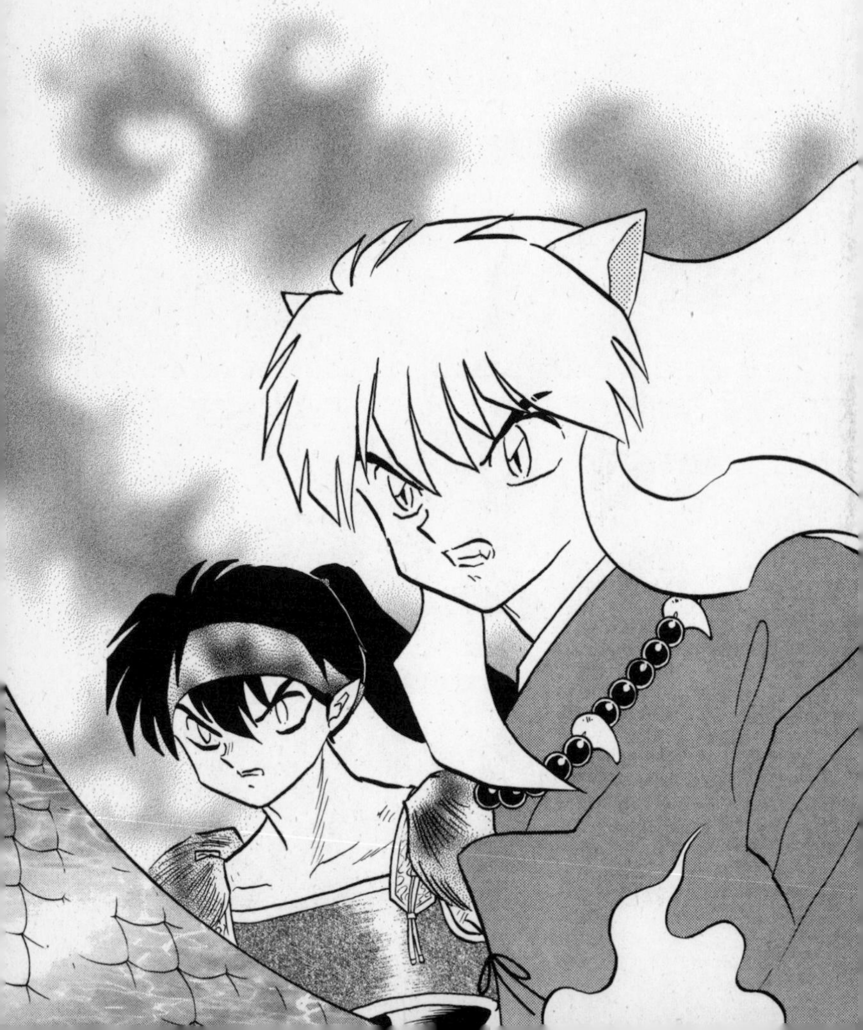

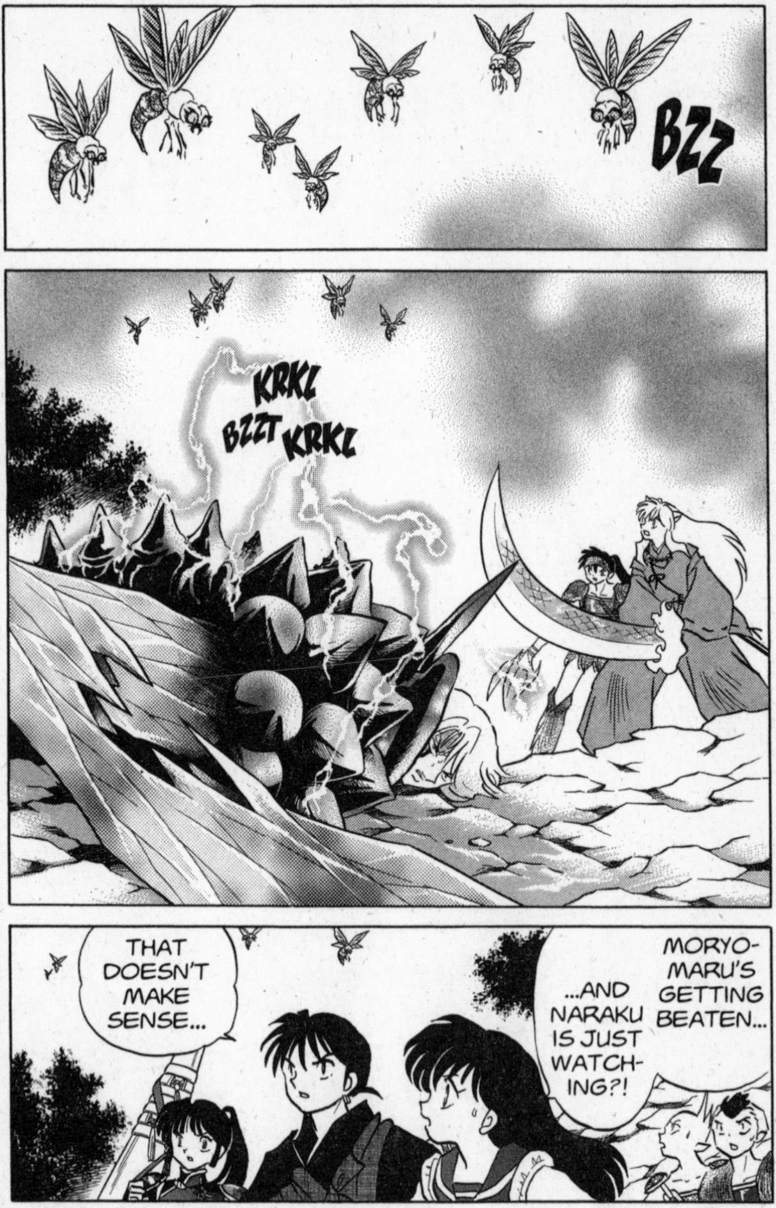
BZZ
KRKL
BZZT
KRKL
MORYO-MARU'S GETTING BEATEN...
...AND NARAKU IS JUST WATCHING?!
THAT DOESN'T MAKE SENSE...

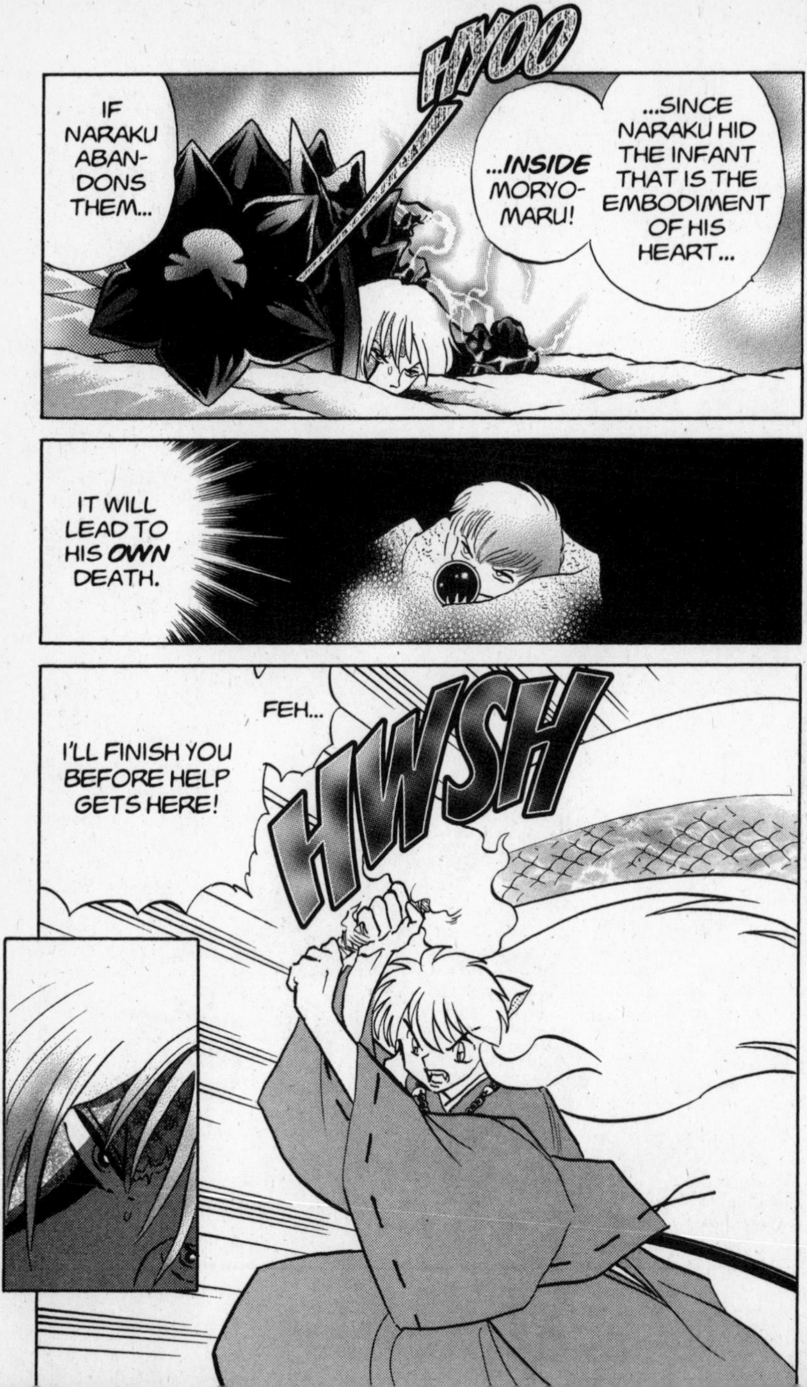
...SINCE NARAKU HID THE INFANT THAT IS THE EMBODIMENT OF HIS HEART...
...INSIDE MORYO-MARU!
HYOO
IF NARAKU ABAN-DONS THEM...
IT WILL LEAD TO HIS OWN DEATH.
FEH...
HWSH
I'LL FINISH YOU BEFORE HELP GETS HERE!

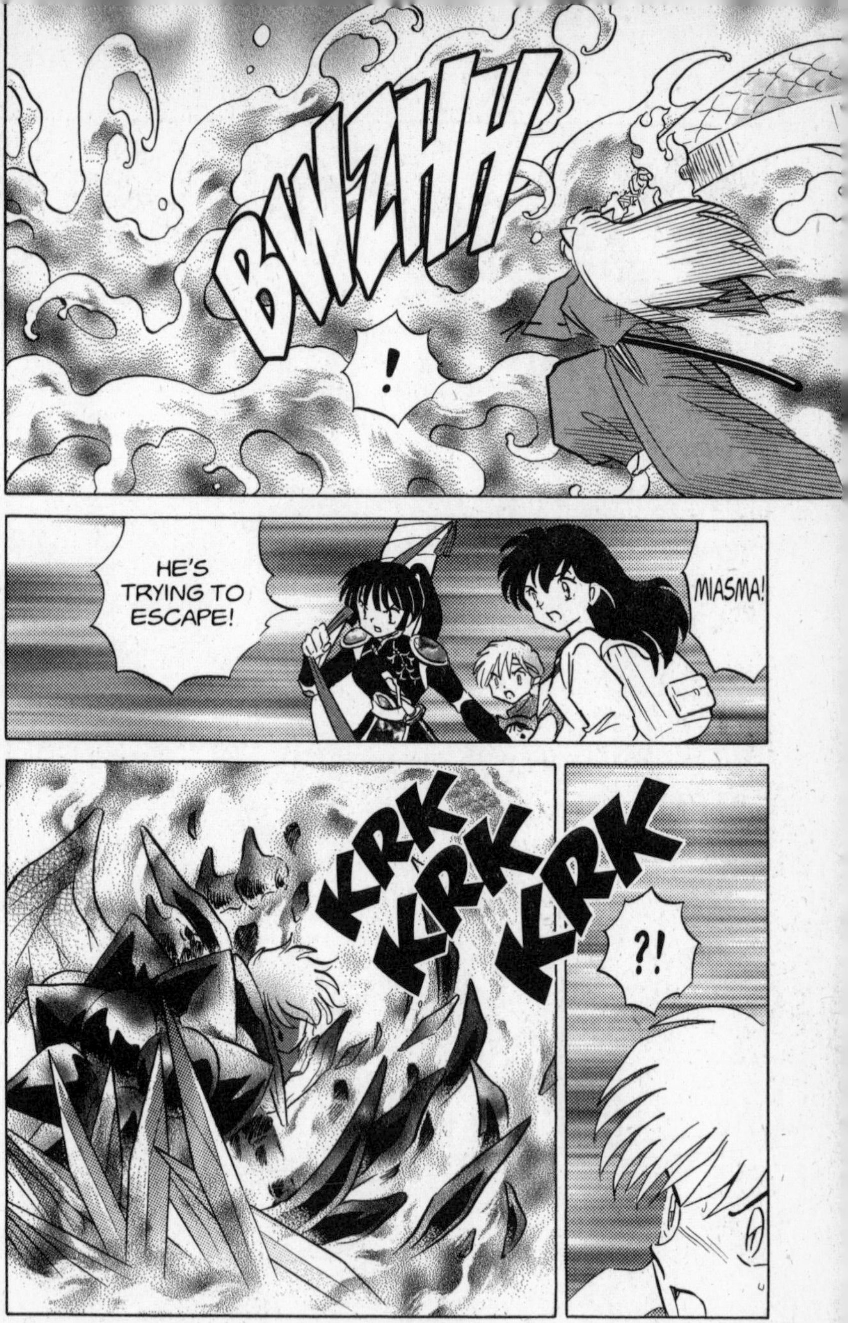
BWZHH
!
MIASMA!
HE'S TRYING TO ESCAPE!
?!
KRK KRK KRK

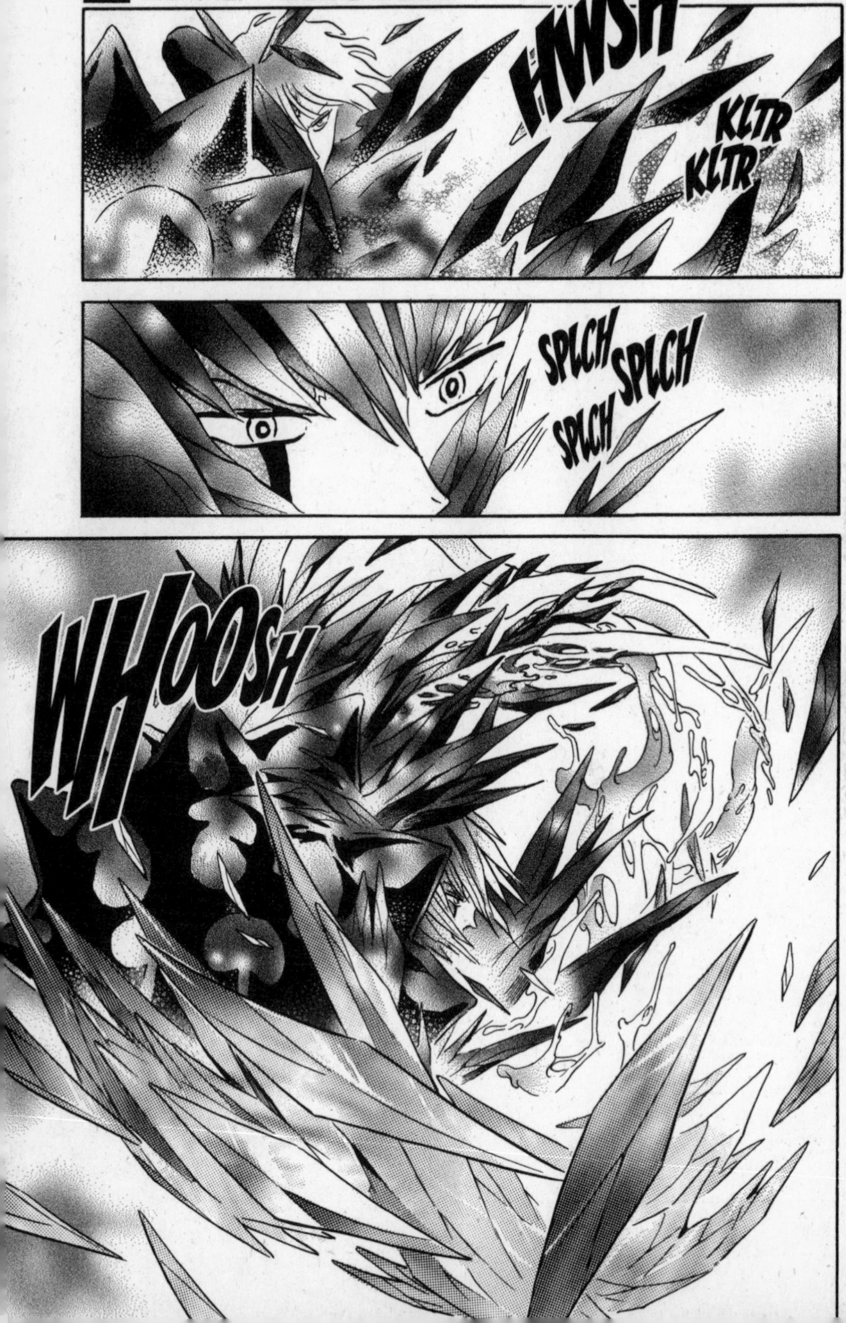
HWSH
KLTR
KLTR
SPLCH
SPLCH
SPLCH
WHOOSH

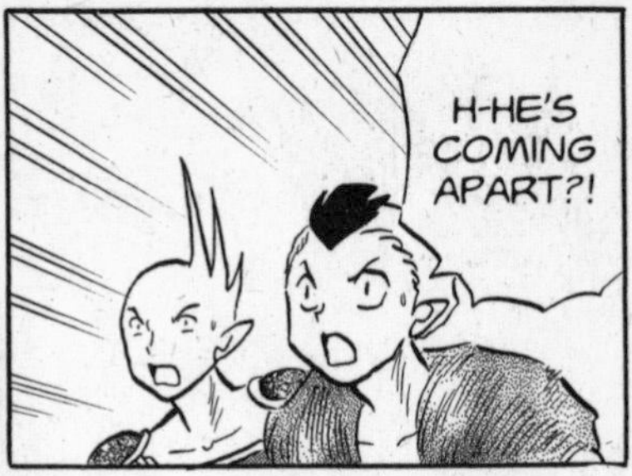
H-HE'S COMING APART?!

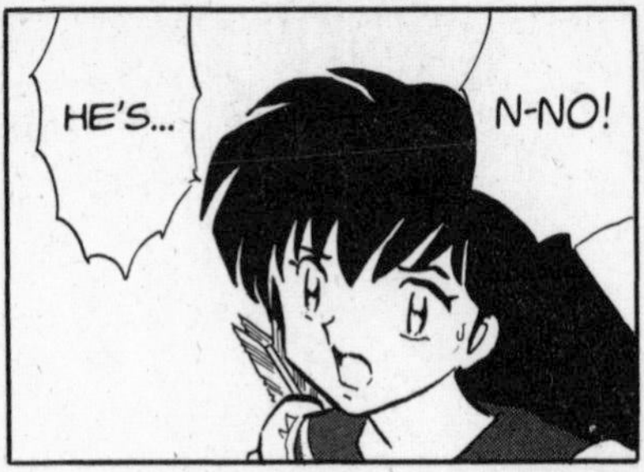
N-NO!
HE'S...

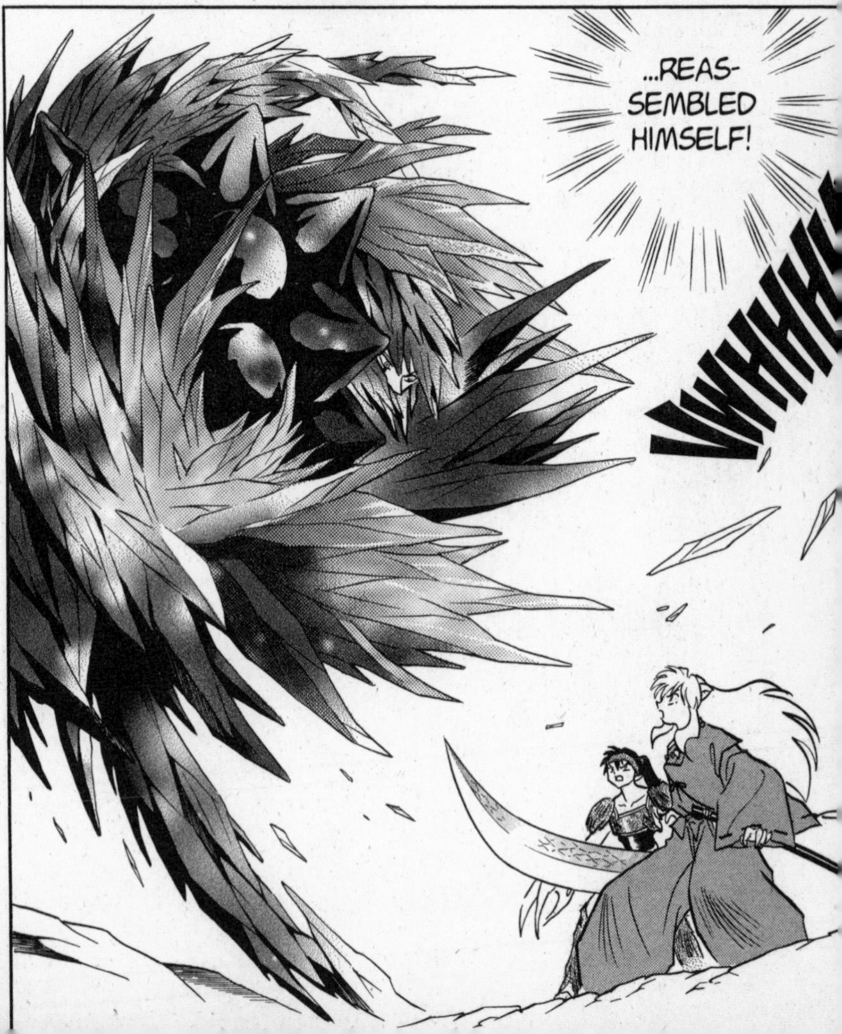
...REAS-SEMBLED HIMSELF!
VWHHH

THD THD THD THD THD
BWHH
SO YOU STILL WANNA FIGHT?!
GORAI-SHI!
FLASH
BZZZZZT
BZZZZZ

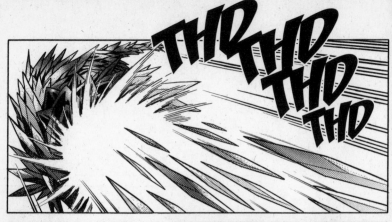

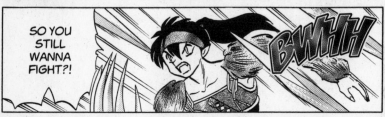

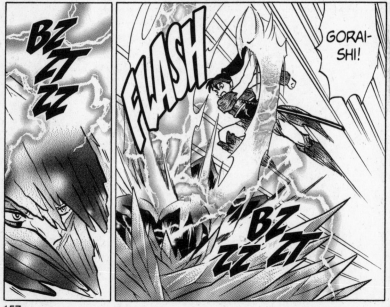

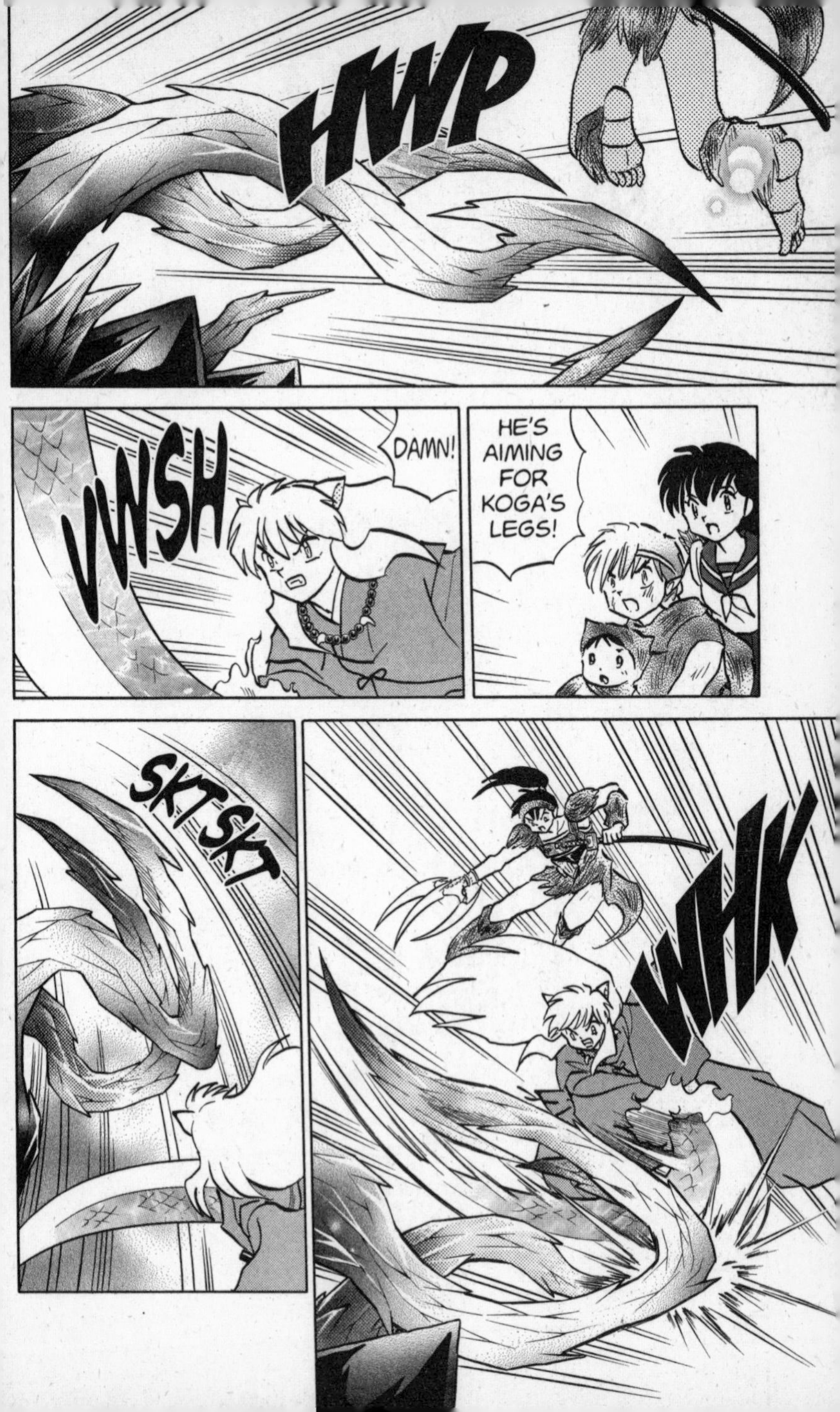
HWP
HE'S AIMING FOR KOGA'S LEGS!
DAMN!
VWSH
WHK
SKT SKT

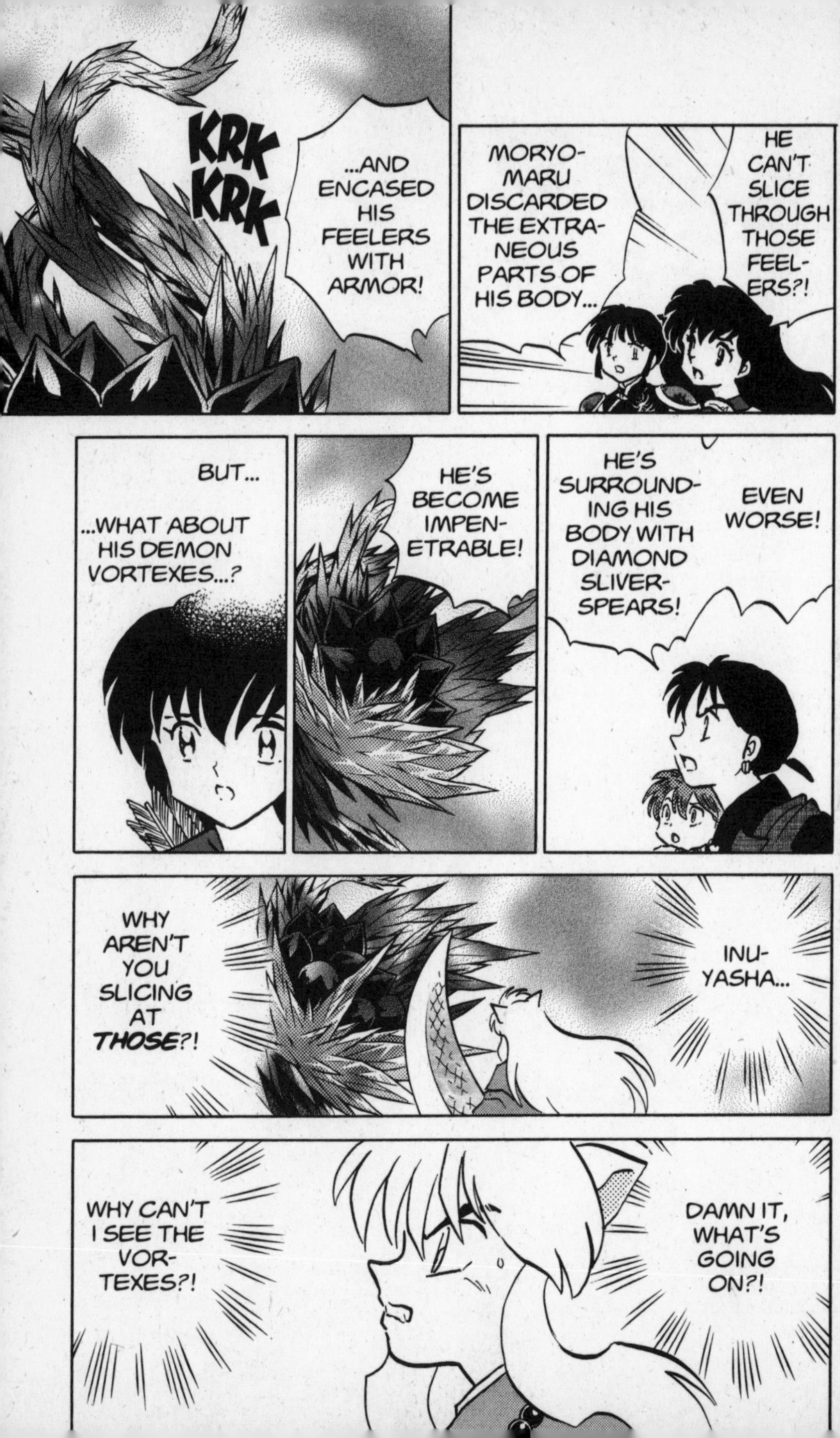
HE CAN'T SLICE THROUGH THOSE FEELERS?!
MORYOMARU DISCARDED THE EXTRANEOUS PARTS OF HIS BODY...
KRK KRK
...AND ENCASED HIS FEELERS WITH ARMOR!
EVEN WORSE!
HE'S SURROUNDING HIS BODY WITH DIAMOND SLIVER-SPEARS!
HE'S BECOME IMPENETRABLE!
BUT...
...WHAT ABOUT HIS DEMON VORTEXES...?
INU-YASHA...
WHY AREN'T YOU SLICING AT *THOSE*?!
DAMN IT, WHAT'S GOING ON?!
WHY CAN'T I SEE THE VORTEXES?!

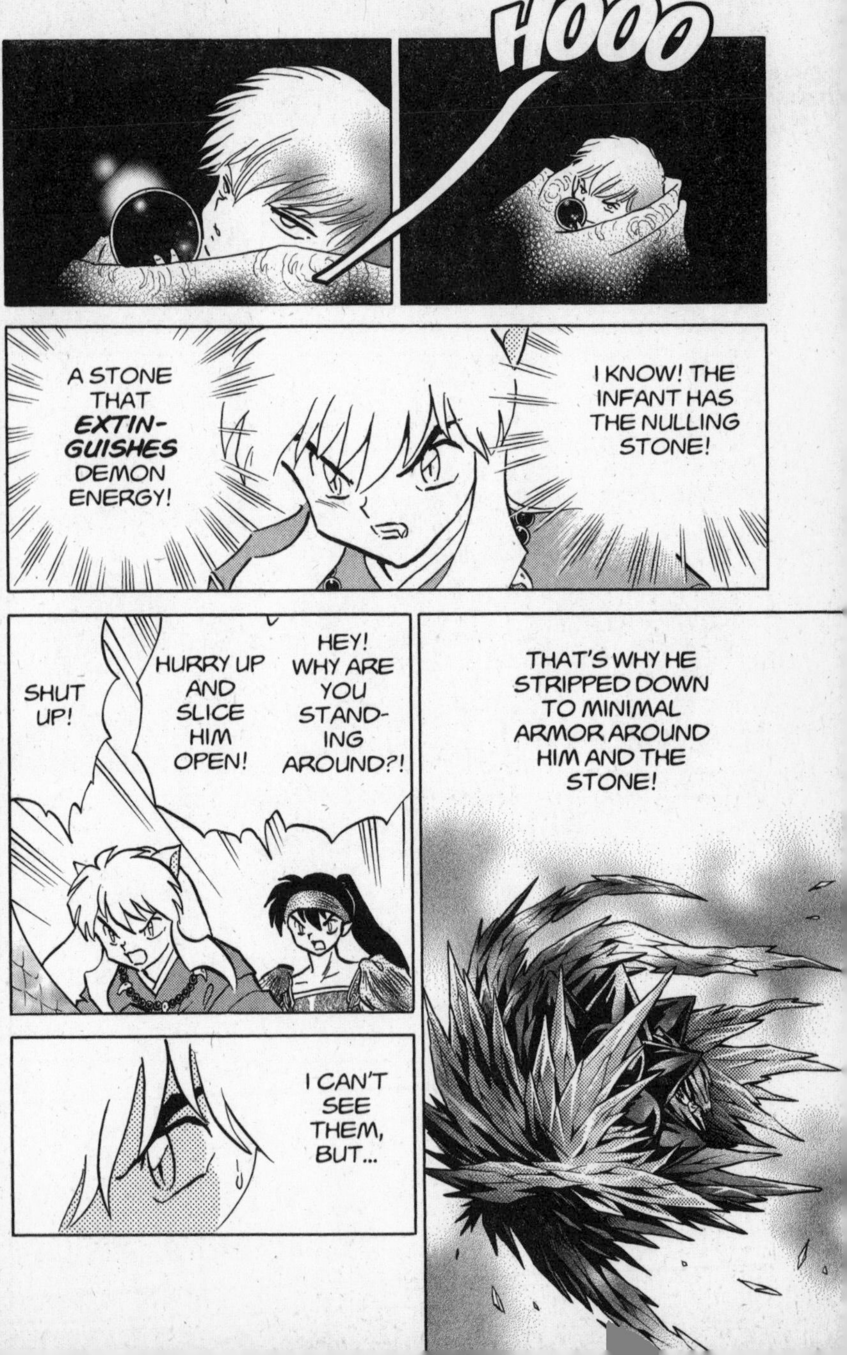
HOOO
I KNOW! THE INFANT HAS THE NULLING STONE!
A STONE THAT EXTIN-GUISHES DEMON ENERGY!
THAT'S WHY HE STRIPPED DOWN TO MINIMAL ARMOR AROUND HIM AND THE STONE!
HEY! WHY ARE YOU STAND-ING AROUND?!
HURRY UP AND SLICE HIM OPEN!
SHUT UP!
I CAN'T SEE THEM, BUT...

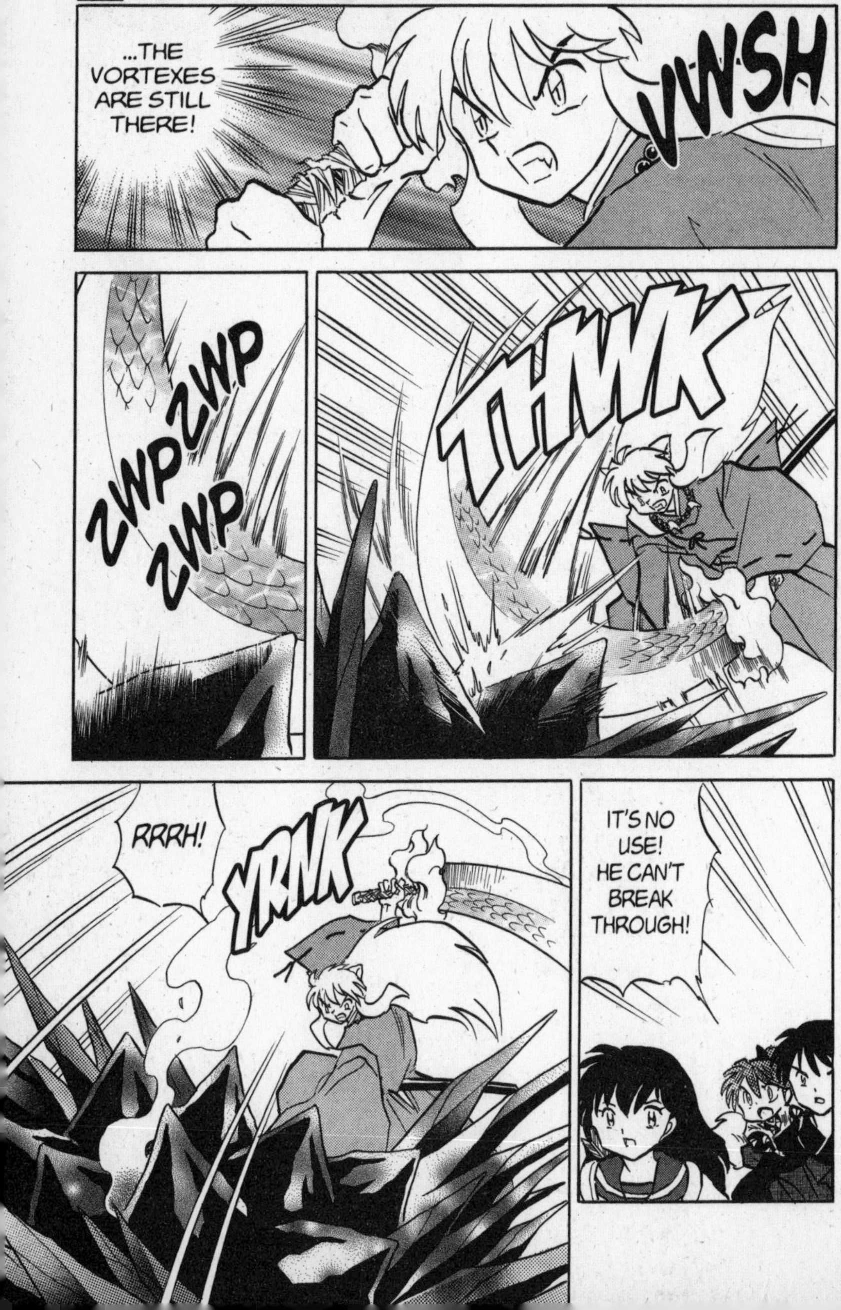
...THE VORTEXES ARE STILL THERE!
VWSH
THWK
ZWP ZWP ZWP ZWP
IT'S NO USE! HE CAN'T BREAK THROUGH!
RRRH!
YRNK

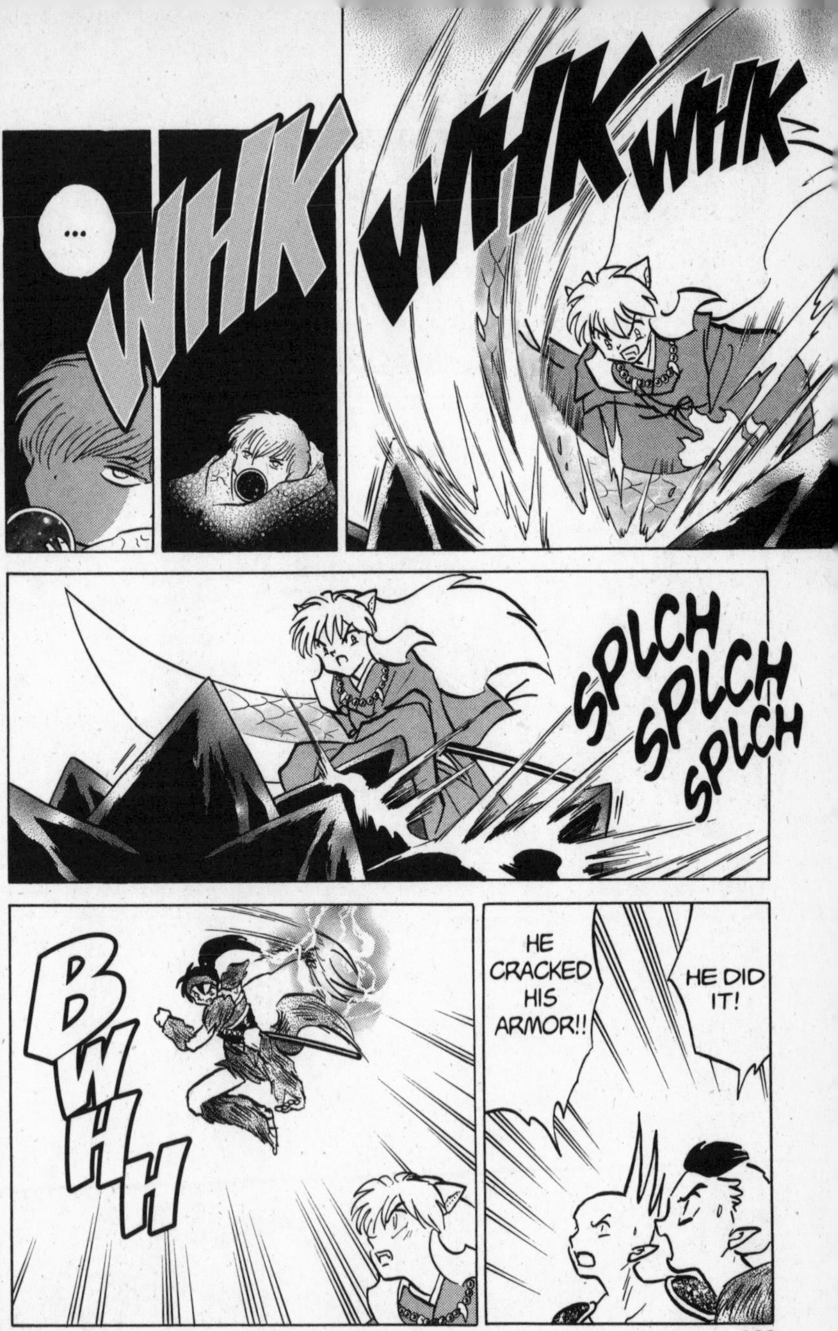
WHK
WHK
WHK
...
SPLCH SPLCH SPLCH
HE DID IT!
HE CRACKED HIS ARMOR!!
BWHHH

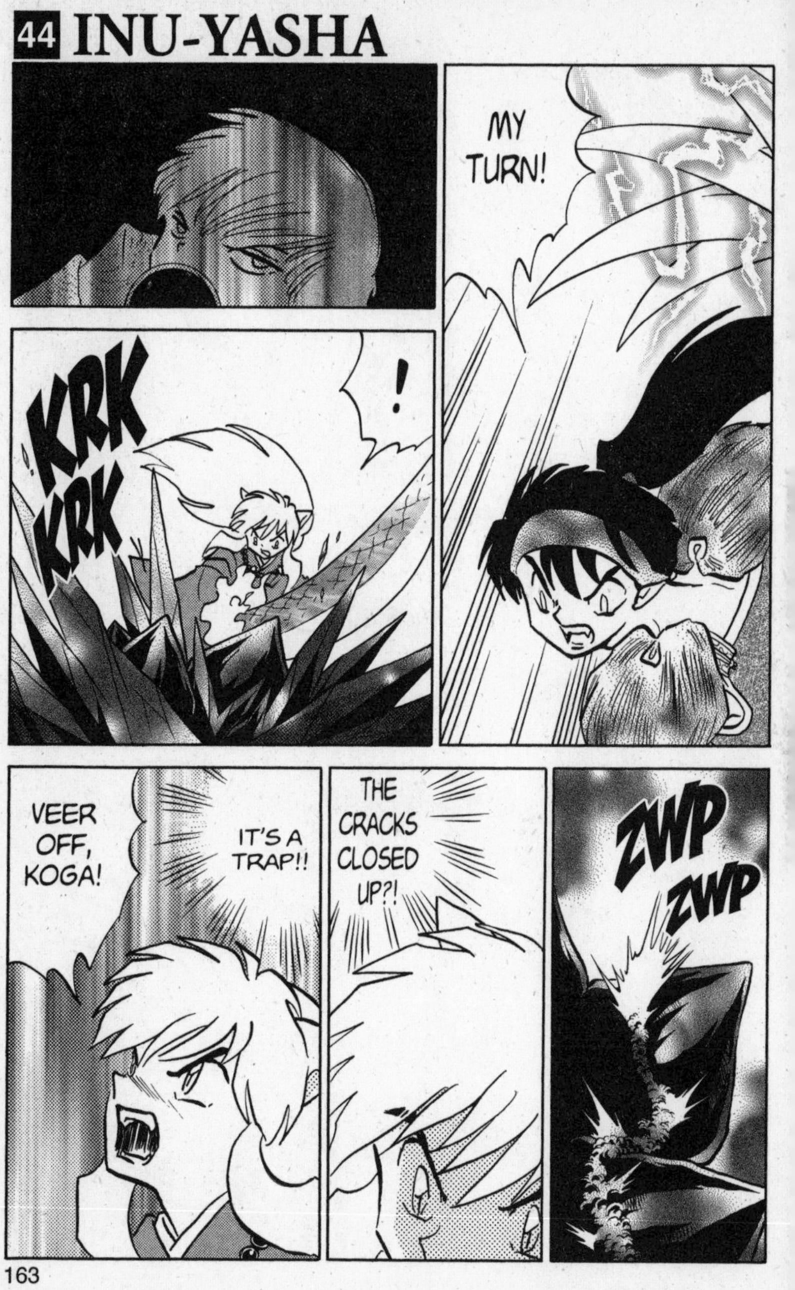
MY TURN!
!
KRK KRK
ZWP ZWP
THE CRACKS CLOSED UP?!
VEER OFF, KOGA!
IT'S A TRAP!!

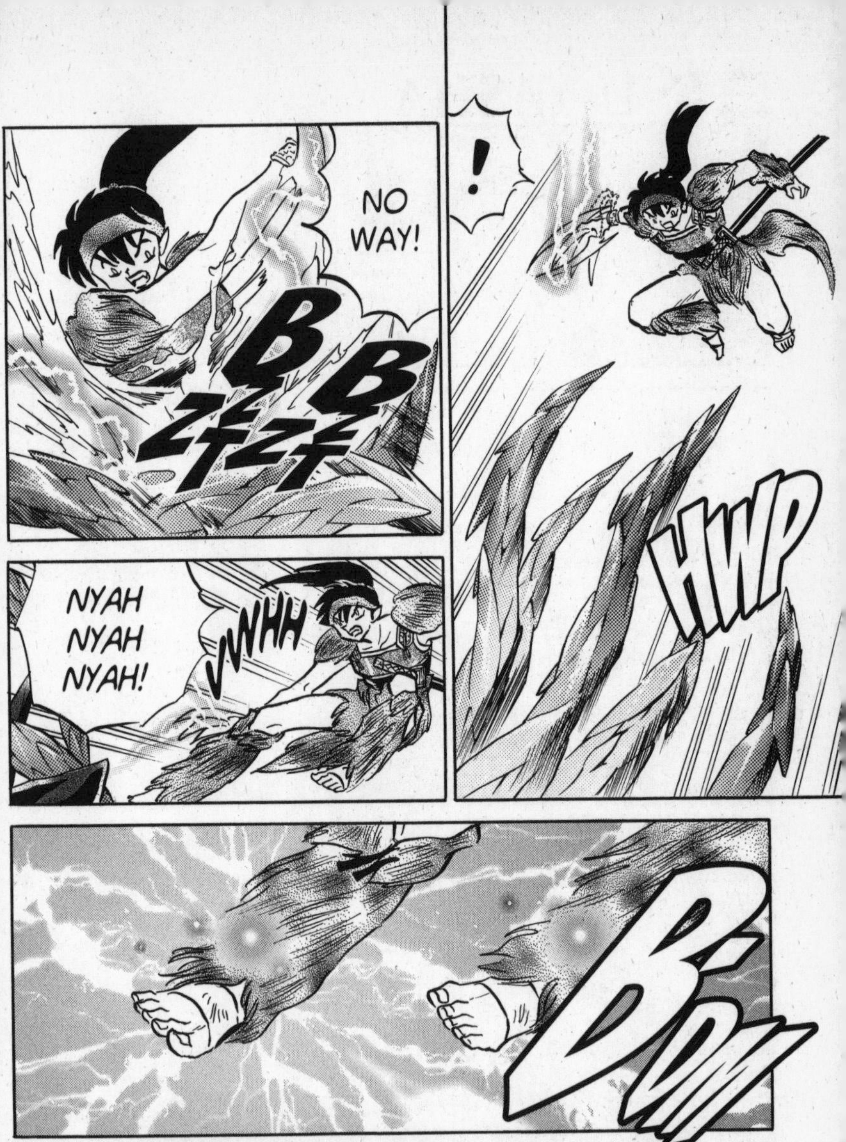
!
HWP
NO WAY!
BBZZZZ
NYAH NYAH NYAH!
WHH
!

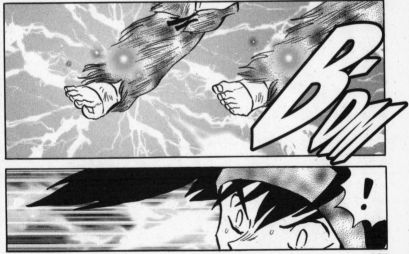

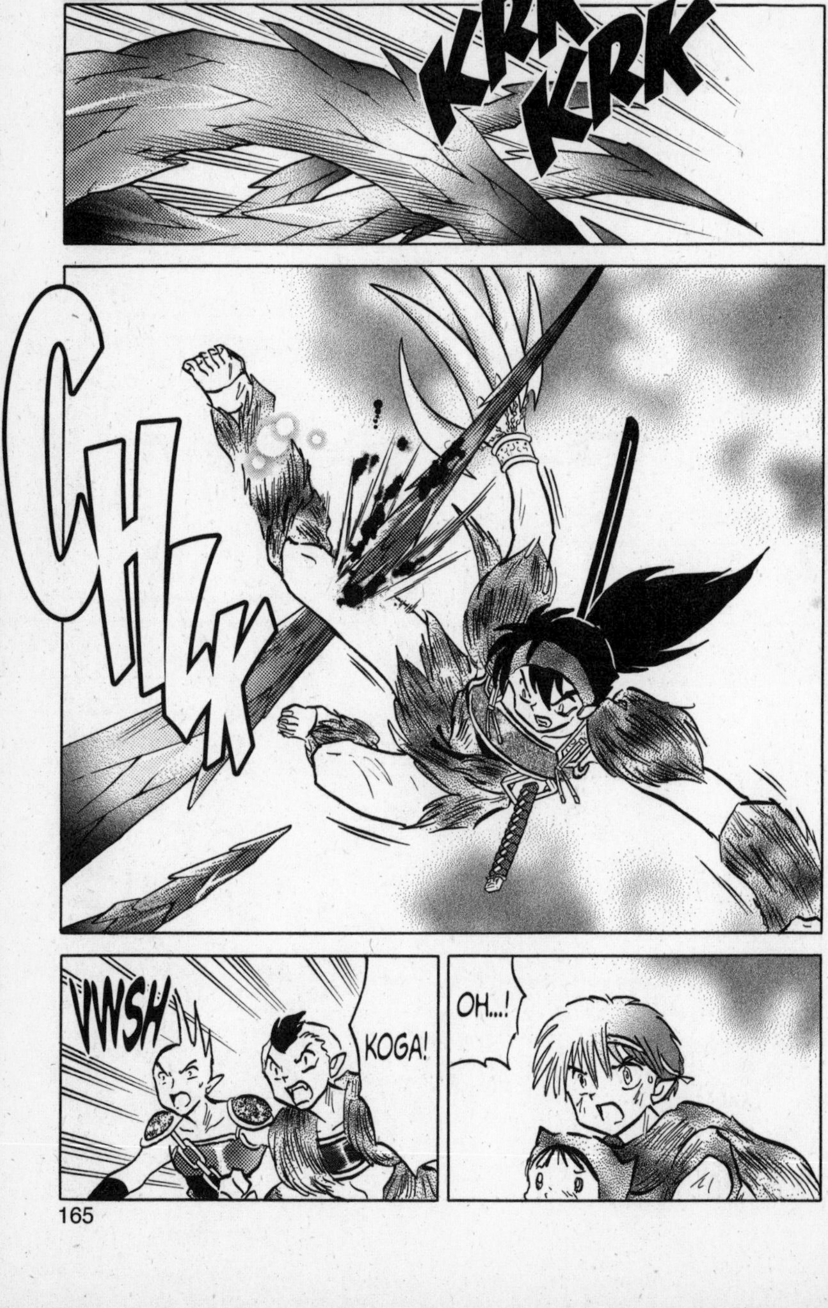
KRK
KRK
CHINK
OH...!
KOGA!
VWSH

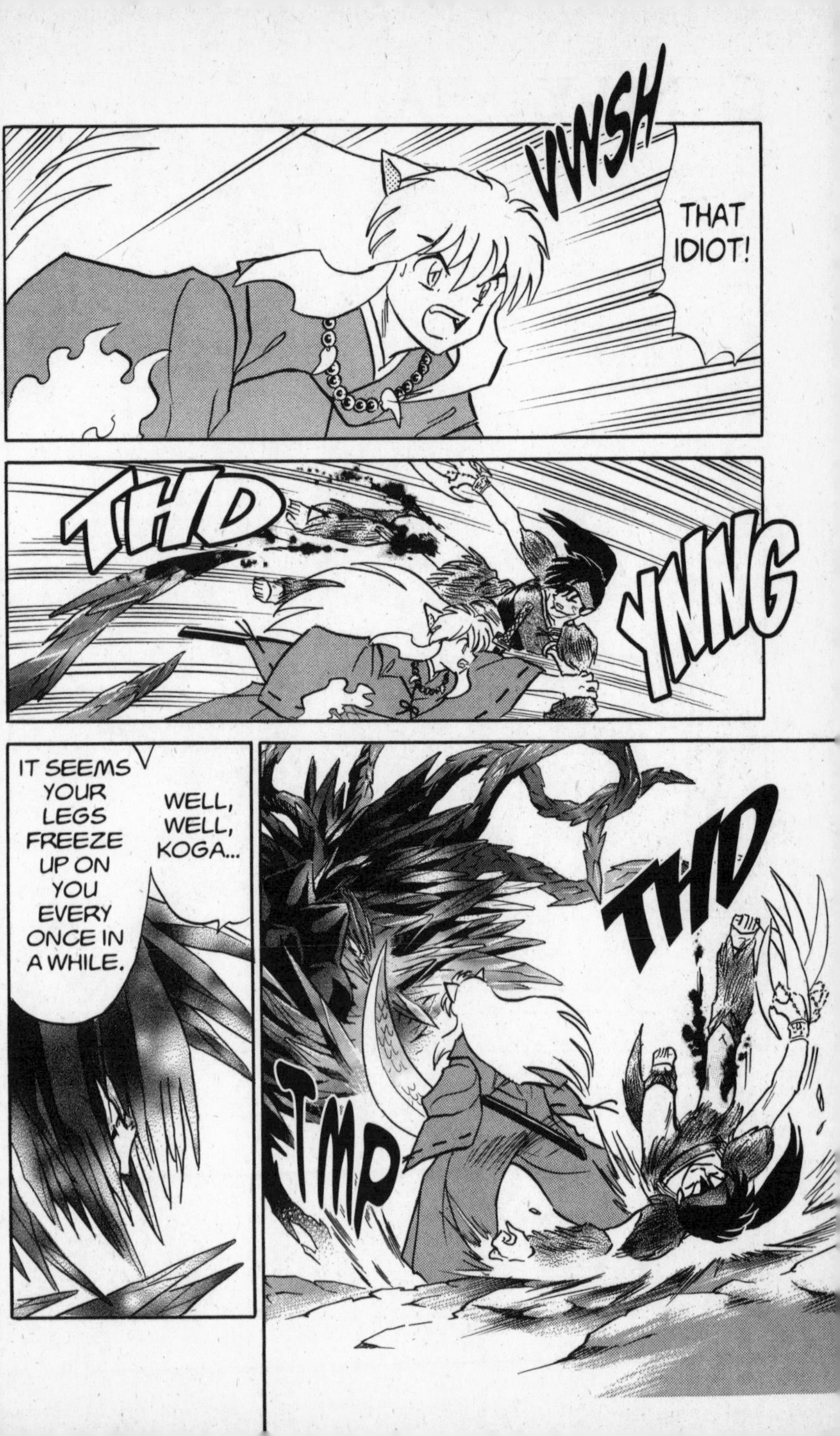
VWSH
THAT IDIOT!
YNNG
THD
THD
WELL, WELL, KOGA...
IT SEEMS YOUR LEGS FREEZE UP ON YOU EVERY ONCE IN A WHILE.
TMP

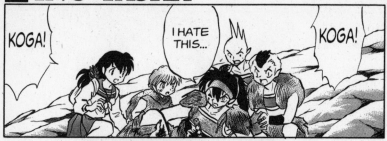

KOGA!
I HATE THIS...
KOGA!
KNNN...
IT'S MIDORIKO'S WILL AGAIN!
HEH HEH HEH... I'VE BEEN WAITING FOR THIS VERY MOMENT...
KRK KRK
ZWRL
VORTEXES OF POWER NEAR THE TIPS OF HIS FEELERS...
THEY MUST HAVE STRAYED BEYOND THE NULLING STONE'S LIMITS!!

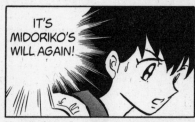

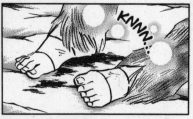

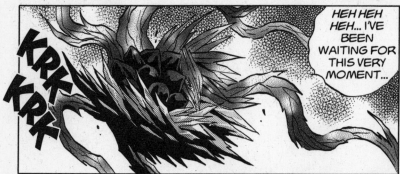

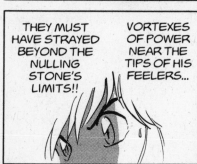

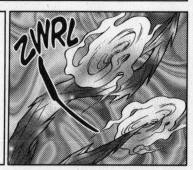

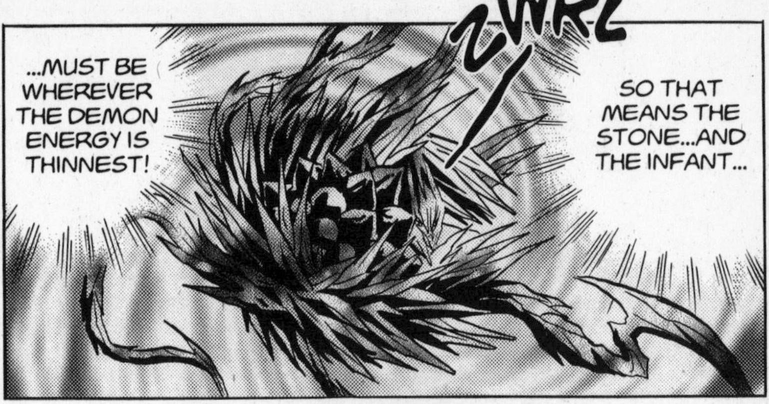
ZWRL
SO THAT MEANS THE STONE...AND THE INFANT...
...MUST BE WHEREVER THE DEMON ENERGY IS THINNEST!
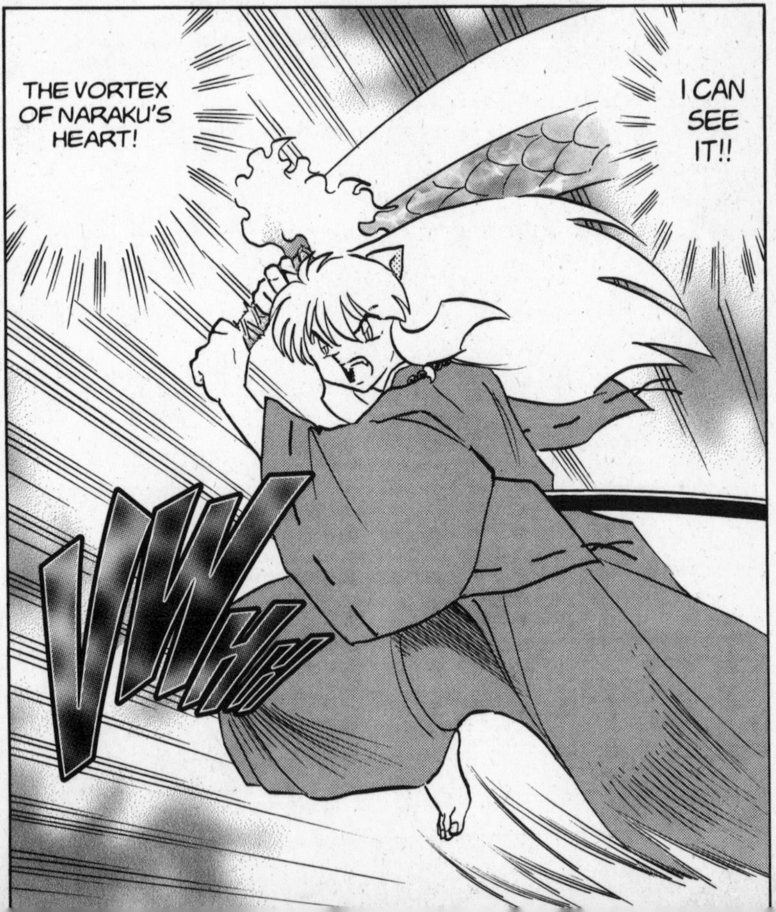
I CAN SEE IT!!
THE VORTEX OF NARAKU'S HEART!

SCROLL 10

KOGA'S DECISION

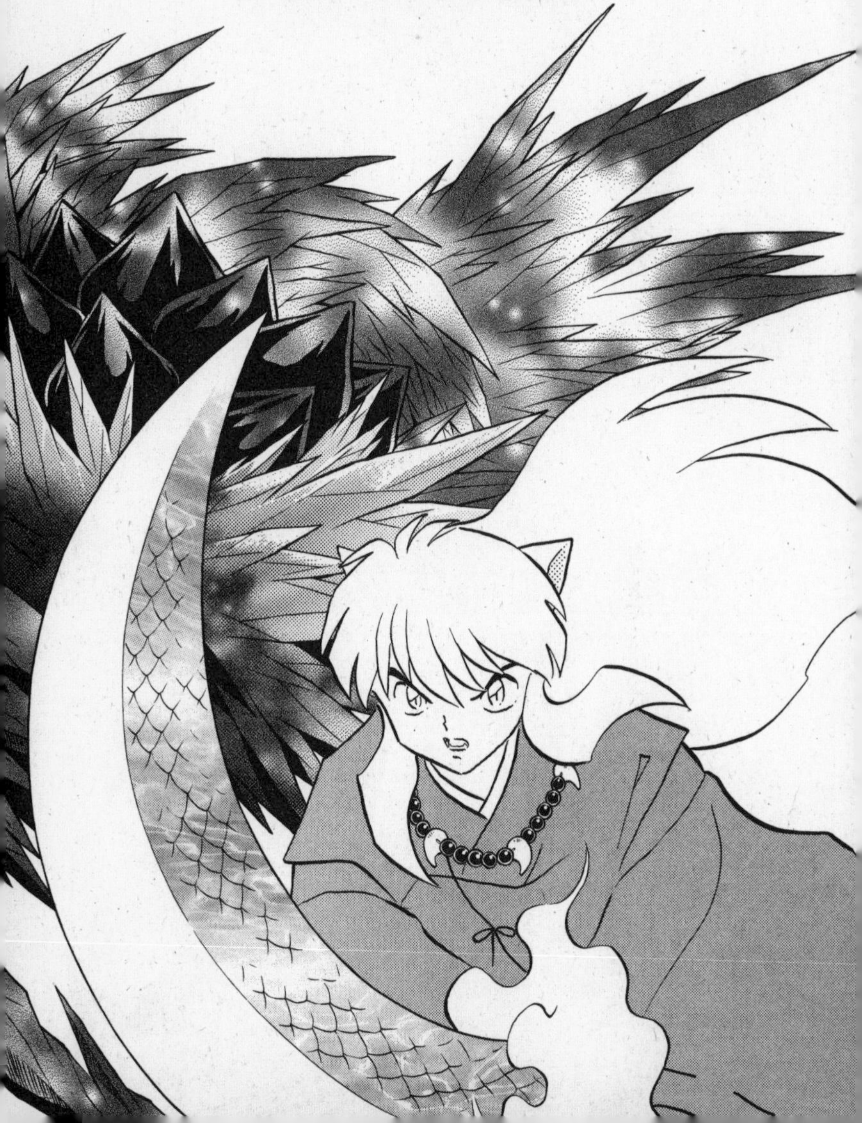

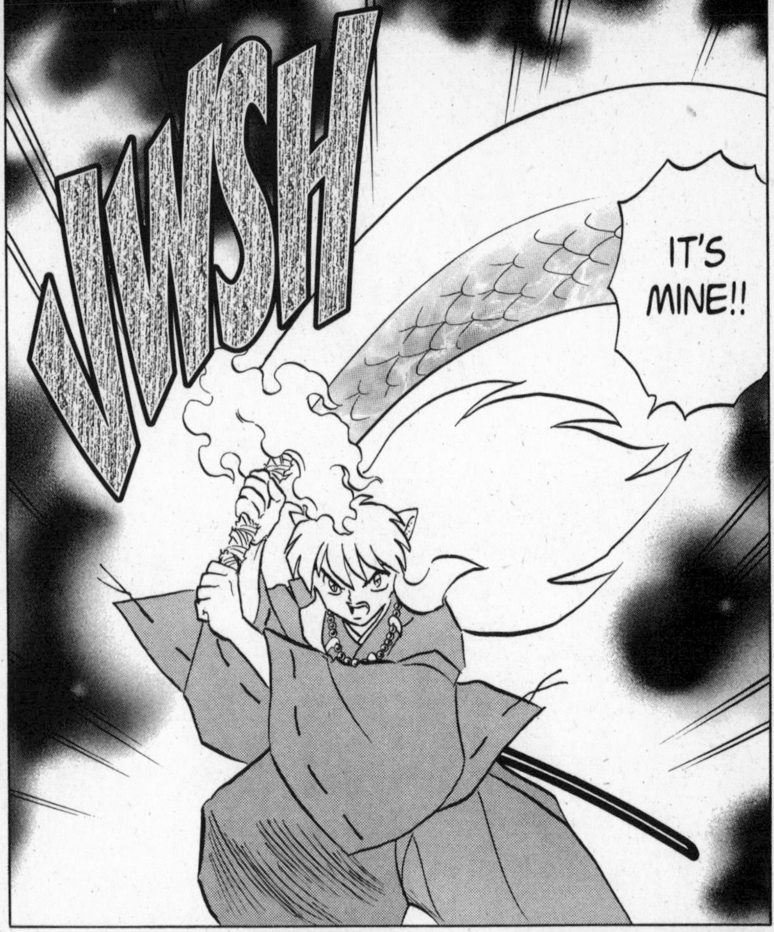
IT'S MINE!!
VWSH
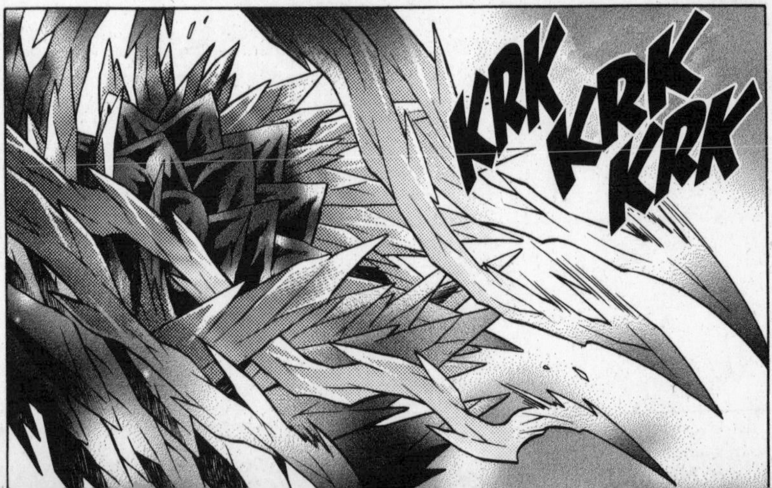
KRK KRK KRK

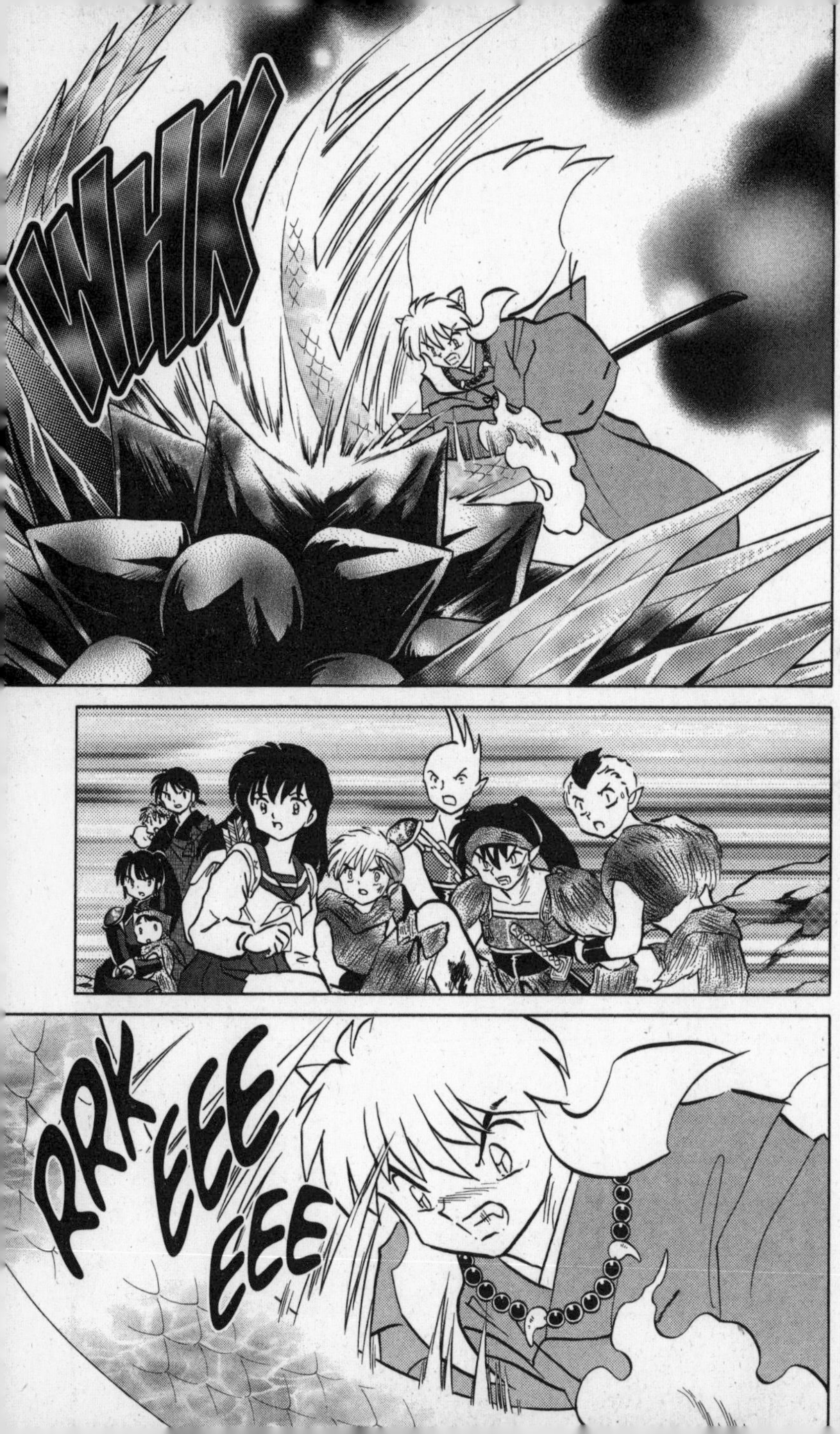
WHH
RRK EEE EEE

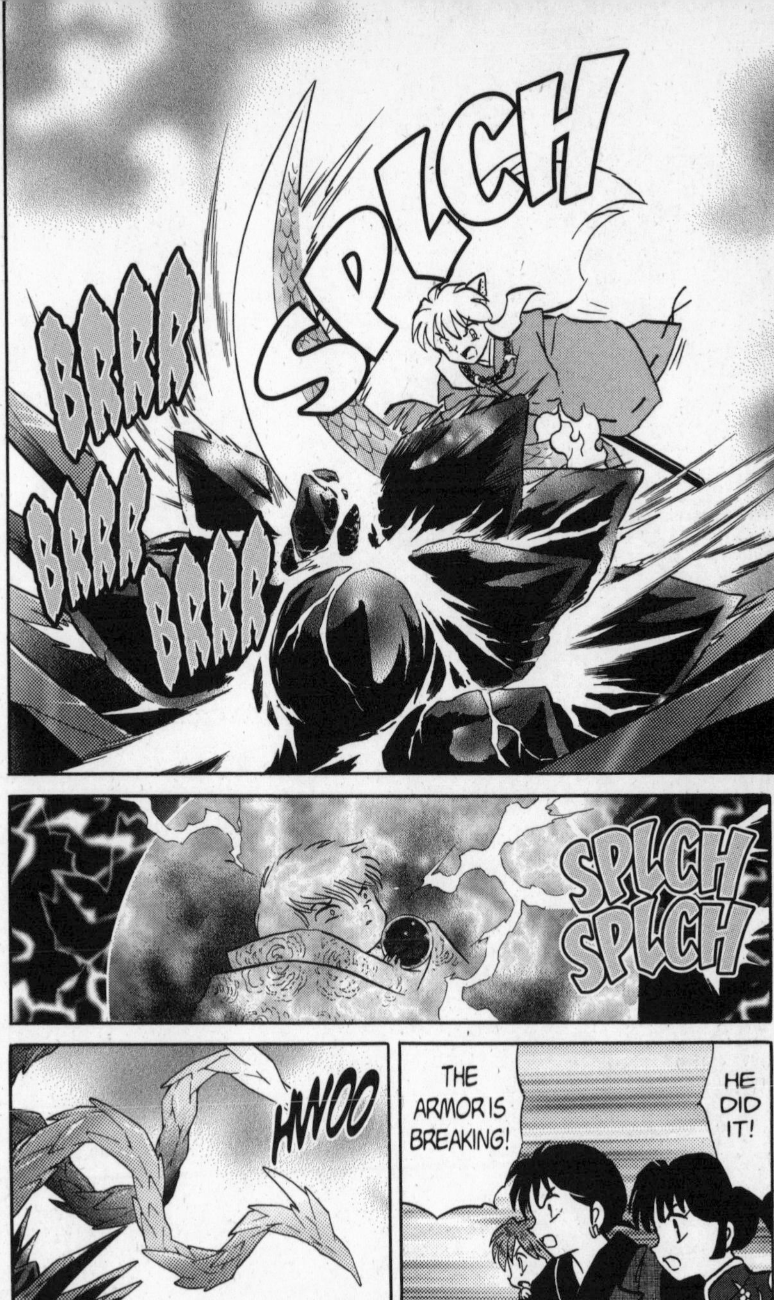
SPLCH
BRRR
BRRR
BRRR
SPLCH
SPLCH
HE DID IT!
THE ARMOR IS BREAKING!
HWOO

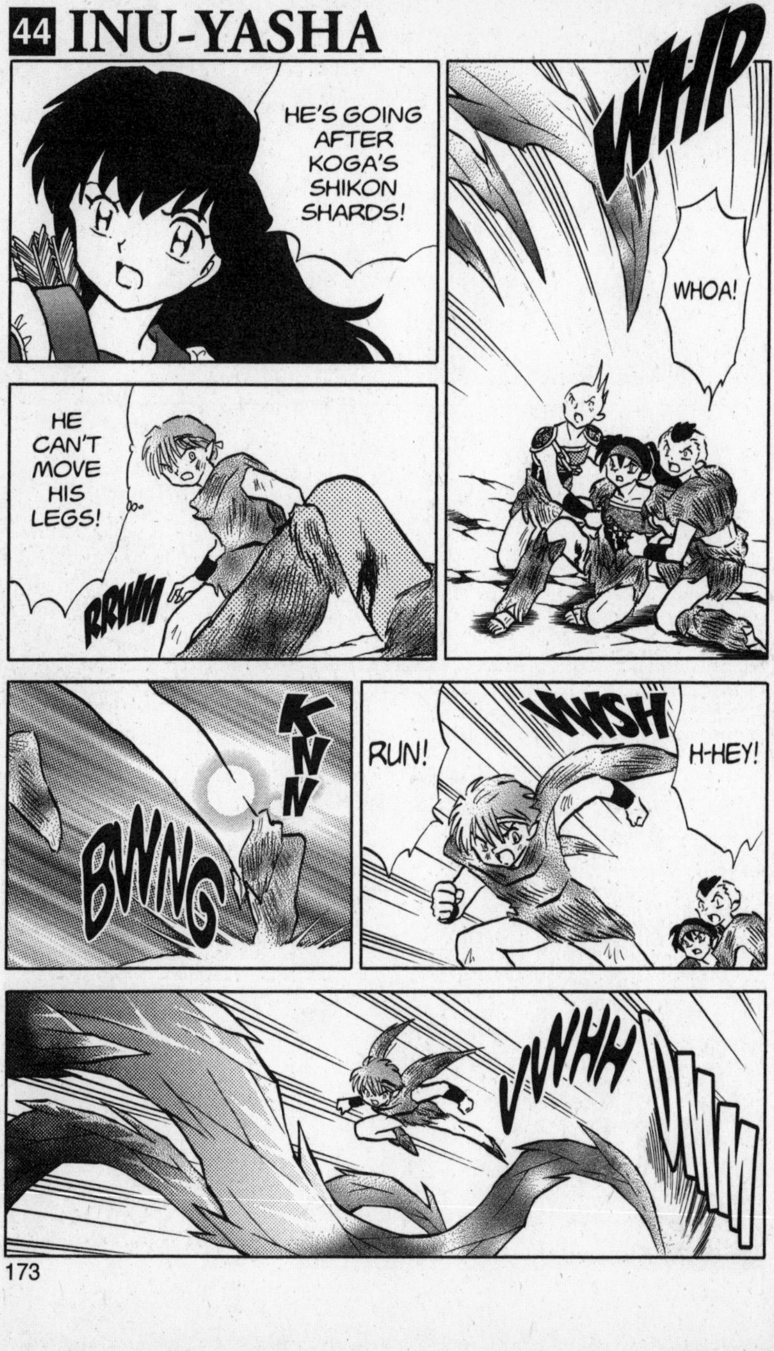
HE'S GOING AFTER KOGA'S SHIKON SHARDS!
HE CAN'T MOVE HIS LEGS!
RRWM
WHIP
WHOA!
KNN
BWNG
RUN!
VWSH
H-HEY!
VVNHH

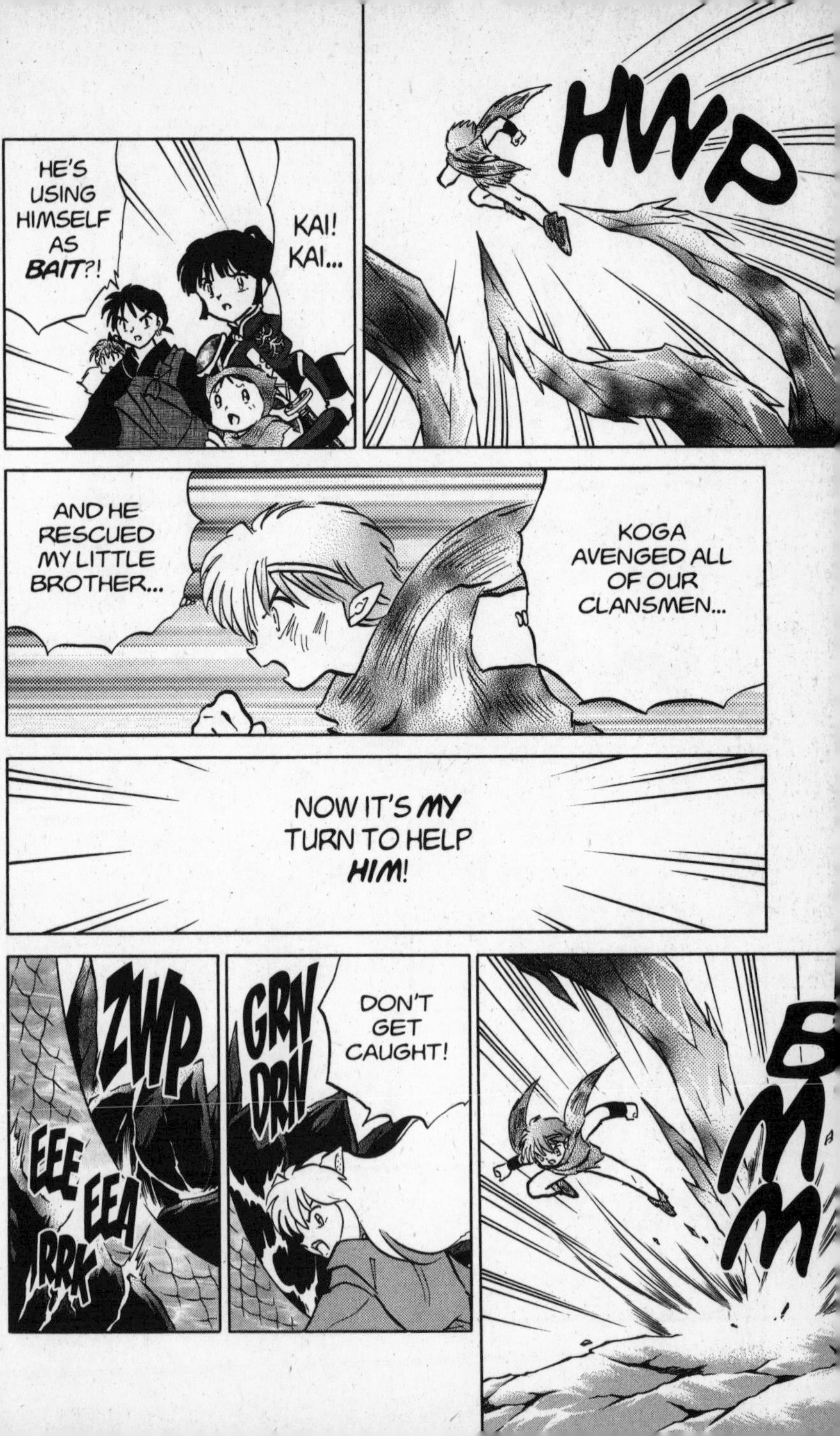
HWP
KAI! KAI...
HE'S USING HIMSELF AS BAIT?!
KOGA AVENGED ALL OF OUR CLANSMEN...
AND HE RESCUED MY LITTLE BROTHER...
NOW IT'S MY TURN TO HELP HIM!
BMMM
DON'T GET CAUGHT!
GRN DRN
ZWP
EEE EEA RRK

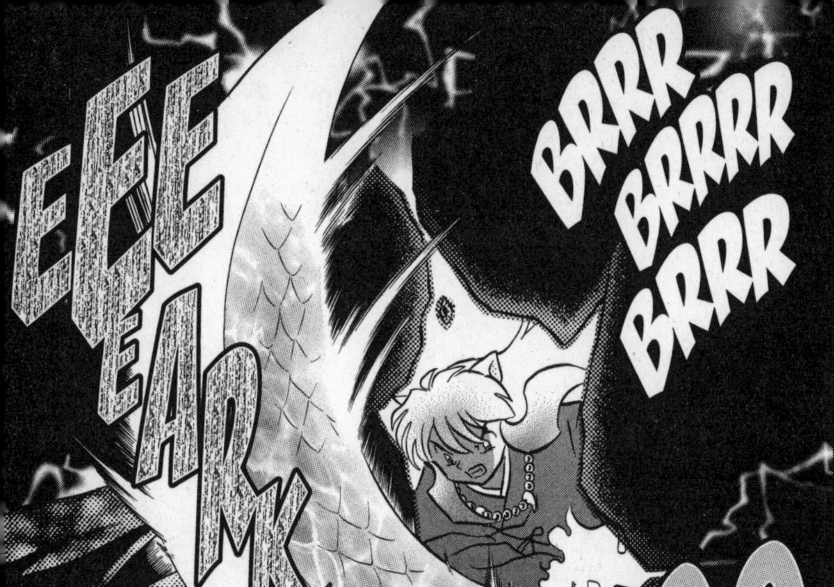
BRRR BRRRR BRRR
EEEEARMK
HYOO

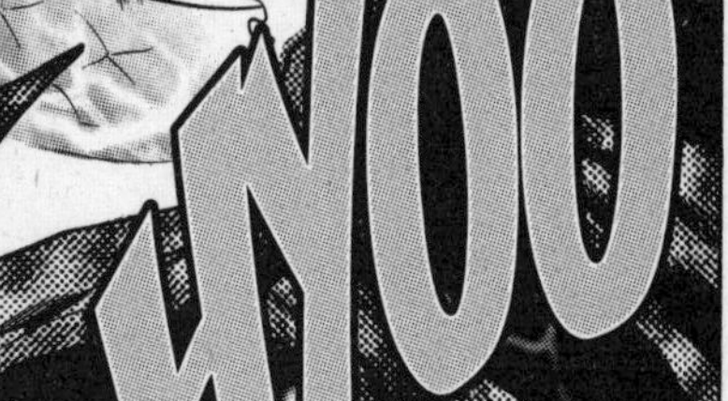
YOUR LUST FOR THOSE SHARDS MADE YOU SLIP UP!

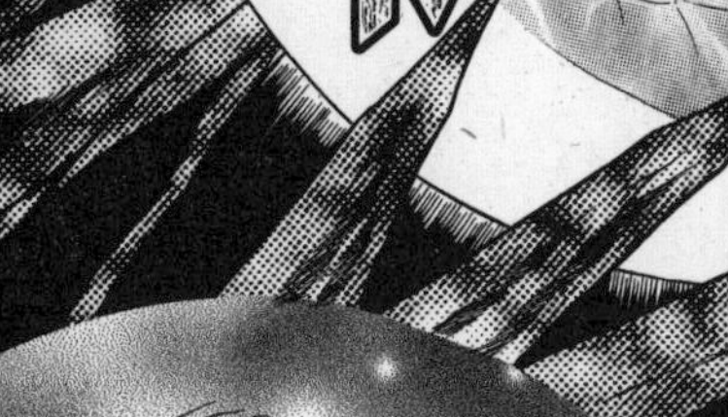
CHURL! HOW DARE YOU ENTER MY ARMOR?

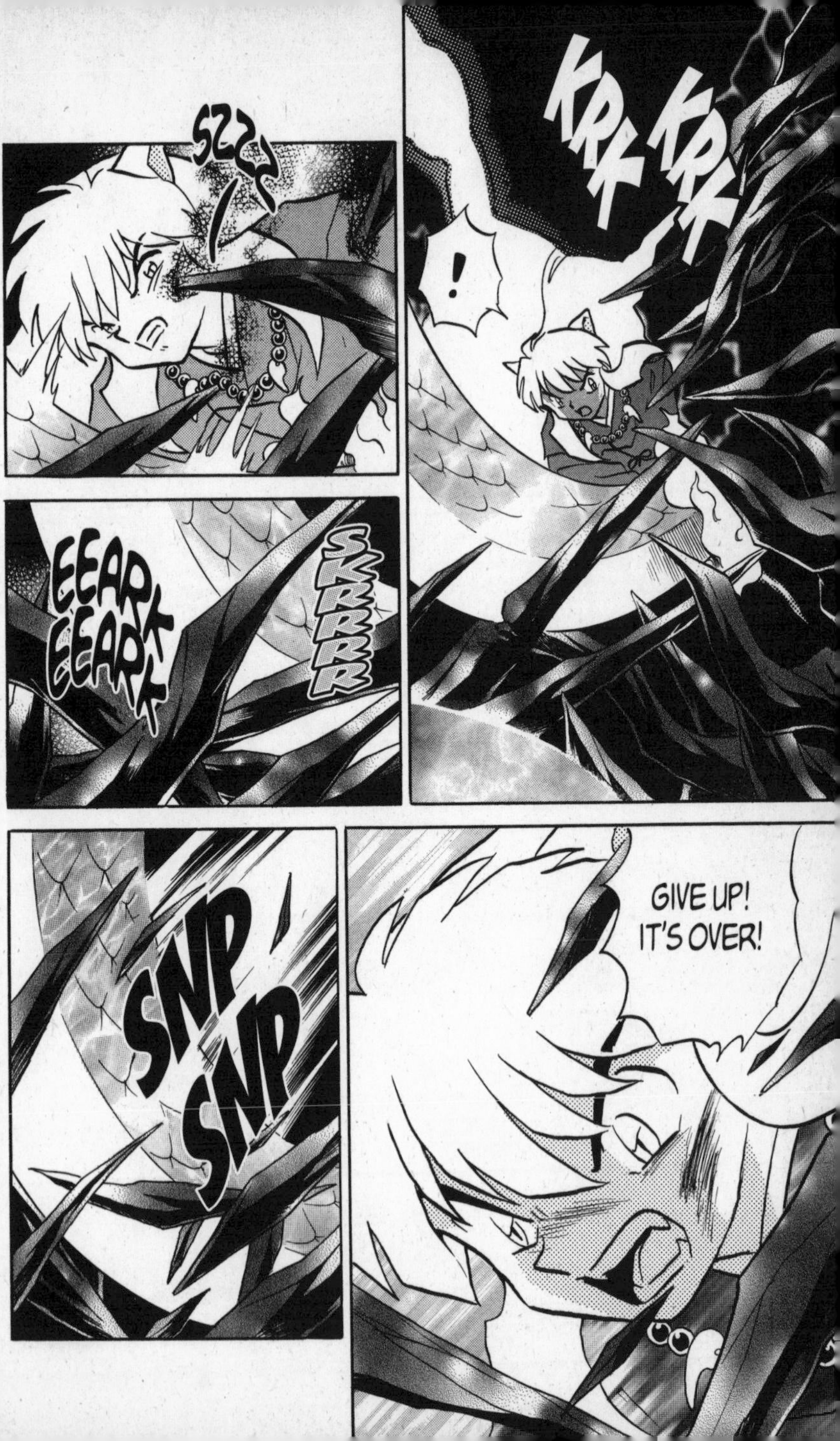
KRK KRK
!
ZSSS
EEARK EEARK
SKRRRR
GIVE UP! IT'S OVER!
SNP SNP

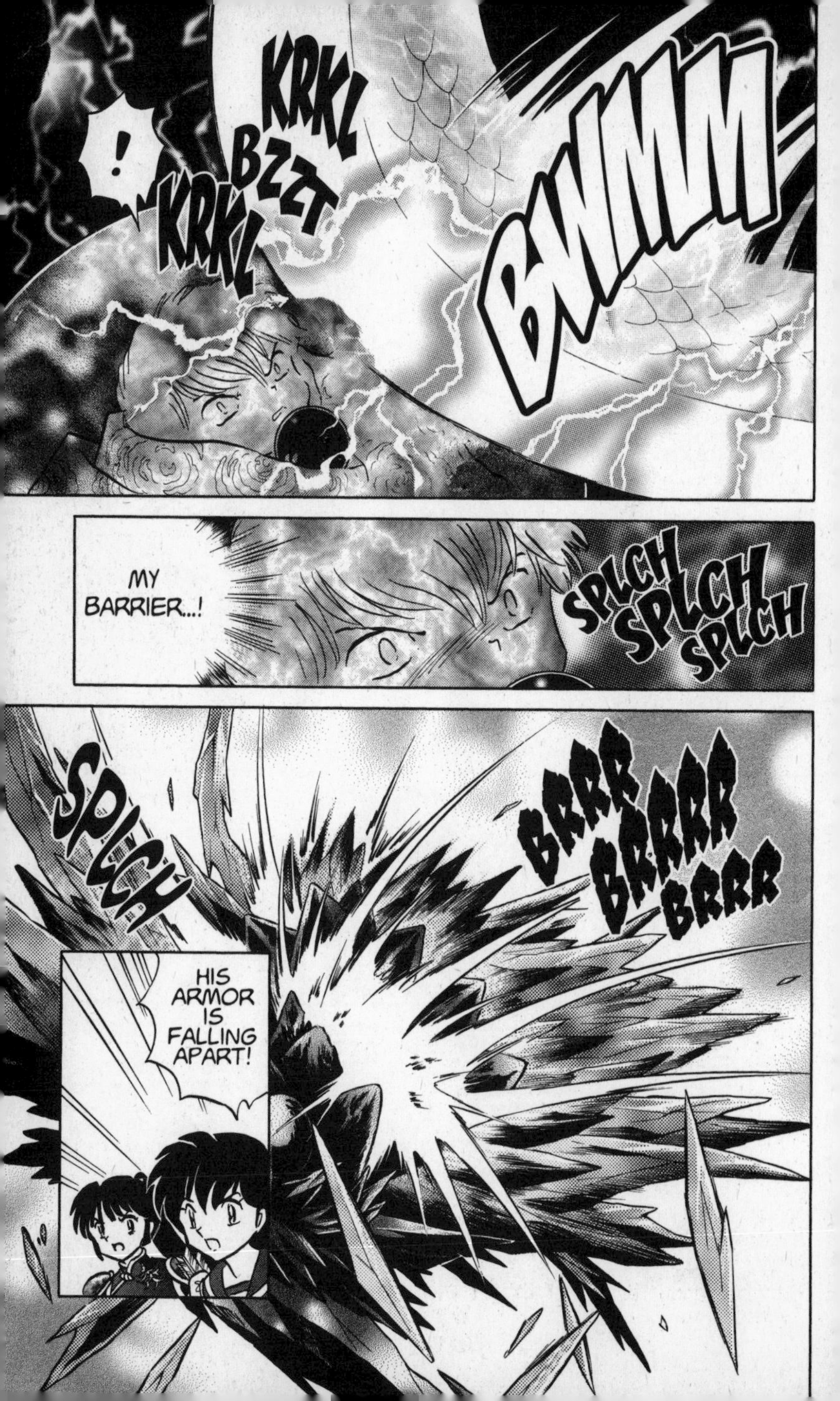
BNMMM
KRKL
BZZT
KRKL
!
SPLCH
SPLCH
SPLCH
MY BARRIER...!
BRRR
BRRRR
BRRR
SPLCH
HIS ARMOR IS FALLING APART!

?!

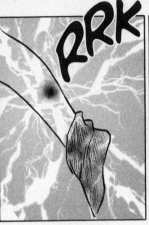

RRK

WE DID IT?!

KNNN

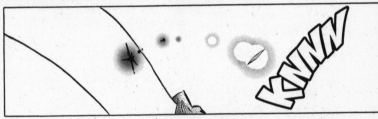

KAI'S SHIKON SHARD WAS RIPPED OUT OF HIM!

HUH...?!

178

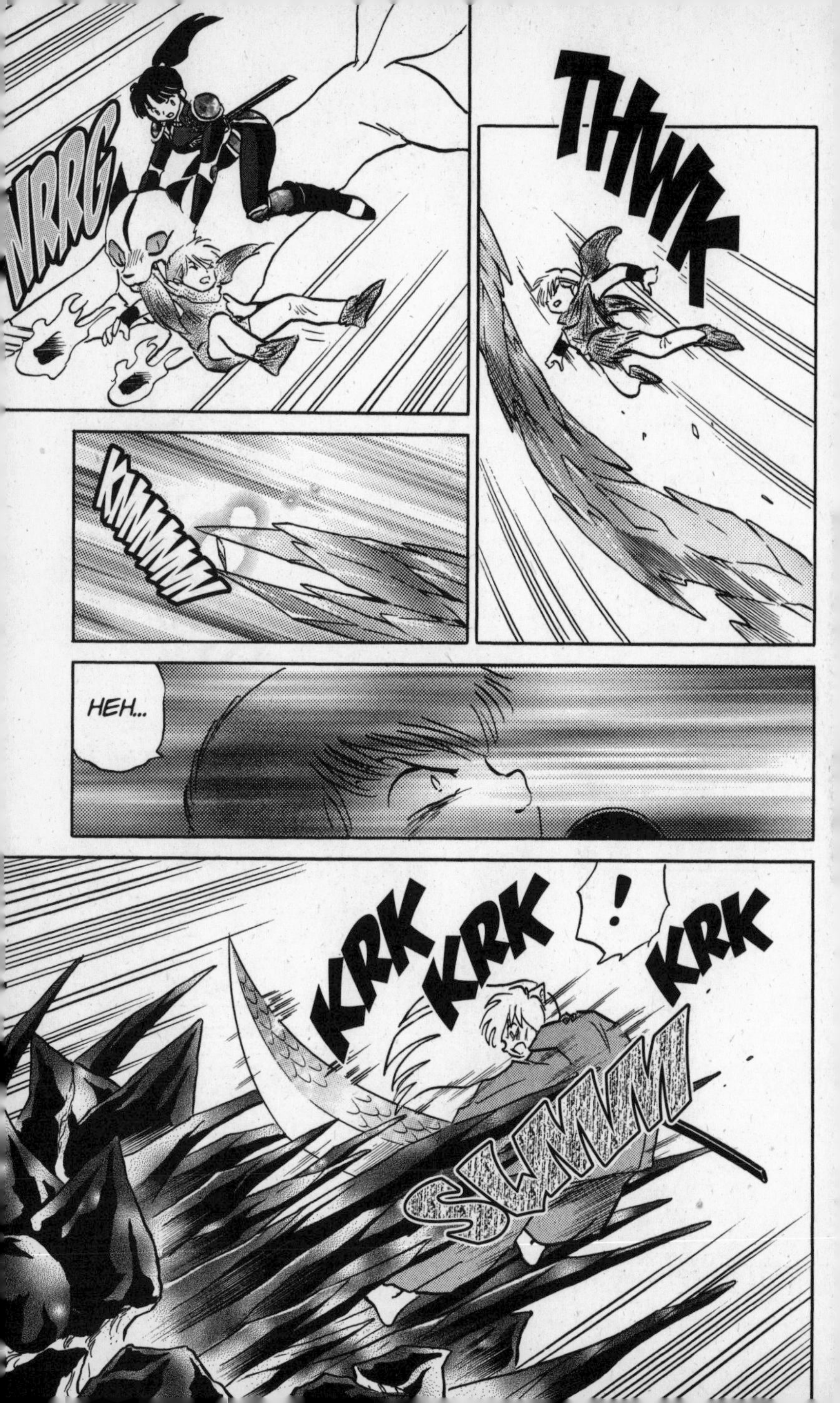
NRRG
THWAK
KWMMMM
HEH...
!
KRK KRK KRK
SWMM

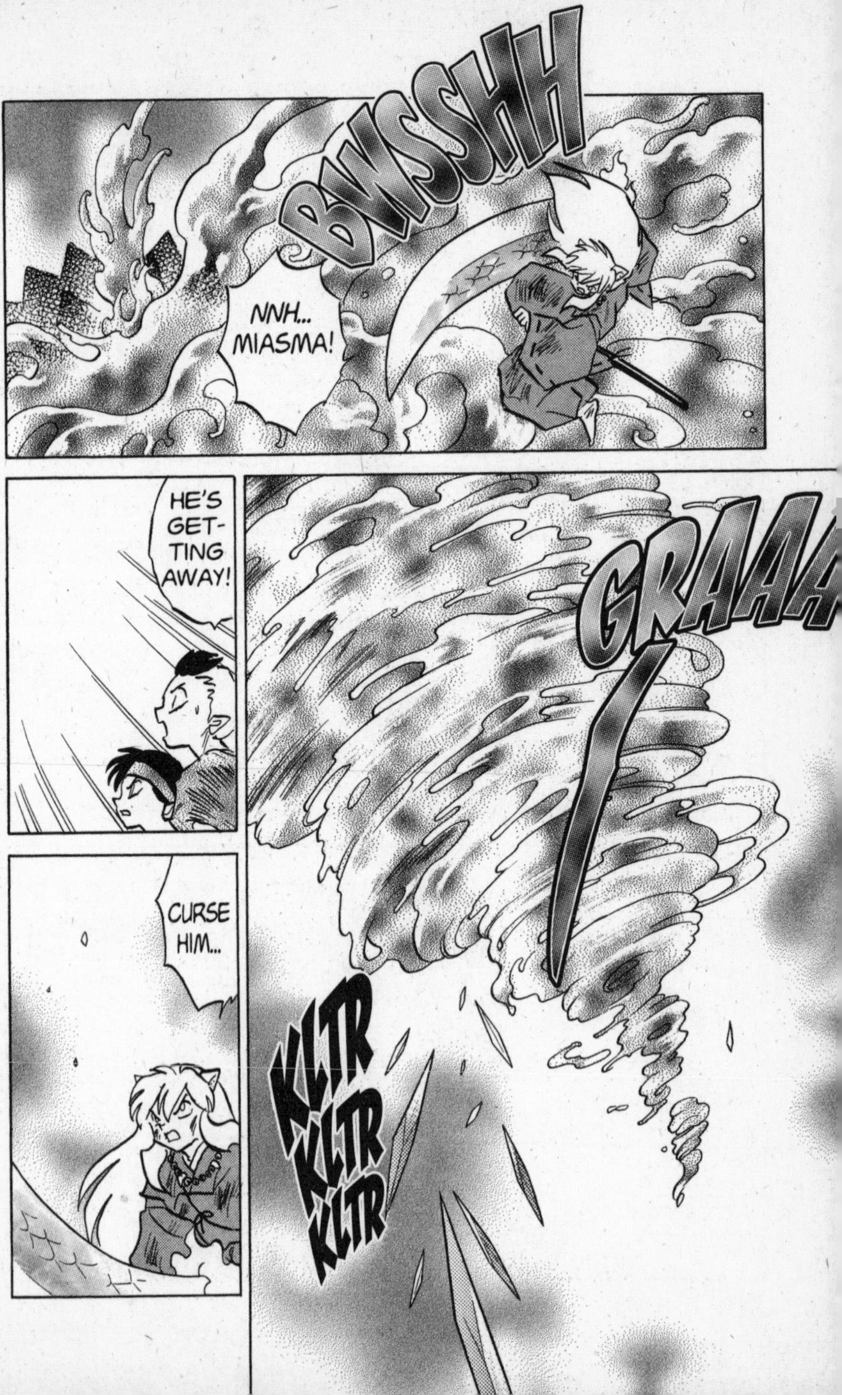
BWSSHH
NNH... MIASMA!
GRAAAA
HE'S GET- TING AWAY!
CURSE HIM...
KLTR KLTR KLTR

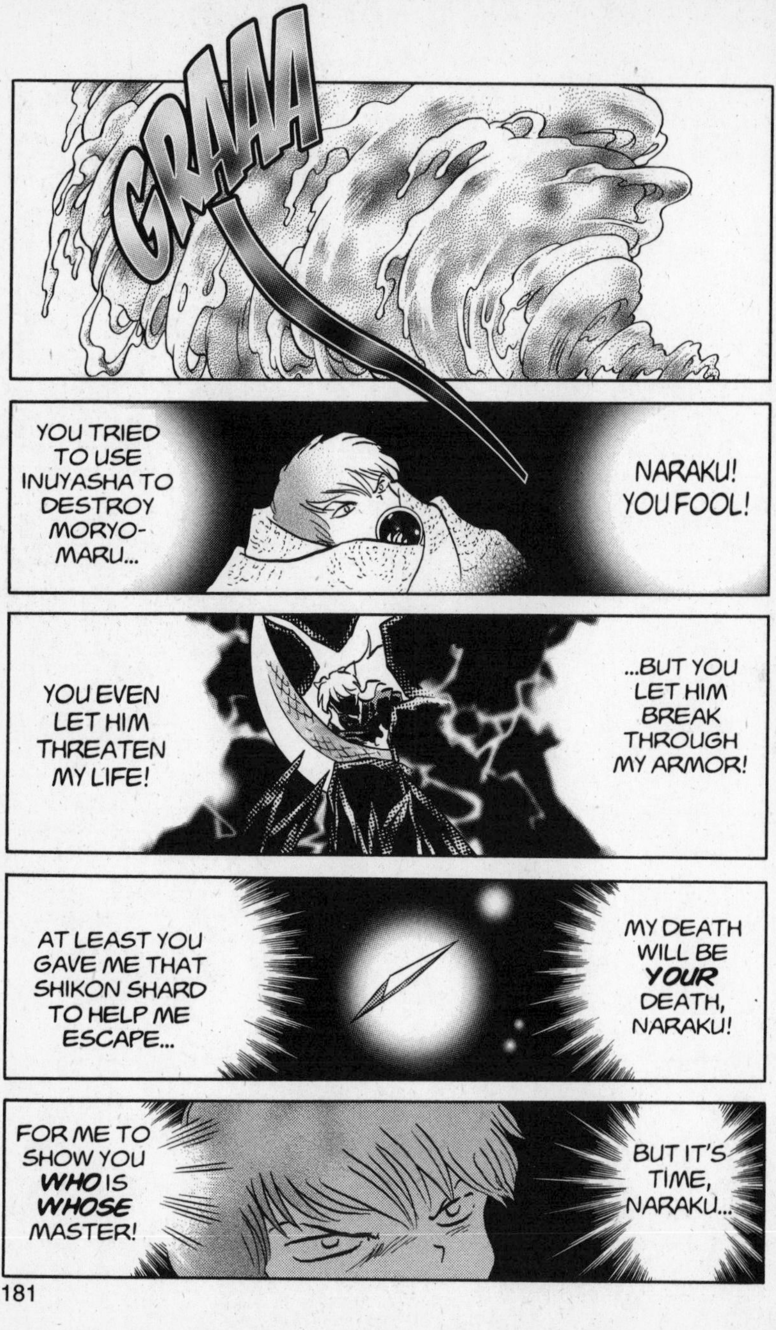
GRAAA
NARAKU! YOU FOOL!
YOU TRIED TO USE INUYASHA TO DESTROY MORYO-MARU...
...BUT YOU LET HIM BREAK THROUGH MY ARMOR!
YOU EVEN LET HIM THREATEN MY LIFE!
MY DEATH WILL BE ***YOUR*** DEATH, NARAKU!
AT LEAST YOU GAVE ME THAT SHIKON SHARD TO HELP ME ESCAPE...
BUT IT'S TIME, NARAKU...
FOR ME TO SHOW YOU ***WHO*** IS ***WHOSE*** MASTER!

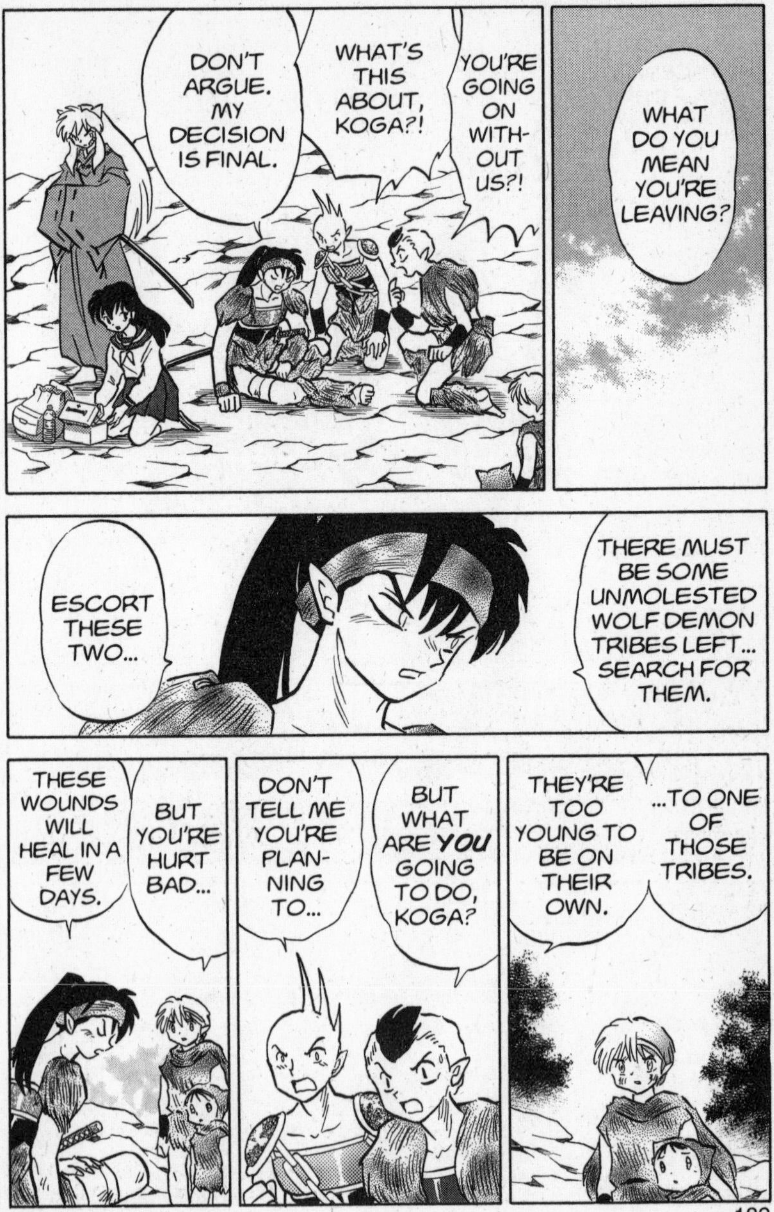
WHAT DO YOU MEAN YOU'RE LEAVING?
YOU'RE GOING ON WITH-OUT US?!
WHAT'S THIS ABOUT, KOGA?!
DON'T ARGUE. MY DECISION IS FINAL.
THERE MUST BE SOME UNMOLESTED WOLF DEMON TRIBES LEFT... SEARCH FOR THEM.
ESCORT THESE TWO...
...TO ONE OF THOSE TRIBES.
THEY'RE TOO YOUNG TO BE ON THEIR OWN.
BUT WHAT ARE ***YOU*** GOING TO DO, KOGA?
DON'T TELL ME YOU'RE PLAN-NING TO...
BUT YOU'RE HURT BAD...
THESE WOUNDS WILL HEAL IN A FEW DAYS.

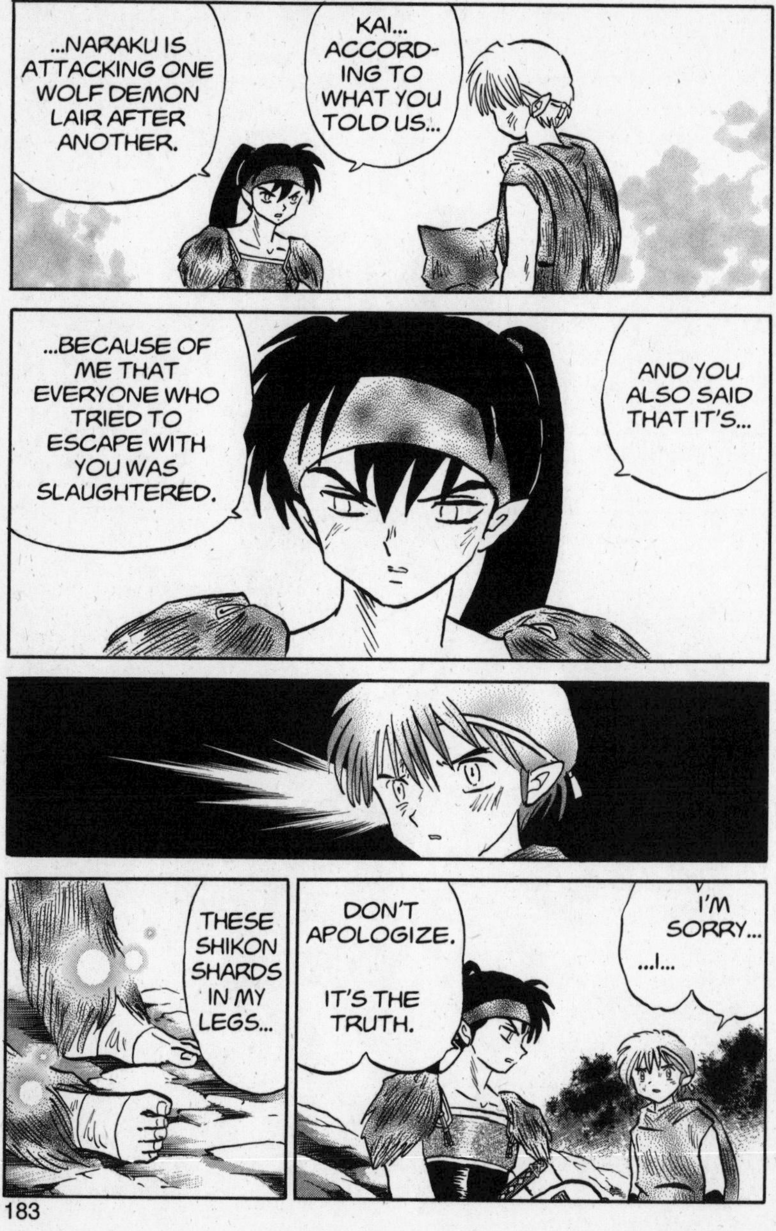
KAI... ACCORDING TO WHAT YOU TOLD US...
...NARAKU IS ATTACKING ONE WOLF DEMON LAIR AFTER ANOTHER.
AND YOU ALSO SAID THAT IT'S...
...BECAUSE OF ME THAT EVERYONE WHO TRIED TO ESCAPE WITH YOU WAS SLAUGHTERED.
I'M SORRY...
...I...
DON'T APOLOGIZE.
IT'S THE TRUTH.
THESE SHIKON SHARDS IN MY LEGS...

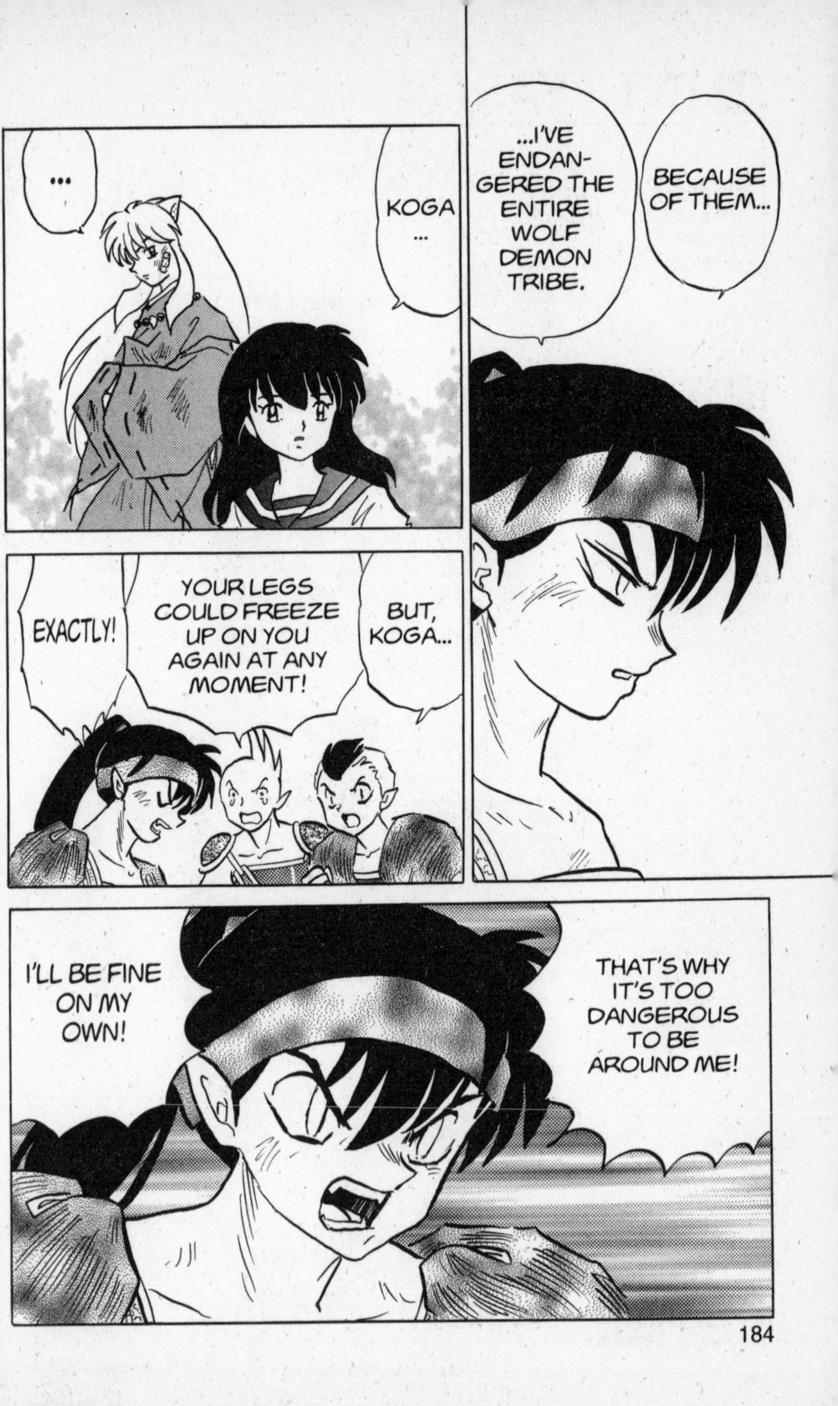
BECAUSE OF THEM...
...I'VE ENDANGERED THE ENTIRE WOLF DEMON TRIBE.
KOGA ...
...
BUT, KOGA...
YOUR LEGS COULD FREEZE UP ON YOU AGAIN AT ANY MOMENT!
EXACTLY!
THAT'S WHY IT'S TOO DANGEROUS TO BE AROUND ME!
I'LL BE FINE ON MY OWN!

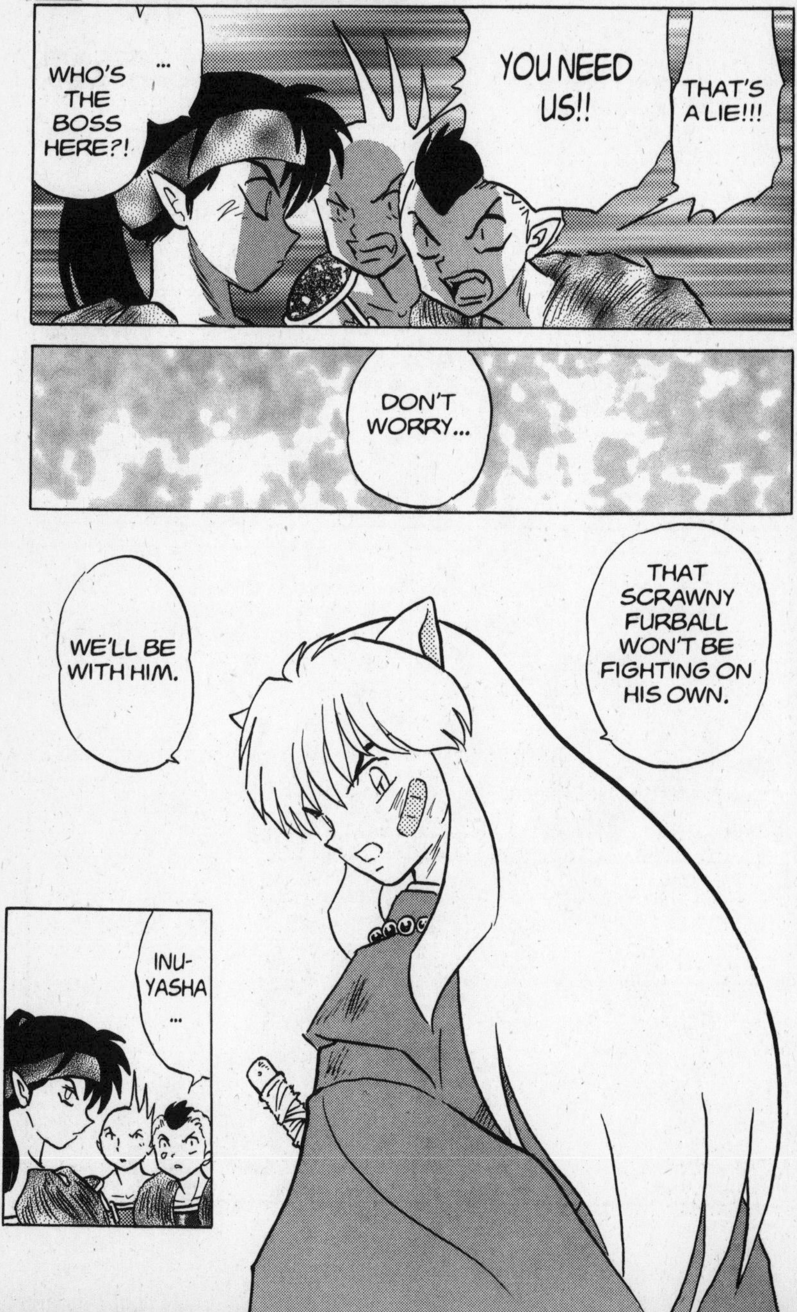
THAT'S A LIE!!!
YOU NEED US!!
...
WHO'S THE BOSS HERE?!
DON'T WORRY...
THAT SCRAWNY FURBALL WON'T BE FIGHTING ON HIS OWN.
WE'LL BE WITH HIM.
INU-YASHA ...

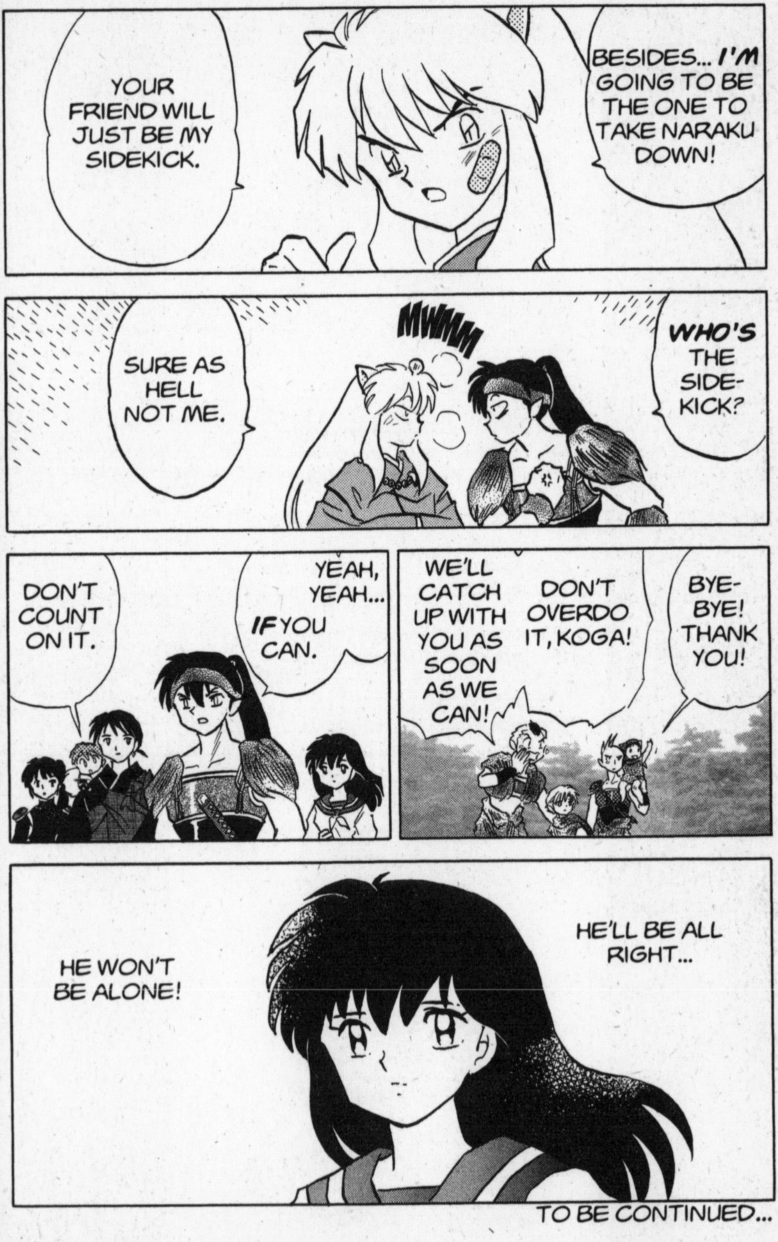
BESIDES... I'M GOING TO BE THE ONE TO TAKE NARAKU DOWN!
YOUR FRIEND WILL JUST BE MY SIDEKICK.
WHO'S THE SIDE-KICK?
MWMM
SURE AS HELL NOT ME.
BYE-BYE! THANK YOU!
DON'T OVERDO IT, KOGA!
WE'LL CATCH UP WITH YOU AS SOON AS WE CAN!
YEAH, YEAH... IF YOU CAN.
DON'T COUNT ON IT.
HE'LL BE ALL RIGHT...
HE WON'T BE ALONE!

TO BE CONTINUED...

INUYASHA

VOL. 44
Shonen Sunday Edition

Story and Art by
RUMIKO TAKAHASHI

English Adaptation by Gerard Jones

Translation/Mari Morimoto
Touch-up Art & Lettering/Bill Schuch
Cover & Interior Graphic Design/Yuki Ameda
Editor/Annette Roman

VP, Production/Alvin Lu
VP, Publishing Licensing/Rika Inouye
VP, Sales & Product Marketing/Gonzalo Ferreyra
VP, Creative/Linda Espinosa
Publisher/Hyoe Narita

Printed in the U.S.A.

Published by VIZ Media, LLC
P.O. Box 77010
San Francisco, CA 94107

10 9 8 7 6 5 4 3 2 1
First printing, January 2010

viz media
www.viz.com

SHONEN SUNDAY
WWW.SHONENSUNDAY.COM

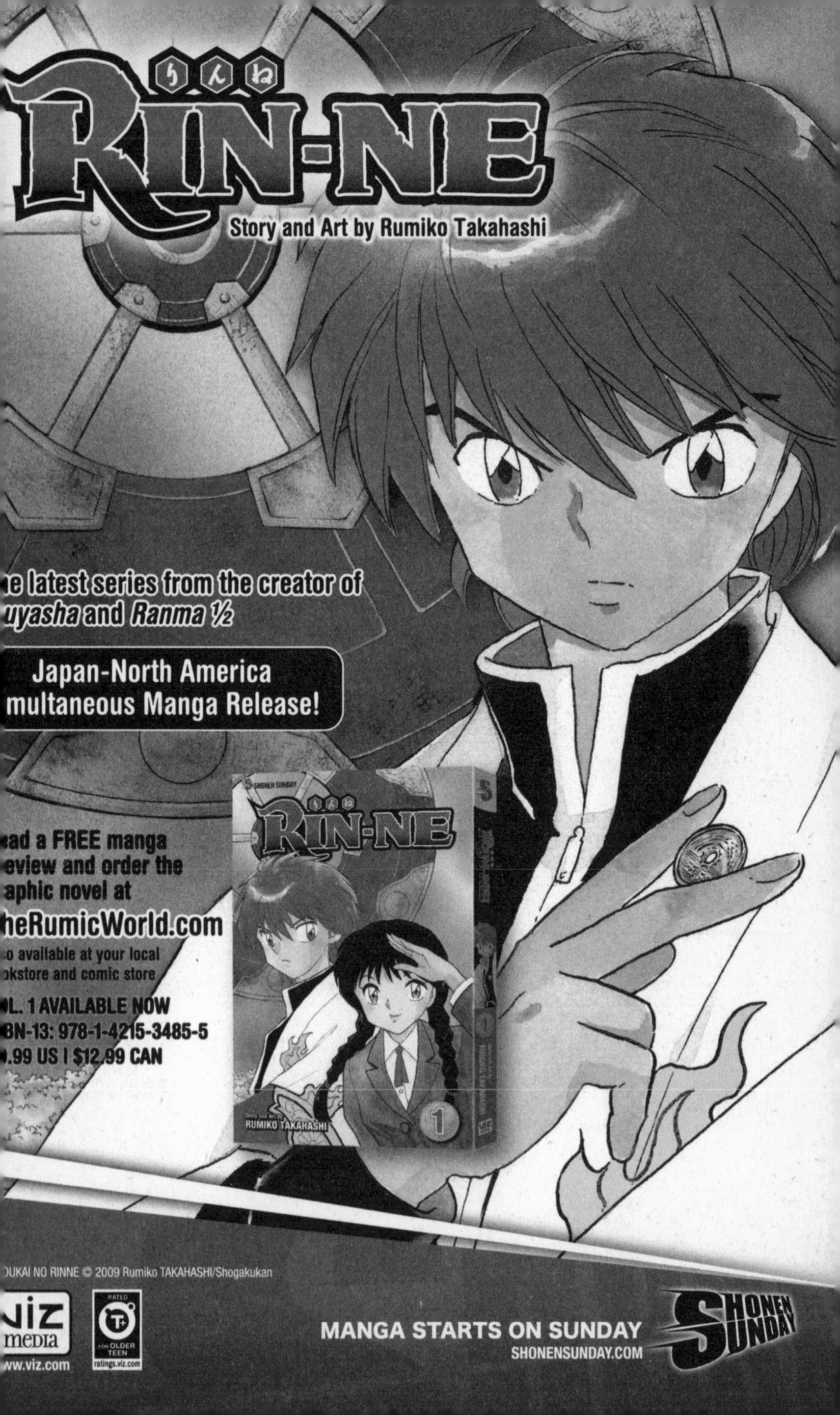

RIN-NE
Story and Art by Rumiko Takahashi
e latest series from the creator of
uyasha and Ranma ½
Japan-North America
multaneous Manga Release!
SHONEN SUNDAY
RIN-NE
Story and Art by
RUMIKO TAKAHASHI
1
ead a FREE manga
eview and order the
aphic novel at
heRumicWorld.com
o available at your local
okstore and comic store
L. 1 AVAILABLE NOW
BN-13: 978-1-4215-3485-5
.99 US | $12.99 CAN
OUKAI NO RINNE © 2009 Rumiko TAKAHASHI/Shogakukan
viz media
ww.viz.com
RATED T+ FOR OLDER TEEN
ratings.viz.com
MANGA STARTS ON SUNDAY
SHONENSUNDAY.COM
SHONEN SUNDAY

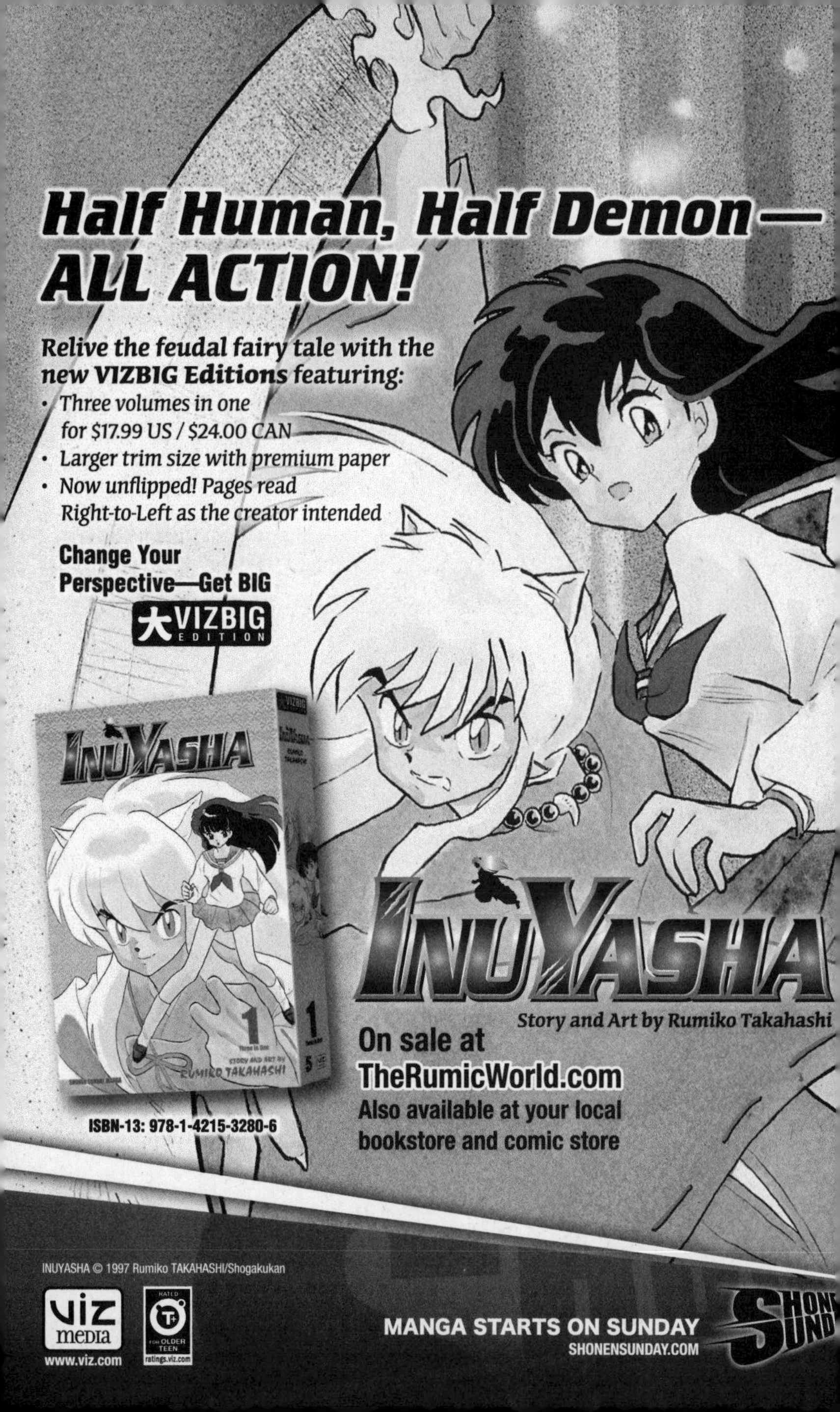

Half Human, Half Demon— ALL ACTION!

Relive the feudal fairy tale with the new **VIZBIG Editions** featuring:

- Three volumes in one for $17.99 US / $24.00 CAN
- Larger trim size with premium paper
- Now unflipped! Pages read Right-to-Left as the creator intended

Change Your Perspective—Get BIG

INUYASHA

Story and Art by Rumiko Takahashi

On sale at
TheRumicWorld.com
Also available at your local bookstore and comic store

ISBN-13: 978-1-4215-3280-6

www.viz.com

MANGA STARTS ON SUNDAY
SHONENSUNDAY.COM

INUYASHA

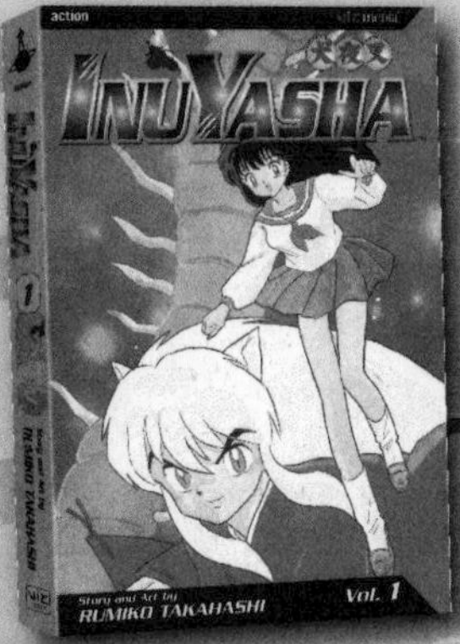
action
INUYASHA
Story and Art by
RUMIKO TAKAHASHI
Vol. 1

Read the action from the start with the original manga series

Full color adaptation of the popular TV series

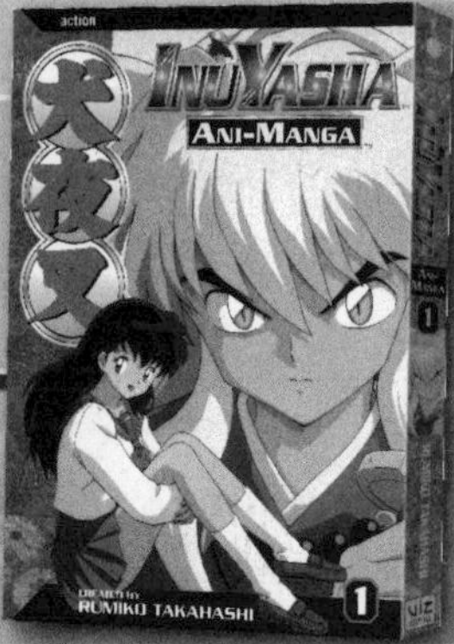
action
INUYASHA
ANI-MANGA
犬夜叉
RUMIKO TAKAHASHI
1

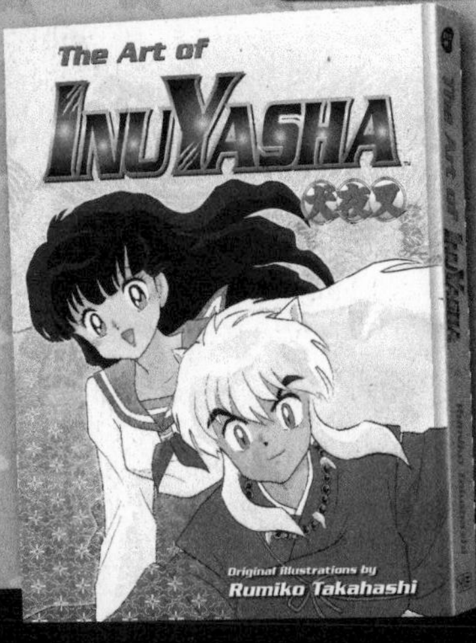
The Art of
INUYASHA
犬夜叉
Original Illustrations by
Rumiko Takahashi

Art book with cel art, paintings, character profiles and more